THE MAJOR POEMS OF TIMOTHY DWIGHT

THE MAJOR POEMS

OF

TIMOTHY DWIGHT

(1752-1817)

WITH

A DISSERTATION ON THE HISTORY,
ELOQUENCE, AND POETRY OF THE BIBLE

FACSIMILE REPRODUCTIONS

WITH AN INTRODUCTION

BY

William J. McTaggart

AND

William K. Bottorff

GAINESVILLE, FLORIDA

SCHOLARS' FACSIMILES & REPRINTS

1969

SCHOLARS' FACSIMILES & REPRINTS
1605 N.W. 14TH AVENUE
GAINESVILLE, FLORIDA, 32601 U.S.A.
HARRY R. WARFEL, GENERAL EDITOR

L.C. CATALOG CARD NUMBER: 68-24207

SBN 8201-1059-0

811.2
D993m

MANUFACTURED IN THE U.S.A.

CONTENTS

INTRODUCTION

Vernon L. Parrington wrote, concerning the poetry of Timothy Dwight, "It is the occasional work of a man wanting humor, playfulness, grace, lacking subtlety and creative suggestiveness, but with a shrewd common sense, a great vigor, and a certain grandiose imagination. . . . His ready versification, one often feels, runs like a water pipe with the faucet off; the words flow in an unbroken stream with never a pause to pick or choose. Yet even in his amazing copiousness there is vigor; a well-stocked mind is pouring out the gatherings of years" (*Main Currents in American Thought,* I). It is refreshing to find a writer, whose own temperament was so uncongenial to Dwight's, describing the poet's work as vigorous and implying it has lasting value, because commentators much more sympathetic to Dwight have found the poetry exceedingly dull. Perhaps the prevailing opinion is best summed up, with the reasons for it, by Francis Parsons: "Their [the Connecticut Wits'] oblivion is as readily comprehended, when we study it for a moment, as their contemporary popularity. It is due to three considerations—first, their work was chiefly inspired by concurrent events which, for the most part, have disappeared from human memory as completely as the verses which they inspired;

and again, because the verse forms which they em-
ployed seem to us so machine-like and wearisome.
Lastly, their poetic units are too long for modern taste.
This carries with it the criticism that they were apt
to be slipshod in technique, prolix, verbose and repeti-
tious" (*The Hartford Wits*, 1936). Nevertheless, today
students of American culture—historians, literary critics,
et al—find themselves increasingly studying those "con-
current events" and "the verses which they inspired"
in a modern, meaningful attempt at grasping what is
valuable and usable in the American past. The works
of Dwight naturally form a distinctive source for such
studies.

This book attempts to supply, in conjunction with
the poems of Dwight included in America's first poetry
anthology, *American Poems* (1793; SF&R reprint, 1966),
a reliable, representative collection of the poetry Dwight
produced. "Of Dwight's minor poems and fragments
of poems, nearly all were written and published before
his accession to the presidency of Yale College" in 1795,
and all the significant minor poems appear in *American
Poems*; here are added the major poems published sep-
arately by Dwight during his career, and "such is nearly
the entire record of Timothy Dwight as a poet" (Moses
Coit Tyler, *Three Men of Letters*, 1895).

One of the most interesting things about eighteenth-
century American poets is that they were consistently
unable to match their critical theories of composition to
their performance as poets. Dwight shared this short-
coming. His theories concerned two primary topics, the
quality of poetry as art, and literary nationalism. In

discussing the art of poetry, he began not with the classics as he saw his British brethren doing, but with the Bible. His *A Dissertation on the History, Eloquence, and Poetry of the Bible* (1772) "formulated a critical point of view which had a permanent influence on his literary judgment" (Leon Howard, *The Connecticut Wits,* 1943). In the *Dissertation* Dwight sets out to assess "the excellencies . . . of the fine writing" of the Bible, where he finds "poetry more correct and tender than *Virgil,* and infinitely more sublime than" Homer. In scripture are "the boldest metaphors, the most complete images," a "passionate Exclamation," epic proportions (as in Job), and the heights of the sublime, a very important aspect to Dwight. It is in each of these key particulars that Dwight falls short as a poet: his metaphors are too seldom "bold" or fresh, his images too often general; he works too little with the passion of expression, whether tender or severe; his is too often the false sublime. And, of course, his metrics and rhythms are far too imitative, too shackled to the standards of a neo-classicism which by his time was quite shop-worn.

In regard to Biblical paraphrase Dwight had more to say about poetics. The long tradition of paraphrasing portions of the Bible—usually involving bathetic expansions that warped the simplicity and diminished the emotional impact of the original—was not a happy one to work in when the poet turned to the heroic couplet for his form. Prefacing Dwight's "The Trial of Faith," paraphrased from Daniel (*American Poems*) is this explanation: "I have long thought that the Bible furnished

many subjects for poetry, far more deserving the ambition and efforts of genius, than those to which it is
commonly dedicated. I do not mean merely that they
are subjects more friendly to virtue, but to poetry.
[This distinction reveals his chief point.] They are
more sublime, novel, beautiful, agreeable, and in every
way interesting." But the couplets destroy their sublimity, novelty, beauty. When, however, Dwight turned from the school of Pope to Milton as exemplar, he
was on his way toward being genuinely a poet even in
the Biblical papaphrase. His Mordecai and Esther
poems (*American Poems*) have a pleasing rhythm and
freshness of expression in their blank verse that allow
a consistent artfulness, as opposed to the rarer patches
of good poetry in his couplets.

In the area of literary nationalism Dwight stood with
other American poets of his time. Almost to a man they
fostered the use of American images, settings, and subjects. But the mere employment of these factors without art seems to us now a small gain. Dwight, who
sometimes thought so too, attributed the lack of a meaningful American expression to a truckling to British
critical opinion (as opposed to simple imitation of the
British poets). In the *Dissertation* he sees a measure of
the greatness of Biblical expression in its writers having been "unincumbered by critical manacles." He approached this problem in its American context in 1789:
"Hence criticism will advance towards a higher perfection, as the varieties of the human mind open new
views of poetical objects, and peculiarity of genius
furnishes new springs and meanderings of delight" ("The
Friend," in Clarence A. Brown, *The Achievement of*

American Criticism, 1954). The "varieties" and "new springs and meanderings" Dwight was most interested in were American ones. "In our own happy state of society," he continues, "disjointed from the customs and systems of Europe, commencing a new system of science and politics, it is to be ardently hoped, that so much independence of mind will be assumed by us, as to induce us to shake off these rusty shackles, examine things on the plan of nature and evidence, and laugh at the grey-bearded decisions of doting authority."

Dwight had done his laughing in 1785, in "The Critics: A Fable" (*American Poems*), where he caustically describes the British critics as various low orders of yelping, cringing, obstinate, wolfish, or pampered creatures, metamorphosed by Juno from the manly state into "Critics, the genuine curs of men." And they are curs because they attack the *"modest young beginners,"* the American poets, who must develop their own distinctive critical stance. At any rate, the American "beginners" continued to write poetry as best they could, including such audacious major efforts as are reprinted here.

"Dwight's 'America' had its thousands of readers," Parsons remarks. *America, or a Poem on the Settlement of the British Colonies, Addressed to the Friends of Freedom and Their Country* (1780, but largely written several years earlier) exhibits Dwight's early ambition toward his several themes or motifs, including the future glory of America (the American era as a new historical period of light and goodness). As did so many of his contemporaries, Dwight early allowed his poetic nationalism to take the form of the "vision poem," prophesying or foreseeing the coming greatness of American culture. "Some readers of the manuscript failed to become enthusiastic," Howard concludes, "but [John] Trumbull, at least, believed that there was 'something original and sublime in his manner of thinking and description' and was confident that 'Mr. Dwight is to be our American poet.'"

Comments on Dwight's longest poem, *The Conquest of Canaan: A Poem in Eleven Books* (1785) have been many. His biographer asserts that "its monumental character made an enormous impression upon his contemporaries" (Charles E. Cuningham, *Timothy Dwight*, 1942). But with time the reputation of the epic faded. Tyler was most unkind in his assessment of 1895: "Surely, 'The Conquest of Canaan,' with its eleven dreadful books of conventional rhymed pentameters,—all tending more or less to disarrange and confuse the familiar facts of Biblical history, as well as to dilute, to render garrulous, and to cheapen, the noble reticence, the graphic simplicity, of the antique chronicle,—is such an epic as can be grappled with . . . by no man who is not himself as heroic as this verse assumes to be." (Tyler also recounts and quotes from Cowper's contemporaneous, favorable review of *Conquest*.) In 1920 Henry A. Beers continued in the same mode: "the epic is unread and unreadable" (*The Connecticut Wits and Other Essays*).

The fullest treatments of the poem come from Leon Howard and George F. Sensabaugh. As always, Howard is accurate and to the point: "Dwight, like most of his contemporaries, was more concerned with the mean-

ing than with the sound of his verse; and when he
considered the subordinate sensory appeal of poetry he
thought of achieving it through 'imitation'—either by
description or by the more 'lively' method of using
rhetorical figures. . . . When he decided that an idea
was good, he usually pushed it to the limit of his own
endurance. . . . [his *Conquest* shows] how emotion
could be strained through his rather pedantic, theory-
ridden mind and so lose all force of reality in its
expression."

In *Milton in Early America* (1964) Sensabaugh
clearly and fully demonstrates that Dwight modelled
"his narrative on what he thought was the most sublime
of all epics, *Paradise Lost*. . . . In deference to pre-
vailing poetic taste, he avoided Miltonic blank verse
and cast his whole epic in heroic couplets; but this was
one of the few concessions he made to Augustan
poetic demands. Language, syntax, narrative machin-
ery, character delineation, and scenes—all came from
Paradise Lost. . . . He failed to amalgamate the Old
Testament story ["of Joshua and his heroic struggles to
bring the Children of Israel into the land of Canaan"],
Milton's symbols and style, and the ideals of the En-
lightenment which animated the American dream. As a
result *The Conquest of Canaan* stands as a monument to
misled ambition and energy, as a signpost to the wrong
turning American poetry took during the patriotic fer-
vor of Revolutionary times."

Dwight's next major effort, *The Triumph of Infidel-
ity: A Poem* (1788), is perhaps just what Parrington
calls it, "solid old-fashioned pulpit-thumping." But here

is Dwight at his most didactic, sharp in his satire and invective. The poem is almost a last-ditch effort, through poetry, to combat what he saw as a waning orthodoxy among Americans of his time and place. Upon his moving into the presidency of Yale, Dwight used sermons and prose tracts increasingly to represent himself in the fight against the infidels. He contributed greatly to the leadership Connecticut took in conservative thought.

"Through their verse we may see their Columbia," writes Mary Dexter Bates of the poets of Dwight's era ("Columbia's Bards: A Study of American Verse from 1783 through 1799," unpubl. diss., Brown Univ., 1954), and Dwight's last major poem, *Greenfield Hill: A Poem in Seven Parts* (1794), is a fine representation of his beloved Connecticut. (For the biographical and cultural background of the poem, see the Cuningham biography; it is interesting to note that Dwight's biographer has very little to say about his subject's poetry, implicitly judging it to be of relatively little importance.) "The emphasis upon such scenes of rural bliss and innocent merriment" as *Greenfield Hill* presents, Bates continues, "was an intrinsic part of the idealization of village and farm life that was already taking shape as part of the American myth." The poem is usually all that represents Dwight in recent anthologies, and perhaps this is just, for "On the whole one prefers him in the pastoral mood when he lays aside his ministerial gown, and *Greenfield Hill,* unless one excepts the *Travels in New England and New York,* remains his most attractive work" (Parrington). Dwight's "fame as a

poet rests primarily upon his *Greenfield Hill*" (Cuning-
ham); it "serves as the best memorial to his poetic
talents," as Howard has said.

Structurally as well as thematically the poem is of
great interest. Beers points out the chief features of
Dwight's plan: "each of its seven parts was to have
imitated the manner of some one British poet. Part
One is in the blank verse and the style of Thomson's
'Seasons'; Part Two in the heroic couplets and the dic-
tion of Goldsmith's 'Traveller' and 'Deserted Village.'
For lack of time this design was not systematically car-
ried out, but the reader is reminded now of Prior, then
of Cowper, and again of Crabbe." And Howard con-
cludes that "the greater part of *Greenfield Hill* repre-
sented for the first time in print a Dwight who was
more interested in his subject than in his reputation,
more natural than affected; . . . the poem itself reveals
Dwight's opinions and beliefs on many subjects better
than almost any of his other works." Thus it seems a
fit coda to the clergyman's career as poet.

As a student and tutor at Yale College, Timothy
Dwight had been a prime mover in the revival of
belles-lettres before the Revolutionary War. Even when
he fixed his career on the ministry, he did not give up
poetry, using his ability as a writer both to teach others
and to satisfy himself. From his classroom and his pul-
pit he could not warn enough people of the heresies,
political and religious, he saw rising around him, so he
used his pen to persuade those out of range of his voice.
In all this Dwight was a typical man of letters in his
time, a writer not by profession but because of what he

considered a necessity. Yet he was no mere propagandist, for he had the creative faculty of the artist even though he was always primarily a teacher and a moralist. If his talent was limited, his influence was large. His works form an interesting panel in the panorama of the American past.

America, Greenfield Hill, and Dwight's *Dissertation* are reproduced with permission from copies held in the Collection of American Literature, Beinecke Rare Book and Manuscript Library, Yale University; *The Triumph of Infidelity* is reproduced with permission from a copy held by the Library of Congress; *The Conquest of Canaan* is reproduced with permission from a copy held by the Massachusetts Historical Society.

WILLIAM J. McTAGGART

University of Toledo　　WILLIAM K. BOTTORFF

Toledo, Ohio

October 24, 1967

AMERICA:

OR, A

POEM

ON THE SETTLEMENT

OF THE

BRITISH COLONIES;

ADDRESSED

To the Friends of Freedom, and their Country.

By a GENTLEMAN *educated at Yale-College.*

NEW-HAVEN:

Printed by THOMAS and SAMUEL GREEN.

A POEM.

FROM *sylvan* shades, cool bowers and fragrant gales,
  Green hills and murm'ring Streams and flowery vales,
My soul ascends of nobler themes to sing ;
AMERICA shall wake the sounding string.
Accept, my native Land, these humble lays,
This grateful song, a tribute to thy praise.

  When first mankind o'er-spread great ASIA's lands,
And nations rose unnumber'd as the sands,
From eastern shores, where AMOUR rolls his streams,
And morning suns display their earliest beams,
TARTARS in millions, swarming on the day,
Thro' the vast western ocean steer'd their way ;
From east to west, from north to south they roll,
And whelm the fields from DARIEN to the pole.
  Sunk in barbarity, these realms were found,
And Superstition hung her clouds around ;
O'er all, impenetrable Darkness spread
Her dusky wings, and cast a dreadful shade ;
No glimpse of science through the gloom appear'd ;
No trace of civil life the desart chear'd ;
No soft endearments, no fond social ties,
Nor faith, nor justice calm'd their horrid joys :
But furious Vengeance swell'd the hellish mind,
And dark-ey'd Malice all her influence join'd.
Here spread broad plains, in blood and slaughter drown'd ;
There boundless forests nodded o'er the ground ;
Here ceaseless riot and confusion rove ;
There savage roarings shake the echoing grove.
Age after age rolls on in deepening gloom,
Dark as the mansions of the silent tomb.

There

Thus wafting Difcord, like an angry fea,
Swept mighty kings and warring worlds away,
And (ages paft) fucceeding times beheld
The fame dire ruin clothe the dreary field.

At length (COLUMBUS taught by heaven to trace
Far-diftant lands, through unknown pathlefs feas)
AMERICA's bright realms arofe to view,
And the *old* world rejoic'd to fee the *new*.

When bleft ELIZA rul'd th' ATLANTIC main,
And her bold navies humbled haughty SPAIN ;
Heaven fent undaunted RALEIGH, ENGLAND's pride,
To waft her children o'er the briny tide,
In fair VIRGINIA's fields to fix her throne,
And ftretch her fway beneath the falling fun.

Then CHARLES and LAUD ufurp'd defpotic powers,
And Perfecution fadden'd ALBION's fhores ;
With racks and flames, Religion fpread her fway,
BRITONS were learn'd to torture, laws t'obey.

Forc'd from the pleafures of their native foil,
Where Liberty had lighten'd every toil ;
Forc'd from the arms of friends and kindred dear,
With fcarce the comfort of one parting tear,
Whilft wives clung round and took a final gaze,
And reverend fires prolong'd the laft embrace ;
To thefe far-diftant climes our fathers came,
Where bleft NEW-ENGLAND boafts a parent's name.
With Freedom's fire their gen'rous bofoms glow'd,
Warm for the truth, and zealous for their GOD ;
With thefe, the horrors of the defart ceas'd ;
Without them, ALBION lefs than defarts pleas'd ;
By thefe infpir'd, their zeal unfhaken ftood,
And bravely dar'd each danger—to be good ;
Th' unfathom'd ocean, roll'd in mighty ftorms,
Want and Difeafe in all their dreadful forms,
The freezing blaft that roar'd through boundlefs fnows,
And War fierce-threat'ning from furrounding foes.

Yet

Yet here Contentment dwelt, and Pleasure smil'd,
And rough-brow'd Labour every care beguil'd,
Made fruitful gardens round the forests rise,
And calm'd the horrors of the dreary skies.

PENN led a peaceful train to that kind clime,
Where Nature wantons in her liveliest prime,
Where mighty *Del'ware* rolls his silver tide,
And fertile fields adorn the river's side.
Peace rul'd his life ; to peace his laws inspir'd ;
In peace the willing savages retir'd.
The dreary Wilderness, with glad surprise,
Saw spacious towns and golden harvests rise.

Brave OGLETHROPE in GEORGIA fix'd his seat,
And deep distress there found a calm retreat ;
Learning and life to orphans there were given,
And drew down blessings from approving heaven.

Happy they liv'd, while Peace maintain'd her sway,
And taught the furious savage to obey,
Whilst Labour fearless rear'd the nodding grain,
And Innocence securely trod the plain :
But soon, too soon, were spread the dire alarms,
And thousand painted nations rush'd to arms,
War's kindled flames blaz'd dreadful round the shore,
And hills and plains with blood were crimson'd o'er.
Where late the flocks rov'd harmless on the green,
Where rising towns and cultur'd fields were seen,
Illimitable desarts met the eye,
And smoking ruins mounted to the sky.

Oft when deep silent Night her wings had spread,
And the vast world lay hid in peaceful shade,
In some lone village mirth led on the hours,
And swains secure to sleep resign'd their powers ;
Sudden the fields resound with war's alarms,
And earth re-echoes —— arms, to arms, to arms ;
Faint through the gloom the murd'ring bands are seen ;
Disploded thunder shakes the darksome green ;

Broad

Broad ftreams of fire from falling ftructures rife,
And fhrieks and groans and fhouts invade the fkies :
Here weeping mothers piercing anguifh feel ;
There fmiles the babe beneath the lifted fteel ;
Here vig'rous youth from bloody vengeance flies ;
There white-hair'd age juft looks to heaven, and dies.

The fons of GAUL in yonder northern lands
Urg'd the keen fword and fir'd the painted bands ;
Priefts, cloath'd in Virtue's garb, deftruction fpread,
And pious fury heap'd the fields with dead.

Rous'd by increafing woes, our fires bade found
The trump of war, and fquadrons gather'd round,
Where LOUISBOURG, adorn'd with towering fpires,
Defy'd the terror of the BRITISH fires ;
Bands, who ne'er heard the thundring cannon's roar,
Nor met a foe, nor view'd a wall before,
By Freedom warm'd, with native brav'ry crown'd,
Bade her proud towers be humbled to the ground.
E'en Heaven itfelf approv'd a war fo juft ;
In Heaven let injur'd nations put their truft.

Yet ftill deftruction fpread around the fhore,
And the dire favage bath'd in BRITISH gore,
'Till WOLFE appear'd and led his freeborn bands,
Like a dark tempeft to yon GALLIC lands :
Then fhook Quebec at his exalted name,
And her high walls already feem'd to flame.
Lo ! where deep forefts roar with loud alarms,
Th' exalted hero fhines in blazing arms ;
His fquadrons, rolling like the billow'd main,
Dart a bright horror o'er th' embattl'd plain ;
Whilft from afcending domes and lofty towers
Pale quivering thoufands view the hoftile powers.
The BRITISH hoft, ftretch'd out in dark array,
Rufh fearlefs on and fweep their foes away ;
From fmoky volumes rapid flames afpire,
And burfting cannon fet the fields on fire ;

Fate

Fate fwells the found ; whole troops of heroes fall ;
And one unbounded ruin buries all.

As o'er the weftern dark clouds arife, *plains*
Involve the fun and blacken all the fkies ;
The whirlwinds roar ; heaven's awful thunders roll,
And ftreamy lightnings flafh around the pole ;
Defcending floods along the meadows flow,
And burfting torrents whelm the world below.

Then glorious AMHERST joins his utmoft force,
And tow'rd CANADIA's realms inclines his courfe ;
Immenfe deftruction marks his dreadful way,
And fmoking towns fpread terror on the day ;
O'er all the land one boundlefs wafte is feen,
And blazing hills and gloomy ftreams between.
The voice of Defolation fills the gales,
And boding Horror fighs along the vales ;
Deep in the woods the *favage* world retires,
Far from the thunder and the wafting fires.
At length thefe realms the BRITISH fcepter own,
And bow fubmiffive at great GEORGE's throne.

Almighty GOD of heaven ! thy wondrous ways
Demand loud anthems and eternal praife.
Through earth, through heaven's immeafurable rounds,
Thy Greatnefs beams ; thy being knows no bounds.
E'er Time began, unbounded and alone,
Beyond the vaft of fpace thy Glory fhone ;
'Till that great moment when th' almighty call
From endlefs darknefs wak'd this earthly ball :
Then Being heard his voice, and round the fky
Glow'd the bright worlds, which gild the realms on high ;
Time then appear'd ; the Seafons deck'd his train,
And Hours and Years danc'd joyous o'er the plain ;
Millions of morning ftars JEHOVAH fung,
And the whole univerfe with praifes rung.

Yon world of fire, that gives a boundlefs day,
From thy effulgence darts the burning ray.

Thou

Thou bid'ſt yon ſtarry flames adorn the pole ;
Thy word ordains, and circling ſeaſons roll :
At thy command awakes the lovely Spring ;
Beauty breaks forth ; the hills with muſick ring :
In Summer's fiercer blaze thy thunders roar ;
Nature attends, and trembling realms adore :
When Autumn ſhines, thy fruits bedeck the plain,
And plenteous harveſts joy the humble ſwain :
On Wintry winds thine awful chariot flies,
When gath'ring ſtorms envelope all the ſkies ;
On Glory thron'd, with flames about thee roll'd ;
Light forms thy robes, and clouds thy wheels infold ;
Around, ten thouſand ſparkling angels glow,
Brighten the heavens, and ſhake the world below.

At thy command, war glitters o'er the plain ;
Thou ſpeak'ſt—and peace revives the fields again,
Vaſt empires riſe, and cities gild the day ;
Thou frown'ſt—and kings and kingdoms melt away.
BRITANNIA's happy iſlands, rais'd by Thee,
Awe the wide world, and rule the boundleſs ſea ;
Led by thine arm, WOLFE humbled haughty GAUL,
And glorious AMHERST taught her pride to fall.
May this bleſt land with grateful praiſe adore
Such boundleſs goodneſs, and ſuch boundleſs power.

See heaven-born Peace, deſcending from the ſky,
Bids diſcord vaniſh, and her horrors fly ;
The wearied nations hear her gentle voice,
Own her glad ſway, and wiſh for milder joys ;
Swift o'er the land, the bliſsful tidings ring,
The vallies brighten and the nations ſing.

As when long night has dwelt on ZEMBLA's ſhore,
Where winter reigns, and ſtorms around him roar,
Soon as the riſing ſun begins to roll,
And gild with fainter beams the frozen pole,
The ſtreams diſſolve, the fields no longer mourn,
And raptur'd regions hail his glad return.

Where

Where once dark Superstition fix'd her throne;
Where soul-exalting science never shone;
Where every social joy was drown'd in blood;
Where Hunger ceaseless rang'd the groves for food;
Where no gay fruits adorn'd the dreary plain;
No mountains brighten'd with the teeming grain;
No flocks nor herds along the hills were seen,
Nor swains nor hamlets chear'd the lonely green:
See num'rous infant states begin to grow;
See every state with peace and plenty flow;
See splendid towns o'er all the land extend;
The temples glitter and the spires ascend.
The rip'ning harvest waves along the hills,
The orchard blossoms, and the pasture smiles.
Unnumber'd vessels skim the liquid plain,
Search every realm, that hears the roaring main,
And fill'd with treasures, bid our shores behold
The eastern spices and the southern gold.

Celestial science, raptur'd we descry
Refulgent beaming o'er the western sky;
Bright Liberty extends her blissful reign,
With all the graces sparkling in her train:
Religion shines with a superiour blaze,
And heaven-born virtue beams diviner rays;
Justice enthron'd maintains an equal sway,
The poor dwell safely, and the proud obey.

O Land supremely blest! to thee tis given
To taste the choicest joys of bounteous heaven;
Thy rising Glory shall expand its rays,
And lands and times unknown rehearse thine endless praise.

As in a lonely vale, with glooms o'erspread,
Retir'd I rov'd, where guiding fancy led,
Deep silence reign'd; a sudden stream of light
Flam'd through the darksome grove & chear'd the night;
An awful form advanc'd along the ground,
And circling glories cast a radiance round:

C

Her

Her face divine with sparkling brightness shone
Like the clear splendour of the mid-day sun ;
Robes of pure white her heavenly limbs infold,
And on her scepter FREEDOM blaz'd in gold.
" Mortal ! attend " (she said and smil'd sublime)
Borne down the stream of ever rolling time,
View the bright scenes which wait this happy shore,
Her virtue, wisdom, arts and glorious power."
  " I see, where Discord thund'ring from afar,
Sounds her shrill trump and wakes the flames of war ;
Rous'd by her voice, vast hosts together driven,
Shake the wide earth, rend air, and darken heaven :
The cannons roar, the fields are heap'd with slain,
And storms of fire are blown along the plain."
  " Behold ! my Heroes lead the glorious way,
Where warring millions roll in dread array,
Awful as Angels, thron'd on streams of fire,
When trembling nations feel the thund'rer's ire :
Before them, Terror wings the rapid flight,
And Death behind them shrouds whole realms in night."
  " Then, white-rob'd Peace begins her milder reign,
And all the virtues croud her lovely train.
Lo ! heaven-born Science every bosom warms,
And the fair Arts unveil their lovely charms."
  " See ! blest Philosophy inspires the soul
To roam from land to land, from pole to pole ;
To soar beyond the sun, to worlds on high,
Which roll in millions round th' unmeasur'd sky ;
To mark the comet thro' his pathless maze,
Whilst his bright glories set the heavens on blaze."
  " Her nobler Sister too shall charm the mind
With moral raptures and with truths refin'd ;
Religion lead whole realms to worlds of joy,
Undying peace and bliss without alloy."
  " See Hist'ry all the scenes of time unveil
And bid my sons attend her wondrous tale !

                                         Led

Led by her voice, behold them mount the throne
And ſtretch their ſway to regions yet unknown !"
  " See all the powers of Poetry unite
To paint Religion,s charms divinely bright ;
To ſing his name, who made yon orbs of fire,
Spread out the ſky and form'd th' angelic choir :
Seraphs themſelves inſpire the ſacred lays,
And ſtoop from heaven to hear their Maker's praiſe !"
  " See Sculpture mould the rude unpoliſh'd ſtone,
Give it new forms and beauties not its own ;
Bid the gay marble leap to life and breath,
And call up heroes from the realms of Death !"
  " Behold the canvas glow with living dies,
Tall groves ſhoot up, ſtreams wind and mountains riſe !
Again the fair unfolds a heaven of charms,
And the bold leader frowns in dreadful arms."
  " Then Eloquence ſoft pity ſhall inſpire,
Smooth the rough breaſt, or ſet the ſoul on fire ;
Teach guilt to tremble at th' Almighty name,
Unſheath his ſword and make his lightnings flame ;
Or reach out grace more mild than falling dews,
While pale Deſpair th' affrighted ſoul purſues."
  " Hail Land of light and joy ! thy power ſhall grow
Far as the ſeas, which round thy regions flow ;
Through earth's wide realms thy glory ſhall extend,
And ſavage nations at thy ſeepter bend.
Around the frozen ſhores thy ſons ſhall ſail,
Or ſtretch their canvas to the ASIAN gale,
Or, like COLUMBUS, ſteer their courſe unknown,
Beyond the regions of the flaming zone,
To worlds unfound beneath the ſouthern pole,
Whoſe native hears Antarctic oceans roll ;
Where artleſs Nature rules with peaceful ſway,
And where no ſhip e'er ſtemm'd the untry'd way."
  For thee, proud INDIA's ſpicy iſles ſhall blow,
Bright ſilks be wrought, and ſparkling diamonds glow ;

Earth's

Earth's richeſt realms their treaſures ſhall unfold,
And op'ning mountains yield the flaming gold ;
Round thy broad fields more glorious ROMES ariſe,
With pomp and ſplendour bright'ning all the ſkies ;
EUROPE and ASIA with ſurprize behold
Thy temples ſtarr'd with gems and roof'd with gold.
From realm to realm broad APPIAN ways ſhall wind,
And diſtant ſhores by long canals be join'd,
The ocean hear thy voice, the waves obey,
And through green vallies trace their wat'ry way.
No more ſhall War her fearful horrors ſound,
Nor ſtrew her thouſands on th' embattled ground ;
No more on earth ſhall Rage and Diſcord dwell,
But ſink with Envy to their native hell."

" Then, then an heavenly kingdom ſhall deſcend,
And Light and Glory through the world extend ;
Th' Almighty Saviour his great power diſplay
From riſing morning to the ſetting day ;
Love reign triumphant, Fraud and Malice ceaſe,
And every region ſmile in endleſs peace :
Till the laſt trump the ſlumbering dead inſpire,
Shake the wide heavens, and ſet the world on fire ;
Thron'd on a flaming cloud, with brightneſs crown'd,
The Judge deſcend, and angels ſhine around,
The mountains melt, the moon and ſtars decay,
The ſun grow dim, and Nature roll away ;
GOD's happy children mount to worlds above,
Drink ſtreams of pureſt joy and taſte immortal love."

THE
CONQUEST
OF
CANÄAN;

A POEM, IN ELEVEN BOOKS.

By TIMOTHY DWIGHT.

Fired, at first sight, with what the Muse imparts,
In fearless youth we tempt the height of arts.
                                        POPE.

HARTFORD:
PRINTED BY ELISHA BABCOCK.
M,DCC,LXXXV.

GEORGE WASHINGTON, Esquire,

Commander in chief of the American Armies,

The Saviour of his Country,

The Supporter of Freedom,

And the Benefactor of Mankind;

This Poem is inscribed,

with the highest respect for his character, the
most ardent wishes for his happiness, and the
most grateful sense of the blessings, secured,
by his generous efforts, to the United States
of North America,

by his most humble,

and most obedient servant,

TIMOTHY DWIGHT.

Greenfield, in Connecticut,
March 1, 1785.

AS this poem is the firſt of the kind, which has been publiſhed in this country, the writer begs leave to introduce it with ſeveral obſervations, which that circumſtance alone may perhaps render neceſſary.

He has taken to himſelf the liberty of altering the real order of the two laſt battles, becauſe he imagined the illuſtrious events, which attended the battle of Gibeon, would make it appear to be the cataſtrophe of the poem, whereever inſerted.

He has varied the ſtory of the embaſſy from Gibeon, for reaſons, which he thinks will be obvious to every reader, and which he hopes will be eſteemed his ſufficient juſtification.

To give entire Unity to the Action, he has made Jabin the Canäanitiſh hero through the whole poem ; and has transferred the ſcene of the battle, between Hazor and Iſrael, from the ſhores of the lake Merom to the neighbourhood of Ai.

In the Manners, he has ſtudied a medium between abſolute barbariſm and modern refinement. In the beſt characters, he has endeavoured to repreſent ſuch manners, as are removed from the peculiarities of any age, or country, and might belong to the amiable and virtuous, of every age : ſuch as are elevated without deſign, refined without ceremony, elegant without faſhion, and agreeable, becauſe they are ornamented with ſincerity, dignity, and religion , not becauſe they are poliſhed by art and education. Of ſuch manners, he hopes he may obſerve, without impropriety, that they poſſeſs the higheſt advantages for univerſal application.

He has made uſe of Rhyme, becauſe he believed it would be more generally reliſhed than blank verſe, even amongſt thoſe who are eſteemed perſons of taſte.

It may perhaps be thought the reſult of inattention or ignorance, that he choſe a ſubject, in which his countrymen had no national intereſt. But he remarked that the Iliad and Eneid were as agreeable to modern nations, as to the Greeks and Romans. The reaſon he ſuppoſed to be obvious--the ſubjects of thoſe poems furniſh the faireſt opportunities of exhibiting the agreeable, the novel, the moral, the pathetic, and the ſublime. If he is not deceiv-ed, the ſubject he has choſen poſſeſſes, in a degree, the ſame advantages.

It will be obſerved that he has introduced ſome new words. and annexed to ſome old ones, a new ſignification. This liberty, allowed to others, he hopes will not be refuſed to him : eſpecially as from this ſource the copiouſneſs and refinement of language have been principally derived.

That he wiſhes to pleaſe he frankly confeſſes. If he fails in the deſign, it will be a ſatisfaction that he ſhall have injured no perſon but himſelf. As the poem is uniformly friendly to delicacy, and virtue, he hopes his countrymen will ſo far regard him with candour, as not to impute it to him as a fault, that he has endeavoured to pleaſe them, and has thrown in his mite, for the advancement of the refined arts, on this ſide of the Atlantic.

THE

CONQUEST of CANÄAN.

BOOK I.

ARGUMENT.

Subject proposed. Invocation. After the battle, mentioned in the beginning of the seventh chapter of Joshua, the Israelites, in correspondence with the sacred history, are represented in circumstances of extreme distress. With this event the poem opens, in the evening. Morning. Scene of war. Story of Zimri, and Aram. Zimri returns to the assembly of Israel, and brings an account of the death of Aram, and of an army, sent by Jabin, king of Hazor, to assist Ai. Distress of the Israelites. Character and oration of Hanniel. After a pathetic address, and rehearsal of their miseries, he attempts to prove the impossibility of succeeding in their present design, because of the strength, skill, and numerous allies of their enemies; foretels their approaching ruin, asserts that GOD is opposed to them, that they were led out of Egypt to silence their murmurs, and, the end being accomplished, ought to return. Panegyric on that country; obviates objections to a return, and informs them that, if they should conquer Canäan, they will be ruined, during the war, by the necessary neglect of arts and agriculture, difficulty of dividing the land, of settling a form of government, and of avoiding tyranny; and concludes with a new exhortation to return to Egypt. Applause. Joshua replies, and beginning to explain the dispensations of Providence, it interrupted by Hanniel, who first obliquely, and then openly accuses him of aiming at the usurpation of kingly authority; and asserts the return to be easy. Joshua vindicates his innocence with severity upon Hanniel; and allowing they can return, paints to them the miseries, they will experience from the Egyptian king, lords, people, and manners, and from providential dispensations terminating in their ruin. He appeals to them to judge of the falsehood of Hanniel's ideas of the purposes of Heaven, in leading them out of Egypt; and declares the certainty of their success from their union, with a few exceptions, their previous prosperity, and the favour and revealed designs of Heaven, and exults in their future glory. Applause. Preparation for war. Caleb opposes immediate war, and advises a fast of two days. Joshua approves of it.

THE CONQUEST OF CANÄAN.

BOOK I.

THE Chief, whofe arm to Ifrael's chofen band
 Gave the fair empire of the promis'd land,
Ordain'd by Heaven to hold the facred fway,
Demands my voice and animates the lay.
O thou, whofe Love, high thron'd above all height, 5
Illumes th' immenfe, and funns the world of light ;
Whofe diftant beam the human mind infpires,
With wifdom brightens, and with virtue fires ;
Unfold how pious realms to glory rife,
And impious nations find avenging fkies :   10
May thy own deeds exalt the humble line,
And not a ftain obfcure the theme divine.
When now from weftern hills the fun was driven,
And night expanding fill'd the bounds of heaven,
O'er Ifrael's camp ten thoufand fires appear'd 15
And folemn cries from diftant guards were heard,
Her tribes, efcap'd from Ai's unhappy plain,
With fhame and anguifh mourn'd their heroes flain,

Line 1.) Wherever *Chief, Hero, Leader,* &c. with a capital, re-
fpect the Ifraelitifh army, Jofhua is intended ; when they refpect the
Canäanitifh army, Jabin is intended. The *Youth,* with a capital,
denotes Irad.

B

Pierc'd with deep wounds the groaning warriors ftood;
Their bofoms heav'd, their tears inceffant flow'd;   20
Their fons unburied on the hoftile plain,
Their brothers captiv'd, and their parents flain.
The tender father clafp'd his lovely child,
That thoughtlefs-fporting innocently fmil'd,
To his fond arms with foft endearments leapt,   25
Gaz'd on his tears, and wonder'd why he wept.
Her woes with his the trembling mother join'd,
Edg'd all his fears, and funk his drooping mind,
Array'd in tenfold gloom th' approaching light,
And gather'd foes unnumber'd to the fight.   30
Thus trembling, fad, of every hope forlorn,
The haplefs thoufands watch'd the coming morn.
  In Jofhua's ear their fad complaints refound,
As flow, unfeen, he trac'd the camp around.
Where'er fhrill cries, or groans diftinguifh'd flow'd   35
Propp'd on his lance, the Hero liftening ftood:
For oft the fecret hour of night he chofe,
To hufh their tumults, and to learn their woes;
Each tear, each cry his feeling mind opprefs'd,
And fchemes of pity fill'd his labouring breaft.   40
  And now bright Phofphor wak'd the dawning day,
The tents all whitening in th' expanded ray;
The fun's broad beam the fcene of war difplay'd,
A wide extent, with diftant groves o'erfpread;
A tall, dark foreft gloom'd the northern round,   45
And caftern hills o'er hills th' horizon bound:
Far fouth, a plain in vivid green withdrew,
And one unvaried level fill'd the view;
Beyond, Ai's grandeur proudly rofe on high,
And azure mountains pierc'd the weftern fky.   50
  Around their Leader's tent, th' unnumber'd train
Throng'd from the camp, and gather'd on the plain.
When Zimri flow approach'd; of Afher's race
The firft in merit, as the firft in place.

Him, not a chief, that dar'd the battling field,   55
In swiftness equall'd, or in strength excell'd ;
Save *Joshua*'s arm, that still unconquer'd shone ;
From every rival every prize he won.

In night's last gloom (so Joshua's will ordain'd)
To find what hopes the cautious foe remain'd,   60
Or what new strength, allied, increas'd their force,
To Ai's high walls the hero bent his course.
Aram, his friend, unknowing vile dismay,
With willing footsteps shar'd the dangerous way.
In virtue join'd, one soul to both was given ;   65
Each steer'd his path, and led his friend to heaven.

O'er earth's dim verge as dawn'd the cheerful day,
Near slumbering Ai they cours'd their fearless way ;
Unseen, in twining shrubs, a heathen sate,
Mark'd their still path, and boded Aram's fate ;   70
Swift hurl'd, his javelin sought the hero's side,
Pierc'd to the heart, he groan'd, and gasp'd, and died.
The heathen flew, fierce Zimri clave his breast,
But Aram's eyes were clos'd in endless rest.

Thus, while fond Virtue wish'd in vain to save,   75
Hale, bright and generous, found a hapless grave.
With genius' living flame his bosom glow'd,
And science charm'd him to her sweet abode :
In worth's fair path his feet adventur'd far ;
The pride of peace, the rising grace of war ;   80
In duty firm, in danger calm as even,
To friends unchanging, and sincere to heaven.

75.) *While, amid,* and *among,* are used throughout this poem,
euph. grat. instead of *whilst, amidst,* and *amongst.*

76. *Hale bright*) The comparisons of this kind were all writ-
ten in the early stages of the late war, and annexed to the poem to
indulge the Author's own emotions of regard to the persons named
in them. As it was impossible to pay this little tribute of respect to
all the deserving characters, who have fallen in defence of American
liberty, the Author determined to desist, after the first attempt. The
lines on Major Andre are an exception to the above remark, as are
those on General Mercer.

How fhort his courfe, the prize how early won !
While weeping friendfhip mourns her favourite gone,
With foul too noble for fo bafe a caufe,   85
Thus Andre bow'd to war's barbarian laws.
In morn's fair light the opening bloffom warm'd,
Its beauty fmil'd, its growing fragrance charm'd ;
Fierce roar'd th' untimely blaft around its head ;
The beauty vanifh'd, and the fragrance fled ;   90
Soon funk his graces in the wintry tomb,
And fad Columbia wept his haplefs doom.

    As now o'er eaftern hills the morning burn'd,
Alone brave Zimri to the camp return'd ;
Pale in his front defpair and anguifh fate,   95
And each kind bofom fear'd for Aram's fate,
When thus, the Leader----Say, exalted chief,
What dire misfortune clouds thy mind with grief?
O beft of men, he cried, my tears deplore
The hero's fate, brave Aram is no more.   100
Weep, weep, my friends : his worthy life demands
This laft, poor tribute from your grateful hands,
Nor weep for him alone : dread fcenes of grief
Surround our fteps, and Heaven denies relief.
Th' infulting wretch, that feal'd the hero's fate,   105
In death proclaim'd what terrors round you wait.
I die, he cried, but know, thou culprit, know,
To the dark tomb thy harbinger I go.
O'er Ifrael's race afcend, from realms afar,
The clouds of ruin, and the ftorms of war.   110
The hofts, that bow to Jabin's great controul
From Hazor's rocky hills, in thunder roll ;
Hofts, that ne'er knew the tender tear to fhed,
Born in the field, beneath the ftandard bred ;
That raptur'd fly, where fhrilling trumpets call,   115
Plunge on the pointed fpear, and climb the kindled wall.
Thefe dauntlefs bands (to Ai the meffage came)
Shall fink in night thy nation's hated name ;

Even now brave Oran, Jabin's martial boaſt,
Speeds his glad courſe and moves a countleſs hoſt : 120
Raptur'd I ſee thy camp in flames ariſe,
And Iſrael's aſhes cloud the angry ſkies.
He ſpoke.   Aſtoniſh'd at th' impending doom,
Round the pale thouſands breath'd a ſolemn gloom ;
Rent were their martial veſtments, torne their hair, 125
And every eye ſpoke pangs of keen deſpair.

    Mid the ſad throng, in mournful robes array'd
Vile duſt beſprinkled o'er his down-caſt head,
Pale Hanniel roſe, and with diſſembled woe,
Clouded his front, and urg'd the tear to flow.   130
Of princely blood, his haughty ſire, of yore
Proud Pharaoh's favourite on th' Egyptian ſhore,
O'er Iſrael's race was ſcepter'd to preſide,
To rule their tributes and their toils to guide.

    In the ſon's mind again the parent liv'd,   135
His pride rekindled, and his art reviv'd.
Where'er pride call'd, his changing ſoul would turn ;
Grieve with the ſad, and with the envious burn ;
Vaunt with the brave, be ſerious with the wiſe,
And cheat the pious with uplifted eyes ;   140
In Youth's fond ſports with ſeeming zeal engage,
Or liſt, delighted, to the tales of Age.

    When Joſhua's hand the ſacred rule adorn'd,
With pangs he ſaw, but ſtill in ſecret mourn'd :
His cloſe revenge the Hero's fate decreed,   145
And ſmooth, ſure ſlander taught his name to bleed.
With friendly graſp he ſqueez'd each warrior's hand ;
With jeſts familiar pleas'd the vulgar band ;
In ſly, ſhrewd hints the Leader's faults diſcloſ'd ;
Prais'd his whole ſway, but ſingle acts oppos'd ;   150
Admir'd how law ſo ſtern a face could wear ;
Stil'd combat raſhneſs, and nam'd caution fear :
With angels then his fame and virtue join'd,
To tempt coarſe ſcandal from each envious mind :

Bleſt his own peaceful lot, and ſmil'd, that Heaven,　155
To minds, that priz'd them, empire's toils had given.
Yet baſe born fear his vigorous ſoul diſdain'd ;
Each danger ſhar'd and every toil ſuſtain'd ;
Joy'd, in terrific fields, the foe to dare,
And claim'd the honours of the fierceſt war.　　　　160

　　Now the bleſt period, long in vain deſir'd,
His fond hope flatter'd, and his boſom fir'd ;
To end his rival's ſway, his own ſecure,
Reſolv'd, his fancy deem'd the triumph ſure.

　　In ſeeming anguiſh oft his hands he wrung,　　165
And words imperfect murmur'd on his tongue ;
At length, with feeble voice, he thus began,
While round the tribes a mute attention ran.

　　Friends ! brethren ! ſires ! or by what tenderer name
Shall I addreſs the heirs of Jacob's fame ?　　　170
Dear to my ſoul, as thoſe red drops, that flow,
Thro' my warm veins, and bid my boſom glow,
If chill'd by grief's cold hand, the vital flood
Still pours its warmth, nor yet forſakes the road !
Long has this heart with deep compaſſion view'd　175
Your generous tribes, by countleſs ills ſubdu'd ;
Ills, theſe pain'd eyes foreboding, long beheld,
And this ſad warning voice in vain reveal'd.
Thoſe counſels, now by ſure experience prov'd,
That voice, alone by Iſrael's welfare mov'd,　　　180
Once more attend.　Ye guardian powers, be near,
Enlarge their minds and give them hearts to hear !
Let baſe-born prejudice no more controul
The native candour of each generous ſoul ;
Aſſert yourſelves ; your future conduct ſcan ;　　185
Reaſon's the nobleſt privilege of man.

　　Long have our feet with reſtleſs error rov'd,
And the ſad waſte with all its miſeries prov'd ;
That waſte, by Heaven's unerring ſentence curs'd
With ceaſeleſs hunger, and eternal thirſt,　　　190

The tyger's rage, the lion's fearful path,
Beftrew'd with bones, and red with recent death,
The fun's keen fury, midnight's gloomy dread,
And all the horrors of th' impoifon'd fhade.

How oft thefe eyes the haplefs child have view'd,   195
By hunger famifh'd and by pain fubdu'd,
While the fond parent o'er his beauties hung,
And look'd diftrefs, that froze his faltering tongue,
Diftrefs, to hear the young, the piercing cry,
That claim'd relief, when no relief was nigh ;   200
To fee the babe, its face with death o'erfpread,
Stretch forth its little hands, and fue for bread :
While friends, all impotent, roll'd down the tear,
Rocks learn'd to feel, and forefts bent to hear.

When pale Difeafe affum'd her fatal reign,   205
Chas'd the warm glow, and rack'd the joints with pain,
Oft have thefe failing eyes the chief beheld,
In counfel fam'd, and glorious in the field,
Condemn'd the pangs of ficknefs to endure,
Far from relief, and hopelefs of a cure ;   210
No downy couch to reft his drooping head,
The fkies his covering, and the earth his bed ;
No foftening plant his ftiffen'd wounds to heal,
Soothe his rack'd nerves, and learn them not to feel ;
Nor fweet, embowering fhade to drive away   215
Night's baleful damps, and fummer's fcorching ray.
But who the various ills can number o'er,
Or tell the fands that form the fea-beat fhore ?
Even now by flow degrees our thoufands fall,
Till one wide, common grave involve us all.   220

For fee what woes furround our daring courfe,
That tempts the terrors of unmeafur'd force ;
Safe in high walls, infulting foes deride,
Our boaftful impotence, and banner'd pride ;
On boundlefs wealth, with carelefs eafe, rely,   225
And hofts unnumber'd never taught to fly ;

Proud of the dreadful steed, the wasting car,
And all the strength, and all the art, of war.
    These foes to aid, what countless throngs will join !
What peopled realms against our arms combine !   230
From Gibeon's walls, and where tremendous powers
Surround imperial Hazor's hundred towers,
Or where proud shores the western main behold,
Or orient Gihon's haughty tides are roll'd,
I see to fearful combat millions rise,   235
Chiefs mount the car, and point the fated prize;
See in the van-guard haughty Conquest ride
Lo, murder'd thousands pour the ruddy tide !
O'er Israel's camp the clouds of vengeance lower,
Fear wings our flight, and flames our race devour.   240
    At that dread season, chain'd in bonds forlorn,
Of men the proverb, and of Heaven the scorn,
Hiss'd by vile slaves, our tribes the rack shall feel,
Or gasp, far happier, on the griding steel :
Slow round the form the fires of Molock burn ;   245
Chiefs mount the pile, and babes to ashes turn:
Impal'd with anguish, bleeding sires behold,
Their wives polluted and their virgins sold ;
Their sons, sweet solace of declining age,
In sport transfix'd, or cleft in causeless rage ;   250
While threats, while insults rend with sore dismay,
And hungry hounds stand gaping for their prey.
But cease my faltering tongue ; ere these befal,
Oh Heaven, let Hanniel's blood bedew yon impious wall.
    And will no happier hand direct the road,   255
And tell, where Quiet builds her sweet abode ?
Where is the sage, on whose angelic tongue
Bright wisdom dwelt, and soft persuasion hung ?
Does no kind breast with patriot virtue glow,
And claim an interest in his country's woe ?   260
Here then, ye heirs of Jacob's name, behold
A friend, whose bosom terror ne'er controul'd ;

Whose voice, though envious thousands dare oppose,
Shall pour the balm, and heal his country's woes.

 How long, brave heroes, shall your feet pursue 265
Such keen distress, as nations never knew ?
How long your host the chains of slavery own,
And millions die, to swell the pride of one ?
'Gainst Heaven's decree let folly cease to rise,
And tempt no more the vengeance of the skies. 270
To other lords that firm decree ordains
Th' expected mountains, and the promis'd plains.
Our every path unnumber'd woes surround ;
Our blood in streams bedews polluted ground ;
No glad success arrays our steps in light, 275
And smiling Victory triumphs in our flight.

 Search ancient years ; thro' time's long course return,
When earth first wanton'd in the beams of morn ;
Success unchang'd attends, when God approves,
And Peace propitious smooths the path he loves. 280
Base flight, and dire amaze, and creeping shame,
Man lost in guilt, and alien'd skies, proclaim.

 If still your fetter'd minds, by folly sway'd,
Doubts wavering toss, and leaden fears invade,
To yon bright dome your eyes convicted turn ; 285
Say why forgets the guiding flame to burn ?
Why round its point forgets the cloud to roll,
Sublime pavilion of th' all-moving soul ?
The dreaded truth must Hanniel singly own ?
Fled is the smile of Heaven, the Guardian gone. 290

 But Virtue asks, Why, led by God's command,
Rov'd this brave host thro' many a weary land ?
Each hour, with pains replete, each field replies,
And with dread language, loud as clarions, cries,
In Egypt's realms, where every pleasure smil'd, 295
And, far from famine, labourers lightly toil'd,
Wanton with feasts, our thankless hearts repin'd,
And tainted prayers provok'd th' all-ruling Mind ;

C

Tir'd by long scenes of woe, th' ungrateful hoft,　299
Learn'd humbler thoughts, and priz'd the good they loft:
Reclaim'd, each fpotlefs mind adores his ways,
And every blefling wakes the voice of praife.
The end thus gain'd, his terrors lifted high
Bid his warn'd fons the unblefs'd purpofe fly.
See, fwiftly borne, the ftorm of vengeance rife!　305
Cloud after cloud invades the angry fkies;
Even now o'er earth, fierce peals commencing roar,
And round the concave flames vindictive pour;
Hark, with what din the diftant whirlwinds roll!
How the floods threaten from the thundering pole!　310
Rife, nimbly rife, burft every dead delay,
And fly, ere fury fweep our race away.

But where, oh where fhall haplefs Ifrael fly?
Where find a covert, when the ruin's nigh?
Will no kind land the wifh'd recefs difclofe!　315
No friendly refuge foothe our long, long woes?
Yes, the fair, fruitful land, with rapture crown'd,
Where once our fires a fweet retirement found,
That land, our refuge Heaven's high will ordains,
Pleas'd with our prayers, and piteous of our pains.　320

Hail favour'd realms, where no rude tempeft blows!
Serene retreats, and fhades of kind repofe!
Ordain'd, the union'd blifs of life to prove,
The wreaths of glory, and the bowers of love!
There the great prince, with awful fplendor crown'd,　325
From foes fhall guard us, and with peace furround,
In no rude combat fated to engage,
Nor fir'd by clarions to vindictive rage.
There cates divine fhall yield the fweet repaft,
Charm the pall'd eye, and lure the loathing tafte;　330
With die refulgent crimfon veftures glow,
And robes of kings fucceed this garb of woe:
Our tribes, in fpicy groves, at eafe recline,
Prefs the fwell'd fig, and pluck the clufter'd vine;　335

Her floods of boundless wealth the river roll,   [the pole.
And spring, with autumn join'd, beam temperate round
   For these bless'd joys, what mind, so left to shame,
Can grudge the tribute, regal glories claim ?
Return, how due ! Devoid of decent show,
How soon would Power to trampled weakness grow ? 340
How soon base minds the feeble judge deride,
And beggar'd rulers quake at wealthy pride ?
Nor the just doom can Avarice' self deny,
Who share the blessing must the tax supply.
No danger now even timid minds can fear,   345
Lest stern Oppression lift her rod severe :
Unlike our sires, who rais'd impatient cries,
A fairer doom awaits us from the skies.
Taught by our hated flight, the nation knows
How, join'd with ours, their vast dominion grows ; 350
Disjoin'd, how swift the weaken'd tribes decay,
To foes a triumph, and to schisms a prey.
   Even now with friendly joy their bosoms burn,
And with fond prescience hail our wish'd return ;
Bid our own hands the grateful covenant frame,   355
Prepar'd to give, what avarice scarce can claim ;
Our sons invite their boundless wealth to share,
Garlands of fame, and sweet repose of care.
   Here, warriors, here the dreaded miseries flow,
Scenes of dire scorn, and seats of thickening woe. 360
For bless'd as hope can paint, o'er all our toil
Let conquest flourish, and let glory smile ;
Still in long train, what ceaseless ills await !
The waste of war, and frowns of adverse fate !   364
   While sheath'd in arms, the conquer'd realms we guard,
End of long pains, and patience' wish'd reward,
Those realms what culturing hand shall teach to bloom ?
Or bid bright vesture purple o'er the loom ?
Unfed, uncloath'd, our tribes shall waste away,
Our lands grow wild, and every art decay.   370

Whofe wifdom then fhall equal lots divine,
And round each province lead the bordering line !
Will none, for fancied wrongs, the falchion draw,
His arm the umpire, and his will the law,
O'er his friend's prize with rude irruption pour, 375
Burft nature's bonds, and bathe in kindred gore ?

 Whofe chofen hand the fceptre then fhall fway ?
What fyftem'd rule the union'd tribes obey ?
To my pain'd eyes what hideous profpects fpread,
When impious Faction rears her fnaky head ! 380
Array'd in favage pomp, Deftruction reigns
O'er flaming cities, and o'er crimfon plains ;
Friends, againft friends, that knew but one fond heart,
Aim the dark knife, and lift the fecret dart ;
In brother's blood unfeeling brothers wade, 385
And parent's bofoms fheath the filial blade.
Let Pity round the fcene extend her veil,
And thrilling virtue fhun the dreadful tale !

 Or fhall one arm the ftate forever fway ?
And, funk to ftocks, our torpid race obey ? 390
One voice, thro' ages, Jacob's pride controul,
Ourfelves the clay, and he th' all-moving foul ?
Perifh the thought ! t' oppofe a tyrant's reign,
One patriot life fhall flow from every vein ;
In Ifrael's caufe fhall burft this fearlefs voice, 395
And this bold arm avenge the free-born choice.

 Rife, warriors, rife ! defert this dreary plain,
Thefe fields of flaughter, and thefe haunts of pain !
To fcenes of brighter name, to happier fkies,
To other Edens lift your raptur'd eyes ! 400
The world's fair Emprefs chides our dull delay,
Spreads her fond arms, and bids us hafte away,
To blifs, to glory ; feize th' aufpicious road,
And claim your intereft in the blefs'd abode !

 The hero fpoke. As when, in diftant fkies, 405
Slow-roll'd, the darkening ftorm begins to rife,

Thro' the deep grove, and thro' the founding vale,
Roar the long murmurs of the fweeping gale :
So round the throng a hoarfe applaufe was heard,
And growing joy in every face appear'd.　　　410

On a tall rock, whofe top o'erlook'd the plain,
The Leader rofe, and hufh'd the reverent train.
By Hanniel warm'd, with airy vifions fir'd,
He faw gay hope their glowing minds infpir'd,
In profpect bright, at hand fair Egypt lay,　　　415
Divine the pleafure, and fecure the way ;
With calm, frank afpect, that ferenely fmil'd,
His port all-winning, and his accent mild ;
Too wife, to thwart at once the general choice,
Or hope to fway alone by reafon's voice,　　　420
He thus began.　Ye heirs of Jacob's name,
Let Jofhua's voice your generous candor claim.
In Ifrael's facred caufe my toils ye know,
My midnight watchings, and my morning woe.
Your long, lone path my wakeful eye furvey'd,　　　425
Charm'd the fad wild, and cheer'd the languid head ;
Sooth'd drooping ficknefs, banifh'd fear's alarms
And clafp'd the orphan with delighted arms ;
'Gainft fierce invafions rais'd a guardian fhield,
The firft to feek, the laft to leave, the field ;　　　430
For all your tribes a parent's fondnefs prov'd,
Fulfill'd each wifh, and even your wanderings lov'd.

In thofe fad fcenes, when pity owns applaufe,
Not Hanniel's tears adorn a fairer caufe.
For Ifrael's woe does Hanniel fingly feel ?　　　435
Are thefe eyes blind ? or is this bofom fteel ?
When ceas'd thefe hands from toil ? or what ftrange fun
Saw Jofhua's feet the haunts of danger fhun ?
Your eyes have feen, thefe honeft fcars proclaim
How oft this breaft has pour'd the vital ftream :　　　440
Still be it pour'd.　A nation's caufe to fave,
Life's a poor price ; the field an envied grave.

Whatever voice your welfare shall divine,
My heart shall welcome and my hand shall join:
But, calmly weigh'd, let Truth our counsels guide,   445
And Reason's choice the destin'd course decide.
So prone the mind in error's path to rove,
'T' explore is wisdom, and 'tis bliss to prove.
Charm'd, at first sight, when pleasures rise to view,
Each painted scene our ventrous thoughts pursue ;   450
In airy visions far-seen Edens rise,
And isles of pleasure tempt enamour'd eyes.
On the calm tide, to aromatic gales,
Our fearless hands exalt impatient sails ;
Thro' sapphire floods the bark foresees its way,   455
While wanton billows smoothly round it play,
Nor heeds the angry storm, that with dread power,
Climbs dark behind the hill, and hopes th' avenging hour,
Warn'd by my voice, such hidden dangers fly,
And each gay prospect scan with searching eye.   460

In realms far distant spreads th' expected shore,
Hills rise between, and boiling oceans roar :
Two tiresome ways invite our wearied bands,
Thro' trackless deserts, or through hostile lands.

Say, shall our steps again the waste pervade,   465
Dare the fierce heat, and tempt th' impoison'd shade ?
Consult yon chief ; his voice again shall tell
Those dreary scenes, he painted now so well.

Or shall our feet, its dangers hid from view,
Thro' peopled realms, a nearer path pursue ?   470
I blush, when falsehood leads the chosen tribes,
Where folly dictates, and where fear prescribes.
One foe to shun, shall fiercer foes be tried ?
Death their delight, and war their earliest pride.   474

Lo the fierce wrath, at Taberah's plain that burn'd,
And Korah's host to instant corses turn'd.
Rous'd to more dreadful flames, our guilt to spy,
And see our feet to hated Egypt fly,

Shall wing Philiftia's hoft to death and war,
And bid fierce Midian whirl the thundering car;   480
Full on her prey avenging Amalek fall,
And guilt and terror every heart appall :
Our wives, our fons, to favage wrath be given,
Feaft famifh'd wolves, and glut the hawks of heaven.

   No fancied doom my boding words declare :   485
Truth, fix'd as mountains, fills your ftartled ear.
To every beaft the lamb prefents a prey,
And coward bands invite the world to flay.

   But will ye tremble for one fhameful fall ?
Shall one loft combat Abraham's race appall ?   490
Is Aram dead ! to rapid vengeance fly ;
By me his orphan babes for vengeance cry ;
Fir'd by his fate, your nerves let ardour ftring,
Exalt the ftandard, and to combat fpring.

   Even Zimri fears, by ftrong affections led,   495
While his fond bofom mourns his Aram dead.
Of all the fympathy, that woes impart
To the foft texture of the good man's heart,
Departed friendfhip claims the largeft fhare,
And forrow in excefs is virtue there.   500
But timid paffion ! Grief, with ftartled eye
Spies fancied ills, and quakes, ere danger's nigh

   Yon chief demands, why fled the guardian fire ?
What unknown folly bade the cloud retire ?
That bafe diftruft, which glorious fight delays,   505
That fmooth, clofe fraud which tempts to dangerous ways,
Thefe claim the foourge of Heaven: be thefe atou'd,
Each fear fhall vanifh, and each hope be crown'd.

   While thus the Chief their bofoms warm'd anew,
And every ear, and heart, to virtue drew ;   510
Their kindfing zeal impatient Hanniel eyed,
Shook for his caufe, and frown'd with ftartled pride:
When thofe, he cried, whofe choice our warriors loft,
Of truth expatiate, and of wifdom boaft,

With juſt diſdain my riſing ſpirits burn, 515
And my pain'd heart, at times, forgets to mourn ;
To ſhame, to flight, does ſacred Wiſdom lead ?
Does ſacred Truth command our ſons to bleed ?
Rouſe then to arms ; lo Ai impatient ſtands,
And yields the doom, our eager wiſh demands ; 520
In wiſdom's cauſe with active zeal engage,
And fall, a ſplendid triumph to their rage.
Far happier lot, to meet the falchion's ſway !
Than, one by one, thus lingering, waſte away.

Far other end yon Chief ambitious eyes ; 525
Conceal'd by virtue's maſk the danger lies.
Unbrib'd, unaw'd, the honeſt taſk I claim,
To burſt the veil, and ward th' impending ſhame.
Long vers'd in wiles, the luſt of power his guide,
He lulls our caution, and inflates our pride ; 530
With ſenſe, that darts through man a ſearching view,
With pride, that reſt, or limits never knew,
To deep deſigns miſtruſtleſs hearts he draws,
With freedom ſoothes, and cheats with flatter'd laws ;
A crown to ſeize, the patriot's fire can claim, 535
And mock with ſeeming zeal the fearful Name.
Full well he knows that, worne by ſlow delay,
Our generous tribes ſhall fall an eaſy prey ;
That long-felt influence, great by habit grown,
Climbs to firm ſway, and ſwells into a throne. 540

Be warn'd, be warn'd ; the threatening evils fly,
And ſeek repoſe beneath a kinder ſky.
Short is the toil, the well-known path ſecure,
The pleaſure endleſs, and the triumph ſure.
Rejoic'd, each land will ope the deſtin'd road, 545
And ſmiling guide us to the wiſh'd abode.
Freed from the fearful ſtorm that round them ſpread,
Their hearts ſhall hail us, and their hands ſhall aid.
No giant chief in terror there ſhall riſe ;
No dreadful Jabin ſpring to ſeize the prize : 550

From Madon's hills, to fierce vindictive war
No frowning Jobab roll his iron car :
From death's alarms the potent king fhall guard,
And bowers of tranfport yield the bright reward.

  He fpoke. Like Angels drefs'd in glory's prime, 555
With confcious worth, and dignity fublime,
While the ftill thoufands gaz'd with glad furprize,
His great foul living in his piercing eyes,
The Chief return'd. By wild ambition tofs'd,
To fhame impervious, and to virtue loft,   560
Here bend thine eye, thy front unblufhing rear;
Let frozen Confcience point no fting fevere ;
Then tell, if falfehood lends thee power to tell,
Thy mind believes one fcene, thy lips reveal ;
One black afperfion, form'd to blot my name ; 565
Or one vain profpect, rais'd for Ifrael's fhame.
Difclofe what dreaded toil this arm has fled ;
On what dire plain this bofom fail'd to bleed :
Tell, if thou canft, when, lur'd by intereft's call,
One nerve, one wifh forgot the blifs of all. 570

  In virtue arm'd, while Confcience gayly fmiles,
I mock thy fraud, and triumph o'er thy wiles :
Thy darts impoifon'd peace and glory bring ;
'Tis guilt alone gives flander ftrength to fting.
Blufh, Hanniel, blufh ; to yonder tent depart; 575
Let humbler wifhes rule thy envious heart ;
Calm the wide luft of power ; contract thy pride ;
Repent thofe black defigns, thou canft not hide ;
Once more to Heaven thy long-loft prayers revive,
And know, the mind that counfels can forgive. 580

  Can I, as God, unfailing blifs affure,
Foil with a wifh, and peace at choice fecure ?
What nature can, this arm unbroke fhall bear,
Whate'er man dar'd, this breaft unfhaken dare
Canäan's hoft, thofe eyes with pain fhall view 585
My falchion vanquifh, and my feet purfue ;

D

On Iſrael's faithful ſons this hand beſtow
The bliſs of quiet, and the balm of woe.

    Should then theſe thoughts, to baſe ambition **grown,**
With impious madneſs build the envied throne,   **590**
To wing my doom let rapid lightnings fly,
And pamper'd hounds the peaceful grave deny.
Mine be the bliſs, the bliſs ſupreme to ſee
My long-lov'd nation bleſs'd, and bleſs'd by **me :**
Let others rule; compar'd with this pure joy,   **595**
A throne's a bubble, and the world a toy.

    In reaſon's face let all thy wiſhes ſpeed ;
Let foes befriend thee, and let Heaven ſucceed :
Then count thy gains ; the mighty prize ſurvey ;
And ſtraws, and bubbles, ſhall thoſe gains outweigh. **600**
Wrought in gay looms, thy golden robes ſhall **glare ;**
Rich banquets tempt, and luſcious wines enſnare :
But to vile ſhow ſhall Men their bliſs confine ?
Or ſink to brutes, and only live to dine ?

    On theſe poor joys what dreadful ills attend ?   **605**
Fears ever riſing ! miſeries ne'er to end !
Tho' whelm'd in floods one impious tyrant lies,
In the thron'd ſon ſhall all the father riſe ;
The ſame black heart ; the ſame beclouded **mind ;**
To pity marbled, and to reaſon blind.   **610**
Search ancient times : the annal'd page run o'er ;
With curious eye the ſun's long courſe explore ;
Scarce can each age a ſingle king confeſs,
Who knew to govern, or who wiſh'd to bleſs :
The reſt, of earth the terror, or the ſcorn,   **615**
By knaves exalted, and by cowards borne.
To lords like theſe ſhall Iſrael's millions bow ?
Bend the falſe knee, and force the perjur'd vow ?
A few ſhort years, our wealth content to ſhare,
The reſt their greedy hands to toil may ſpare :   **620**
But ſoon, full ſoon, their envious minds ſhall know
Our growth their ruin, and our peace their woe.

Then all the plagues, from jealous power that spring,
And death, the tender mercy of a king,   624
Your breasts shall feel ; and, rack'd with anguish, mourn
The day, when madness counsell'd to return.

Can I forget, how, from the dunghill rais'd,
Villains who bow'd, and sycophants who prais'd,
O'er Jacob's heirs were scepter'd to preside,
Their tributes gather, and their labors guide ? 630
From them, each cruel pang your heart shall rive,
That coward minds, or offic'd slaves, can give :
Their daring hands prophane the spotless charms,
That yield soft transport to your melting arms ;
Each generous thought the brandish'd scourge controul
And Insult rend the agonizing soul.   636

Then too shall Egypt, fir'd with wrath, recal
The plagues they felt, their king's, their nation's fall ;
Against your race, while Vengeance spreads the wing,
With fury arm them, and to torture spring ;   640
Your sacred dome shall burn ; your altars rend ;
Your priests destroy ; your hated worship end.

In that dread period, what auspicious shore
Shall banish'd Virtue's lifted wings explore ?
In what new realm, when, crush'd, her votaries fail, 645
Build the bright dome, and spread the hallow'd veil ;
Her priests inspire ; her altars teach to rise,
And waft her morning incense to the skies ?
Her final flight your hearts in vain shall mourn ;
In vain, with anguish, call her wish'd return ; 650
In vain the hour extatic sigh to find,
And the sweet sabbath of a guiltless mind.

To Egypt's crimes our sons shall fall a prey,
And learn her manners, while they own her sway :
From many a bower obscene the poison glide,   655
Taint the young soul, and freeze the vital tide ;
The sacred Law our rising hope forsake,
And lisp out curses, ere they know to speak :

Sad Conscience bow beneath an iron rod,
And torpid Reason own a reptile God.   660
   Then, rous'd to wrath, shall Heaven refuse to hear;
Mock all your pangs, and hiss your bitter prayer:
In poison'd gales, its wasting curses rise;
The plague empurpled taint the sickly skies:
The fields all wither, famine rend the breast,   665
And babes, sad victims! yield the dire repast.
   Then from Sabean climes, with hideous sound,
Swift cars shall roll, and savage war resound;
To blood, to vengeance, chiefs their hosts inspire,
Spread boundless death, and wrap the world in fire: 670
Our sons, bless'd refuge of the waning year!
Charm of sad toil, and sweet repose of care!
'Gainst their own hapless fires with foes combine,
And with new anguish point the dart divine.
   Thus o'er our race shall matchless misery roll,   675
And death, and bondage blast the rising soul;
Till the last dregs of vengeance Heaven expend,
Blot out our race, and Israel's glory end;
In final darkness set our sun's pale beam,
And black oblivion shroud our hapless name.   680
   For this dire end, were such bright scenes bestow'd?
For this, th' eternal covenant seal'd by God?
For this did ocean's trembling waves divide,
And o'er pale Egypt roll their whelming tide?
For this, the seraph lead our sacred bands?   685
For this loud thunder speak the dread commands?
From the hard rock refreshing waters rise?
The food of angels shower from balmy skies?
The sun-bright waste its flaming heats allay,
And Jordan's parting billows yield our way?   690
   But Hanniel cries, These wondrous signs were given,
To scourge our guilt, and bend our hearts to Heaven.
Were this the end, fierce famine had annoy'd;
The plague had wasted, or the sword destroy'd.

To fairer bliss he led the chosen train   695
Thro' the dark wave, and o'er the howling plain,
Ordain'd, when yon proud towers in dust are hurl'd,
To found an empire, and to rule a world;
O'er earth's far realms bid truth and virtue shine,
And spread to nature's bounds the Name divine.   700

    What tho' a few base minds the course oppose,
Slaves of poor pride, and Israel's bitter foes;
For pomp, for banquets would their race destroy,
And smile, to sell a nation for a toy;
What tho' of lifeless mold, a feeble race   705
With souls of maids the shape of men disgrace;
Think life no life, unbless'd with torpid ease,
Shrink from a shield, and shiver at a breeze:
'Gainst those let Justice' angry falchion flame,
And hissing Vengeance blast their impious name: 710
These dress th' inglorious loom; in sleep decay,
And to their kindred nothing fleet away,

    Far other mind our true-born race inspires;
Keen bravery prompts, and Abraham's virtue fires:
I see to combat ardent heroes rise;   715
I see bright glory flash from sparkling eyes;
Hark a glad cry! that every danger braves,
" Perish the day, ere Israel's sons be slaves;"
Swift pour new transports thro' my thrilling veins;
Heaven's voice in thunder calls to hostile plains: 720
Mark, mark the sound divine! cease every care;
Gird on your arms, and wake to manly war:
To bright possessions glory points the way,
And calls her sons, her heroes, to the prey.

    By friendship's ties, religion's bands combin'd,   725
By birth united, and by interest join'd,
In the same view our every wish conspires,
One spirit actuates, and one genius fires;
Plain, generous manners vigorous limbs confess,
And vigorous minds to freedom ardent press;   730

In danger's path our eyes ferenely fmile,
And well-ftrung finews hail accuftom'd toil.

   'Gainft hofts like thefe what foe with hope can arm?
What numbers daunt them? or what fears alarm?
To reeds before them deadly fpears fhall turn,   735
Swords blunt their edge, and flames forget to burn;
To the flight mound defcend the heaven-topp'd wall,
The floods grow dry, and hills and mountains fall.

   Rife then to war; awake to bright alarms;
Hail the glad trump, and feize your eager arms!   740
Behold, my fons, behold with raptur'd eyes,
How flight the toil, how vaft the glorious prize!
Thefe golden robes the fate of Sihon tell,
How Midian yielded, and how Amalek fell;
How funk proud Jericho's invaded wall,   745
And wide Canäan trembled at her fall;
How through each region rings the dreadful cry,
And their wild eye-balls fee deftruction nigh.
That faith, that arm of fteel, that dauntlefs foul
That bade o'er Bafhan's walls deftruction roll,   750
O'er fields, o'er towers, fhall Ifrael's ftandard bear,
Turn realms to flight, and wreft the prize of war;
Fill life with glory; Heaven's complacence gain,
And call fair Peace to cheer the crimfon plain.

   Then o'er wide lands, as blifsful Eden bright,   755
Type of the fkies, and feats of pure delight,
Our fons, with profperous courfe, fhall ftretch their fway,
And claim an empire, fpread from fea to fea:
In one great whole th' harmonious tribes combine;
Trace Juftice' path, and choofe their chiefs divine;   760
On Freedom's bafe erect the heavenly plan;
Teach laws to reign, aud fave the rights of man.
Then fmiling Art fhall wrap the fields in bloom,
Fine the rich ore, and guide the ufeful loom;
Then lofty towers in golden pomp arife;   765
Then fpiry cities meet aufpicious fkies:

The foul on Wifdom's wing fublimely foar,
New virtues cherifh, and new truths explore:
Thro' time's long tract our name celeftial run,
Climb in the eaft, and circle with the fun;   770
And fmiling Glory ftretch triumphant wings
O'er hofts of heroes, and o'er tribes of kings.
   The Leader fpoke; and deep in every breaft
A thrilling joy his cheerful voice imprefs'd.
Round the wide train, late drown'd in fad difmay,   775
His eyes refulgent caft a living ray:
Soul caught from foul the quick, enlivening charm;
Each parent's vifage bade his children arm;
In every heart th' undaunted wifh began;
O'er the glad field a pleafing murmur ran;   780
On Ai's high walls they caft a longing eye,
Refolv'd to conquer, or prepar'd to die.
So, when the northeaft pours a deepening ftorm,
Night fhades the world, and clouds the heaven deform,
Loud on fome fhip defcends the driving rain,   785
And winds imperious tofs the furging main;
Diffolv'd in terror, failors eye the wave,
Lift ardent prayers, and wait the gaping grave:
If chance in beauty's bloom the morn arife,
Still the rough roar, and charm the troubled fkies,   790
Serenely opening, far the billows o'er,
The blue-feen mountains, and the native fhore;
Raptur'd the new-born day with fhouts they hail,
And ftretch their canvas to the joyous gale.
   When fickening Hanniel faw their bofoms glow,   795
Their fierce eyes burn, and tears of tranfport flow,
The lov'd, the fond defign, his changeful mind,
With fecret pangs, to happier hours confign'd.
High o'er the reft his fhouts diftinguifh'd rofe;
With well feign'd fmiles his artful vifage glows,   800
And thus his voice---When pierc'd with Ifrael's grief
I ftrove in vain to lend the wifh'd relief,

BOOK I.

Perhaps this heart, by nature prone to know
The good man's interest in his country's woe,
Of peace, and prosperous arms too soon despair'd,   805
Unreal ills foresaw, and fancied dangers fear'd.
Yet still those views a kind indulgence claim,
Your fame their glory, and your bliss their aim.
Should this bold course be doom'd to woe severe,
Pure is my warning voice, my conscience clear;   810
On destin'd fight should friendly Conquest smile,
With joy, my soul shall welcome every toil ;
In Israel's cause, to scenes of danger driven,
To war is transport, and to die is heaven.

The hero ceas'd : a faint applause was heard,   815
And half-form'd smiles around the plain appear'd,
With startling sound the trump's deep voice began ;
To seize their arms the raptur'd thousands ran ;
When Caleb, reverend chief, all white with age,
Serenely rose, and hush'd the tumult's rage.   820
Deep thought sate musing on his furrow'd face ;
Calm wisdom round him cast an awful grace ;
With smiles just Heaven survey'd his constant truth,
Innerv'd his limbs, and lengthen'd out his youth :
Even now his arm rejoic'd the sword to wield,   825
To lead the contest, and to sweep the field.
Near the great Chief, in purple robes he stood ;
Sense, from his tongue, and sweet persuasion flow'd ;
Round the wide plain attentive silence hung,
And thus sage counsels sway'd the listening throng.   830

My voice impels to arms ; but let the sky
Lead on our host, and bid the heathen fly.
Were Israel spotless in the ETERNAL's sight,
Ai had not boasted a victorious fight.
When Virtue dress'd us in divine array,   835
Joy cheer'd each hour, and smooth'd the rugged way :
To scenes of fame each warrior ardent ran,
And claim'd the glories of the dreadful van.

But when black Vice our breasts with poison stain'd,
We shook for dangers timorous Fancy feign'd ;   840
Each shameful field beheld our squadrons fly,
And heroes arm'd for battle but to die.

And now some sin, some folly, not bemoan'd,
Rebellion bold, or injury unaton'd,
Pours on our heads their flood of grief and care,   845
Bids Ai exult, and all our sons despair.
Else round the heavenly dome the cloud had spread,
And sacred fires illum'd the nightly shade.

Let the whole race to God submissive bend ;
Let ceaseless prayer to Mercy's throne ascend ;   850
'Till the third morn, the pious fast endure ;
Each deed be holy, and each bosom pure ;
Then o'er our path with joy shall HEAVEN preside,
Our guilt discover, and our counsels guide.
Then, nor 'till then, to war let trumpets call ;   855
Lead forth these bands, and mount the yielding wall.
But should our course, this day, to fight be driven,
Should arms be brandish'd in the face of HEAVEN,
Look round your steps ; survey the dreadful road ;
Think if the sword and shield can war with God.   860

Thus spoke the sage.   Blest man ! the Chief replied,
The war's first honour, and the council's pride !
Thine is the voice of God : th' inspiring ray
Shines thro' thy breast, and gives the brightest day.
Two days shall combat cease.   The camp around,   865
Let the sad fast in every tent be found :
Two days to HEAVEN be rais'd by pious fear
The grateful tribute of a humble prayer.
So shall we wipe away the crimson stain,
And Israel's glory gild the conquering plain.   870

He spoke.   Each warrior with delight obey'd ;
Each cheerful face th' obsequious mind display'd.
The host dispers'd ; and prayers, and reverent sighs
Rose in soft incense to th' approving skies.

E

THE

CONQUEST of CANÄAN.

BOOK II.

ARGUMENT.

Morning. Gibeonites assemble for the worship of the Sun. Mina refuses to join them in this worship; the king enquires the reason. She mentions her adoration of the true GOD. *The king being anxious to know more of the matter, after an apology for speaking in such an assembly, she gives a general account of the Deity, and his dispensations. As he is still further inquisitive, she gives him a more minute account of the Divine works, in a history of the creation---our first parents---the fall---general succeeding apostacy---deluge---second apostacy---calling of Abraham ---Israelites journeying into Egypt---oppression and plagues of Egypt---Israelites' deliverance---journey through the wilderness---promulgation of the divine law --destruction of Sihon, and Og---last prophecy, death, and burial of Moses, and the commission of Joshua. The Gibeonites being much afflicted at the prospect of their destruction, Mina proposes an embassy to Joshua, to solicit peace. The king approves the proposal. Conclusion.*

The CONQUEST of CANÄAN.

BOOK II.

BEYOND thofe weftern hills, whofe haughty brow,
To heaven exalted, fcorn'd the world below,
A plain outfpread, with growing verdure bright,
And ftole, extenfive, from the aching fight.
Here, in proud pomp, adorn'd with countlefs fpires,   5
That mock'd the glories of the folar fires,
Gibeon's imperial towers fublimely rofe,
And fpurn'd the terrors of furrounding foes.
   Now o'er the hills red ftreams began to burn,
And burfting fplendors ufher'd in the morn;   10
With living dies the flowers all-beauteous glow'd;
O'er the glad fields etherial odours flow'd;
The foreft echoed with a boundlefs fong,
And rifing breezes pour'd the ftrains along.
   Adorn'd with green, before the palace lay   15
A fpacious fquare, and fmil'd upon the day.
Here, ere the dawn the kindling fkies illum'd,
Or opening flowers the fragrant gales perfum'd,
Of every age, a vaft, affembled train
Pour'd from the lofty domes, and fill'd the plain.   20
   High in the midft two facred altars fhone,
Adorn'd with honours to their God, the Sun.
This, deck'd with art, and bright in royal pride,
With fable gore the quivering victim died:

On that gay flowers in rich profusion lay,   25
And gales of Eden bore their sweets away.

Here, white with age, in snowy vesture dress'd,
Aradon stood, their monarch, and their priest;
Red in his hand a torch refulgent shone,
And his fix'd countenance watch'd the rising sun.   30

When first the flaming Orb, with glorious rays,
Roll'd o'er the hills, and pour'd a boundless blaze;
Charm'd at the sight, the monarch stretch'd his hand,
And touch'd the tributes with the sacred brand;
Through freshen'd air perfumes began to rise,   35
And curling volumes mounted to the skies.
Thrice to the earth the raptur'd suppliants bow'd,
Then struck the lyre, and hymn'd the rising God.

O thou, whose bursting beams in glory rise,
And sail, and brighten, thro' unbounded skies!   40
The world's great Parent! heaven's exalted King?
Sole Source of good! and life's eternal Spring!
All hail, while cloath'd in beauty's endless ray,
Thy face unclouded gives the new-born day!

Above all scenes is plac'd thy heavenly throne;   45
Ere time began, thy spotless splendor shone:
Sublime from east to west thy chariot rolls,
Chears the wide earth, and warms the distant poles;
Commands the vegetable race to grow,
The fruit to redden, and the flower to blow.   50
This world was born to change: the hand of Time
Makes, and unmakes the scenes of every clime.
The insect millions scarce the morn survive;
One transient day the flowery nations live:
A few short years complete the human doom;   55
Then pale Death summons to the narrow tomb.

Line 28. *Aradon stood, their monarch,*) Gibeon is generally sup-
posed to have been a commonwealth. But as most nations, in that
early age, had a chief magistrate, vested with more or less civil and
religious powers, I have supposed such a magistrate, and given him
the usual epithets.

BOOK II.

Lash'd by the flood, the hard rocks wear away;
Worne by the storm, the lessening hills decay;
Unchang'd alone is thine exalted flame,
From endless years to endless years the same;   60
Thy splendors with immortal beauty shine,
Roll round th' eternal heavens, and speak thy name divine.
    When thy bright throne, beyond old ocean's bound,
Thro' nether skies pursues its destin'd round,
Lost in th' ascending darkness, beauty fades;   65
Thro' the blank field, and thro' the woodland, spreads
A melancholy silence.   O'er the plain
Dread lions roam, and savage terrors reign.
    And when sad Autumn sees thy face retire,
And happier regions hail thy orient fire,   70
High in the storm imperious Winter flies,
And desolation saddens all the skies.
But when once more thy beam the north ascends,
Thy light invigorates, and thy warmth extends;
The fields rejoice, the groves with transport ring,   75
And boundless nature hails the sky-born spring.
    Nor even in winter's gloom, or night's sad reign,
Darts the warm influence of thy beams in vain.
    Beyond the main some fairer region lies,
Some brighter isles beneath the southern skies,   80
Where crimson War ne'er bade the clarion roar,
Nor sanguine billows died the vernal shore:
No thundering storm the day's bright face conceals,
No summer scorches, and no frost congeals;
No sickness wastes, no grief provokes the tear,   85
Nor tainted vapours blast the clement year.
Round the glad day-star endless beauties burn,
And crown'd with rainbows, opes th' imperial morn;
A clear unbounded light the skies display,
And purple lustre leads the changing day.   90
O'er conscious shades, and bowers of soft repose,
Young breezes spring, and balmy fragrance blows;

The fields all wanton in fereneſt beams,
Wake fairer flowers, and roll diviner ſtreams;
Thro' the long vales aerial muſic roves,   95
And nobler fruitage dies the bending groves.

     Thro' ſpotleſs nations as the realm refin'd,
Thine influence there ſublimes th' immortal mind;
Its active pinions ſwift thro' nature roam,
Loſe the low world, and claim a nobler home.   100
Their limbs, of endleſs life, with glory crown'd,
New youth improves, and growing charms ſurround:
On the bleſs'd ſhore thy ſplendors love to ſhine,
And raiſe thy ſons each hour, to raptures more divine.

     Thus ceas'd the ſound: the harp's melodious ſtrain 105
Join'd the glad hymn, and charm'd the liſtening train;
A ſparkling joy each ſpeaking face diſplay'd,
While light expanding leſſen'd every ſhade.

     Fair as the lucid ſtar, that up the ſky
Leads the gay morn, and bids the darkneſs fly,   110
Beſide the king a lovely Virgin ſtood,
Nor join'd the ſong, nor with th' aſſembly bow'd.
A ſweet diſpleaſure ting'd her melting eye,
And her ſad boſom heav'd th' oppreſſive ſigh.
Her ſoft diſtreſs the watchful king ſurvey'd,   115
And thus, with friendly ſmile, addreſs'd the maid.

     Say, lovelieſt fair one, whence the meaning gloom,
That damps our joys, and clouds thy roſy bloom!
Why does thy ſoul the reverence due deny
To yon bright orb, that gilds the orient ſky?   120

     Far other God, replied the fair, demands
My vocal tranſports, and my ſuppliant hands;
A GOD, whoſe power rais'd high yon azure round,
Form'd the wide earth, and fix'd the ocean's bound;
Who more the ſun tranſcends, than his gay glare   125
The tranſient glimmerings of ſome half-ſeen ſtar.

     Strange ſcenes, the monarch cries, thy voice declares,
And breathes ſweet muſic thro' our raptur'd ears.

BOOK II.

But canſt thou, unconvinc'd, yon orb behold,
O'er earth, o'er heaven, in endleſs triumph roll'd? 130
What boundleſs joy his gladſome courſe attends !
What glory brightens ! and what good deſcends !
Round the blue void his beams unchanging ſhine,
And ſpeak his nature, and his name, divine.
Yet ſtill my curious thoughts the tale demand, 135
And aſk improvement at thy lovely hand.
Say then, O fair, what all-exalted Power
Thy wiſhes reverence, and thy hands adore.

   With down-caſt eye, and cheek of crimſon bright
That ſweetly mingled with the ſpotleſs white, 140
Replied the virtuous maid.   To bolder tongues
Of man's bold ſex, the arduous taſk belongs.
But thy fond cares, that ſav'd my life, demand
Toils far ſuperior from my grateful hand.
Thy bliſs, thy endleſs bliſs, my voice ſhall bribe 145
To paſs the bounds, the maiden's laws preſcribe.

  Far, very far beyond this lower ſky,
Beyond the ſun, beyond the flames on high,
Dwells in pure light, in heaven's ſerene abode,
The Source of life, the Spring of endleſs good ; 150
All ſcenes, all heights above, ſublimely reigns ;
All worlds created, and all worlds ſuſtains.

  Yon orb, whoſe brightneſs wakes thy raptur'd praiſe,
Is but a beam of his unbounded blaze.
His breath illum'd, his hand exalted high, 155
And roll'd him flaming thro' th' expanded ſky.

  His bounteous influence, thro' all nature driven,
Warms the wide earth, and cheers the wider heaven.
All ſcenes, all beings his pure ſight ſurveys,
Where morn begins, and where pale eve decays ; 160
Where hell's dark ſhores the glooms of night diſplay ;
Or heaven's broad palace glows in laſting day :
Thro' worlds of endleſs youth, where angels ſhine,
And unknown nations rove in light divine.

He moves, informs, directs, and rules the whole;　165
Their cause, their end, their guardian, and their soul.

　　He wakes the beauties of the vernal morn;
He bids the flames of sultry summer burn;
He showers th' autumnal wealth; and his dread power
Sounds in the wintry storm, and bids the wild waves roar.

　　In these vast regions countless beings move,　171
Live in his smiles, and wanton in his love:
In all, his power, and boundless wisdom, shine,
The works, the glories of a hand divine.

Thron'd in high heaven, in starry mansions reign,　175
Of purest intellect, th' angelic train
All sense, all soul, all love, eternal power
Their thoughts contemplate, and their songs adore.

　　Thro' earth's wide realms unnumber'd tribes we find,
Of different ranks, for different ends design'd.　180
On every leaf the insect millions swarm,
Hum round the flower, or in the sun-beam warm;
The birds, on painted pinions, gayly fly
Thro' the wide regions of the sapphire sky;
Beasts climb the cliff, or walk the savage wood;　185
And fishes sport around the foamy flood.
These, with the reptile race, to time a prey,
Of dust were fashion'd, and to dust decay.

　　To man of nobler rank, two parts were given,
This form'd of earth, and that inspir'd by heaven.　190
Such as the texture, such th' allotted doom;
His body moulders in the narrow tomb:
But the wing'd soul, when earth in dust is hurl'd,
Shall spring, immortal, from the sinking world;
Ordain'd, if crimes its earthly course distain,　195
To bathe in fire, and waste with endless pain;
If cleans'd from guilt, with active joy to rise
To the pure transports of angelic skies;
But man, unmindful of his nobler birth,
In vain seeks pleasure from surrounding earth.　200

Far different, far, the scenes by Heaven defign'd
To fill the wifhes of the active mind.
This bounded point is but our being's morn ;
To endlefs life th' etherial Soul was born.
Upward with nimble flight her thoughts fhould foar, 205
And, wing'd by virtue, brighter worlds explore ;
Earth's groveling joys difdain with confcious pride,
Like angels fafhion'd, and to heaven allied.

For this fair train our nature to prepare,
And the pure fragrance of immortal air, 210
To raife the downward heart from earthly toys,
And mould our wifhes to fublimer joys,
Thro' earth's wide realms, afflictions firft began,
The nobleft bleffings HEAVEN beftows on man.
Toil, difappointment, hunger, thirft, and pain, 215
A long, long, difmal, melancholy train,
Cleanfe the dim eye, diffolve the powerful luft,
And loofe the chains, that bind our hearts to duft.
From forrow's fire, like filver well refin'd,
Freed from vile earth, fhall rife th' undrofty mind, 220
Each hour, with beams of clearer beauty fhine,
And ceafelefs claim an image more divine.
At length, when ficknefs brings th' expected doom,
Its powers fhall rife triumphant o'er the tomb,
Forward to nobler scenes with rapture fpring, 225
And hail the meffage of th' undreaded king ;
While life's long ftream its fartheft fhore fhall lave,
And feek the bofom of th' eternal wave.
Then fhall we fee diviner winds arife,
The main grow calm, and fmiles inveft the fkies : 230
Then fhall our happy hands exalt the fail,
Launch on the deep, and call th' etherial gale ;
With joy, our fpirits leave the fading fhore,
And hear the leffening ftorms at diftance roar.
Inwrapp'd in beams of uncreated light, 235
All heaven, difclos'd, fhall burft upon the fight ;

Streams of immortal blifs in vifion roll,
And hofts of angels hail the kindred foul.

　　With rofy fmiles, thus fpoke the lovely maid,
While o'er the plain a boundlefs filence fpread.　　240
Like the tun'd lyre, the mufic of her tongue
Pour'd foft perfuafion on the truths fhe fung :
Pleas'd, her fweet grace, and fparkling eye, they view,
And the frank mein, that Falfehood never knew.

　　To all, Aradon bent a yielding ear ;　　　　245
For Heaven infpir'd his honeft heart to hear.
Mid favage realms, fair Gibeon's fons inclin'd
To manners gentler, worfhip more refin'd :
Each focial art adorn'd the generous door ;
The ftranger welcom'd, and reliev'd the poor ;　　250
And hence they liv'd.　From nature's bounteous Lord,
Even virtue's femblance finds a fure reward.

　　A calm delight exulting in his eyes,
With gentleft voice, the monarch thus replies.

　　O brighteft of thy fex, an angel's tongue　　255
Alone can boaft the fweetnefs of thy fong.
Led by thy voice, my raptur'd mind would know
The mighty Power, from whom all bleffings flow ;
Would learn what holy feers his will explain,
What prayers delight him, and what offerings gain ; 260
Safe in his fmiles, beyond the grave refpire ;
Exult o'er death, and flee from endlefs fire ;
To thofe immortal regions fpeed my flight,
And prove fome humble feat, amid the fons of light.

　　But fay, O fair, when form'd the Power divine　265
The lamps that round yon fky forever fhine ?
Know'ft thou the day when earth's wide realms were made,
The hills exalted, and the ocean fpread ?
Whofe hand thine infant mind to reafon wrought,
In virtue nurs'd thee, and in wifdom taught ?　　270
Tho' age my trembling brow has whiten'd o'er,
Strange unknown fcenes thy curious thoughts explore,

Return'd the lovely maid, Thy glad requeſt
Wakes my fond hope, and warms my grateful breaſt---
Know, mighty prince, when Elam's deathful ſpear   275
Pierc'd the fell foe, and loos'd my ſoul from fear,
From Iſrael's camp, thro' unknown paths, I ſtray'd,
My lone ſteps wandering round the woodland ſhade.
'Twas there, the ſacred truths the prophet ſung,
And thus ſweet muſic tun'd his heavenly tongue.   280

From realms divine high-rais'd beyond all height,
Th' almighty Parent caſt his piercing ſight;
With boundleſs view, he ſaw the etherial vaſt
A clouded gloom, an undelightſome waſte:
Around the extended wild, no ſun's broad ray   285
Mark'd the clear ſplendor of immortal day;
No varying moon, ordain'd at eve to riſe,
Led the full pomp of conſtellated ſkies;
No day in circling beauty learn'd to roll;
No fair ſpring ſmil'd, nor froſt congeal'd the pole;   290
Subſtantial darkneſs ſpace unmeaſur'd fill'd,
And nature's realms lay deſolate and wild.

He ſpoke: at once, o'er earth's far diſtant bounds
The heavens wide-arching ſtretch'd their ſapphire rounds
With hoary cliffs the far-ſeen hills aſcend;   295
Down ſink the vales, and wide the plains extend;
Headlong from ſteep to ſteep the billows roar,
Fill the broad main, and toſs againſt the ſhore.

He ſpoke; and beauty thro' all nature flow'd;
With ſpringing verdure earth's wide regions glow'd;300
Forth ruſh the flowery tribes, and trees on high
Shroud their tall ſummits in the ambient ſky.

He ſpoke; the heavens with ſudden glory ſhone;
In godlike pomp burſt forth the golden ſun;
Far thro' immenſity his kindling ray   305
Shot life and joy, and pour'd the new-born day;
With milder luſtre roſe the charms of even,
The moon's broad beam, and all the pride of heaven.

He ſpoke; and fiſhes fill'd the watry rounds,
Swarm'd in the ſtreams, and ſwam the Ocean's bounds;
The green ſea ſparkled with unnumber'd dies,   311
And varying beauty wav'd upon the ſkies;
Whales through the foaming billows proudly rode,
And unknown monſters gambol'd o'er the flood.
From the deep wave, adorn'd with nobler grace,   315
In countleſs millions ſprang the feather'd race;
Thro' the far clouds the eagle cleft his way,
And ſoar'd and wanton'd in the flames of day;
Full on the morn the peacock op'd his beams,
And ſwans majeſtic row'd th' expanded ſtreams.   320

He ſpoke; and, wondering, from diſparted plains
In throngs unnumber'd roſe the beſtial trains:
Their ſnowy robes the harmleſs flocks reveal'd;
Gay ſteeds exulting pranc'd the vernal field;
The lion glar'd, and mid the gazing throng   325
Shook his rough main, and grimly ſtalk'd along.

The wide earth finiſh'd, from his weſtern throne,
In ſplendid beauty look'd the gladſome ſun;
Calm were the ſkies, the fields with luſtre crown'd,
And nature's incenſe fill'd th' etherial round.   330
Enſhrin'd in ſacred light, the Maker ſtood,
Complacent ſmil'd, and own'd the work was good.
Then from his hand in ſilent glory came
A nobler form, and Man his deſtin'd name;
Erect, and tall, in ſolemn pomp he ſtood,   335
And living virtue in his viſage glow'd.
Then too a fairer being ſhew'd her charms;
Young Beauty wanton'd in her ſnowy arms;
The heavens around her bade their graces fly,
And Love ſate blooming in her gentle eye.   340
O pair divine! ſuperior to your kind;
To virtue faſhion'd, and for bliſs deſign'd!

He, born to rule, with calm, uplifted brow,
Look'd down majeſtic on the world below;

BOOK II.

To heaven, his manfion, turn'd his thought fublime; 345
Or rov'd far onward thro' the fcenes of time;
O'er nature's kingdom caft a fearching eye,
And dar'd to trace the fecrets of the fky
On fancy's pinions fcann'd the bright abode,
And claim'd his friend, an Angel, or a God. 350
  Her he indu'd with nature more refin'd,
A lovelier image, and a fofter minb.
To her he gave to kindle fweet defire,
To roufe great thoughts, and fan th' heroic fire:
At pity's gentle call to bend his ear; 355
To prompt for woe the unaffected tear;
In fcenes refin'd his foftening foul improve,
And tune his wifhes with the hand of love.
To her he gave with fweetnefs to obey,
Infpire the friend, and charm the lord away; 360
Each bleeding grief with balmy hand to heal,
And learn his rending finews not to feel;
Each joy t' improve, the pious wifh to raife,
And add new raptures to his languid praife.
  To this lov'd pair a blefs'd retreat was given, 365
A feat for angels, and a humbler heaven;
Fair Eden nam'd: in fwift fucceffion, there
Glad fcenes of rapture led the vernal year;
Round the green garden living beauty play'd;
In gay profufion earth her treafures fpread; 370
The air breath'd fragrance; ftreams harmonious rung,
And love, and tranfport, tun'd th' aerial fong.
  With tranquil beams the feventh bright morn appear'd
And thus, from firey clouds, a voice was heard.
This day, O Man, to facred tranfports rife, 375
And pafs the hours in converfe with the fkies:
To prayer, to praife, be all thy wifhes given;
Soar from the world, and here begin thy heaven!
So fhall thy fons purfue the virtuous road,
And, each returning fabbath, wake to God. 380

40

The sovereign voice the reverent pair obey'd ;
A solemn beauty earth and heaven array'd :
With joy the pinion'd tribes, in every grove,
Hymn'd the blest influence of immortal love :
Man join'd the concert, and his raptur'd lays   385
Charm'd the gay fields when angels ceas'd to praise.

Mid Eden's groves the tree of glory stood,
That taught the unalter'd bounds of ill, and good :
Its fruit, all beauteous to the ravish'd eye,
Denied to man, and sacred to the sky :   390
Denied alone ; a boundless store was given,
Food for bright angels, transcript fair of heaven.
And thus the law---If vain desire to taste
Prompt thee, rebellious, to the dire repast ;
Hear, hear, O man ! on that tremendous day,   395
Thy life, thy bliss, thy virtue, pass away ;
No more the heir of endless joys refin'd,
But guilty, wretched, to the dust consign'd ;
Toil here thy lot, thine end the dreary tomb,
And hopeless anguish thine eternal doom.   400
The sovereign voice the pair obsequious heard,
Th' injunction reverenc'd, and the danger fear'd :
'Till urg'd by impious lust, by hell insnar'd,
They pluck'd the fruit ; the guilt, and sentence shar'd,
For one poor banquet, one unreal joy,   405
Rebell'd, and yielded bliss without alloy ;
To howling deserts were from angels driven,
And lost the sweet society of heaven.

Then ills on ills unnumber'd rose forlorn ;
No more the orient beam'd th' angelic morn ;   410
Fragrance and Beauty clos'd their blissful reign
Nor Spring perennial danc'd along the plain.
Cold Night her fearful clouds around them spread,
And gave new terrors to the howling shade.
Lost in the bosom of th' ascending storm,   415
The sun's faint beam in winter ceas'd to warm ;

BOOK II.

O'er plains, and hills, the chilling froft congeal'd;
The fnow tempeftuous fadden'd all the field;
On the wide wave the headlong whirlwind pour'd,
And all the thunders of the ocean roar'd. 420
Where late gay bloom'd the harveft's waving pride,
And purpled fruits the bending branches died,
Impervious thorns, and clinging brambles fpread,
And unblefs'd famine gloom'd th' autumnal fhade:
For blood, the raging wolf began to arm; 425
Fierce, hungry tygers rung the dread alarm;
The lion's fovereign voice, with thrilling found,
Clear'd the wide grove, and fhook the hills around.

 The facred ftamp the mind forever loft,
The fkies' perfection and the angel's boaft: 430
Elfe had our life roll'd on, from forrow clear,
A femblance bright of heaven's eternal year.
Now ftain'd with guilt, the foul to hatred turn'd;
With pride was lifted, and with envy burn'd.
Fierce bickerings rofe; with conqueft noife was crown'd,
And Reafon's ftill, fmall voice in curfes drown'd: 436
In vain fweet Friendfhip charm'd the ftubborn ear;
She fung, and wondering found no heart to hear.

 By hands, not wifdom, next the caufe was tried,
And blows obtain'd what argument denied. 440
Revenge foon taught to point the murdering knife,
And fecret ambufh hedg'd the hated life.
The villain's gloomy path black night conceal'd,
And virtuous blood bedew'd the lonely field.
Then roufing banners War with tranfport rais'd; 445
Forth flafh'd the fteel; the far-feen fignal blaz'd:
O'er the fcar'd hills the warning clarion rang,
And fwift to combat ftartled nations fprang;
In floods of ftreaming gore the fields were drown'd,
And flaughter'd thoufands heap'd th' embattled ground.
The regal dome, the turret's golden gleam 451
Grac'd the fad triumphs of th' imperious flame;

G

From wall to wall insulting engines frown'd,
And all the pride of art fell crumbling to the ground.

To earth's wide realms, from scenes above the sky, 455
Th' Almighty Ruler turn'd his searching eye:
Deep sunk in boundless guilt the regions lay,
And vice exulting claim'd a single sway.
Her countless millions, lur'd by Pleasure's charms,
Bask'd in her smiles, and sported in her arms; 460
The song, the feast, inspir'd the jocund hours,
And Lewdness wanton'd in luxurious bowers.
In vain from door to door the beggar stray'd;
His portion hunger, and the frost his bed:
In vain sad Sickness rais'd her feeble cry; 465
No friendly hand appear'd, nor melting eye:
Virtue, fair pilgrim, cast a wishful view,
And spread her wings, and sigh'd a last adieu.

He saw, while terror veil'd his awful face,
And bade fierce ruin wrap the guilty race, 470
Borne by the vengeance of his lifted arm,
Far roll'd the black immensity of storm;
From east to west were pour'd the glooms on high,
And cloudy curtains hung th' unmeasur'd sky.
Shook by the voice that rends th' immortal plain, 475
In one broad deluge sunk th' etherial main;
Huge floods, imprison'd in the vaulted ground,
With wild commotion burst the crumbling bound;
O'er earth's broad climes the surging billows driven
Climb'd the tall mountains, and invaded heaven: 480
The pride of man, the pomp-embosom'd tower,
Towns wrapp'd in gold, and realms of mighty power,
All plung'd at once beneath th' unfathom'd wave,
And nature perish'd in the boundless grave.

From realms, where suns with milder glory shine, 485
His voice awak'd the western wind divine.
At once the balmy wind obedient blew,
And springing beauty cloth'd the world anew;

In rosy youth her climes emergent smil'd,
And flowery visitants rejoic'd the wild.   490

How, doom'd to pass beyond the liquid grave,
The ark's rich treasure triumph'd o'er the wave;
How the bless'd favorite, rising from the main,
Rul'd orient lands, and peopled earth again,
Thou know'st. The wonderous tale, thro' every clime,
Tradition wafts along the stream of time.   496
With circling splendor, and etherial die,
The covenant bow spread sudden round the sky,
From those gay heavens, that arch'd with pomp divine,
Fair o'er the angelic world forever shine,   500
To earth remov'd, and fix'd by God's decree,
An endless barrier 'gainst th' ambitious sea.

Safe in the sacred sign, ungrateful man
New scenes of guilt with eager zeal began.
Again black Vice o'er nature stretch'd her sway,   505
And magic Pleasure charm'd the foot astray.
No sacred anthems climb'd the bright abode;
Nor Reason blush'd to hail a golden god:
With rage, and conflict, earth was cover'd o'er;
Towns sunk in flames, and fields were drench'd in gore.
With impious jests they mock'd a future doom;   511
Sung o'er the shroud, and danc'd into the tomb.
From land to land the clouds of death unfurl'd,
And one wide lethargy benumb'd th' oblivious world.

Then too, proud Ashur, queen of realms, began   515
To forge her chains, and bind inglorious man.
Hence, tyrants sprang, and dar'd with impious claim,
Demand the honours of the sacred Name;
Hence stern Oppression rais'd his iron rod,
Hence crimson Slaughter wrapp'd the world in blood:
Thro' every clime the night of slavery spread.   521
And Heaven repenting griev'd that man was made.

From this black mass, this mingled host of foes,
One sainted friend th' Almighty Ruler chose;

For him, bleſs'd champion of his yielding cauſe !   525
He chang'd the ſtable courſe of nature's laws ;
(An hundred ſummers ſaw the circling morn,
Ere his firſt hope, the promis'd heir was born)
To him, to his he gave Canäan's ſhore,
'Till the bright evening gild the weſt no more.   530
To Idol guilt the world beſide was given,
Their name, their memory blotted out of heaven.

    When the dire famine o'er all nations ſpread,
His hand the favorite race to Egypt led.
As ſome fair tree, where fruitful ſtreams are roll'd,   535
Lifts ſpiry ſhoots, and bids its leaves unfold ;
O'er the green bank ambitious branches riſe,
Enjoy the winds, and gain upon the ſkies ;
While opening flowers around it gayly ſpring,
And birds with tranſport clap the painted wing :   540
So each fond ſun, and each ſucceſſive ſhade
Beheld with ſmiles the infant nation ſpread ;
From field to field the riſing boughs expand,
Share the glad ſmiles of heaven, and fill the jealous land.

    Their ſudden growth the envious tyrant view'd,   545
And impious hands in infant gore imbru'd,
With bold oppreſſion bath'd the ſtreaming eye,
Rack'd the ſad ſoul, and rous'd the ſuppliant cry.

    Their bleeding wrongs the omniſcient Mind ſurvey'd,
And bade fierce Vengeance bare her flaming blade.   550
No more the limpid wave ſerenely flow'd ;
But thro' ſad ſhores the river roll'd in blood ;
Unnumber'd reptiles climb'd the ſtately dome,
Croak'd o'er the feaſt, and crawl'd the pillar'd room ;
Inſects in countleſs millions earth o'erſpread ;   555
The ſickening murrain gloom'd the paſtur'd ſhade ;
From darken'd ſkies the ſtorm's red bolts were hurl'd,
And hail, and lightening ſwept the waſted world ;
Like cloudy curtains, locuſts hung the day ;
Pale death, and famine mark'd their baleful way :   560

Three days blank midnight wrapp'd the realm in gloom,
And all her first-born sunk in one broad tomb.
  Then, high in air his lucid banner spread,
To the bright sign collected Israel fled,
With transport trac'd the finger of the sky,   565
Wing'd their glad path, and hail'd redemption nigh.
In vain its countless ills the waste disclos'd ;
In vain the sea their sacred path oppos'd ;
Back roll'd th' instinctive main ; and round their side
In crystal splendor stood the conscious tide.   570
In the bright front, a cloud his dark abode,
Thron'd on the rushing winds, an angel rode,
The spreading volumes mark'd their path by day,
And guiding flames illum'd their nightly way.
Behind, the tyrant, urg'd by Heaven's decree,   575
Drove his pale host, and trembled thro' the sea.
On the tall shore sublime the Prophet stood,
And stretch'd his hand above the eager flood ;
Wide-circling all, far clos'd the billow'd womb,
And Egypt's glories found a watery tomb.   580
Thro' spacious climes of fierce and scorching day,
The cloud expanded led their lonely way,
'Till, white with cliffs, and crown'd with many a shade,
In cloudy pride fam'd Sinai rear'd its head.
On this lone mount, the all-discerning Mind   585
To teach his name, t' unfold his law, design'd ;
On earth to witness truth and power divine,
And bid o'er Jacob's sons his splendors shine :
Beneath its haughty brow the thousands lay,
And hop'd the wonders of th' expected day.   590
  Fair rose the dawn : from heaven's sublime abode,
Th' almighty Power in boundless glory rode ;
Long dusky folds a cloud around him spread,
His throne surrounding with impervious shade.
Its flame-bright skirts with light excessive shone,   595
A noon-tide morn, that dimm'd the rising sun.

Forth from its womb unusual lightnings fly,
And thunders, hurl'd on thunders, rock the sky:
To Sinai's top the wonderous scene descends;
Down plunge his cliffs ; his tottering summit rends;   600
O'er all the mountain burn devouring fires,
Wreath'd in dread smoke, and crown'd with lofty spires.
Loud as hoarse whirlwinds earth and heaven deform,
Loud as the thousand thunders of the storm,
With clear, dread voice, in pomp tremendous, roll   605
The trump's long-sounding terrors thro' the pole.
The Seer majestic climbs the towering height,
And, bosom'd deep in glory, leaves the sight.

There, while the world was hush'd in silent awe,
The Sovereign Mind disclos'd th' eternal Law;   610
And thus the dread commands. O Israel, know,
I am the Lord, who snatch'd thy sons from woe,
From Egypt's bondage trac'd thy various ways;
Nor shall base Idols share my sacred praise.
Let no vain words my fearful Name prophane;   615
Nor toil, nor sports my holy sabbaths stain.
Thy parent's voice with reverent mind obey:
Thy hand from dire revenge, and murther stay:
Let not a thought thy neighbour's couch ascend;
And not a wish to others wealth extend: 620
Let truth thy converse, truth thy oaths confine:
And every passion to thy lot resign.

Unnumber'd statutes then his voice ordain'd,
The poor protected, and the rich restrain'd;
And taught, what manners prosperous rule assure,   625
Their foes to vanquish, and their peace secure.

Then thro' long, weary climes their course was turn'd,
Still mov'd the cloud, and still the glory burn'd.
With ceaseless care he fill'd their hearts with good;
The skies dissolving shower'd immortal food: 630
With wondering joy they saw the streamy rain
Pour from the rock, and spread along the plain:

And clonds of quails, from every region driven,
Blacken'd the fields, and fill'd the bounds of heaven.
    'Twas then, near Edom's realms the thousands lay, 635
And her proud prince denied th' expected way.
Whate'er their state, whate'er their God concern'd,
From their great Seer my curious parent learn'd ;
Charm'd with the scene, he left his native soil,
Shar'd all their wants, and barter'd ease for toil.   640
    Thro' long, lone paths we bent our circling course,
Untir'd by winter's rage, or summer's force ;
Bright angels led the van ; and round the road
Dread scenes of terror mark'd the present God.
    Even now I see fierce Sihon's hostile train,   645
Sheath'd in dire arms, and frowning o'er the plain.
In childhood then, around my sire I clung,
Danc'd in his arms, and in his bosom hung.
With nimble steps the sacred warriors sped,
Blew the shrill trump, and fill'd the field with dead. 650
Like drifts of rushing dust, that sweep the skies,
On fear's light pinions swift the remnant flies ;
From town to town we wing our rapid way,
And the wide region sinks an easy prey.
    Then giant Og his heroes drove to arms,   655
Whirl'd his proud car, and thunder'd hoarse alarms :
In distant fields I saw the storm ascend,
Its shades all darken, and its clouds extend ;
Down the grim hills I heard the volumes roll,
And bursting terrors rend the shuddering pole.   660
As snows, slight fabric, in warm suns decay,
The impious squadrons sudden melt away.
    Now o'er the Seer had six-score summers run,
And hoary locks around his temples shone,
When sounds melodious, opening from the sky,   665
To the sad train declar'd his end was nigh.

* See Book IV, Line 239.

His mind infpir'd with more than mortal fight,
Saw future fcenes and ages rufh to light ;
And thus his voice.   On Ifrael's chofen train,
Like vernal fhowers let endlefs bleffings rain :   670
Each rifing age, afcend thy glory higher,
With time roll on, and with the fkies expire !
But oh, my fons, this voice attentive hear ;
Let thefe laft ftrains command the liftening ear !

    To unborn years I ftretch my raptur'd eyes ;   675
I fee the promis'd feed in glory rife !
The etherial ftar triumphant mounts on high,
And fairer beams adorn the unmeafur'd fky :
All heaven impatient waits the facred morn ;
Jefus defcends ; the filial GOD is born :   680
Hofts of bright angels round the favorite fhine,
And earth is ravifh'd with their hymns divine.
'Tis he, whofe offering guilt fhall wafh away,
And raife Mankind to climes of ceafelefs day ;
The blifs of truth, and virtue, fhall infpire,   685
And warm the bofom with feraphic fire.
Hafte, hafte, ye days of heaven ! with rapid wing,
To this fad world the hope of nations bring !
Defcend, O Prince of peace ! thy love beftow ;
Cleanfe the dark foul from feeds of endlefs woe ;   690
With all earth's myriads Jacob's fons unite,
And bid immortal glory fpring to light.
No more the gentile realms in duft fhall mourn ;
Nor evening altars to th' infernals burn ;
But wak'd, reviv'd, by thy celeftial name,   695
One cloud of incenfe, one unbounded flame,
To heaven afcend : the fun fhall brighter rife,
And peace, and light, and glory gild the fkies.

    Thus the great Seer ; and warm'd with heavenly grace,
Befought all bleffings for his darling race ;   700
Then up fam'd Pifgah's fide ferenely drew,
Where all Canäan met his rapturous view ;

Thence his glad foul explor'd her native day,
And left, for blifs, the tenemental clay:
His foul, fcarce lower than the angels made,   705
With glory mitred, and with truth array'd.
As the bold eagle, borne from humble vales,
Lifts his ftrong wings, and up th' expanfion fails;
O'er groves, o'er hills, o'er mountains, wins his way,
And climbs exulting in the noon-tide ray;   710
Now far beneath him fees each birdling fly;
Now clouds light-floating fkim the lower fky;
In profpect wide, with piercing ken, defcries
Far, leffening towns, and fpacious empires rife;
Here rivers wind, the lakes their borders fpread;   715
And there the blue-feen ocean fmooths his bed;
In pride fublime, he holds his upward way,
And bafks, and triumphs, in the flame of day.
So, borne with angel-flight, his mighty mind,
Afcending, left the common wing behind;   720
Full on the fun's great Source fuperior drew,
'Till truth's wide regions ftretch'd in glorious view;
There fair Creation fpread her boundlefs plan;
There op'd, myfterious, all the world of man:
With every fplendor bright Redemption fhone;   725
And, one immenfe of beauty, God the Son.
Still up the heavens he wing'd his folar flight,
And foar'd, and mingled with unborrow'd light.

Far in a wild vale's folitary gloom,
Jehovah form'd his favourite's lonely tomb;   730
For life diftinguifh'd, there his limbs refine,
'Till morn's laft beams in purple glory fhine;
Then, rob'd in beauty, fhall the Prophet rife,
And fail, the peer of angels, thro' the fkies.

But, ere his fpirit fought celeftial day,   735
To Jofhua's hand he gave the deftin'd fway,
A Chief divine! with every virtue crown'd,
In combat glorious, and in peace renown'd,

H

To him the Almighty voice---Thy chosen hand
Shall guide my sons, and rule the promis'd land.　　740
That land, where peace, and every pleasure reigns,
O'er heaven-topp'd hills, and fair, extended plains ;
Where countless nations build the lofty dome,
Nurse purpling vines, and teach the vales to bloom ;
That land is thine.　Where'er thy foot shall tread,　745
From the parch'd climes where Midian's thousands spread,
To realms, where Hazor, arm'd with potent sway,
Bids kingdoms bow, and conquer'd chiefs obey :
Or where Euphrates winds his gentle flight ;
Or the broad ocean rolls in evening light ;　　　750
All, all is thine.　Who dare thy course withstand,
Shall feel the fury of th' Eternal hand.
Lost in black crimes the torpid nations lie,
And claim fierce vengeance from an injur'd sky.
Rise, rise to arms ! o'er Jordan's yielding flood　755
My guardian hand shall point the destin'd road.
　Thus spoke the fair : and while th' etherial strain
Breath'd a soft music o'er the wondering train,
With anxious look th' impatient monarch cried---
O best of maids, thy sex's noblest pride !　　　760
Far round the neighbouring realms by fame is rung
The wonderous race, thy lovely voice has sung.
Oft have I heard, how, arm'd with dreadful rod,
Before his votaries march'd their mighty God ;
How kings in vain their rapid course oppos'd,　765
Their hosts all vanquish'd, and their empire clos'd.
But still, misled by Rumour's dubious tongue,
In sad suspense my mind all-anxious hung.
Now with clear truth the scenes tremendous shine ;
Of force convinc'd, I own the Power divine.　　770
And must our race with one wide doom expire ?
These turrets sink ? these walls be wrapt in fire ?
Must yon bright maid, whose soft and lovely smile
Could murderers charm, and wolves of rage beguile ;

These beauteous infants, scarce to reason born,   775
Sweeter than flowers perfume the vernal morn,
To war's unpitying fury yield their breath,
And helpless close their little eyes in death?
O thou great God, whose sway o'er heaven presides,
Whose searching eye the world's vast empire guides: 780
Stay, stay thine hand; this guilty nation spare;
Let these sweet babes thy boundless pity share!
Unform'd our infant prayer--but cries sincere
And honest hearts will find a bounteous ear.

He spoke; around, the melting voice of woe   785
Breath'd sad complaints, and tears began to flow;
When thus the Prince again--O loveliest maid!
Where, where shall Gibeon find the needed aid?
Can no kind hand the friendly refuge give?
No pitying saviour bid my children live?   790
Say, loveliest fair, canst thou no succour lend?
Our teacher thou--be thou our guardian friend.
Perchance thy bounteous Ruler, form'd to bless,
O'er suppliant realms may lift the branch of peace.

The maid return'd--perhaps a virgin's mind,   795
Though wisdom fail, the wish'd retreat may find.
To Israel's camp two trusty heroes send;
Let me, restor'd, their peaceful steps attend.
The maid, thou seest by blest adoption shares
Their mighty Leader's fond, parental cares.   800
Pleas'd with the offering, Joshua's hand may give
The palm of peace, and bid thy nation live.

Charm'd with the thought, joy sparkling in his eyes,
With voice exulting, strait the king replies.
O fair divine! thy mind, with wisdom bright,   805
Even age out-soars and climbs an angel's flight.
Let peace thy life surround.   The task be mine
Soon to prepare, and end the blest design.
Thy lovely voice must find a generous ear;
So sweet a strain even oaks would bow to hear.   810

The Monarch fpoke; and o'er the circling throng
Bright fmiles broke forth, and pleas'd applaufes rung;
A beauteous femblance of the fields around,
Starr'd with young flowers, and with gay verdure crown'd,
Where airy fongs, foft proof of raptur'd love,　　　815
Wav'd on the gale, and echo'd thro' the grove;
While the clear fun, rejoicing ftill to rife,
In pomp roll'd round immeafurable fkies.

THE

CONQUEST OF CANÄAN.

BOOK III.

ARGUMENT.

Characters of Hezron, Irad, and Selima. Morning. Irad and Selima walk out on the plain, northward of the camp, and hold a conversation on the justice of the War. As they are returning to the camp, they overhear two Israelites conversing on a design of returning into Egypt. Irad communicates the discovery to Joshua. The alarm is given, and an army perceived, coming from Ai to attack the camp. Joshua goes out to the place of rendezvous, marshals a body of troops, and sends them, under the command of Zimri, to meet the army of Ai. In the mean time the camp is in a general uproar, and a large body of the Israelites assembled, westward of the camp, for the purpose of returning into Egypt. After the confusion is in a degree allayed, Tadmor harangues the insurgents, with a list of grievances, and stimulates them to perseverance. Caleb who, with Hezron, had been sent by Joshua, upon Irad's information, to watch the motions of the camp, replies to him. Ardan answers him, with impudence, and Hezron him, with severity. Insurgents march. As they are quitting the plain, Joshua comes out, with a body of troops to attack them. The chieftains set their forces in array. Joshua orders them to disperse. Ardan affronts him, and is killed. The insurgents disperse, and the chiefs return to the camp. Irad goes out to view the battle. Armies engage with violence, and equal success; until the chiefs of Ai, influenced by superstitious fears, excited by the appearance of a thunder storm, order a retreat. Zimri also retires. Scene of the beauties of an evening after the storm concludes the book.

THE CONQUEST OF CANÄAN.

BOOK III.

OF Judah's thousands Hezron held the sway;
And love, and reverence, bade them all obey.
The chief, of simple manners, knew no art;
Truth was his language; honesty his heart:
To bless mankind his life's unvaried end;   5
His guest the stranger, and the poor his friend.
So fair his strong, and stubborn virtue shone,
Heaven crown'd his wishes with a lovely son.
To mould young Irad was his darling care;
To form for peace, to animate for war;   10
His limbs t' innerve; his vices to controul,
And lead to wisdom's fount his thirsty soul.
In earliest years, the favourite Youth began
To shew those charms, which rarely grace the man.
To rashness brave, his bosom burn'd for fame;   15
Yet knew a milder, and a nobler flame:
Love's gentle fire his passions could controul,
And pure Religion warm'd his manly soul.
Not that, which broods upon the surly brow,
Or walks on frozen joints, demure, and slow;   20
At truth, and virtue, points the fatal wound,
Swells on the tongue, and vanishes in sound:
But that, whose influence fires th' angelic band;
Smooths the rough bosom; opes the narrow hand;

Serenely brightens in the cheerful face ;   25
Cafts round each act unutterable grace ;
With rifing morning, bows the secret knee,
And wafts, great God! the humble foul to thee.

His raptur'd father wifh'd no fecond fon ;
But found both parents' charms combin'd in one ;   30
His own ftrong fenfe, and daring thought, refin'd
By the foft graces of a mother's mind.
His lively duty cheer'd the waning year ;
With hand all gentle wip'd the aged tear ;
Explor'd each wifh, prevented each requeft,   35
And thought it heaven to make a parent bleft.
Nature's politenefs, unaffected eafe,
Mov'd in his limbs, and fram'd his foul to pleafe ;
To worth complacent gave the juft reward,
And notic'd humble life, with kind regard.   40

Nature can form the foul, or rough, or fine ;
But all her clouded beauties faintly fhine :
Religion bids a new creation rife,
Fragrant as fpring, and fair as fpangled fkies.
Thus, on the canvas, Weft, with raptur'd view,   45
Sees new-born worlds his magic hand purfue ;
Th' impaffion'd forms diffolve in foft defire,
Or glow, and tremble, with feraphic fire ;
They breathe, they fpeak, they move, the field around,
And the ear liftens for th' expected found .   50
But thefe muft fade : while Virtue's ftrokes fhall live,
Tranfcend earth's fky-built tomb, and with the heavens
        Beyond his peers, by nature, Irad fhone ;   [revive.
By virtue, ripen'd to the duteous fon ;
By virtue, aim'd at life's fublimeft end,   55
Rofe to the faint, and foften'd to the friend :
Pleas'd his fond nation faw his glories rife,
And a new Joshua charm'd their raptur'd eyes.

The virgins view'd, how could they not approve ?
Efteem's the filent harbinger of love.   60

BOOK III.

The kind eye, glistening with a frequent tear,
The conscious blush, that saw discovery near,
Th' unbidden sigh, that swell'd the beating breast,
And the fix'd gaze, that scarce could be repress'd,
The soft emotions to his eye reveal'd, 65
And new, strange tremors through his bosom thrill'd.
But far o'er all Selima's charms prevail'd,
When his pleas'd heart her piercing eyes assail'd.
His youngest birth, bless'd Caleb own'd the fair,
His life's chief solace, and his favorite care. 70
Not nature's hand her beauty could improve ;
Her voice was melody ; her mind was love ;
Her stature tall ; her air intrancing ease ;
Her skin the lilly, opening to the breeze ;
Her cheek was health's inimitable die, 75
And the bright soul sate sparkling in her eye.
No vile cosmetic stain'd her lovely face ;
No affectation murder'd real grace :
Her robes all neatness, told the world how fine,
How pure, th' angelic habitant within. 80
Sweetness etherial majesty controul'd,
And form'd an Irad of a softer mould.
Such was her soul, as when, of darkness born,
O'er young creation rose beginning morn,
Fair, in her front, a blushing Virtue stood, 85
Just sprung to life, and ey'd the forming God ;
From grace to grace with glowing wisdom grew,
And smil'd, and triumph'd, in the rapturous view.
Now twice nine years had o'er the fair-one roll'd,
Illum'd her eyes, and bade her charms unfold ; 90
When her quick fancy, self-inspir'd to rove,
Attun'd her feelings to romantic love.
Oft on the youth she fix'd a secret gaze,
And oft, with transport, listen'd to his praise.
The charms of face, the beauty of desert, 95
Stole soft, and silent, through her yielding heart.

I

Efteem, which hermits fcarce could difapprove,
Bloom'd in his fmiles, and open'd into love.

Nor fhone her glances on his breaft in vain;
The gaze, that gave, return'd the pleafing pain.　　100
Judgment, in both, the fpotlefs flame improv'd;
They lik'd from fancy, but from reafon lov'd.

Oft would each fire his tender wifh declare,
To fee one band unite the lovely pair.

Oft figh'd the youth t' unfold his anxious mind;　　105
But ftill a modeft fear his lips confin'd:
In pleas'd attention on her charms he hung,
And half-heard wifhes trembled o'er his tongue.
At length, kind Heaven, propitious to the pair,
Led his fond fteps, where love had led the fair.　　110
In a lone walk, far-diftant on the plain,
Surpriz'd, his tongue unbidden told his pain.
The beauteous maid, of frank and gentle mind,
Smil'd in his hopes, and blefs'd with love refin'd,
In truth's mild beam the fpotlefs union grew,　　115
And gave fuch joy, as youthful angels knew.

Now wak'd the dim-feen dawn. O'er hills afar
Rofe in gay triumph morn's refulgent ftar;
Up the gay fkies fore-running beauty fpread;
The grey mift fail'd along the mountain's head;　　120
In clouds th' embofom'd lark her matin fings,
And from his couch impatient Irad fprings,
To morn's unnumber'd fweets invites the fair,
Gay profpects, magic fongs, and fragrant air.

Rapt with the charms, which nature gives to view　　125
The great, the high, the beauteous, and the new,
To her foft power they bow'd the yielding mind,
Warm'd as they heard, and as they gaz'd refin'd;
In flowery tribes, where thoufand fplendors play;
When magic profpect holds the lingering day;　　130
When brighten'd Evening fpreads her gayeft train,
And hails young Hefper to his native main;

BOOK III.

In cloudy wilds, where gloomy thunder lies,
The pale moon mourns, and mountains prop the ſkies.

O'er northern plains ſerene the lovers ſtray,   135
And various converſe charms their eaſy way---
How ſweet, O fair---the Youth with rapture cries---
Earth's beauteous ſcenes, and wonders of the ſkies !
The folding clouds ! the gates of morn unbarr'd !
The dewy plains, with flowery gems inſtarr'd !   140
The cliff-topp'd mountain ! the deep-waving grove !
The air all odour ! and the world all love !

Thrice fair are nature's works---the maid replied,
And her face bloom'd in beauty's living pride---
When round her fields my thoughts untroubled roll,   145
An eaſy joy ſteals ſoftly on my ſoul :
Fir'd as I gaze, my breaſt with rapture warms,
Her glories raviſh, and her muſic charms.
But oh the fate of Ai's unhappy field,
That every joy, and every hope, diſpell'd !   150
Fled are the charms, that nature once attir'd
And loſt the ſweets, that ether once inſpir'd.
As now through well-known paths, retir'd I ſtray,
And ſeek accuſtom'd beauties round my way ;
At every turn, the ſeeming trump alarms,   155
Pale corſes riſe, and groans. and claſhing arms ;
From my pain'd boſom heaves th' unbidden ſigh ;
The ſtill tear trembles in my labouring eye ;
Loſt, but to grief, my feet bewilder'd rove,
And my heart deadens to thyſelf, and love.   160
O fatal hapleſs combat ! cauſe unjuſt !
That blends the nobleſt heroes with the duſt ;
From ſad Canäan's ſons their wealth demands,
The flocks they tended, and their cultur'd lands ;
Bids o'er their peaceful domes deſtruction flame,   165
And blots with deep diſhonour Iſrael's name.

The Prince rejoin'd, By all-creating Heaven,
To Abraham's ſons theſe ſruitful fields were given.

Whate'er he made, the Maker claims his own ;
Gives, and refumes, advis'd and rul'd by none.   170
By him beſtow'd, a righteous ſword demands
Theſe flocks, theſe cities, and theſe promis'd lands,
Yet not 'till crimes, beyond long-ſuffering great,
Had fill'd their cup, and fix'd their changeleſs ſtate,
Would Heaven permit our race its gift to claim,   175
Or ſeal the glory of th' almighty Name.
In vain mild Mercy hop'd their hearts to gain,
And Patience look'd for Penitence, in vain.
As rolling ſtreams one courſe eternal keep,
All ruſh impetuous down the guilty ſteep.   180

    The maid return'd, The nations' foul diſgrace,
Stain'd with black guilt, I grant Canäan's race.
But not alike are all from virtue driven ;
Some, more than others, claim the ſword of Heaven :
Yet undiſtinguiſh'd falls the general doom,   185
The beſt, the worſt, we deſtine to the tomb.

    Where Hazor's hundred towers majeſtic riſe,
Frown o'er her plains, and dare avenging ſkies ;
In all that elegance of artleſs charms,
Which prompts mild love, and rival hate alarms ;   190
In that ſweet union of ſerene deſires,
Which blows with fragrant breath unmingled fires ;
Young, beauteous fair-ones, through her regions known,
Outvie the maid, thou lov'ſt to call thy own.
To theſe bright virgins choſen Irads bow ;   195
Leſs wiſe, leſs virtuous, and leſs fair than thou ;
But crown'd with many a grace ; of thoughts refin'd,
Of pleaſing perſon, and of dauntleſs mind.
Shall this bleſs'd train, ſo young, ſo fair, ſo brave,
Fall, with black wretches, in a firey grave ?   200
Or round wild regions muſt they hapleſs roam,
Exil'd from joy, and forc'd from cheerful home ?
To hunger, thirſt, and ſorrow, ſink and pray,
And breathe, with lingering death, their lives away,

BOOK III.

Should'st thou, when war to Salem drives her course,
Seize the keen steel, and join the conquering force,   206
While thy bold breast with glory's warmth beats high,
And wreaths well-twin'd approach thy ravish'd eye,
To some lone hamlet loosely wandering come,
Where simple swains had built their peaceful home,   210
Where care in silence smoothly pass'd away,
And home-bred happiness deceiv'd the day;
Should there sweet, helpless children meet thy view,
Fair as young rosebuds look thro' early dew,
With infant wonder, on thine armour gaze,   215
And point, with artless hands, the steely blaze:
Say could thy heart one angry purpose know,
Or doom such cherubs to a single woe?
Charm'd by soft smiles, I see thy heart retire,
And mild compassion breathe a gentler fire;   220
Thy love parental o'er them kindly yearn,
Prompt pleasing hope, and all their wishes learn;
Thy bounteous hand each needed bliss bestow,
And in the angel lose th' intended foe.

Yet should dread war o'er these fair regions fly,   225
Unnumber'd virgins, bright as those must die;
To flames unnumber'd babes resign their breath,
And ere life blossoms, meet untimely death.

To thee, O prince! without a blush, I own
Such woes tremendous freeze my heart to stone.   230
Ere Irad's arm such precious lives destroy,
Let me, far guiltier, cease from every joy;
Quick to the dreary grave my form descend,
Our love all vanish, and our union end.

The Prince replied, Bless'd gentleness of mind!   235
The grace, the glory of a heart refin'd!
When new-born, helpless beings meet our eyes,
In noble minds, such thoughts resistless rise:
Even brutes, when young, our tender wishes try,
And love forbids the infant whelp to die.   240

Yet oft this kindeſt impulſe of the ſoul
Bids wild deſire in murmuring tumults roll,
And blames the Power, whoſe love alone, to earth,
And all earth's drear and dark events, gave birth.

   In thy pure boſom, angels muſt approve.   245
For ſad Canäan's youth, this generous love.
But once as fair, as young, as ſoft as they,
As white with innocence, with ſmiles as gay,
Were thoſe black throngs, whoſe crimes as mountains riſe,
And wipe out pity from th' all bounteous ſkies.   250
As eggs innoxious, oft in meadows ſtrew'd,
Break into aſps, and pour the viper's brood;
Nurs'd in rank ſoils, to ſtrength the reptiles grow,
Reſound the hiſs, the ſting of vengeance throw,
Uprear the creſt, inroll the ſnaky ſpire,   255
Light the keen eye-ball with terrific fire;
From fields, and foreſts, death, and poiſon gain,
And ſcatter wide deſtruction round the plain:
So, harmleſs once, by vile affections lur'd,
In guilt, and years, thoſe babes alike matur'd;   260
Athirſt for ſin, all patterns left behind,
The form all putrid, poiſon'd all the mind,
To every crime, to every madneſs, driven,
Curs'd the ſad world, and hiſs'd the name of Heaven.
There the ſot reels, the murderer prowls for blood; 265
There the ſtarv'd orphan ſues in vain for food;
For man man burns, with Sodom's tainted flame,
And the world ſickens with inceſtuous ſhame.
Even nature's ties their boſoms bind no more,
Wives wade in nuptial, ſires in filial gore;   270
To howling Molock blooming babes expire,
And mothers round them dance, and light the funeral fire.
   Should then theſe infants to dread manhood riſe,
What unheard crimes would ſmoke thro' earth and ſkies!
What hoſts of demons ſin's dark realm would gain! 275
How hell gape hideous round Canäan's plain!

This sea of guilt unmeasur'd to prevent,
Our chosen race eternal Justice sent,
At once the bright possession to reclaim,
And 'gainst its victims point the vengeful flame,   280
Thus crimes their due and dire reward shall know;
Thus God be witness'd sin's unchanging foe;
From land to land Jehovah's glory shine,
And fear, and homage, wait the Name divine.

But, O unrivall'd maid! the kindest doom   285
These babes may destine to an early tomb.
To manhood risen their guilt, beyond controul,
Would blot their names from life's celestial roll.
Now, in fair climes, their souls, forever bless'd,
May bloom in youth, and share immortal rest;   290
And hail the boundless grace, that snatch'd its foes
From sins unnumber'd, and from lasting woes.

And, O bright maid! whate'er high Heaven design'd
Is just, is glorious to th' omniscient Mind.
When Heaven commands, the virtuous ask no more: 295
His will is justice, as his arm is power:
Led by his voice, our cause divine we know;
We tempt no evil, and we fear no foe.

All gentle Youth! Selima soft replied---
How well thy words from falsehood truth divide!   300
With what sweet tenderness, thy voice displays
The truth, the lustre, of th' Eternal ways.
But say, bless'd Prince! will Heaven our race succeed?
Shall we victorious gain the darling meed?
So oft our host rebellion blackens o'er,   305
I fear, lest triumph crown our arms no more.
When will the friendly cloud again return?
When o'er yon dome the nightly glory burn?

Rejoin'd the smiling Prince; too anxious maid,
Let faithless terror ne'er thy heart invade,   310
To Abraham seal'd the sacred covenant stands---
Thy countless sons shall rule Canäan's lands.---

Guilt's impious train these tumults shall destroy;
Too vile, too base, to share the promis'd joy.
And he, whose soul, a plant for earth too fair,   315
Has grown, and ripen'd for a kinder air,
Full soon may feel the hand of blasting time,
By Heaven transplanted to a nobler clime,
Pass the cold winter of the frozen tomb,
And rise, and flourish in eternal bloom.   320

But to glad fields, beyond those hills that lie,
And drink mild influence from the western sky,
The rest triumphant soon shall wing their way,
Seize their vast towns, and reign from sea to sea.

Then join'd in love, in bands connubial join'd,   325
Each passion calm'd, and every taste refin'd,
Our fears shall end, unclouded hope begin,
Peace' gentle morning o'er Canäan shine;
In soft beatitude the seasons roll,
And growing union mix the kindred soul.   330

The maid return'd---O day supremely fair!
Not blooming Eden own'd a happier pair.
But, Youth belov'd! my bosom, rack'd with pain,
Tells me, sad tale! the darling wish is vain.
Tells me that chosen mora will never come,   335
Nor bliss be finish'd, but beyond the tomb.
For earth too bright were these love-lighted fires!
Too bless'd th' indulgence of such pure desires!
Here unallay'd, no lot, no joy appears;
Grief poisons hope, and pleasures mix with tears.   340

Ah fairest, wisest, loveliest of thy kind!
Of form all finish'd' and of matchless mind!
Sweet-smiling visitant from yonder sky!
Too bright to live, and O too dear to die!
Why, hapless Mina! why from friends, and home,   345
Didst thou, unguided, in the wild wood roam?
Perhaps the hungry wolf around thy way
Lurk'd with grim rage, and seiz'd his helpless prey.

Perhaps, O lot of anguiſh ! brutal men
Thy path unguarded, with fell eyes, have ſeen.   350
Or doſt thou pale, unſeen, unburied, lie,
Sad ſorrow's victim, in th' inclement ſky ?
How ſoon is thy fair courſe of glory run !
Thy hopes all ended ! all thy duties done !
Sleep, lovely maid ! in hollow'd ſilence reſt,   355
Let fragrant gales thy form with leaves inveſt ;
There with new ſweets, the lovely wild-roſe bloom,
And pitying ſtrangers raiſe thy verdant tomb.

 Ah hapleſs maid ! the tender prince rejoin'd---
How thy rich graces charm'd each generous mind !   360
Even Joſhua's love how nobly didſt thou claim,
Thy wiſhes virtue, and thy actions fame !
When his toils roſe, when dangers dire oppreſs'd,
And Iſrael's griefs hung heavy on his breaſt,
Thy gentle mind, a ſoul-ſupporting ſtay,   365
Seren'd thoſe toils, and charm'd thoſe griefs away ;
A calm retreat from fear, and doubt, and ſtrife,
And all the hidden pangs of ſcepter'd life.
Reſt in mild ſlumbers, lovely maiden ! reſt ;
Thy life be copied, and thy memory bleſs'd !   370
Each ſoft-eyed virgin bid thy fame revive,
Attune her lyre, and in her actions live ;
So, join'd with thee, in beauty's diſtant clime,
Her praiſe ſhall triumph o'er the death of time.

 As thus the converſe paſs'd, with many a tear,   375
To the ſtill camp approach'd the ſadden'd pair.
In th' utmoſt ſkirt, a tent at diſtance ſtood ;
Whence mingling voices, ſcarce-diſtinguiſh'd, flow'd.
Heard'ſt thou--a warrior low his zeal expreſs'd--
When generous Hanniel Jacob's ſons addreſs'd ?   380
How on his words the thouſands liſtening hung !
How ſweet perſuaſion charm'd us from his tongue !
From pride, from pomp, from love of titles free,
He loves the poor ; he feels for thee and me.

K

Oh, could our tribes by fad experience learn   385
What children tell, and what the blind difcern,
Him for their leader would they raptur'd claim,
And fly from endlefs toil, and endlefs fhame.
From hideous war my wearied foul recoils ;
I afk no treafures rais'd from battle's fpoils.   390
To painful arms let fons of flaughter run ;
By them be glory's painted bubble won :
To peace, of aims far different, would I fly,
In peace inglorious live, inglorious die :
While peace, while plenty, much-lov'd Egypt knows,
Hears no fhrill trump, and dreads no banded foes,   396
Thefe boafted flocks, and towns, and promis'd fields,
To them my firft, laft wifh delighted yields.

     With earneft voice, his fellow pleas'd replies---
Since toil and pain have taught thee to be wife,   400
Know, my brave friend, a fecret, faithful band
Soon point their courfe to Egypt's darling land.
When firft to combat Jofhua bends his way,
To guard the camp thefe bold affociates ftay ;
With one firm heart, our path we then begin,   405
And noble Hanniel leads the blefs'd defign.
But hufh'd in filence muft thefe counfels reft,
Scarce even to tried, and faithful friends confefs'd ;
Left the dread Chief's all-watchful, piercing eye,
With fun-like ken, the hated plot defery.   410
Thou know'ft what ills a plot difclos'd attend ;
Our names muft perifh, and our lives muft end.

     His friend return'd---The lov'd, the bold defign
My glad foul welcomes, and my hand fhall join.
Hail happy tidings ! hail aufpicious fields !   415
Where genial nature every pleafure yields---
Too blefs'd, to that fweet native land I fly,
That cot, that heritage, that friendly fky---
Dear fcenes of youth ! where peace and pleafure mild,
With cheerful health, and ceafelefs plenty fmil'd---   420

Might these, O envied lot! again be given,
'Twere bliſs too great ; I claim no higher heaven.
   This heard, Selima to her tent withdrew ;
While ſtrait to Joſhua ardent Irad flew,
To him, apart, the dangerous plot diſclos'd,   425
And what the tribe, and where the tent, expos'd.
As ſome fond parent eyes his darling child,
Pleas'd, the great Hero on the favourite ſmil'd,
His zeal, his prudence prais'd, and on his head
Beſought the Heavens their choiceſt bliſs to ſhed.   430
   Mean time from diſtant guards a cry aſcends,
And round the camp the dinning voice extends :
Th' alarming trump reſounds ; the martial train
Pour from the tents, and crowd th' accuſtom'd plain,
In mazy wanderings, thickening, darkening, roll,   435
Fill all the field, and ſhade the boundleſs pole.
As where proud Erie winds her narrowing ſhores,
And o'er huge hills a boiling ocean pours,
The long white-ſheeted foam, with fury hurl'd,
Down the cliffs thundering, ſhakes the ſtable world,   440
In ſolemn grandeur clouds of miſt ariſe,
Top the tall pines, and heavy, ſeek the ſkies :
So ſpread the volumes of the duſt afar ;
So roar the clamors of commencing war.
   Anxious, and active, there the Leader ſtrode.   445
Nerv'd every heart, and ſteel'd for death and blood ;
From rank to rank, he huſh'd the tumult's ſound,
And ſpread deep ſilence o'er th' attentive ground :
Then while the chiefs combin'd the dread array,
Tow'rd a high rock he bent his rapid way ;   450
From the tall height, to Ai he caſt his eyes,
And ſaw, in ſouthern fields, her ſquadrons riſe ;
A cloud, far-ſpreading, o'er the plain impell'd,
Roll'd up th' expanſe, and wrapp'd the gloomy field ;
Approaching, widening, ſlow the darkneſs came,   455
Emblaz'd with gleams of intermitted flame.

BOOK III.

So, long and black, like skirts of rising oven,
Thick clouds, now gathering, fill'd the northern heaven;
Borne on slow winds, that ceaseless chang'd its form,
O'er the dark mountains sail'd th' expanding storm; 460
In rising grandeur far-off thunders roll,
Dim lightnings flash, and gild the clouded pole;
More wide, more vast, the solemn gloom ascends,
And frowning, deepening, round th' horizon bends.

    At once the Hero gave the loud command; 465
In awful silence mov'd the chosen band;
Compact, to Ai they cours'd their dreadful way,
And generous Zimri rul'd the long array,

    Mean time new scenes around the camp began,
The tribes all motion, man confus'd with man; 470
From tent to tent swift-hastening feet appear'd;
Low-murmuring voices, mingling sounds were heard,
Loud, and more loud, the earnest clamors grow,
Hum through the tents, and all the camp o'erflow.
To Egypt's realms---resounds the general cry--- 475
From these sad scenes, with prosperous feet, we fly,
These hosts of foes, these fields of ceaseless fight,
This sway of bondage, and this war of flight.
Haste, freedom's sons, and seize her happy shores,
For all her peace, and wealth, and joy, are yours. 480
Thus round the host the mingled clamor flew,
And loud, and fierce, debates tumultuous grew;
They urg'd, persuaded, threaten'd, flatter'd, cried,
With love conjur'd, with stubborn breast denied;
Friends left their friends, with answering look severe, 285
Sigh'd sad departure, dropp'd th' expressive tear;
From parents children headlong burst away,
While groans recall'd them from the dire affray;
To brothers brothers gave the parting hand,
And Virtue eyed, with tears, the swerving band. 490

    All dress'd in arms, and cloth'd in rich array,
Forth from the camp the warriors bent their way;

Their hands their gold, and favourite treasures bore,
And each fond bosom hail'd th' Egyptian shore.
O'er the broad circuit of the western plain,   495
From all sides gathering, mov'd the numerous train,
This way, and that, in thousand paths impell'd,
Immingling, rushing, darkening, hid the field,
To one great central phalanx swiftly driven,
Gloom'd the sad ground, and cast a shade on heaven, 500
Frowning, and fierce, expanded o'er the plain,
And, proud of numbers, deem'd resistance vain.

Of name obscure, before th' increasing throng
Two haughty chieftains proudly stalk'd along ;
Felt all the joys, which little minds o'errun,   505
From sway first tried, and influence scarce begun ;
Look'd wise, inportant hurried o'er the field ;
Commanded, question'd, with loud threats compell'd ;
Spoke with stern voice ; advising, wavering stood,
And scarce the ground was printed, where they trode. 510

Far round the plain the mingled tumult ran,
Chief answer'd chief, and man rehears'd to man.
Thro' each small circle loud the murmur spread,
Of spoils ungiven, virtues unrepaid,
Woes unextinguish'd, labours ne'er to end,   515
The starving houshold, and the naked friend---
Where now's the heart, that bless'd the prophet's sway,
That sooth'd the tribes, and bade the soul obey,
Swept Bashan's fields, o'erthrew proud Sihon's throne,
And to poor warriors left the spoils they won ?   520

But now new chiefs, in wiles and learning train'd,
Wield a dread sceptre, with an iron hand ;
All, all but Hanniel ; Hanniel singly glows
With Israel's good, and weeps for Israel's woes.
Hail then, oh hail the bless'd, auspicious day,   525
That opes to brighter realms our happy way !
The chiefs, we chose, the glorious path shall guide,
Uncurs'd with learning, and unstain'd with pride.

Thus round the plain the tumult shrill resounds;
Of different note, immix unnumber'd sounds;   530
High toss'd in ether helms confus'dly fly,
And clashing shields to clashing shields reply:
Loud, hoarse, and rough, wide jars discordant noise,
And raging passions swell the clamorous voice.
So, where on ocean's brim the long beach winds,   535
Breaks his proud waves, and all his fury binds,
Unnumber'd fowls, of various wing, arise,
And toss in wild gyrations to the skies;
From each harsh throat hard strains of discord roar,
Break with dire din, and grate along the shore;   540
Loud, and more loud, the nations heaven deform,
Or gloom the strand, and croak the coming storm.

As round the plain the mingled tumult ran,
Tadmor, the elder chieftain, thus began---
Hail, sons of freedom ! Jacob's fairest boast !   545
Heirs of the sky, and virtue's genuine host !
Well did brave Hanniel teach, in words divine,
How fast our tribes, with toils, and griefs, decline;
Full well he mark'd what deep designs are laid
By chiefs, of man, nor truth, nor Heaven, afraid;   550
That, swell'd with pride, and train'd in artful lore,
O'erleap all right, and crush the hapless poor.
To us no leader tells the deep design,
What hosts oppose us, and what lands combine;
What towns are next besieg'd; what dangers tried;   555
What spoils are won, and who those spoils divide.
In Egypt's realm the long-wish'd rule to gain,
They found each art, and each bold effort, vain:
Thence thro' the waste they urg'd our fatal way,
And hop'd, in this dire land, untroubled sway;   560
Yet there the poor a lot far happier found,
With fasts unburden'd, and with rites unbound:
Our tribute paid, at plenteous feasts we sate,
Stretch'd in soft ease, and every dainty ate.

Oh, why from those fair regions did we come ?   565
Why, blind and headlong, leave our darling home ?
Here our own leaders Egypt's kings outdo,
And change of lords is all the good we know.

Haste then, from these dread fields of misery fly ;
With chiefs you chose again to Egypt hie ;   570
Where ease, and wines, and feasts, and soft delight,
Earth ever fruitful, skies forever bright,
Awake sweet pleasure, raptur'd love revive,
And teach poor mortals what it is to live :
Now seize the hour, by Joshua's folly given,   575
Or op'd for Israel by a pitying Heaven.
Ai's gallant sons will sweep his host away,
Worne by long labours, and to fasts a prey ;
Or, scap'd the field, their weary feet must fail ;
Or, join'd in fight, our arms will soon prevail ;   580
This day beyond persuit our course removes,
And leaves the tyrant to the slaves he loves.

He spoke ; at once, from all th' impatient train,
A bust of triumph shook the sounding plain ;
Thence rose the shout ; as oft the heavens replied ;   585
And, borne thro' fields, and woods, the far-off murmur died.
Thus, when the vernal storm forbears to rave,
And the wild river swells his torrent wave,
Huge isles of ice, along the clifted shore.
Float slow, and cumbrous ; solemn thunders roar;   590
In deep gradations, rise, and burst, and roll,
Wave o'er the sounding hills, and lessen to the pole.

When first from Joshua faithful Irad went,
He summon'd Judah's heroes to his tent,
Bade them the tribes with prudent caution eye,   595
Pursue their motions, and their views descry,
Their tumults hush, or should their efforts fail,
With speed to him convey th' unpleasing tale.
When round the camp disorder'd scenes began,
Strait to the sound th' attentive heroes ran ;   600

Watch'd all the murmurs of the gathering train,
And follow'd anxious to the troubled plain ;
But first the tidings to the Leader sped,
What bands assembled, and what chieftains led,
Urg'd him with haste to arm a numerous force,   605
And 'gainst th' insurgents bend his rapid course.

  And now, when Tadmor ceas'd, the shouts decay'd;
With sweet, mild accent, thus grave Caleb said---
How slight the toil, mistaking chief, to prove
'Tis wisdom's voice directs the path, we love !   610
Though thorns, though serpents hedge the fatal way,
The fond heart bids, and answering feet obey.
Each truth, each argument, thy voice runs o'er,
Forbids our host to seek th' Egyptian shore.
The waste's dire ills thy plaintive words resound,   615
Yet through that waste the darling realm is found ;
Again those countless woes our race must try ;
Again with toil, and thirst, and famine, die.
Or shall we flee, by Hazor's bands compell'd,
To meet fierce Amalek, in the hostile field.   620
Will hosts that tremble, where Ai's sons appear,
Abide the conflict, when Philistia's near.

  But to what end, against unnumber'd foes,
Shall Israel war to gain Egyptian woes;
Shame, vice, idolatry, and bondage, join'd,   625
The wrath of Heaven, and hissing of mankind ?
If war is destin'd Israel's fearful doom,
With war, let freedom, wealth, and glory come:
Let peace, let realms, let empire crown the toil ;
The world applaud us, and th' Eternal smile   630
In this fair land, shall each poor warrior reign
Lord of himself, and monarch of the plain.
His house, his herd, his harvest all his own,
And changeless law transmit them to his son.
But Egypt's wealth her king alone commands,   635
Her sons, her gold, her products, and her lands.

BOOK III.

For him our hands, in flavish woe, muft toil,
And pamper fplendor on the beggar's fpoil,
Poor beyond thought, fufpended on a breath,
Our life a fufferance, and a nod our death.　640

But Ifrael's chiefs are train'd in dangerous lore,
And hence regardlefs of the humble poor.
Say, Tadmor, fay, the wiles of art to fhun,
To Egypt's realms impatient doft thou run ?
To courts, to lords, with fmooth deceit o'erhung,　645
Where art firft budded, and where learning fprung ?
Truth, confcience, Heaven, thine idle dreams deny;
Repent, return ; nor, fnar'd by treafons, die.

The hero fpoke.　From all the angry train
A rifing murmur wav'd along the plain :　650
As 'twixt tall hills, where rufhing torrents roll,
A flow, and lingering groan afcends the pole;
Thro' gloomy caverns hums the folemn found,
Fills all the hollow realm, and fhakes the fhady ground.

Ardan, the younger chieftain, quick return'd,　655
And from his eye-balls kindling fury burn'd---
Imperious prince, I know thy heart of fteel
Ne'er lov'd the poor, and never knew to feel.
But that proud voice, which aw'd my breaft before,
Now fails to rule, and guides the hoft no more.　660
I mock thy threats, thy utmoft power defy,
Thy reafons trample, and thy words deny.
Chang'd is the fcene.　Thy pride muft now obey
In worth thy betters, and thy lords in fway.
Go tell yon flaves, that bafe, and beftial train,　665
Thy arts, thy arguments, and threats are vain ;
Bid them their friends, their gallant brethren foe,
A hoft of heroes, daring to be free,
Of numbers countlefs, bravery never aw'd,
Dup'd by no laws, and blinded by no God,　670
Their courfe now bending to the blifsful fhore,
Where peace and plenty bid the cup run o'er :

L

While they, poor reptiles ! in dread bondage lie,
Drag life in mifery, and unburied die.
Hafte, hafte, ere vengeance on thy helmet light,   675
And plunge thee fwift to everlafting night.

Bafe, reptile mifcreant !---Hezron fierce replied---
Go dream of Egypt ; fwell thine infect pride ;
Thy wings expand ; around thy dunghill fly ;
Buzz thy fmall moment, and forgotten die.   680
For know, vain wretch ! the voice of peace is o'er ;
The hand of Mercy lifts her branch no more ;
To fpeed thy doom impatient Juftice flies,
And wings the vengeance of affronted fkies.

The hero fpoke.   A rifing hifs began,   685
And round the plain contemptuous murmurs ran :
Quick tow'rd the camp the princes bent their courfe,
And, turn'd to Egypt, mov'd the rebel force.
Their ftandard rofe : a fhout to heaven afcends,
And wide, and deep, the gloomy hoft extends.   690
Far round the files each cafts exulting eyes ;
Each feels the prowefs of his arm arife :
By pride their force, their numbers doubled o'er,
All foes defpis'd, and Jofhua fear'd, no more ;
From voice to voice the haughty tale rebounds,   695
And air re-echoes with the mingling founds.

As near the diftant groves the warriors drew,
And homeward caft a lingering, parting view ;
Behold ! in eaftern fields, a numerous train
Pour'd from the camp, and haften'd o'er the plain.   700
There trembled Ephraim's enfign in the fkies ;
There the bull's vengeance blaz'd from wrathful eyes ;
In act to wound, with threatening horns, he ftood,
Felt his vaft ftrength, and fnuff'd his rival's blood.
Behind the mighty Chief, in pomp, impell'd,   705
The darkening phalanx widen'd o'er the field ;
Sublime, the Hero wing'd his dreadful way,
And round the rebels fhed a dire difmay.

Amaz'd, the chieftains faw his haftening courfe,
And rang'd, with active fpeed, their numerous force; 710
In wild, diforder'd ranks, confus'd they ftood,
Spoke founding boafts, and thirfted loud for blood.

As near the noify fquadrons Joshua drew,
Round the rude files he caft a fearching view;
For Hanniel's fteps he gaz'd; but gaz'd in vain, 715
Nor found the hero on the troubled plain.
For well his mind, by fad experience, knew
What fearful ills defeated plots purfue,
How fway accuftom'd, faction wild o'erthrows,
And fudden tumults end in certain woes. 720
Thence, to his tent by cautious thoughts confin'd,
Disjointed counfels throng'd his reftlefs mind;
He view'd, he wifh'd; but knew the wifh was vain,
And boded ruin to his favorite train.
Too wife the Chief, too fix'd the hoft, he faw; 725
Too firm th' obedience to the facred law;
In fullen filence mourn'd his lot fevere,
And wail'd devoted treafon, with a tear.

High in the van, the Leader rais'd his voice,
The hofts all trembling at the dreadful noife--- 730
Hafte to your tents, with fwift obedience hafte,
That Mercy's veil may hide the follies paft;
Hafte, ere this hand, by injur'd juftice driven,
Plunge in your breafts, th' avenging fword of Heaven:
Your Maker's voice, with confcious fpeed, obey, 735
And let deep forrow wafh your guilt away.

Thus he. Bold Ardan with fhrill voice replied---
Let no vain hope inflate thy fwelling pride---
Know, proud, mif-deeming leader! Heaven defign'd
Jacob's brave fons to bow with willing mind; 740
The chiefs, we freely chofe, our hearts obey,
And crouch no more, obfequious to thy fway.
To happier realms, with profperous feet, we go,
And leave thy bondmen here to every woe;

Leave them to toil, to groan, to mourn their doom, 745
Languish out life, and die without a tomb :
While we, fair freedom's sons, superior fly
To peace, and transport, in a kinder sky.
   The Chief disdain'd return. With wrathful look,
His eyes stream'd terror, as the culprit spoke ;   750
Forth from the van, with awful port, he strode ;
O'er his bright arms reflected lightnings glow'd ;
With lifted hand, he drove th' avenging blade,
And plung'd proud Ardan swift to endless shade.
Th' astonish'd train, like hunted harts impell'd,   755
Scatter'd in headlong terror, o'er the field.
So, on heaven's plain when war and tumult sprung,
By Britain's pride, and earth's bright Phœnix, sung,
When Satan, madden'd with Tartarean rage,
Dar'd Michael's sword, and Michael's might engage ;
In pomp divine the great Archangel stood ;   761
A sun's broad splendors round his forehead glow'd ;
Down his long wings thick, branching lightnings fell ;
Dire as ten thunders, rush'd his flaming steel ;
Th' Apostate sunk ; fear wing'd the rebel train,   765
Swift as the rapid whirlwind, o'er th' empyreal plain.
   Pleas'd, the great chief, and Judah's heroes view'd
The flying train, by guilt and fear subdued ;
While to high heaven their grateful praises rose,
Whose guardian hand had sav'd from countless woes. 770
Then loud the cries proclaim---to Egypt's land
Whatever wretch shall lure a guilty band,
By stones oppress'd, his life shall fall a prey,
And dread oblivion sweep his name away.
   While thus the rod of vengeance Joshua sway'd,   775
And the dread tumults of the plain decay'd,
Th' approaching hosts, at distance, Irad view'd,
And Zimri's thousands, with glad feet pursued,
Trac'd all the pomp of war, with wild delight,
And wish'd, unarm'd, to share th' impending fight. 780

BOOK III.

Like ocean's waves, the sons of Ai were driven,
And lowering Israel cast a gloom on heaven ;
Proud chiefs, in golden splendor, trod the plain,
And tower'd majestic o'er the vulgar train.
So, straight and tall, beyond the forest fair,   785
The pine, ambitious, stands without a peer ;
O'er every grove beholds his boughs ascend,
Oaks climb beneath, and humble cedars bend ;
Shares the mild winds, the sullen storm defies,
And towers, and waves, and wantons, in the skies ; 790
In pride sublime, demands the sylvan reign,
And glows, and triumphs, in immortal green.

   As now the tempest hid the orb of day,
The threatening fronts approach'd, in dark array ;
Swift through th' expansion clouds of arrows fly ; 795
Stones shower on stones, and whizz along the sky ;
Sing the shrill strings ; the hissing darts resound ;
From clanging bucklers rattling pebbles bound ;
Now here, now there, the warriors fall ; amain
Groans murmur ; armour sounds ; and shouts convulse the
   With deep amaze, the sons of Ai beheld   [plain. 800
Their foes, with ardour, tempt the deathful field.
For now, elate, they sought the early fight,
To certain victory march'd with fierce delight ;
And fondly hop'd, ere Oran's hosts should come,   805
To seal devoted Israel's hapless doom.
But vain their hopes ; for with firm duty strong,
Undaunted Zimri fir'd the martial throng---
Now, warriors, now--the glowing leader cried---
Shall Israel's arms regain their ravish'd pride ;   810
Ai now shall learn, untaught our force to slight,
What virtue warms us to the generous fight ;
That one lost field shall ne'er our race dismay,
Nor shame, nor terror, stain the glorious day.

   While thus untroubled thoughts his words confess'd, 815
All-anxious fears disturb'd his boding breast.

The hoft he knew diftruftful of the fky,
Propenfe to terror, and prepar'd to fly ;
He faw them fad move lingering o'er the plain,
New arm their foes, and double all their train :   820
And the great Chief a ftrong injunction gave,
Each poft with care to guard, each band to fave,
Each opening fair for wife retreat t' imbrace
To tempt no lofs, and hazard no difgrace.
But far beyond his thoughts, the found of war,   825
The clafh of arms, the fhouts that rend the air,
Th' infpiring tumults of the dreadful plain,
New ftrung their nerves, and rous'd their hopes again.
In quick oblivion, flight and fear were loft;
Increafing ardours every bofom tofs'd ;   830
Firm-wedg'd, unfhaken, rufh'd the darkening train ;
Spears flew ; air murmur'd ; corfes heap'd the plain ;
One flight of twinkling arms, all ether fhone ;
Earth roar'd one fhout confus'd, one mingled groan ;
Each hoft prefs'd eager ; each difdain'd to fly ;   835
And wide confufion blended earth and fky.
    Mean time the ftorm, along dark mountains driven,
Hung o'er the plain, and wrapp'd the mid-day heaven ;
More frequent lightnings blaz'd the fkies around,
And peals more dreadful fhook the folid ground.   840
From the black clouds the whirlwinds burft amain,
Scour'd all the groves, and rag'd along the plain :
Beneath, huge fhouts the murmuring concave rend,
And drifts of duft in gloomy pomp afcend.
    With boding hearts, the chiefs of Ai furvey'd   845
The fun's pure fplendor loft in cloudy fhade ;
The fun, their god, his fmiling face withdrew,
And round the world a fearful darknefs flew :
Hence unapprov'd they deem'd the doubtful day,
And fcann'd, with careful looks their homeward way : 850
As thus they backward gaz'd, the driving rain
Rufh'd, with impetuous fury, o'er the plain ;

Fierce down th' expanſion ſtreaming torrents ſhower'd,
And blood-ſtain'd brooks along the champain pour'd.
The claſh of arms, the long-reſounding cries   855
Wav'd o'er the world a hoarſe, tumultuous noiſe;
From heaven's huge vault loud-rolling thunders came,
And lightnings blaz'd inſufferable flame.
Then ſad, diſhearten'd, from the dreadful fire
Ai's generous leaders bade their hoſt retire.   860
Reluctant, ſlow, diſdaining baſe defeat,
From Iſrael's ſons the griſly ranks retreat;
Surpriz'd, fierce Iſrael ſee their backward courſe,
Hang o'er their rear, and preſs with gathering force;
Intenſer ſhouts aſcend; the lightning's flame   865
Caſts o'er the ſhields a ſtrong alternate gleam;
Loud thunders roll; the fields all quake around:
And the rain ruſhing roars along the ground.
Then Zimri's piercing voice, with ſtern commands,
Reſtrains the fury of his eager bands.   870
So fierce the thouſands burn for raging war,
Even ſingle warriors urge their foes afar;
'Till near the chief, they ſee the ſtandard riſe,
While yet the tempeſt fills the midway ſkies,
Then deep-emboſom'd in th' obſcuring rain,   875
Their foes untroubled croſs the homeward plain.
     Mean time the winds were paſs'd, the ſtorm was o'er,
And ſtreaming torrents ceas'd from heaven to pour;
Strait to the camp, by Zimri's voice compell'd,
The bands ſlow-moving croſs'd the ſpacious field.   880
With joy, the chief revolv'd the troubled day,
The fate, and influence of the fierce affray;
Ai, in fierce conflict, fail'd the wreath to gain,
And Iſrael, dauntleſs, trod the ſkirmiſh'd plain;
He ſaw the hoſt again to combat won   885
Their hopes new-kindled, and their terror gone;
Thence his own boſom boding fear diſpell'd,
And promis'd triumph on the future field.

And now the Youth they pass'd, as, with fond eyes,
He saw the varying fate of combat rise ;   890
To him, deep-pondering, blew the storm in vain,
Scarce heard the peals, or mark'd the battering rain :
'Till Ai, retir'd, the doubtful strife resign'd,
And calm'd the tumults of his anxious mind.

Then gentler scenes his rapt attention gain'd,   895
Where GOD's great hand in clear effulgence reign'd,
The growing beauties of the solemn even,
And all the bright sublimities of heaven.
Above tall western hills, the light of day
Shot far the splendors of his golden ray ;   900
Bright from the storm, with tenfold grace he smil'd,
The tumult soften'd, and the world grew mild.
With pomp transcendant, rob'd in heavenly dies,
Arch'd the clear rainbow round the orient skies ;
Its changeless form, its hues of beam divine,   905
Fair type of truth, and beauty ; endless shine,
Around th' expanse, with thousand splendors rare,
Gay clouds sail'd wanton through the kindling air ;
From shade to shade, unnumber'd tinctures blend;
Unnumber'd forms of wonderous light extend ;   910
In pride stupendous, glittering walls aspire,
Grac'd with bright domes, and crown'd with towers of fires
On cliffs cliffs burn ; o'er mountains mountains roll :
A burst of glory spreads from pole to pole :
Rapt with the splendor, every songster sings,   915
Tops the high bough, and claps his glistening wings :
With new-born green, reviving nature blooms,
And sweeter fragrance freshening air perfumes.

Far south the storm withdrew its troubled reign ;
Descending twilight dimm'd the dusky plain ;   920
Black night arose ; her curtains hid the ground ;
Less roar'd, and less, the thunders solemn sound ;
The bended lightning shot a brighter stream,
Or wrapp'd all heaven in one wide, mantling flame ;

By turns, o'er plains, and woods, and mountains, spread
Faint, yellow glimmerings, and a deeper shade.   92 6
  From parting clouds, the moon out-breaking shone,
And sate, sole empress, on her silver throne ;
In clear, full beauty, round all nature smil'd,
And claim'd o'er heaven, and earth, dominion mild; 930
With humbler glory, stars her court attend,
And bless'd, and union'd, silent lustre blend.
  All these bright scenes revolv'd, his raptur'd mind,
With sweet transition, heaven in all divin'd ;
Where, round the prospect, grandeur, beauty, glow'd,
They shone, the grandeur, beauty, of a God ;   936
God look'd through all, as, with resplendence gay,
They rais'd, and bore him from himself away.

THE

CONQUEST OF CANÄAN:

BOOK IV.

104

Argument.

Morning. Tribes assemble. Story of Achan. Embassy from Gibeon. Story of Mina, Joshua gives her to Elam, prince of Gibeon, in marriage, and makes peace with the Gibeonites. Feast. Joshua's prayer. Cloud descends on the tabernacle. Elam sollicits leave to return to Gibeon. Joshua consents. Sports of the Israelites. Conduct of Hanniel. Walls built around the camp. Story of Helen.

The CONQUEST of CANÄAN.

BOOK IV.

NOW the third fun illum'd the azure main,
And Ifrael anxious gather'd on the plain.
In every face fufpenfe and grief appear'd,
Each fon was doubted, and each parent fear'd:
Brothers on brothers caft a fide-long eye,   5
And trembling fair-ones prefs'd the rifing figh.
   Mid the wide concourfe great Eleazar fhone,
The facred minifter of Heaven's high throne.
White were his aged locks, and round his face
Calm contemplation caft a folemn grace;   10
O'er his pure vefture fhining unguent fpread,
And breath'd the fragrance of th' Arabian fhade:
Full on his breaft the ftar-bright Urim glow'd,
And o'er his brow beam'd HOLINESS TO GOD.
   The facred rites perform'd, he bent his way   15
To the bright dome that mock'd the rifing day.
The train with reverence bow'd. Around his head
Red fpires of lambent flame ferenely play'd;
On the clear fplendors gaz'd the crowd around,
And deep attention hufh'd the fhady ground.   20
   Now in the facred place the Prieft ador'd,
And thus his voice Jehovah's fmiles implor'd.
O thou, whofe wifdom built the bright abodes,
Great KING OF KINGS, and fovereign GOD of GOD's,

BOOK IV.

Almighty Father hear! Let grace divine 25
Shower on our hoſt, and cleanſe from every ſin!
Thou ſeeſt, Omniſcient Mind! what guilt unknown
Pollutes our race, and dares inſult thy throne:
Thou ſeeſt; and oh may thy all-gracious voice
That guilt declare, and bid thy ſons rejoice! 30
  He ſpoke. A ruſhing ſound of winds began,
Sung in the vail, and thro' the temple ran;
A ſapphire flame, unutterably bright,
Shot from the gloom, and wrapp'd the walls in light;
The dome all trembled; earth beneath it ſhook; 35
And o'er the ark a voice in thunder ſpoke---
To Iſrael's thouſands, from th' Eternal throne,
This mighty mandate by thy voice be known.
Of Judah's race, a wretch, by madneſs driven,
With impious hand, hath dar'd the wrath of Heaven:
Stones ſhall his houſe deſtroy, and flames devour; 41
I AM commands; let all my ſons adore.----
Not more; an awful darkneſs round him ſpread,
Still as the gloomy manſions of the dead.
  All ſad, all ſlow, return'd the mournful prieſt, 45
And ſtrong impatience every eye expreſs'd---
What the decree of Heaven! the Leader cried---
With ſolemn voice, the ſacred Seer replied---
Of Judah's race, a wretch, by madneſs driven,
With impious hand, hath dar'd the wrath of Heaven:
Stones ſhall his houſe deſtroy, and flames devour; 51
I AM commands; let all his ſons adore.
  He ſpoke; and ſorrow gloom'd the plain: in haſte,
So Joſhua's voice decreed, the lots were caſt;
The wretch, ſo long conceal'd, aroſe to view, 55
And *Achan's* name to fearful vengeance drew.
Forth from the crowd, with languid ſteps, and ſlow,
The victim ſtrode, and look'd unutter'd woe:
His uſeleſs hands hung feebly by his ſide;
His tottering knees their wonted aid denied; 60

BOOK IV.

His front was clouded with a wild difmay;
For haftening ruin darken'd o'er his way.
    And thus the youth forlorn----My hated name
Sinks in the mifery of undying fhame.
Pafs'd is the day of grace: my dimmed light   65
Fades in the fkirt of everlafting night.
From the rich fpoils my hand a ftore convey'd,
Help'd by the night, and fafe in covert laid.
Beneath my tent the mifchief may be found,
Where fpreads the flooring o'er the fecret ground.   70
Why did my heart refift that lovely fair,
Who fweetly warn'd me of the tempting fnare?
Hear, all ye warriors! fly the fatal road,
And learn, that vengeance waits the foes of God!

    Great Joſhua heard; and tho' his feeling mind   75
To crimes was gentle, and to mifery kind;
Fierce on the youth he caft a dreadful eye,
That wither'd all his ftrength, and bade him die.
And could no honour, and no law, controul
The groveling wifhes of thy gloomy foul?   80
How durft thou, impious, face th' Almighty rod,
Put forth rebellious hands and fteal from God?
Didft thou not know, weak man! th' avenging Sky
Trac'd thy dark footfteps with all-fearching eye?
Didft thou not fear, amidft the gloomy deed,   85
Its vengeance burfting on thy guilty head?
Didft thou not fear the ftings of confcious fhame?
The thunder's terror; or the lightning's flame?
Go, raife to Heaven the fad, repenting eye,
A Heaven that hears, when Mifery lifts her cry!   90
Perhaps foft Mercy yet may lend an ear,
While thy fun glimmers in his laft career.
Not pity's wifh, but folly's, hides from view
The wretch, whom Juftice' awful feet purfue.
Go then, unpardon'd, fink in fhame forlorn,   95
Of Heaven the victim, and of earth the fcorn;

A warning lamp, o'er guilt's benighted way,
To light bewilder'd error back to day.
    He spoke.   The victim, with dread horror pale,
Walk'd trembling onward to a diftant vale;   100
His look of anguifh afk'd a hand to fave,
And Pity's eye purfued him to the grave.
    Mean time around their Chief the princes ftood,
And kind compaffion in their bofoms glow'd;
When rob'd in fair attire, two ftrangers came,   105
And bow'd refpectful, at the Hero's name.
One, pafs'd his ftrength, was grac'd with manly fcars,
Crown of the brave, and palm of glorious wars;
Tall was his frame, his countenance roughly kind,
And his calm front with honeft boldnefs fhin'd.   110
Drefs'd in light robes, as flowers adorn the wild,
In nature's prime his young companion fmil'd
Sweetnefs ineffable.   Devoid of art,
His eye, foft-glowing, look'd the friendly heart.
    Hail ftrangers, hail! the mighty Hero cried,   115
Whofe port befpeaks a nation's faireft pride.
Bring your kind hands the peaceful branch from far?
Or pant your bofoms for the fate of war?
The elder chief replied---From Gibeon's king
Our friendly hands no hoftile meffage bring.   120
Tho' once in fight renown'd, now filver age
Serenes his brow, and cools ambition's rage.
'Tis his firft glory, Gibeon's weal t' encreafe,
To foothe fad woe, and widen human blifs.
    Pafs'd are five morns, fince round th' extended plain,
With fond impatience, rufh'd a chofen train,   126
O'er rocks, and ftreams, the nimble deer purfued,
'Trac'd the wild marfh, and fcour'd the devious wood.
From the lone manfions of the unpierc'd fhade,
At once deep cries our wondering ears invade.   130
Led by the unknown voice, we nimbly hied
Thro' the thick grove, and ftrait the fcene defcried.

'Twixt two rough favages, whofe hungry eyes
Lower'd death, and ruin, o'er their helplefs prize,
Fair as the ftar of morn, a lovely maid,   135
In pangs of terror, call'd in vain for aid.
Her robes embroider'd loofely met the view;
Her hair, unbound, in wild diforder flew;
All pale fhe ftood, and to the pitying fky
Stretch'd her white hands, and rais'd a piercing cry.   140
In vain, on terror's wings, the caitiffs flew;
His eager fword this generous hero drew;
Their heads in twain the fteely vengeance clave,
And hungry vultures yield the horrid grave.

To Gibeon's domes we led the beauteous fair,   145
Repos'd on down, and nurs'd with tendereft care.
Pleas'd with our pains, her fweet, angelic tongue
Strange truths divine, with heavenly mufic, fung.
Of nature's Sovereign Lord, the tale began,
How earth was form'd, and how created man;   150
How the tall mountains heav'd their cloud-wrapp'd fpires,
And heaven was ftarr'd with thoufand thoufand fires.
Then too fhe told how, rous'd to fearful ire,
Jehovah bade the delug'd world expire;
Thy nation's rife; the rod of Sovereign power,   155
That fhook proud Egypt's realms from fhore to fhore,
The cleaving main; the wonders of the wild,
Where hard rocks flow'd, and fands with verdure fmil'd;
Food, fhower'd from heaven, perfum'd the morning blaft,
And quails in millions peopled all the wafte.   160
In thefe dread fcenes, Aradon's mighty mind
The clear difplays of boundlefs power divin'd;
Scenes nobler far than ancient fages knew,
Than age e'er taught, or airy fancy drew.
At once, infpir'd with eager zeal to learn   165
What wondrous truths the glorious fcheme concern,
This prince, his only hope, the monarch chofe,
And join'd with me, his pleafure to difclofe.

N

Sweet peace by us his friendly heart demands ;
His gold he proffers, and his warlike bands ;   170
At thy requeſt, to arms the thouſands fly,
With thee we conquer, or with thee we die.
Shouldſt thou conſent, ſome bright, and generous Sage,
Fam'd for pure manners, and grown wiſe with age,
Skill'd with unſeen, yet all-perſuaſive art,   175
T' inform the mind, and ſoftly win the heart,
Whoſe tenets, nobly rais'd o'er pride, and ſtrife,
Grace the fair conduct of a virtuous life,
He aſks, to ſpread Religion's ſacred ſway,
To lure his ſons to heaven, and point the way.   180
And O what price immenſe canſt thou demand !
What golden hoards ? or boundleſs breadth of land ?
One precious prize our grateful hands reſtore,
Unbought by gems, or loads of ſhining ore,
In thy own tent, behold thy favorite fair,   185
Child of thy choice, and darling of thy care !
    Thus ſpoke Hareſhah.   While glad ſmiles expreſs'd
The Leader's joy, he thus his chiefs addreſs'd.
Even now, propitious, on our lengthen'd toils
Behold th' all-watchful Eye complacent ſmiles !   190
In other realms our growing fame is heard,
Our triumphs number'd and our Guardian fear'd.
But ſay, brave princes, ſhall theſe bands be tied ?
And Gibeon's ſons to Jacob's heirs allied ?
Shall ſome bleſs'd ſage her thouſands teach to riſe   195
To peace, to truth, to virtue, and the ſkies ?
Your choice I wait---he ſaid.   Quick Hanniel roſe,
Whoſe life was conteſt, and whoſe joy t' oppoſe.
To ſave the ſuppliant race his wiſh inclin'd,
For Heaven had form'd him with a feeling mind :   200
But well he knew how fair his matchleſs art
Could gild the latent miſchiefs of his heart ;
How thouſands on his words inchanted hung,
Touch'd by the magic of his wily tongue.

All paths with him were fmooth, that fhew'd a name, 205
Tho' flaughter'd nations pav'd the road to fame.
Thrice rofe the chief to thwart the Leader's choice,
And thrice ftrange faltering feiz'd his opening voice ;
Far round he cafts his keen, experienc'd view,
And peace, the wifh of every bofom, knew ;   210
With fhame his dauntlefs front was cover'd o'er,
And the cheek blufh'd, that never blufh'd before.

Pleas'd the great Leader faw his failing eye,
And voice, in vain, attempt a bafe reply,
Then fmiling thus---Uutaught the wiles of art   215
I fee mild afpects fpeak the friendly heart.
Yes let fair Peace, o'er Gibeon's happy land,
Raife her fweet voice, and lift her facred wand.
'Gainft hoftile realms alone our falchions rife,
Foes to high Heaven, and victims of the Skies.   220
But far remov'd from Ifrael, very far,
Be every wifh t' extend the wafte of war :
To footh vain pride with conqueft's dreadful name ;
To pamper avarice with the fpoils of fhame ;
To take one hour from man's too hafty doom,   225
Or force one widow to a hufband's tomb.
From death's fad fcenes, and battle's horrid toils,
The real hero's generous mind recoils :
When fwords alone can plead the righteous caufe,
The crimfon fteel his hand reluctant draws ;   230
Grief walks his partner to the dreadful plain,
And glory's manfions prove the haunts of pain.

'Tis Ifrael's boaft, the human weal t' increafe ;
To ftretch the reign, and nurfe the arts, of peace ;
The fierce, the wild, to tame ; the weak defend ;   235
Late to begin, and foon the ftrife to end ;
To teach vain man the blifs to virtue given,
And with new faints t' enlarge the bounds of heaven.

But now, brave chiefs, to Jofhua's tent repair---
My fond heart pants to find the lovely fair---   240

Her fire, in Edom's realm, our nation join'd,
Urg'd by the dictates of a virtuous mind :
Her, a fweet babe, his hand indulgent bore,
To virtue form'd, and nurs'd in facred lore.
As fome bright lilly, daughter of the morn,   245
Swells its young leaves, and bids its fplendors burn ;
Fair, and more fair, th' expanding beauties glow,
Dance in the fun, and fhame the driving fnow ;
So, born for heaven, ftill brightening to the view,
From truth to truth, from charm to charm, fhe grew; 250
Soft was her temper ; all her thoughts refin'd ;
Beauty her form, and virtue was her mind.

    Now at the tent arriv'd, the fair they found ;
With many a lovely maid incompafs'd round ;
With fmiles of joy, their friend the virgins hail'd,   255
And gentle tears on every cheek prevail'd.
When firft her Sire appear'd, around his form
She caft, with fweeteft grace, each fnowy arm ;
Pleas'd the great Hero eyed his lovely child,
And gave the fond embrace, and o'er the charmer fmil'd.

    Sweet maid! he cried, where rov'dft thou from the plain?
With tears we fought thee, but we fought in vain.   262

    Far in the wood, replied the fair, I ftray'd,
No care difturb'd me, and no fear difmay'd ;
Charm'd with the flowers, that, undiftinguifh'd, fmil'd
With folitary beauty round the wild.   266
A plum'd mufician, on her verdant throne,
Hymn'd, with foft tranfport, to the falling fun.
Slow I approach'd ; the bird before me flew ;
I heard the found ; how could I not purfue ?   270
So long I wander'd, day forfook the fky ;
I gaz'd, and gaz'd ; but found not where to fly.
In different paths, I roam'd the woody plain ;
But faint, and trembling, ftill return'd again.

    Line 243, *Her, a fweet babe,*] This epithet is given merely from
tendernefs.

BOOK IV.

The wolf began to howl ; and all around, 275
The hungry panther ſhook the ſhuddering ground ;
Loud roar'd the approaching lion's dread alarms,
And death ruſh'd by me, in a thouſand forms.

 The long, long, diſmal night at length was gone ;
And cheerful day with pleaſing beauty ſhone. 280
Huſh'd was the world, ſave where, along the wood,
Rung the ſoft current of a ſilver flood.

Down verdant banks, with trembling ſteps I ſtray'd ;
Each breeze alarm'd me, and each leaf diſmay'd ;
Till, near the confines of the lonely ſtream, 285
Ro ſe two barbarians, as the tyger grim.
My hated garb diſpleas'd their ſavage eyes,
And female weakneſs bade their luſt ariſe.
O why was ſtrength to miſcreant villains given ?
Why lovely virtue left unarm'd by heaven ? 290
Why muſt the helpleſs fair-one's glory ſtand
A prey. for every monſter's brutal hand ?
Thus mourn'd my heart ; when Elam ruſh'd to fight,
Clave the dire foes, and calm'd my wild affright ;
At once low-whiſper'd Virtue's heavenly friend--- 295
Weak are the fair, that heroes may defend.

 She ſpoke. The bluſh that gives the brighteſt charm,
Glow'd in her face, and told her heart's alarm.
Skill'd in the ſcience of the human ſoul,
Th' experienc'd Chief beheld her paſſions roll, 300
Smil'd at th' expreſſive language of her eye,
The dancing boſom, and the deep drawn ſigh.

 On Elam's face he turn'd a ſearching view,
Trac'd his young flame, and all his wiſhes knew.
Oft on the virgin glanc'd his earneſt gaze ; 305
She glance for glance, and bluſh for bluſh, repays ;
Their eyes prove faithful to the melting heart,
Waft the fond wiſh, and all the ſoul impart.

Line 287. *My hated garb,*) She wore the Iſraelitiſh dreſs

No pride of beauty wak'd his young defires ;　　　　310
Nor eye that fparkles, fraught with lambent fires ;
Nor cheek, that gaily fhines with morning glow ;
Nor downy bofom, dipp'd in fpotlefs fnow.
He figh'd for charms of nature more refin'd,
The Maker's image, in the fair one's mind ;
Such charms, as found in heaven, delight improve,　315
And plac'd in angels prompt an angel's love.

　　Thus while they paus'd ; with fweet, and modeft grace,
Fear in his eye, and blufhes o'er his face,
The trembling youth began---O Chief divine !
My parent's voice thou heard'ft, difdain not mine.　320
To this bright maid my wifhes would afpire---
O blame not ! frown not on the fpotlefs fire !---
Thou know'ft the joy her virtues yield to thee ;
Then think her hand were paradife to me.

　　Pleas'd the Chief faw his eyes with fondnefs fhine, 325
And mien all modeft, merit's faithful fign,
And thus---O fair ! 'tis thine alone to choofe.
Say, muft this heart fo foon its darling lofe ?
Canft thou to Elam yield a willing hand,
And feek a guardian in a diftant land ?　　　　330

　　With voice fincere, unus'd her thoughts to hide,
And bofom frank, the virgin's lafting pride,
The guife, low-creeping Cunning muft approve,
Fair mark of worth, and friend to virtuous love,
The maid replied---O fire ! 'tis blifs to me,　　335
To be by him belov'd, approv'd by thee.

　　The Chief return'd ; Blefs'd heir of fpotlefs fame !
Thy choice and wifdom ever afk the fame.
Receive, brave Elam ! Jofhua's favourite care,
As angels virtuous, and as Eden fair.　　　　340
Her hand, her heart fhall heal thy bleeding mind,
Warm'd with pure love, and grac'd with truth refin'd,
Thy fainting ftrength, thy languid eye infpire,
Improve thy joys, and wake the hero's fire,

Charm, with foft tendernefs, thy griefs away,　345
And gild alike the darknefs and the day.
And thou, brave Elam ! ftill, as morn returns,
While early tranfport in thy bofom burns,
On firm foundations let thy fondnefs reft,
Nor cold indifference canker in thy breaft.　350
Know, all the vows by heedlefs lovers given,
Though oft on earth forgot, are feal'd in heaven :
Then let thy fond connubial actions fhow
Truth was the language of the lover's vow.
And thou, my child, to Heaven thyfelf approve ;　355
Act all the foft commands of duteous love:
So fhall your lives ferenely dance away,
And blifs unclouded light the fetting day.
But now, brave friends, let pleafure round us roll ;
Enjoy the genial feaft, and fhare the bowl ;　360
Three days, with me, and every pleafure, ftay ;
The fourth glad morn fhall gild your homeward way.

　　Thus he.　The feelings of each grateful breaft
With manly dignity the chiefs confefs'd.
In converfe mild they fate.　With bufy care,　365
Th' attendant train the cheerful feaft prepare ;
With kindly warmth the fmoaking cauldrons glow,
And fweet thro' ether rifing odours flow.

　　So vaft, fo various, was the Leader's mind,
It rov'd through every region, unconfin'd ;　370
From fcenes fublime, with foft tranfition, ran
Thro' all the duties, all the weal, of man ;
At once his friends, his race, his Maker, ferv'd ;
At once his own domeftic blifs preferv'd ;
In nice dependence rang'd the fervant train,　375
And o'er his houfe bade beauteous order reign.
Thro' all their minds Religion's influence ran---
Men, true to Heaven, he knew were true to man---
Her fons he chofe ; and with all-bounteous fway,
Rewarded, rul'd, and led in virtue's way:　380

　　　　B O O K IV.

Hence, rich return of all his watchful toil,
No murmur pain'd him, and no houfhold broil.
Peace round his manfion fhed her influence mild,
And cheerful, friendly, each domeftic fmil'd.
　　Now the lov'd maid had 'fcap'd from favage bands, 385
With twofold pleafure, wrought their active hands.
So juft, fo gentle was her angel mind,
To want fo bounteous, and to all fo kind,
Her, as the Leader, each alert obey'd,
And thought it blifs to pleafe the heavenly maid,　　390
　　Mean time, felected for the genial feaft,
To Jofhua's tent came many a princely gueft ;
Their courteous hearts the noble ftrangers greet,
And hail the fair with gratulation fweet.
　　O'er a vaft board a wide pavilion fpread,　　　395
With grandeur fhin'd, and caft a pleafing fhade.
There fate the guefts ; there cates delight the foul ;
There wines infpiring tinge the fpacious bowl :
They tafte, enjoy, and, with light converfe gay,
In calm oblivion roll their cares away.　　　　400
　　O'or all great Jofhua fhone, with afpect mild,
Cheer'd every gueft, and with foft fplendor fmil'd :
Touch'd by his eyes, each heart with rapture glow'd,
And fweet complacence every face o'erflow'd.
So round th' immenfe the fun's broad glories ftream, 405
Spread boundlefs life, and pour the etherial flame ;
Warm'd with pure light, the golden planets roll,
And fmile foft-beaming joy from pole to pole,
In endlefs pride, at beauteous diftance, rife,
Swell the great pomp, and glad the earth, and fkies. 410
　　There, like the day-ftar, beauteous Irad fhone,
His fplendors leffening in the nearer fun ;
Full on the Chief a fparkling eye he turn'd,
And as he gaz'd, with bright ambition burn'd,
Mark'd all the glories of his awful face,　　　415
His folemn grandeur, and his matchlefs grace ;

B O O K IV.

While hoary Hezron watch'd with boding eyes,
And saw, well-pleas'd, the future hero rise.

   There too, in transport brighten'd Caleb's pride,
With tears, embracing Elam's lovely bride ;   420
Yet felt soft pain, to see her favourite's charms,
The destin'd treasure of a stranger's arms,
To see her days at distance doom'd to roll,
And mingling friendship soothe no more the soul.

   In easy converse pass'd the hours away ;   425
Each face shone cheerful, and each heart was gay ;
In glad succession went the goblets round,
And blended voices gave a jocund sound.

   Mean time throng'd numerous round the Leader's door;
The stranger, orphan, widow, and the poor ;   430
Call'd from each tribe; by Joshua's kind command,
A rare-felt joy inspir'd the friendless band ;
They feasted, sang, and in the dance combin'd,
Pour'd forth the raptures of th' oblivious mind:
Then, moving various, o'er the camp they spread,   435
Each bliss imploring on the Leader's head.

   When now the feast was o'er, the sun drew nigh
The gilded borders of the western sky :
Forth to the temple march'd th' illustrious train,
The thousands gathering o'er th' extended plain.   440
From a tall rock, amid the silent crowd,
The suppliant Hero rais'd his voice aloud---

   O thou, whose hand illum'd yon rolling fire,
Stretch'd the wide plains, and bade the hills aspire,
Rul'd by whose power, the stars unnumber'd rise,   445
And swift-wing'd lightnings flame athwart the skies,
Storms ride majestic o'er th' etherial plain,
And wake the sleeping thunders of the main !
Empires, at thy command, arise, and fall ;
And flight and triumph hasten at thy call !   450
Disclose, O Power Divine ! thy sovereign voice---
Does combat please thee ? combat is our choice---

Does peace delight thee? peace alone we prize,
Led by thy will, and guided by thine eyes.
By thee this land to Abraham's race was given, 455
'Till suns withdraw, and stars are lost in heaven:
If now the bright possession God ordain,
And crowns await us, on the crimson plain,
By some great sign th' eternal smiles display,
And point our footsteps to the fierce affray! 460

 At once a hollow wind began to roll,
As distant thunders rumble round the pole;
The fields grew black, the forests felt th' alarm,
And swift through ether rush'd a cloudy storm,
High heaven all trembled with the dreadful sound, 465
And peals on peals, convulsive, shook the ground.
Far round the sacred dome the darkness spread;
The sun's clear splendor vanish'd in the shade:
Red flames burst forth; the conscious mountains nod,
And the world smokes beneath th' approaching God.

 In silent awe, the camp astonish'd stood; 471
And each burn'd fiercely for the day of blood.
Fix'd in still wonder, gaz'd the stranger pair,
And mark'd, with anxious mind, the darkening air,
The dome, invelop'd in the sable shroud, 475
And peals deep-murmuring in the hollow cloud:
With solemn look, each frequent eyed his friend,
And felt, instinctive, half-form'd prayers ascend.

 Mean time the Leader every chief commands---
Two days, let peace refresh the fainting bands; 480
The third glad sun, awak'd by trumpet's sound,
Shall light our falchions to the deathful ground.
Sleep, hapless Ai! thy last returning day
Soon gilds thy turrets with a pitying ray.
And let the chief, th' important charge who owns, 485
Of all our wealth, our wives, and blooming sons,
Bid a long trench wind through the tented ground,
And guardian walls the spacious camp surround.

BOOK IV

He fpoke.   With joy th' attendant chiefs obey'd,
And round the camp the glad commands convey'd.   490
The fquadrons ardent wait th' appointed morn,
Cleanfe their blue fhields, and polifh'd coats adorn.
So Jofhua will'd ; for well the Hero knew
How glittering fteel allur'd the ravifh'd view ;
Thence prais'd the chief, in fhining neatnefs arm'd,   495
Averfe from toys, but with true beauty charm'd ;
And thence in glorious panoply he blaz'd,
A great example, acting all he prais'd.

Now round the world pale Eve her fadnefs threw ;
Still, folemn darknefs cloudy curtains drew :   500
Through the wide camp the Leader trac'd his way,
To learn what wifhes mark'd the bufy day.
Ai, full in view, each heart to combat fir'd,
And with gay profpects every breaft infpir'd.
No thought of Egypt boding minds embrac'd ;   505
No childifh fear even vulgar fouls difgrac'd :
In deep oblivion funk the painful wound,
And fierce impatience hop'd th' embattled ground.
Pleas'd the great Hero heard th' exulting ftrain,
And wandering, liftening, fought his tent again.   510

When now the morn look'd mildly from the eaft,
To Jofhua Elam thus his voice addrefs'd---
O Chief of Ifrael, crown'd with grace divine !
Let health's green garland round thy temples twine.
To blefs mankind be ftill thy lov'd employ ;   515
To ferve thy Maker ftill thy facred joy ;
No hour of thine to wafting grief be given ;
Let each more brightly roll, and antedate thy heaven !
But now, his years impatient of delay,
My hoary father hopes our homeward way.   520
Indulge, great prince, our eager wifh to bear
The rapturous tidings to his longing ear.
His foul rejoic'd will fmile at nature's pains,
And life flow fwifter through his icy veins.

Bid us with fpeed our deſtin'd path reſume,   525
And bleſs a parent, ſinking in the tomb.

He ſpoke.   Hareſhah join'd the youth's requeſt:
Even Mina's eyes a ſecret wiſh confeſs'd.
In love's kind heat, like ice in ſummer's ray,
All former ties, diſſolving, paſs away ;   530
To new-found friends the ſoul oblivious flies,
New objects charm us, and new paſſions riſe.
The Hero ſaw, and kindly bade depart
The lov'd, the long-loſt favourite of his heart ;
With arms impaſſion'd claſp'd the bright-eyed fair,   535
Kiſs'd with fond look, and dropp'd a tender tear.
On gay-dreſs'd camels, toward the ſetting day,
With converſe ſweet, the lovers bent their way ;
Like two fair ſtars, that ſhed a lonely light,
And ſink in clouds, above the mountain's height.   540
Two ſeers their ſteps attend, to point the way,
That ends in manſions of unchanging day.

And now, o'er all the camp, the raptur'd throng
Crowd the wide plain, and wake th' enlivening ſong.
Here cheerful thouſands bid the walls aſcend ;   545
And broad, and deep, the lengthening trenches bend.
Here the ſtrong arm the falchion learns to wield,
Or hurls the javelin o'er the meaſur'd field.
With ſhouts of praiſe the conquerors oft are crown'd,
And clanging bucklers ſwell th' applauding ſound.   550
Part, join'd in crowds, in mimic fight engage,
Range their ſmall hoſts, and ſport with ſeeming rage ;
From force unequal here the vanquiſh'd fly ;
There, with deep groans, diſſembling victims die.

Mean time all-watchful.   Hanniel, round the plain,
From crowd to crowd, inſpir'd the buſy train.   556
He knew the plot, the generous Youth diſclos'd,
To dark ſuſpicion ſaw his name expos'd ;
To wipe diſgrace, his influence to recall,
And, with light, ſecret ſnares, to gather all,   560

From tent to tent he urg'd his active way,
And blam'd with words severe, the wild affray.
Me, cried the hero, Israel's thousands know
A fair unchanging friend, or open foe.
To generous war since Israel's voice is given,   565
To war I fly, and hope the smiles of Heaven.
Rouse then to arms ; for glorious fight prepare ;
Each thought of peace, each terror vile forbear :
Let glory's fire each warrior's breast inflame,
And deathless deeds shall brighten Jacob's name.   570
  Thus he.   The wile the thoughtless thousands drew,
Snar'd by soft words, and caught by gilding shew ;
For war, invigor'd, glow'd th' undaunted mind,
And kindling eye-balls with new lustre shin'd.
No walls they need, to stay th' impending foe ;   575
Yet, with light labour, swift the barriers grow ;
Hope high in view display'd unmeasur'd spoil,
Sooth'd every pain, and lessen'd every toil.
  As thus serenely pass'd the cheerful day,
And care, and grief, oblivious roll'd away,   580
At once shrill rang, from eastern woods afar,
The cry of foes, and growing sound of war.
The sporting warriors, prompt at dread alarms,
Ceas'd from each game, and brac'd for fight their arms ;
O'er eastern fields, with rapid steps they hied.   585
And bands conjoining swell'd th' embattled pride.
  From the wood hastening, flew, with wild surprize,
Two timorous youths, and rais'd lamenting cries,
With trembling voice, they said---Of nought afraid,
Through yonder grove, with easy course, we stray'd ;   590
A savage band, by twining shrubs conceal'd,
Burst on our path, and half enclos'd the field.
Amaz'd we flew.   Snar'd by the tangling vine,
Our heedless Partner fell ; of Simeon's line ;
Helon his name : they seiz'd him fallen ; in vain   595
Uplifting cries, and bore him o'er the plain.

Quick, at the found, a warrior rais'd his voice---
'Tis my own fon; the fpring of all my joys---
Hafte, hafte, brave friends, my darling Helon fave;
Nor yield your faithful Shallum childlefs to the grave.
The train, infpir'd, with nimbler footfteps flew;   601
Each prefs'd his fhield, and each his falchion drew;
The youths, before them, fhew'd the fadden'd way,
Where the fell heathens bore their haplefs prey;
Where the clofe thicket wrapp'd the ambufh'd force, 605
And bending fhrubs, and footfteps mark'd their courfe.
Thence the glad train, with eafe, the foe purfued,
And hoping, haftening, fcower'd the devious wood.

   Now, where all-anxious through the favouring fhade,
Their haplefs prize the heathens fwift convey'd;   610
Weening, ere morn, through Oran's camp to bear
The youth, with tidings of th' expected war,
The heroes rufh'd: his friends glad Helon knew;
Loud rofe his voice; the warriors eager flew;
While the bold heathens ftay'd their ufelefs flight, 615
New-brac'd their fhields, and ftrung their nerves for fight.

   Shrill through the woods the clafh of arms arofe;
Thefe, fix'd to hold, and fierce to refcue, thofe;
The foreft fhook. In front, confefs'd to view,
Full on the heathens raging Shallum flew.   620
One with his lance, and one with griding fteel,
He flew: the victims gave a hideous yell.
To his fon's voice he wing'd his furious courfe;
Nought ftay'd his fpeed, and nought withftood his force.
Where two huge heathens ftruggling Helon led, 625
He wildly fprang; one flew; the other bled:
With frantic joy he feiz'd his raptur'd hand,
And urg'd him trembling toward the friendly band.
There fcarce arriv'd, a javelin pierc'd his fide;
He groan'd, he funk, grew pale, and fainting died. 630
Aghaft, his darling's fate the fire beheld,
Then rufh'd delirious round the woody field;

B O O K IV.

On the fled heathens ſtretch'd his raging courſe,
O'ertook, and ſingly drove the gather'd force :
Three fierce he flew ; the reſt, in devious ways,   635
Fled o'er the field, and 'ſcap'd the hero's chace.
At length return'd, with a deep, burſting groan,
In ſtrong embrace he claſp'd his hapleſs ſon,
Preſs'd to his boſom, bore him o'er the plain,
And, mid the weeping warriors, ſought the camp again.

THE

CONQUEST OF CANÄAN.

BOOK V.

ARGUMENT.

Evening. Irad and Selima walk out on the plain south-ward of the camp, and begin a conversation concerning the nature and defignation of the vifible heavens. Original ftate of Man, and of Creation. Reflections on the fall of Man. Wifdom and benevolence of the prefent fyftem afferted. Threefold ftate of man, emblematized in the but-terfly. Fanciful ideas of Heaven. An old man, in the habit of a beggar, follicits alms of Irad, and is directed to repair to Hezron. The old man informs him that his requeft was but a pretence, and he came out of the Camp to ftimulate him to the war, and ufes a variety of argu-ments to accomplifh the defign. He retires, and Irad and Selima, terrified by the appearance of a meteor, return to the Camp. Morning. Irad goes to his father, and with earneft follicitations, obtains leave to go out to the next battle. He communicates the intelligence to Selima. A thoufand young volunteers choofe him their leader. Even-ing. Joshua fends Zimri with a body of troops to lie in ambufh on the weftern fide of Ai.

The CONQUEST of CANÄAN.

BOOK V.

NOW funk the fun beneath the weftern main,
  And deepening twilight fhaded every plain.
To the known tent untroubled Irad fped,
And forth, with proffer'd hand, Selima led.
Through fouthern fields they trac'd their eafy way,   5
And love, and rapture, chang'd the night to day.
The weftern beam decay'd : th' expanding fky
Spread clear, and boundlefs, to th' attentive eye :
Scarce fill'd, the moon afcends the vaulted even,
And flow behind rolls on the pride of heaven ;   10
With joy, th' unenvious planets round her play,
Join their glad beams, and fwell the mimic day ;
From ftar to ftar the mingling luftre flies ;
Unmeafur'd beauty clothes the lucid fkies ;
Hufh'd in calm filence fleeps the world ferene,   15
And floating fplendor gilds the fhadowy fcene.
 Round the mix'd glories of the fpacious fky
The pair inftinctive turn'd a raptur'd eye,
From fcene to fcene with rifing wonder ran,
And mild, with accent fweet, the maid began—   20
In yon broad field what fcenes of glory fhine !
The bright effufions of a fource divine !
Great as the hand, that form'd yon lucid way !
Fair as the morn, that op'd immortal day !

In earlieſt youth, when firſt my feeble mind   25
In nature's works celeſtial power divin'd,
To thoſe gay regions fancy ſtretch'd her ſlight,
And rov'd, and ſported, mid the gems of light.
For whom, I cried, aſcend you glowing fires ?
What favourite firſt-born of th' angelic choirs ?   30
Thoſe azure curtains ? that ſublime abode ?
A tent of glory for ſome darling God !
Say, lovelieſt Prince ! for thy ſuperior mind
Walks, with ſure ſtep, in wiſdom's path refin'd,
Why rove ſo far th' unnumber'd flames on high ?   35
Why caſt their endleſs beauty through the ſky ?
Is yon blue frame, that limits morn and even,
The ſapphire pavement of ſome nobler heaven ?
Are ſtars but gems of unborn light, that ſpread
With duſt of gold the ſtreets where angels tread ?   40
Or if for man theſe works of glory ſhine,
For earth-born reptiles furniture divine ;
Say why ſo ſtrange the acts of Heaven appear,
There ſuch bright pomp, ſuch wondrous meanneſs here.

          The Youth return'd---Fair as thoſe lucid eyes,   45
All lovely maid ! thy bright ideas riſe.
In vain proud man, with ſelf-applauſe runs o'er
His arts of Egypt, and his Eaſtern lore,
Thy ſoul, on nature's pinions, takes her flight,
And, ſelf-inſtructed, gains a nobler height.   50
          When from the deep, aſcended earth, and heaven,
To man, ſole heir, the mighty boon was given.
Unlike his ſons, no guilt his mind deform'd ;
His life, his limbs, no fierce diſcaſes ſtorm'd ;
Nor death's cold poiſon pal'd his growing bloom,   55
Nor knew his feet the journey to the tomb.
Young beauty's purple ſplendor round him play'd ;
Immortal Health his vigorous limbs array
Life, eldeſt heireſs of th' empyreal ſky,
Smil'd on his cheek, and bloſſom'd in his eye.   60

BOOK V.

Array'd in endless light, his infant mind
Shone with fair truth, and glow'd with grace refin'd;
Her robe sky-tinctur'd, Virtue round him threw;
Unchanging jubilee his passions knew;
Heaven's living lamp, with clear, and constant shine,
Sunn'd the pure regions of the world within.　　66

 Far other glories then arose to view;
Parts answering parts, and beauties ever new.
With strong, bright charms the heaven angelic shin'd;
The varying prospect charm'd th' inchanted mind;　　70
Soft strains of rapture bade all ether ring;
The gales, all fragrance, shed the light of spring;
From stars, from moonbeams, life's sweet influence flew,
Inspir'd the streams, and glow'd in foltering dew;
Bade with strong life the purpling fruits refine,　　75
And warm'd the bosom with a youth divine.

 Then reign'd fair Love, th' immortal bliss of heaven;
Then social angels came on clouds of even;
Here trac'd new wonders of th' omniscient Mind,
Strange to their world, and first on earth design'd;
In countless forms, where love and beauty glow'd,　　80
And stamp'd a rival of the bright abode.

 His hand such nature to the man assign'd,
His form so temper'd, and so wrought his mind,
All gave delight; where spring display'd her prime;　　85
Or where blank winter froze the desert clime;
The vale's soft pride; the flower's etherial form;
The mountain's grandeur, and the solemn storm.

 But when foul guilt debas'd the beauteous mind,
The skies grew dim, and sickening nature pin'd.　　90
With converse sweet, no more kind angels came:
No blissful morning shed th' eternal beam;
No more from starry realms life's influence fell,
And peace, and Eden bade the world farewell.

 Yet still with clear, though faded lustre, glow'd　　95
The love, the greatness, of a bounteous GOD.

What though cold east winds wither'd all the plain;
Though blasts, and mildews shrunk the golden grain;
Pale evening's, skirts the frost, and damp o'erhung;
Air bred disease, and worms the fruitage stung: 100
Still o'er the mountains stars serenely rise;
Still the soft moonbeam trembles from the skies;
The sun, fair image of unborrow'd day,
Lights heaven, and earth, and cheers the boundless sea;
Reviving seasons, crown'd with lustre, roll,   105
And plains of plenty glad th' expecting soul.

   These splendid scenes surprize thy curious mind;
For worms too noble, and for foes too kind.
But not too noble, or too kind, they shine,
The works of wisdom, power, and love, divine.   110
From morn's gay bounds, to skirts of distant even,
They teach the hand, and spread the name, of Heaven;
In beauty, grandeur, make JEHOVAH known,
But mark, with faded charms, a world undone.
Yet these, could man the common bliss pursue,   115
Would gentle peace, and smiling joy, renew,
Light, with soft-beaming hope, the cheerful day,
And drive grim war, and cankering hate, away.

   Thus spoke the Prince. The tender maid replies,
While her sad bosom heaves unbidden sighs.   120
Fair scenes of bliss thy living words disclose,
Realms of gay youth, and times of sweet repose.
Oh had our sire! but hence, ye wishes vain!
No fancied joy shall edge returning pain---
Yet too, too blissful is the fond employ,   125
To nurse gay hope, and dream unreal joy;
Abroad in fields of airy light to roam,
And fly th' envenom'd grief, that lurks at home.
Ah, had the fatal fruit, untasted hung,
What bliss had brighten'd! and what glory sprung! 130
In gentlest union these bless'd hands had join'd,
One wish inform'd us, and one soul intwin'd;

BOOK V.

On some lone hill our envied mansion stood,
There rich perfumes in morning breezes flow'd;
Sweet Peace around it wav'd her balmy wing,   135
And Youth unchanging dress'd eternal spring.
There, O bless'd lot! each innocent employ
Had form'd, and cherish'd mild, domestic joy :
The walk all-pleasing, virtuous love refin'd ;   139
Our flocks, our prospects, sooth'd th' improving mind;
For me, the garden op'd its spicy bloom ;
For thee, soft vesture whiten'd o'er the loom :
Our growing bliss the sun delay'd to see,
And the poor heathen been as bless'd as we.
Ah dire reverse ! while round this field of gore,   145
War's hoarse rough-grating clangors ceaseless roar ;
While sons, and fathers, in one hour are slain,
And each bright youth must tempt the fatal plain ;
While the sad virgin sees, with wearied eye,
No hope remains her, but to weep, and die ;   150
While pain, and grief, and half-form'd joy invade,
And suns gay-rising set in mournful shade.
   Kind, tender maid ! the smiling Prince return'd—
The hapless fall how sweetly hast thou mourn'd!
Thy voice, all music, wins the raptur'd ear ;   155
Yet more persuasive drops that melting tear.
But, O bright maid ! by strong affections driven,
Let no fond wish oppose the choice of Heaven.
To man's first guilt ten thousand ills adjoin'd,
Writhe the torn limbs, and agonize the mind :   160
Pain, famine, toil, the sword, the ruthless wave,
Care, envy, broken faith, sad sorrow, and the grave.
Yet God's high acts unerring wisdom guides,
And boundless love his every choice decides.
Hence all events, and hence all beings right,   165
Best in their places, to best ends unite.
Hence from small ills unmeasur'd good shall flow;
Hence joys unnumber'd spring from every woe:

Through the vaſt whole th' eternal glories ſhine,
One great I AM, all-beauteous, all divine.   170
    Taus the great Prophet ſung ; and oft my ſire
With theſe bleſs'd truths my tender heart would ſire,
When, won to virtue, on his lips I hung,
And learn'd pure wiſdom from his friendly tongue.
    Heaven's high beheſt, had faithleſs man obey'd,   175
A peaceful earth his eye had ſtill ſurvey'd ;
Mild hours and ſeaſons ſoft o'er nature run ;
His ſons, in millions, ſpread to lands unknown ;
To Eden's bowers the filial nations come,
Hail'd their great ſire, and own'd their happier home.
While ſrom his throne, ſupreme of all below,   181
He ſaw well pleas'd, his mighty kingdom grow ;
His ſubjects children, love his potent ſway,
And one vaſt houſhold ſpread to every ſea.
    But, ſprung from earth, and ſtill to earth confin'd, 185
No fairer bliſs had flow'd for poor mankind :
No law had given the high, ſtupendous claim,
To ſoar, and brighten in th' immortal flame.
Now to thoſe climes where, 'twixt delight and pain,
Expands, untravers'd, night's eternal main,   190
Worms, born of duſt, may point their lofty way,
And ſeize the bliſs of ever-riſing day.
    Oft on the flower, emboſom'd in perfume,
Thou ſeeſt gay butterflies in beauty bloom ;
With curious eye, the wondrous inſect ſcan,   195
By Heaven ordain'd a threefold type of man.
Firſt from the dung-hill ſprang the ſhining form,
And crawl'd to view, a hideous, loathſome worm ;
To creep, with toil, his inch-long journeys, curs'd ;
The ground his manſion, and his food the duſt :   200
To the next plant, his moment o'er, he drew,
And built his tomb and turn'd to earth anew.
Oft, from the leaf depending, haſt thou ſeen
Their tombs, with gold bedropp'd, and cloth'd in green ;

There flept th' expectant, 'till the plaftic beam　205
Purg'd his vile drofs, and bade his fplendors flame.
Then burft the bonds : at once in glory rife
His form etherial, and his changing dies,
Full on the lucid morn his wings unfold,
Starr'd with ftrong light, and gay in living gold;　210
Through fields of air at large the wonder flies,
Wafts on the beams, and mounts th' expanded fkies,
O'er flowery beauties plumes of triumph waves ;
Imbibes their fragrance, and their charms out-braves ;
The birds his kindred, heaven his manfion, claims,　215
And fhines, and wantons, in the noon-day flames.
　So man, poor worm ! the nurfling of a day !
Springs from the duft, and dwells in humble clay ;
Around his little mole-hill doom'd to creep,
To drag life's load, and end his toil with fleep,　220
In filence to the grave his form defcends,
And waits the trump, that time and nature ends,
There ftrength imbibes, the beam of heaven to bear;
There learns, refin'd, to breathe its fragrant air ;
Of life the bloom, of youth the fplendor, gains,　225
And, cloth'd in beauty, hopes empyreal plains.
Then, wing'd with light, the deathlefs man fhall rife,
Sail through yon ftars, and foar from fkies to fkies ;
See heavens, o'er heavens, beneath him leffening roll,
And feel the Godhead warm his changing foul;　230
From beauty's fount inhale th' immortal ray,
And grow from light to light, in cloudlefs day ;
Mid morn's fair legions, crown'd with grace, be known,
The peer of angels, and of GOD the fon.
　But O what fcenes in that far region glow !　235
What crowns of patience ! what rewards of woe !
　From yon tall hill, when morn's inviting air
To woodland wandering lur'd thy chofen fair,
Thou know'ft how fweet gay profpects to defcry,
And catch new Edens with the ravifh'd eye.　240
Q

BOOK V.

In living green, the lawns at distance lay,
Where snowy flocks mov'd round in vernal play ;
High tower'd the nodding groves ; the cliffs sublime
Left the low world, and dar'd th' assaults of time ;
Huge domes heav'd haughty to the morning fires,   245
And the sun trembled round a thousand spires :
All heaven was mild ; and borne from subject vales,
A cloud of fragrance cheer'd th' inchanting gales.

　　Such pleasing scenes if this drear earth supply,
What scenes, what glories bloom beyond the sky !   250
There with strong life the plains immortal glow ;
There Beauty bids her streams of rapture flow :
There changing, brightening, reigns th' extatic power ;
Smiles in each fruit, and burns in every flower ;
In solemn domes, with growing pride, aspires ;   255
Gems with fair stars, and robes in living fires ;
Round the trees wantons ; on the mountains blooms ;
Charms in new songs, and melts in strange perfumes.
And O, of liquid light what seas extend !
What skies impurple ! and what stars ascend !   260
But cease, my tongue ! nor headlong rush too near
The sun, that kindles heaven's eternal year.

　　When great Messiah shall those gates unbar,
Where grief recedes, and pain, and death, and war ;
Then freed from dross, from every stain refin'd,   265
And dress'd in all the elegance of mind,
To her own mansion shall thy Soul aspire,
And add new raptures to the sainted choir.
With love divine thy heart has learn'd to glow ;
Smil'd at each joy, and wept at every woe ;   270
In each soft station amiably stood,
And shewn the bright ambition to be good ;
The best, the loveliest daughter, sister, friend ;
Thy life all virtue, and the heavens thine end.
Scarce, of thy years, can blooming cherubs claim   275
A purer conscience, or a fairer name.

BOOK V.

Pleas'd as he spoke, an aged Form drew near,
The moon-beams whitening o'er his silver hair.
His quivering limbs a tatter'd garb array'd ;
A staff his slow, and faltering footsteps stay'd--- 280
Oh youth ! he said, in wealth thy lot is cast ;
Let humble Poverty thy bounty taste.
Large as thy treasure be thy heart to give ;
Thy bread impart, and bid my children live.

Sire ! cried the Youth, to Hezron's tent repair ; 285
The poor, unfriended, never enter'd there.
To share his wealth the Heaven-sent strangers come ;
There orphans, beggars, find a constant home.
His pious acts in sweet memorial rise,
And prayers of thousands bless him from the skies. 290

Return'd the sage. To life's far distant end,
On thee may Judah's envied bliss descend !
From Asher's race I spring, nor of thy sire,
Nor thee, fair Prince ! or clothes, or food require.
My highest wish the gifts of Heaven exceed ; 295
Though small my portion, yet far less my need.

But O lov'd Youth ! my faithful counsels hear ;
Let hoary Age command thy listening ear.
Thy growth, thy beauty, nobler than thy peers,
Mine eyes attentive mark'd from earliest years : 300
I saw thy limbs in fair proportion rise,
And thy face smile the image of the skies.
Thy mind all-lovely, every voice proclaim'd ;
For sense distinguish'd, and for virtue fam'd ;
Bounteous and brave thy heart ; thy tongue discreet ; 305
Thy manners courteous, and thy temper sweet.

Oft on these plains when gathering armies spread,
The long van darken'd, and proud ensigns play'd ;
Absorb'd, I saw thee war's gay splendors view,
Trace the deep files, and moving chiefs pursue ; 310
I saw the martial flame instinctive rise,
And growing lightnings tremble in thine eyes ;

I faw, and fmil'd ; and Ifrael's voice approv'd,
That deftin'd empire to thine arm belov'd.

But ftill, impell'd by ftrong defire to find   315
If Fame well fung the beauties of thy mind,
I watch'd thy fteps, when evening hid the main,
Affum'd thefe rags and fought thee on the plain.
For know, fair Prince ! in Truth's unbiafs'd ftate,
The proud are little, and the lowly great ,   320
From man, man claims, of high, or low degree,
The courteous manners, I have found in thee.

Now o'er thy head have twice ten fummers run;
The Youth is ripen'd, and the man begun :
Thy fhapely limbs are finew'd into force,   325
To hurl the dart ; to fpeed the nimble courfe :
Yet on what plain in triumph haft thou ftood ?
When, bold and active, dar'd the ftrife of blood ?
No fcar of thine attefts the patriot wound ;
Thine arm inglorious, and thy wreaths unbound: 230
Should'ft thou, when Jofhua fleeps, the fceptre bear ;
How fhall thy untaught mind conduct to war ?
How know what counfels wifdom bids embrace ?
What ftrength to arm ? the ambufh where to place ?
Where on the field to ftretch the dreadful wing ?   335
Or with what words of fire the languid arm to ftring ?
Rife then, brave Youth ! from eafe unhonour'd rife !
Let fun-bright glory tempt thine eager eyes !
When next approaching combat threats the field
Seize the ftrong lance, and grafp the fheltering fhield ;
If Hezron grant, the van's bright ftation claim,   341
And leave the foremoft in the chafe of fame !

Ill fits vile eafe a Prince of worth divine,
Whofe countlefs graces fair as angels fhine ;
At home, unnotic'd, ftretch'd in floth, to lie,   345
While friends, while fathers toil, and bleed, and die :

Line 323. *Twice ten fummers*) This is a miftake of the Sage.

B O O K V.

To ſhare the ſpoils diſtain'd with others' gore,
A mean, falſe plunderer, when the battle 's o'er.
Then while to war thy bold companions run,
While deeds of glory, wreaths of life, are won ;   350
On the dread ſword while Iſrael's cauſe ſuſpends ;
While empire victory, ruin flight attends ;
While in full view the field of promiſe lies,
And the brave arm ſhall win th' unmeaſur'd prize ;
Demand thy ſhare, thy ſhare of danger claim ;   355
The toils of danger give the crown of fame.
To thee, through tribes, through nations yet to come,
Let grateful Iſrael owe her proſperous doom ;
Her endleſs rule ; her land in beauty dreſs'd ;
Her ſtream of glory, and her ages bleſs'd.   360
Thus, in far diſtant times, when Joſhua's name
Shall paſs, all-fragrant, down the tide of fame ;
When future heroes to their ſons ſhall tell
How Hezron triumph'd, and how Sihon fell ;
Combin'd with theirs, thy deeds ſhall waft along,   365
Swell the glad theme, and mingle in the ſong.
  No ſhameful ſloth, no dread of manly toil,
No mean, falſe wiſh to ſhare in others' ſpoil,
No love of eaſe, the generous Youth replied---
To tents confine me, and to Hezron's ſide.   370
Far other wiſh my glowing mind inſpires ;
Fame wings my thoughts, and war my boſom fires.
When Glory's ſons aſſembling hoſts array,
Th' extatic view bears all my ſoul away.
My pulſe beats high ; my briſtling hair aſcends ;   375
My heaving heart a thrilling anguiſh rends :
Sighs, prayers, and tears confeſs the growing pain ;
But ſighs, and prayers, and melting tears are vain.
By love, beyond my higheſt claim impell'd,
My ſire conſtrains me from th' embattled field.   380
Youth, frowns the chief, to ruin heedleſs flies ;
From arms refrain, 'till years ſhall make thee wiſe.

Go tell thy fire, the kindling fage return'd,
Thy hated abfence Ifrael long have mourn'd.
In forceful language, afk their wondering eyes,　385
Why funk in floth, their darling Irad lies,
Their voice demands thee to th' important plain,
To generous toils, and glories bought with pain:
They pant, they burn, to fee thy fplendors fhine,
Thy falchion triumph, and thy garlands twine.　390
Not fame alone, but duty points the way,
And truth and virtue chide the dull delay.

This faid, the Ancient o'er the plain withdrew,
And, fading from the moon-beam, left the view.

As loft in filence ftood the wondering pair,　395
Or maz'd, bewilder'd, rov'd they knew not where,
A cloud afcending eaftern fkies o'erfpread,
Involv'd the moon, and wrapp'd the world in fhade:
A dim-feen luftre cloth'd all heaven around,
And long, black fhadows floated o'er the ground.　400
As deep and folemn the far whirlwind roars,
Or waves run rumbling under cavern'd fhores,
With murmuring noife, o'er weftern mountains came
A broad, and dark-red meteor's awful flame:
Far o'er the woods, and plains, its fanguine hair　405
Stream'd wild, and dreadful, on the burden'd air.
As eaftern groves its leffening light abforb,
Like thoufand thunders, burfts the rending orb;
Wide-fhooting flames the glimmering fky furround;
A gloomy glory fpreads the twilight ground;　410
Loud o'er the world a long, hoarfe echo roars,
And fad Canäan groans through all her fhores.

Quick to the camp return'd th' aftonifh'd pair,
And half, in broken flumbers, loft their care.
O'er anxious Irad hovering visions play'd,　415
Call'd up fair fcenes, or difmal terrors fhed;
Oft from his couch, in act to fmite, he fprang,
And oft his voice in fhouts imperfect rang.

BOOK V.

When firſt through broken clouds the morning ſhin'd,
In purpoſe firm he fix'd his doubtful mind ;   420
At Hezron's feet, with graceful reverence ſtood,
And claim'd the bleſſing, e'er with joy beſtow'd.
With dawning ſmiles, he bleſs'd his lovely ſon,
And ſweet complacence round his aſpect ſhone.
Will Hezron bend his ear ? the favourite cries--- 425
Speak, my belov'd---th' indulgent ſire replies.

 Thou know'ſt my boſom feels the warrior's flame,
Sighs for gay arms, and pants for generous fame ;
For Iſrael weeps, to aid her cauſe aſpires,
And burns tumultuous with reſiſtleſs fires.   430
When next our hoſt the ſhining falchion wield,
Bleſs'd ſire ! command me to th' embattled field.
Youths, o'er whoſe heads a few more months have run
In ſport, the peers, the rivals of thy ſon,
In glory's bright career with heroes join,   435
And their fair names even now begin to ſhine.
Grant, beſt of parents ! grant one bliſsful day,
And threefold duty ſhall thy love repay.

 Why doſt thou bring---the anxious ſire replied---
The dread requeſt, my love has oft denied ? 440
Why muſt thy ſire his favourite treaſure loſe ?
Why will thy heart the path of danger chooſe ?
That path, conceal'd where various evil lies,
And the brave periſh, while the daſtard flies.
More circling ſummers have thoſe youths beheld ; 445
Th' accuſtom'd age commands them to the field.
Scarce nineteen ſuns thine infant eyes have ſeen ;
Secure from ſhame, enjoy thy hours ſerene.
Let truth, let wiſdom be thy virtuous care ;
And the ſweet converſe of thy darling fair. 450
Still with thy partners draw the mimic field ;
The javelin hurl, the heavy falchion wield :
So taught their uſe, ſhalt thou, when battles join,
With fairer names, with veteran heroes ſhine ;

B O O K V.

In marſhal'd hoſts a nobler office claim,   455
And ſtride more ſwiftly in the chaſe of fame.
   Return'd the favourite---To thy faithful ſon
Whene'er thy choice, indulgent ſire, was known,
No counter choice unduteous words confeſs'd,
But my ſole anſwer was obedience bleſs'd.   460
When laſt mild evening cloſ'd the cheerful day,
O'er ſouthern plains I trac'd my careleſs way ;
There as I gaz'd the works of Heaven around,
A chief, of Aſher's race, my footſteps found---
Youth, cried the hoary ſage, the changing ſun   465
Beholds, well pleaſ'd, thy riper years begun.
The ſcenes of dangerous war thy breaſt demand,
And thy lov'd nation aſks thine aiding hand ;
Their eyes require thee on the hoſtile plain,
Nor let a nation claim thy aid in vain.   470
Go tell thy ſire, while friends, while brothers die,
'Tis ſhame, 'tis guilt, in torpid eaſe to lie.
His duty bids him dreſs thy limbs in arms,
And thine ſtrait ſummons to the trump's alarms.
Haſte, virtuous Youth ! thy nation's voice obey,   475
And fly, where Glory points her envied way.
Ah ſire belov'd ! to ſhame, to fatal ſhame
Yield not thy darling Irad's opening name.
Think, beſt of parents ! with what ſtings of gall,
Contempt and ſcorn a generous mind appall.   480
Save me from piercing ſcorn ; from ruin ſave ;
From daſtards ſnatch me ; rank me with the brave ;
Thy nation's call, more loud than thunders hear ;
Though Irad fail, let Iſrael gain thine ear.
   With anxious look, th' unwilling ſire replies,   485
The tears faſt-ſtreaming from his reverend eyes---
O ſon belov'd ! beyond expreſſion dear !
The ground of every joy ! and every fear !
This painful tale diſparts my troubled ſoul ,
And bids my tears in large effuſion roll.   490

BOOK V.

How can my heart to favage war refign
My wealth, my boaft, my glory, all that's mine ;
The child, the joy, the image, of my mind ;
The beft, the only trace, I leave behind ;
To prayers long-tried, all-fervent, kindly given ;   495
The richeft bounty of indulgent Heaven ?

  From infant years thy lovely form to raife,
To lure thy mind to all that merits praife ;
'Gainft fatal fnares thy youthful heart to arm,
With truth illumine, and with virtue warm,   500
Ten thoufand fighs I breath'd, ten thoufand prayers,
Watch'd countlefs nights, and felt unnumber'd cares.
Each opening wifh, each rifing thought, I fcann'd ;
Each new-born virtue nurs'd with foftering hand :
The flower etherial faw, with rapture, bloom,   505
Glow with ftrong light, and charm with choice perfume,
And each glad morn beheld my praifes rife,
A grateful tribute to the bounteous fkies.

  As, touch'd with joy, thy beauties I behold,
Thy limbs invigorate, and thy thoughts unfold ;   510
Thy pure complacence eye the all-lovely Mind ;
Thy love, thy goodnefs flow to all mankind ;
Thy aims expand beyond the flight of youth ;
Thy tongue unvarying yield the voice of truth ;
Thy cheerful bounty make the poor thy care ;   515
Thy fpotlefs mind affect fo bright a fair ;
Thy fweet obedience every wifh forerun,
And my blife double in my darling fon ;
Too blefs'd, I wifh, my pains, my toils review'd,
Each pain repeated, and each toil renew'd.   520

  But chief, when that bright fair, who gave thee breath,
Sunk, pale and haplefs, in the arms of death,
Thy hand fo gently footh'd her long decay ;
So fweetly guileful lur'd her pains away ;
Whole nights, whole days, fuftain'd her drooping head ;
Dried her fad tears, and watch'd her weary bed ;   526

R

Like fome mild angel, fent from pitying fkies,
Shed dewy flumbers on her languid eyes ;
Illum'd the grave, feren'd the rugged way,
And cheer'd each fainting Hope of future day :   530
Me from myfelf thy matchlefs duty ftole,
And chain'd thee lovely to my inmoft foul.

Now to far regions is that parent gone,
And, but for thee, thy fire were left alone :
From thee remov'd, no fecond felf I know ;   535
And, O blefs'd favourite ! folitude is woe.

When wing'd, my fweet companion trac'd her flight,
A wildering gloom obfcur'd the cheerful light ;
Each joy was banifh'd from my haplefs doom,
And not a wifh remain'd me, but the tomb.   540
Her tent, forfaken, feem'd in fhades to mourn ;
Her empty feat implor'd her blefs'd return :
Friends grac'd my board ; her vacant place I view'd ;
Down rufh'd the tear, and every pang renew'd.
Through diftant fields I roam'd ; the fields were fad :
No more her prefence bade the flowers be glad :   546
A folemn twilight round all nature fpread,
Drear as dun caves, that houfe the filent dead.
Alone in crowds I ftood, in fields alone ;
My hope, my friend, my lovely folace gone.   550

But thou waft left.   In thy angelic face
Smil'd her lov'd image, glow'd her matchlefs grace :
To thee I flew ; and, in thy duty, view'd
Her power to charm, her wifh to blefs, renew'd.
That peace, the world befide could never give,   555
I found in thee, and lov'd again to live.
Too rich, too great, I own my Heaven-lent ftore ;
On earth, if thou may'ft live, I afk no more.

Shall then thy fire that dread perfuafion hear ?
Or feel the urgence of that forceful tear ?   560
Ah ! how can Hezron thy lov'd life deftroy,
And yield th' infatiate grave my only joy ?

For, O fond Irad! all the pride of ſtate,
Fair dreams, and painted bubbles, of the great,
No real joy, no gentle peace, contain,   565
But gay deceit, and undiſcover'd pain.
Whate'er in Wiſdom prompts a wiſh to live,
Soft, calm domeſtic ſcenes alone can give.
Should'ſt thou be ſlain, even theſe muſt ceaſeleſs mourn;
No joy betides me, and no hopes return;   570
A poor, deſpairing ſtranger, here I ſtay,
'Till Death's loud voice ſhall ſummon me away.

    But ah! to combat Iſrael Irad calls---
The piercing ſound my ſtruggling heart appalls---
Was all my bliſs for Iſrael's weal beſtow'd?   575
And is a nation's voice the voice of GOD?
Go then, my ſon, may he thy boſom guard,
To triumph lead thee, and with fame reward;
Bright, and more bright, extend thy proſperous doom,
Or ſpeed my footſteps to an early tomb.   580

    Thus the great chief; and riſing as he ſpoke,
In his right hand a ſword ſuſpended took;
Forth from the ſheath the blade refulgent drew,
And his ſad eye-balls kindled at the view.
Behold, brave youth---with earneſt voice he cried---   585
Thine is the ſword, thy ſire's, thy grandſire's pride;
By death of kings, and generous chiefs, renown'd,
With wreaths ennobled, and with triumphs crown'd.
When Egypt's ſons, on proud Sabea's plains,
By Moſes guided, pour'd their countleſs trains;   590
High in his haughty car a chieftain rode,
Bore down whole troops, and roll'd through brooks of blood;
Deep in his breaſt, while thouſands round him fell,
Thy generous Grandſire lodg'd this ſhining ſteel;
Then ceas'd the fight; Sabea's millions fled,   595
And the earth groan'd beneath the piles of dead.

    Line 589. *Egypt's ſons*) See the account of the event referred to
in Joſephus.

To Jahaz' deathlefs field when Sihon drew,
When combat thicken'd, and when dangers grew,
This arm, this falchion clave the monarch's fide,
And low on earth abas'd his impious pride.　　　　600
　　From Hezron's hand the honour'd gift embrace-
Dread of thy foes, and glory of thy race ;
And while thy arm their weapon learns to wield,
Let the fame fpirit prompt thee to the field.
Each wild excefs, each ufelefs danger fhun ;　　　605
But firft in virtue's courfe aufpicious run :
Outftrip thy peers ; To Jofhua's height afpire ;
Let real glory all thy wifhes fire :
Let mine, my fire's, my tribe's, my nation's fame
Imbibe new fplendors from thy added name.　　　610
Yet not one fear my boding mind alarms,
Left Irad's deeds diftain his parent's arms ;
I know thy generous mind ; and, forc'd to yield,
Affur'd, behold thee grace th' embattled field.
And oh ! wilt thou, whofe hand from every foe　　615
My life preferv'd, and footh'd in every woe,
My darling fon defend ! from thee he came ;
Scarce born, I gave him to th' eternal Name ;
Thine are his virtues ; round his youthful head
A guardian fhield may thy good angel fpread.　　　620
　　Thus fpoke the chief.   In Irad's feeling foul
A ftrange, tumultuous joy began to roll :
As oft t' unfold his grateful heart he tried,
The fuffocated founds in filence died.
Down dropp'd the fword ; and ftrait, with homage due,
The Youth enkindling from the tent withdrew ;　　626
Quick to the lovely fair-one trac'd his way,
And ftrove the tumult of his thoughts t' allay.
Her in the tent, with maidens compafs'd round,
Select companions of her fports, he found.　　　630
There, fweetly welcom'd with inftinctive fmiles,
He fmooth'd his face with new, but harmlefs wiles,

BOOK V.

And, while soft art her tender mind prepar'd,
His own design, his sire's consent declar'd.
With guarded lips he spoke; but dire surprize   635
Pierc'd her sad heart, and gloom'd her starry eyes;
With one deep sigh, she felt her strength decay,
Slid to the ground, and breath'd her life away.
Quick to her aid the Youth impassion'd flew:
And, with the virgins, bade her life renew;   640
Again reviv'd the splendor of her eye,
And ting'd her cheek with health's transcendent die.
O best belov'd! with tender voice he said---
Let not such anguish wound my beauteous maid!
Let cheerful hope thy timorous thoughts inspire,   645
And thine eye languish with a brighter fire!

  When o'er my head a few short days shall roll,
My hastening feet must reach th' appointed goal;
To manhood grown, the law, from heaven reveal'd,
Resistless calls me to th' imbattled field.   650
If Israel's sons my falchion earlier claim,
And kindly summon to the path of fame,
Why should'st thou mourn? 'tis duty points the way;
When duty calls us, safety bids obey.

  Thou know'st when evening last the skies attir'd,   655
The sage, reproving, generous thoughts inspir'd;
First from his mouth my nation's choice I knew;
And swift to war my soul obsequious flew:
No place, no hope, to vile delay was given;
The call of nations is the call of Heaven.   660
Led by his voice, I trust his guardian care;
With equal ease he saves in peace, and war.
The same good hand, that thro' the woodland shade,
To friends, to safety, loveliest Mina led,
Though thousands fall, may Irad's bosom shield,   665
And wing th' averted javelin through the field.

  Thus he, with softest voice, and fondest eye---
Then stopp'd; and anxious, hop'd the maid's reply.

She, plung'd in grief, and loft in dread amaze,
Sate filent, folemn, fix'd in mournful gaze:　　　670
With tendereft action on her looks he hung,
And thus vain folace tunes again his tongue.

But, doom'd to fall, fhould Heaven my life **demand**,
And death betide me from a heathen's hand,
I fall in virtue's caufe. Far happier doom,　　　675
In that blefs'd path, to find a fpeedy tomb!
Than, loft in fports, or funk in fhameful eafe,
To drag a worthlefs life, and fwell in glorious days.
And O bright maid! without one guilty fear,
My thoughts can view refiftlefs death draw near.　　　680
In that far clime, where joy extends her reign,
My pinion'd foul fhall fpring to life again;
Strong with empyreal youth, fhall trace her way,
And join the nations of immortal day.
Thence, when thy form is fummon'd to the tomb,　　　685
Perchance my fpirit, wing'd with light, fhall come,
Hail thy releafe from toil, and grief, and pain,
And raptur'd guide thee o'er the tracklefs main;
In bonds etherial there our fouls be join'd,
And prove th' extatic nuptials of the mind.　　　690

With filent, fad, and difcontented air,
And face averted, fate the liftening fair.
While the deep woe her feeling bofom mourn'd,
With a long, heavy figh, fhe thus return'd.
With boding heart I heard the fage's tale,　　　695
But felt fond hopes the dire defign would fail;
That Hezron's choice, fo often tried in vain,
Would ftill confine thee from the fatal plain.
Yet thy lov'd maid, with gentle words, defign'd
To change thy wifh, and footh thy eager mind,　　　700
But my foul trembled at the dreadful light,
And every fenfe was loft in wild affright.

Now to dire fate my fondeft hope muft yield,
While empty fame allures thee to the field.

BOOK V.

But O bless'd youth ! by soft intreaties won,　　705
Where duty calls not, hideous danger shun.
Let not thy ardour fame's high impulse feel,
Tempt nearer fight, and try the deathful steel.
The fatal front to veteran warriors give ;
Be thy rich boon, thy bless'd reward, to live.　　710
I know thy bosom burns with glory's fire ;
I know what visions war's bright beams inspire.
I fear, would Heaven the cause were less to fear,
Lest thy bold footsteps headlong rush too near ;
Lest, wing'd with zeal, on instant death thou fly,　　715
And leave thy hapless maid to weep, and die.
　For ah ! on Irad all my joys suspend ;
Grow with thy bliss, and with thy life extend.
Should then dread war compel thee to the grave,
The sad, untimely portion of the brave,　　720
Whither, ah whither can Selima fly ?
Where find a friend, to bid her early die ?
Robb'd of thy face, the world's a desart drear ;
The house of pain, and grief, and cankering care ;
Forlorn, and friendless, life's lone path I tread,　　725
And ask no lot, but with the silent dead.
Nor all those joys, thou know'st to paint so fair,
Can sooth sad woe, or lighten dark despair.
With thee conjoin'd, I claim my only doom,
Alike well-pleas'd, or here, or in the tomb.　　730
Scarce would my soul, without thee heaven explore,
Where the first joy shall be to part no more.
　Oh, would the Chief thy anguish'd maiden hear,
And mark thy station in the humbler rear !
There no fell heathen would thy life annoy ;　　735
Nor fatal danger threat Selima's joy :
'Till age, 'till art, from sure experience won,
Had taught thee caution's every wile to shun.
And then, ah then might peace our days serene ;
War cease to rage, and foes no more be seen ;　　740

B O O K V.

Blifs, in glad ftreams, around our land extend,
And every figh, and grief, and terror end.
　　Thus fpoke the faddening maid.　With pleafing guile,
The tender Prince recall'd her vanifh'd fmile ;
With tales amufive lur'd her grief away,　　　　745
And cheer'd her foul with hope's inlivening ray.
　　Meantime, through Ifrael fpread the rumour far,
That matchlefs Irad join'd the coming war.
Charm'd with the tale, a bold, and generous train
Of youths, his rivals, throng'd the vacant plain ;　750
And there, with one glad voice, the hero chofe
To guide their footfteps 'gainft th' expected foes.
To him too youths the flattering meffage bare ;
With modeft grace, and fweet, becoming air,
Surpriz'd he heard, and while their hearts he won,
Affum'd the truft, and own'd the honour done.　756
　　And now decay'd the founds of bufy day ;
The fun defcending beam'd his final ray ;
In ftarry grandeur rofe the bonndlefs night,
And temper'd ether with a milder light.　　　　760
As through the hoft a general filence flow'd,
To Zimri's tent the watchful Leader ftrode,
And thus---Brave chief, to Ai direct thy courfe ;
Thy fole command awaits a chofen force :
Through the deep foreft fteer thy fouthward way,　765
Where ftately portals hail the fetting day.
When firft the clarion's voice to conflict calls,
Forfake thy ambufh, and afcend her walls ;
O'er all her domes let fudden flames afpire,
And her proud turrets fink in hoftile fire :　　780
Then through her northern gates direct thy way,
And lead thy fquadrons to the fierce affray.
　　I go---the chief replied.　The moon's broad round
Look'd in full luftre on the tented ground ;
Fair o'er the fhadowy hills fhe gently rofe,　　　785
And fhew'd a path for Ai's exulting foes.

B O O K VI.

In glimmering steel, a long, refulgent train,
Stretch'd in just files, and dazzled all the plain.
Slow to the wood their fading steps they press'd,
The Chief, in silent joy, retir'd to rest.

T H E

CONQUEST of CANAAN:

B O O K VI.

Argument.

Morning. Army assembles under the command of Hezron, and Joshua. Irad sollicits, and obtains a post, in the front of the western division. Orders. Israelites march. Army of Ai. Characters of Oran, and Carmi. Battle. Feigned retreat of the Israelites. Hanniel's disobedience, and overthrow. Joshua rescues him. Signal of return to battle. Joshua's address. Battle renewed. Joshua retires, and gives Caleb the command. Exploits of Irad. Exploits of Hezron, and of Caleb. Death of Ludon. Oran. Death of Hezron. Exploits of Carmi. His death. Irad rallies Judah. Joshua descends to battle, kills Oran, and puts the Heathens to flight. Zimri, having set Ai on fire, comes out upon the rear of the enemy. Final rout, and overthrow of the Heathens. Irad's distress at the fate of his father. Interview of Irad and Selima. Evening.

THE CONQUEST OF CANÄAN.

BOOK VI.

NOW dawning light conceal'd the worlds on high,
  And morn in beauty cloth'd the cloudlefs fky:
Loud o'er the field the trump's fhrill found began,
And fwift to arms the ftartled thoufands ran;
From all the camp burft forth the numerous throng,   5
Shook their tall fpears, and wak'd the martial fong;
Wide wav'd their plumes, refulgent flafh'd their fhields,
And fpiry banners trembled o'er the fields,
South of the camp, in two deep fquares they ftood,
And fierce for combat, fac'd the plain of blood.   10
  Before the weftern band great Hezron rofe,
Joy of his race, and terror of his foes:
Averfe from pomp, in ufeful fteel array'd,
Pleas'd, his juft ranks the mighty chief furvey'd;
Pleas'd to the well-known field of combat drew;   15
When duty call'd, his foul no terror knew
  Of equal ftrength battalions eaftward ftood,
And high in front exalted Jofhua ftrode.
By nature fafhion'd millions to controul,
In peace, in war, the great all-moving foul,   20
His mind expanded look'd exiftence through;
His heart undaunted danger never knew;

With calm endurance, toils and fears engag'd,
Climb'd as they rofe, and triumph'd as they rag'd;
Patient, ferene, as ills and injuries tried,   25
Meek without meannefs, noble without pride,
Frank yet impovious, manly yet refin'd,
As the fun watchful, and as angels kind.
His Maker firft, his confcience next he fear'd,
All rights kept facred, and all laws rever'd;   30
Each wandering friend, with faithful friendfhip blam'd;
Each foe applauded, as fair merit claim'd:
Alike his kingdom wealth and want approv'd;
The noble reverenc'd, and the peafant lov'd.
His form majeftic, feem'd by GOD defign'd   35
The glorious manfion of fo vaft a mind:
An awful grandeur in his countenance fate;
Calm wifdom round him caft a folemn ftate:
His deathful arm no fingle force withftood;
His fpeed, his fkill, no vigor could elude;   40
His piercing eye his mighty foul difplay'd;
His lofty limbs refplendent arms array'd;
With varied lightenings his broad falchion fhone,
And his clear buckler mock'd the rifing fun.

 Fair in the front of Judah's manly train,   45
A young gay band, adorn'd the gladfome plain.
Bright was their fteely mail; their polifh'd fhields
With dazling fplendor ftreak'd the fmiling fields;
Soft breezes fported through their plumy pride;
Their trembling falchions glitter'd by their fide;   50
Equal their bravery, and their thirft of fame;
Their age, their ftature, and their arms the fame.
 In the fair front, more beauteous than the morn,
When cloudlefs fplendors orient fkies adorn,
Firft of his race exalted Irad ftood,   55
His foul inflam'd, his falchion drawn for blood;
On Jofhua's fteps his ceafelefs eye was turn'd,
Charm'd with the pomp, that round the hero burn'd;

BOOK VI.

Tall was his stature, lofty was his mien,
His eye refulgent, and his brow serene:
Topp'd with two snowy plumes, that play'd in air, 60
A silver morion crown'd his auburn hair:
Far o'er the train his form sublimely shone,
By nobler arms, and manlier beauty, known.
So, when calm spring invests the sparkling plain, 65
And night sails silent up th' etherial main,
Round the broad azure stars unnumber'd glow,
And shadowy lustre robes the world below:
Thron'd in the western heaven young Hesper shines;
His silver car to nether realms declines; 70
O'er the gay mountains smiles his living eye,
And sinks, in splendor, down the gladsome sky.

From host to host the Chief majestic strode,
Inspir'd their hopes, and steel'd their souls for blood;
Their perfect ranks his skilful eyes divide, 75
And his great bosom swells with manly pride.
As tow'rd the western square he bent his way,
Where hoary Hezron led the long array;
To meet his steps impatient Irad ran,
And bent one knee before the godlike man; 80
And thus---To youth will Joshua lend an ear?---
---Speak my brave son; thine every wish declare---
---With gentle voice, he said---The Youth replied---
See that fair train, inwrapp'd in steely pride!
In war, though young, our bosoms pant to shine, 85
And feel the wish, that brighter glows in thine.
Give, best of men! this brave, though youthful band
In the bright front of charging fight to stand.
Oh, by my father's toils in fields of blood,
Whose love this freedom, and this sword bestow'd, 90
Indulge this ardent wish! nor let thy frown
Quench a young flame, that emulates thy own.

I grant thy wish---the mighty Chief replied,
Smiling superior o'er his manly pride,---

Go, firſt of youths, defend thy Maker's laws,   95
And lift the falchion, in thy country's cauſe.
May God's good hand thy tender footſteps guard,
With caution bleſs thee, and with fame reward !
He ſpoke, and kindly raptur'd Irad rear'd ;
His ſwimming eye the grateful mind declar'd ;   100
Swift he return'd, on high his ſhield diſplay'd,
Shook his blue ſword, and thought the fight delay'd.
Near the bleſs'd ſcene enraptur'd Hezron ſtood,
And life ran nimbler thro' his languid blood ;
Charm'd with the kind regard, to Irad given,   105
He kneel'd to earth, and bleſs'd all-bounteous Heaven,
That Heaven which gave, his every wiſh to crown,
The Chief to Iſrael, and to him the ſon.
Now, rang'd for combat, wait the warrior bands,
And his brave leaders Joſhua thus commands---   110
'Till this right hand exalt the javelin bright,
Let every rank conduct a mimic flight :
Slow, firm, and cloſe, be mov'd the fair retreat ;
Nor wing'd with ruin wild, and foul defeat :
Meantime a miſſive death let arrows rain,   115
And ſlings unnnmber'd tempeſt all the plain.
But when the javelin's beams in ether burn,
Swift to the fight let every rank return ;
Each vigorous arm the ſword's broad terrors rear,
Or hurl the vengeance of the ſlaughtering ſpear ;   120
Brace firm the ſpacious ſhield ; diſdain to fly ;
Ruſh to glad conqueſt, or with glory die.
He ſpoke : o'er ſouthern plains, in long array,
To Ai's high walls the ſquadrons bent their way.
Undaunted Ai, th' approaching ſtorm beheld,   125
And rous'd her heroes to the darkening field :
Her chiefs command, her northern gates unfold,
Bright arms burſt forth, and hoſts to fight are roll'd ;
Like gloomy clouds, the blackening thouſands riſe,
And ſhrill-voic'd clarions thunder in the ſkies.   130

Two warlike chiefs th' embattled heathens guide,
Their forms majeftic cloath'd in golden pride.
Wrapp'd in blue mail, infufferably vain,
With cruel front, that frown'd a ftern difdain,
Around, dark Oran caft a fanguine eye,   135
Wav'd his broad fhield, and dar'd th' avenging fky.
Grim in the van, with lofty ftalk, he ftrode,
And fhook his fpear diftain'd with drops of blood,
Blood, by his hand, in ancient battles fhed,
In wafted realms, and fields beftrew'd with dead.   140
Sheath'd, in his hall the crimfon'd weapon lay,
Left cankering time fhould cleanfe the ftain away;
There, oft retir'd, he turn'd it o'er, and o'er,
And with fierce tranfport view'd the purple gore,
There call'd to mind the orphans of his fpear,   145
Smil'd horrid o'er the fcene, nor knew to drop a tear.

Behind him darkly roll'd a cloudy band,
Rous'd to the war from many a diftant land,
With various arms in one great hoft combin'd,
And various banners ftreaming on the wind.   150
'Gainft Jofhua's hoft the chief imperious ftrode,
And with fond prefcience hail'd the fcenes of blood;
A gloomy fmile array'd his fhaggy brow,
And thus his horrid joy began to flow.
Blefs'd be the Gods, who gave this rapturous hour!   155
For this their fires fhall many a youth devour;
While their gor'd children bleeding parents view,
And tears in vain their lifelefs forms bedew.
Warriors rejoice; yon troop forgets the day,
When Ai's brave fquadrons fwept their hoft away;   160
Soon fhall our fpears be bath'd in brooks of blood,
And fields grow fruitful with a genial flood.

'Gainft Judah's hofts, inclos'd in burnifh'd arms,
With matchlefs bravery and unrival'd charms.
Ai's dauntlefs fons to fight young Carmi led,   165
And now the helm firft fparkled on his head.

T

Mov'd by his ceaseless sighs for martial fame,
His royal fire the parent's fears o'ercame.
Reluctant sent him to the deathful plain,
And fondly hop'd his lovely steps again.   170
There pleas'd with fame's imaginary charms,
He clasp'd the phantom in his eager arms,
On the bright glories turn'd a raptur'd eye,
And gaz'd, and gaz'd, and fancied bliss was nigh.

  Now, mid the grandeur of the deep array,   175
A dreadful space in gloom tremendous lay :
No banners wave in air, nor trumpet's sound ;
But silent terror saddens all the ground.
Loud burst the clarion's voice, and trembling far,
Shoot the broad ensigns o'er the frowning war ;   180
As thousand stars thro' kindling ether stream,
Bright showers of arrows cast a transient gleam :
From slings tempestuous countless pebbles rain,
Whizz thro' the skies, and whiten all the plain ;
The shrill helms clatter, death pursues the wound,   185
And prostrate heroes cloth'd the sprinkled ground.
So, when red summer burns the sultry pole,
O'er darkening hills a cloud's black volumes roll ;
Hoarse rush the winds ; hoarse drives the rattling hail,
Batters the craggs, and tempests all the vale ;   190
Deep groan the forests, torne their branches fall,
And one tumultuous ruin buries all.
Ere the loose combat long suspense had hung,
" Retire," the great command around them rung ;
Then, closely wedg'd, recedes the yielding fight,   195
And well-feign'd terror clothes the mimic flight.
Swift tow'rd their yielding foes the heathens spring,
Their bucklers blaze, their flashing lances sing :
Oft they rush forward, oft the bands retreat ;
For Israel's host disdains a base defeat ;   200
From ranks behind unnumber'd arrows shower,
And stones unnumber'd down the concave pour ;

Thick fall the foremost, clanging arms refound,
And streams of crimson die th' embattled ground.
 Meantime, fierce Hanniel, burning still for fame, 205
And sickening still at Joshua's envied name,
Deem'd this the destin'd hour, to pluck the crown
From the Chief's head, and plant it on his own.
Oh heaven, he cried, shall Israel ever flee,
The dupe of cunning, and the coward's prey ?   210
Must these pain'd eyes again our ruin view,
Curse our wild counsels, and our follies rue ?
Come every generous chief, whose bosom brave
To foul disgrace prefers a hero's grave,
Join Hanniel's path ; and soon proud Ai shall see 215
A few, bold warriors yet disdain to flee.
Whate'er my voice commands, my hand shall dare,
My deeds unspotted, as my dictates fair ;---
Far nobler doom, to fall in manly fight,
Than share, with titled names in splendid flight.— 220
This said his course the hero forward bends,
No chief applauds him, and no chief attends :
Two vulgar warriors, sad rebuff to pride !
Alone rush on, and clamour at his side.
Their dauntless course their raptur'd foes descry, 225
And well-aim'd lances glitter thro' the sky ;
Thick round the warriors, sinks the hissing steel,
And death's cold hand the brave attendants feel ;
In Hanniel's thigh expands a painful wound,
And the stunn'd hero raging bites the ground.   230
 Swift to his aid, impassion'd, Joshua flew,
Tho' well proud Hanniel's dark designs he knew,
Heard all the vaunts, the close injustice saw,
And felt th' infractions of his prudent law :
Yet now the chief lay weltering in his gore ;   235
Foes in distress to him were foes no more---
O'er the pale form he threw his guardian shield,
And bore him languid thro' the dreadful field :

Thick shower the stones, the flashing javelins sing;
And his bright arms with ceaseless murmurs ring.   240
Borne by four warriors o'er the distant plain,
Reluctant Hanniel sought the camp again:
There friendly plants his dying strength renew,
And sleep's soft influence aids the balmy dew.
While Joshua thus--Hence taught, ye warriors, know, 245
Wild, headstorng wishes guide to certain woe,
In peace, laws only claim a righteous sway;
In war, one voice commands, the rest obey.
Proud disobedience Heaven consigns to shame;
The path of duty leads alone to fame.   250
He spoke---With awe the silent squadrons heard,
The precept reverenc'd, and the teacher fear'd;
Each saw, abash'd, the terrors of his frown,
And pleas'd, condemn'd rebellion, not his own.

Meantime, brave Irad, on the western plain,   255
With pangs retir'd from Ai's contemptuous train,
As oft th' imperious taunt his rage inspires,
And his scorch'd bosom flames with eager fires,
Their utmost strength his vengeance promps to try,
He longs, he pants, to bid th' insulters fly: 260
Oft toward the host his course instinctive turns;
His drawn sword trembles, and his buckler burns;
But still his soul, in child-hood taught t' obey,
Restrains the wish, and backward turns his way.

Now with pure splendor glow'd meridian light,   265
And Ai triumphant chas'd th' imagin'd flight,
When gay in dazzling arms, great Joshua turn'd:
His eyeballs sparkled, and his bosom burn'd:
The glittering lance his mighty hand uprear'd;
Loud rose his voice, and distant squadrons fear'd.   270
Behold, he cried, yon sheets of smoke ascend!
What heavy volumes round the skies extend!
Brave Zimri's conquering arm, while Heaven inspires,
Bursts Ai's proud portals, and her turrets fires;

Now wheel your courfe ; to active vengeance fpring : 275
Brace the ftrong hand ; the bloody falchion wing ;
See, Heaven's propitious finger points the way !
Fear chains their limbs, and terror yields the prey ;
O'er our glad courfe commencing grory fmiles,
And boundlefs treafures crown triumphant toils.   280

   He fpoke ; the warriors eyed th' exalted fign ;
And thrilling bofoms own'd the voice divine ;
Swift wheel'd, the ranks to combat vigorous rife ;
Red lances fhower, and fhouts convulfe the fkies.
An equal ardour Ai undaunted brings,   285
Fronts the dire foe, and fierce to danger fprings---
As, borne by warring winds, thro' ether roll
Two rifing ftorms, and cloud the northern pole ;
O'er fome dark mountain's head their volumes driven
With floods of livid lightening deluge heaven ;   290
Peal following peal, careering thunders fly,
Burft o'er the world, and rend the fhuddering fky.
With equal noife the ftorms of war refound ;
The blackening volumes cloud the hoftile ground ;
Thro' the fhock'd air in mingled tumult rife,   295
The conqueror's triumphs, and the victim's cries.

   And now the chief to prudent Caleb's charge,
While the cloud thickens, and the founds enlarge,
Commends the hoft that own his mighty fway,
And bends to diftant rocks his backward way.   300
Here high in air he lifts the lance's beam,
And power divine fupplies a ceafelefs ftream ;
With pointed circles glows the weapon bright,
And cafts th' effulgence of exceffive light.

   Long o'er the plain, impatient to purfue,   305
Had panting Irad fix'd an anxious view,
Sigh'd the great Leader's warning voice to hear,
Or catch the radiance of th' expected fpear :
The ready fword his hand all eager prefs'd ;
The well-brac'd buckler glitter'd o'er his breaft :   310

In th' utmoſt weſtern ranks he ſilent ſtood
And look'd far onward thro' the field of blood ;
Pain'd, leſt the deſtin'd ſign, forgot ſhould fail,
Or ſome baſe dart the Leader's life aſſail.
But when the ſun-bright point inſtarr'd the air,   315
The blooming hero kenn'd the beam afar ;
To his brave peers, with ardent joy he cries,
And all the warrior ſparkled in his eyes.
Lo, generous youths, on yon delightſome plain
Shines the fair javelin, wiſh'd ſo long in vain !   120
Now ſpurn the hated flight ; to combat ſpring ;
Let virtue rouſe you, and let glory wing.
Now ſhall our ſires, and now the Leader, know
What flames heroic in our boſoms glow ;
Ai now ſhall learn, untaught our ſtrength to ſlight   325
Not fear, but wiſdom plann'd our ſeeming flight,
On their own heads redoubled vengeance feel,
Or fly inglorious from the conquering ſteel.
Riſe then, brave youths, their impious ſcoffs repay ;
My arm to triumph leads the envied way.   330
   He ſpoke ; the voice each active hero warms ;
With dreadful din they claſh their glittering arms,
Full on their dauntleſs foes impetuous fall,
And break reſiſtleſs o'er th' embodied wall.
As winter's ſhrilling blaſt begins to roar,   335
And drives, in gloomy rage, along the ſhore ;
Torne, in it's path, the trees confus'dly lie :
The white waves roll, the boughs tumultuous fly,
Not with leſs force, o'er piles of warriors ſlain,
Pours the bold band acroſs the bloody plain ;   340
Death leads their way : with youthful vigor light,
They deal ſwift vengeance thro' the duſty fight,
Regardleſs of the ſtorm, that round them flies,
Of dying murmurs, and of conquering cries.
   High in the van exalted Irad ſtrode,   545
And now commenc'd the toils of death and blood.

When firſt his arm, immingling in the ſtrife,
Drew the red ſtream, and ſpilt a human life,
(A lovely youth oppos'd his hapleſs head,
And with pure crimſon died the infant blade)   350
Thro' his chill'd veins a new, ſtrange horror ran,
And half-ſorm'd tears in either eye began ;
In his young heart, unus'd to create woe,
Inſtinctive ſympathy began to glow ;
The dreadful ſcene he gaz'd, and ſhook to hear   355
The hollow groan and ſee pale death ſo near.
But ſoon freſh tranſports in his boſom riſe,
Rous'd by ſhrill arms, and fir'd by barbarous cries :
Again his ſpirit claims th' imbattled foe ,
And bids two heroes to his falchion bow ;   360
Thro' cleaving ranks he wings a dreadful way,
And clouds of rolling duſt obſcure the day.
    Meantime in Judah's van great Hezron ſped,
His voice arous'd them and his footſteps led ;
With fix'd firm courſe, the hoary hero ſtrode,   365
His brown arms purpled with the burſting blood ;
Ranks after ranks againſt his falchion riſe,
And chief on chief in ſwift ſucceſſion dies.
For now each breaſt ſuch active vengeance warms ;
They ſpurn the trifling toil of miſſive arms ;   370
Each braces firm the ſhield, and joys to wheel
The ſurer vengeance of the griding ſteel.
Full on great Hezron's courſe the heathens ruſh'd,
And the firſt chiefs by following chiefs were cruſh'd :
In ſolemn pomp, againſt the growing ſtorm   375
The mighty hero rear'd his moveleſs form.
In vain bright ſwords around him ceaceleſs hung,
Troops preſs'd in vain, and clattering armour rung.
So, on ſome hill, while angry tempeſts lower,
In ſtately grandeur, ſtands the moſs-grown tower ;   380
Loud roar the winds ; impetuous drives the rain,
And all the fury of th' etherial main ;

Still, rear'd to heaven, it frowns with pride sublime,
Spurns the fierce storm, and mocks the waste of time.

Far distant, Caleb swept the crimson plain,   385
Guided the fight, and pil'd the numerous slain;
Round his great arm the cloudy squadrons hung;
Clash'd on his buckler countless weapons rung;
Chiefs after chiefs oppos'd his wasting course,
Met his broad steel, and felt its fatal force.   390

Ludon, the Hivites' prince, his arm defied
All rough with gold, and gay in barbarous pride;
With giant strength the heathen hurl'd his spear,
Its terrors quivering through the parted air;
Loud o'er brave Caleb's shoulders sung the steel,   395
And pierc'd a warrior's breast; the warrior fell;
His blue mail clang'd; to rise he tried in vain,
But writh'd in dying anguish on the plain.
The mighty leader rais'd his sword on high,
Its transient lightnings circling in the sky,   400
Full on the Heathen's neck a griding wound
Sunk; the loos'd head fell spouting to the ground.
Amaz'd, the Hivites saw their monarch lost.
And deathlike murmurs groan'd around the host.

Near the bold leader Oran rear'd his steel,   405
Where the storm thicken'd, and the fiercest fell;
Imperious taunts provoke the rage of war,
Loud threats insult, and tumult sounds afar;
Wedg'd in a moveless throng, the battle grows,
Cries deeper roar, and shriller ring the blows.   410
With joy, unfeeling Oran strides the slain,
And hails the ruins of th' accustom'd plain;
No anguish melts, no wound his pity charms,
No fate impassions, and no groan alarms;
Thro' the red scenes he hews a raptur'd way,   415
And mingling darkness intercepts the day.

Meantime fierce Irad o'er the field is driven,
And boasts th' assistance of a favouring heaven

BOOK VI.

Though new to war, with war his bosom glows,
And knows no transport, but the flight of foes. 420
 In scenes of distant death bold Hezron stands,
Dies his blue arms, and pains his aged hands;
Full many a chief his veteran falchion crowns,
Thick flit the shades, and blood the verdure drowns.
Impetuous Carmi springs the chief to meet, 425
Conscious of youth, and light with nimble feet;
His arm all active strews the sanguine ground,
Wakes the deep groan, and deals the frequent wound:
Full on his angry sword the warriors rush,
Impel th' upright, the falling heedless crush: 430
No chief the fury of his arm withstands,
And ruin widens o'er bold Hezron's bands.
Amaz'd, the hero saw the deluge spread,
And wide, and wider rise the piles of dead,
Flight first commence in hosts that own his sway, 435
And proud Ai hail a second conquering day:
From his sad bosom heav'd a heavy groan;
Round the whole war he miss'd his favourite son:
Untaught to droop, he hopes congenial fire
May yet ward shame, and yet the troops inspire.--- 440
Where now, he cries, are fled the boasts of morn?
The towering stalk? the brow of lifted scorn?
Then Judah's warriors promis'd deeds of fame,
Hiss'd impious flight, and spurn'd the dastard's shame.
Far other scenes now rend these hapless eyes; 445
The foe advances, and the boaster flies;
Broke but by fear, ye wing inglorious flight,
Giants in words, and maidens in the fight;
Oh had kind Heaven dispens'd a speedier doom,
And this frail form in Bashan found a tomb! 450
Then had these palsied limbs, in peace repos'd;
Unpain'd with shame, these eyes in triumph clos'd;
Pleas'd to the last, survey'd my favourite race,
View'd no base flight, and bled for no disgrace.---

U

Hence, hence, ye timorous souls, to Joshua fly,   455
And tell the Chief, ye saw your leader die.

　The hero spoke ; and urg'd by passion's force,
On furious Carmi bent his aged course ;
Awful in gleam of arms, the chiefs appear,
Here the bold youth, the white-hair'd hero there: 460
But ere his sword great Hezron could extend,
Or circling bands their ancient chief defend,
A long, bright lance his wary foe beheld,
And snatch'd it glittering on the bloody field ;
Swift through the hero's side he forc'd the steel ;   465
Pierc'd to the heart, the aged warrior fell ;
There lay, a corse, bespread with purple stains,
The form, that triumph'd on a hundred plains.

　On Ridgefield's hills, to shame to virtue dead,
Thus dastard bands the foe inglorious fled ;   470
When Wooster singly brav'd the deathful ground,
Fir'd hosts in vain, and met the fatal wound.
In dangers born, to arms in childhood train'd,
From Gallia's heroes many a palm he gain'd ;
With freedom's sacred flame serenely glow'd   475
For justice arm'd, and sought the field for God ;
With steady zeal his nation's interest lov'd ;
(No terror touch'd him, and no injury mov'd)
Far in the front, with dauntless bosom bled,
And crown'd the honours of his hoary head.   480

　Bent o'er his foe, the lovely Carmi stood,
And view'd, with tears of grief, his bursting blood ;
And thus---Unhappy sire, he sadly cried---
Perhaps thy monarch's joy, thy nation's pride.---
How like my father's bends thy hoary brow ?   485
His limbs, his countenance, and his locks of snow,
All in thy venerable face I see---
Perhaps the parent of a son like me---

　　He spoke ; and fiercely wheel'd his bloody sword,
Sprang to the fight, and many a hero gor'd ;   490

His voice, his eyes the joyful hoſt inſpire,
And through the ſweetneſs flames a dreadful fire.
Active as light, o'er trembling ranks he hung ;
Shouts ſhook the plains, the frighted foreſts rung :
Unnumber'd ſullen groans were heard around ;   495
Unnumber'd corſes cloath'd the purple ground :
From poſt to poſt retir'd pale Judah's train,
And chief on chief increas'd the piles of ſlain.
Dark as an evening cloud, bold Ai was driven,
Gloom'd all the fields, and caſt a ſhade on heaven ;   500
Wide roll'd the ſtorm ; wide drove the duſt along,
And ruin hover'd o'er the flying throng.

 Meantime, brave Irad turn'd his ſparkling eyes,
And ſaw in diſtant fields the clouds ariſe ;
Sad flight and terror fill'd the backward plain,   505
And the foe ſhouted o'er his kindred ſlain.
As, when autumnal clouds the ſkies deform,
Burſts the wild whirlwind from the gloomy ſtorm ;
Hoarſe craſh the pines ; oaks ſtiffly ſtubborn fall,
And ſudden thunders liſtening ſwains appall :   510
So, wing'd by Heaven, impetuous Irad flew ;
As ſwift their darling chief the youths purſue ;
Whelm'd in their path, the falling bands expire,
And crowds of warriors from their ſteps retire.

 Now, where brave Carmi ſwept the purple ground,
Terrific Irad ſhook his buckler's round ;   516
Alike in years they ſeem'd, alike in arms,
Of equal ſtature, and of rival charms :
Nor this, nor that, the dangerous fight can yield ;
But each demands the empire of the field.   520
From the fierce chiefs the wondering bands retreat ;
Blows following blows their ſounding ſhields repeat ;
Uncleft, each faithful orb the ſtroke rebounds,
Blunts the keen blade, and intercepts the wounds :
'Till Irad's nimble arm, with ſudden wheel,   525
Through Carmi's ſide impels the fatal ſteel,

Pure ftreams of crimfon ftain the fubject ground,
And the freed foul pervades the gaping wound.

 Not that fair pride, that foul-fupporting flame,
That lights the fplendors of th' immortal name ; 530
Not all the bravery nature can impart,
Nor the fond wifhes of a virgin's heart,
Nor parents' vows, nor nations' prayers could fave,
The young, bright hero from an early grave.
He fell, with beauty's faireft beams adorn'd, 535
While foes admir'd him, and while Irad mourn'd.
Ah youth, too foon allotted to the tomb ;
Oh had kind Heaven difpens'd a fofter doom,
On thy fair deeds a fweet reward beftow'd,
And op'd the manfions of the blefs'd abode ! 540

 Thus, where fad Charleftown lifts her hills on high,
Where once gay ftructures charm'd the morning fky,
Ere Howe's barbarian hand in favage fire
Wrapp'd the tall dome, and whelm'd the facred fpire,
In life's fair prime, and new to war's alarms, 545
Brave Warren funk, in all the pride of arms.
With me, each generous mind the hour recall,
When pale Columbia mourn'd her favourite's fall ;
Mourn'd the bright ftatefman, hero, patriot, fled,
The friend extinguifh'd, and the genius dead ; 550
While he, the darling of the wife, and good,
Seal'd his firm truth, and built his name in blood.

 Loud as the rufhing ftorm, the din of war
Burft o'er the plain, and fhook the fields afar ;
Fierce Irad rais'd a loud, diftinguifh'd cry--- 555
Here fee, my friends, their gafping leader lie.---
Through Ai's wide hoft my fword fhall hew your way ;
Shall Jndah's fons alone defert the day ?
Shall Jofhua know you fled ? to glory rife ;
Lift all your arms, and pierce the knave that flies. 560

 The hero fpoke : abafh'd the warriors heard,
Rung their blue arms, and high the ftandard rear'd ;

Aloft in air a Lion's gloomy form
Lower'd, like the darkneſs of a ſullen ſtorm ;
Around his head his ſhaggy terrors frown'd, 565
And his red eyeballs gleam'd deſtruction round,
Swift from the bearer's hand fierce Irad drew
The banner'd ſtaff, and mid the heathens threw ;
With joy they ſprang to ſeize the glittering prize,
And ſmiles of triumph ſparkled in their eyes. 570
Shame fluſh'd the cheeks of Judah's glowing train ;
Their boſoms heav'd ; their faces flaſh'd diſdain ;
To ſeize the ſhining ſpoil each warrior ſprang ;
The combat thicken'd ; and all ether rang ;
Far roll'd the darkneſs of the duſty cloud ; 575
Loud roſe their cries, and armour claſh'd aloud.
The blackening tempeſt Ai undaunted kenn'd,
Pleas'd to procure, and ſtubborn to defend ;
Scarce Irad's arm could cleave the firm-wedg'd train,
As fierce he ſtrove the ſtandard to regain ; 580
Through ranks on ranks he forc'd a ſanguine way,
Ere his red falchion won the ſplendid prey ;
With ſmiles, he ſaw the crimſon tumult grow,
And hail'd the vengeance gathering o'er the foe.

From the tall rock great Joſhua caſt his eyes, 585
And ſaw the varying ſcenes of combat riſe.
To Carmi's force beheld pale Judah yield,
And roſe to ſave the triumphs of the field ;
But ſoon new ſhouts aſcend the clouded ſky,
His friends now triumph, and the Heathens fly. 590

Now nearer ſcenes his ſearching view demand,
Where mighty Caleb rules the warrior band ;
Fierce Oran's ſword begins inglorious flight,
And his loud clamours animate the fight :
Scarce Caleb's arm the conflict can ſuſtain, 595
His voice arouſe, or deeds inſpire, the train ;
So fierce the heathens throng th' embattled ground,
So thick the warriors fall, the groans reſound.

The Hero view'd, and tow'rd the fainting throng,
Swift as a rapid whirlwind, rush'd along ;   602
As 'gainst a mound, when tempests ride the gale,
The raging river foams along the vale ;
Down the wall crumbles, and with dreadful reign
Sweeps a wild deluge on the wasted plain.
Bursting upon the dark embodied throng   605
Thus the wide ruin Joshua drove along ;
Around his course increas'd the piles of dead,
The brave sunk fighting, and the coward fled.

Now, where unfeeling Oran crush'd the slain,
All grim with dust, and red with many a stain,   610
While smiles of transport gather'd on his brow,
His fierce eye sparkling o'er the bleeding foe,
While high for death he rear'd his sanguine arm,
And a brave warrior bow'd to shun the storm,
Great Joshua's full-orb'd buckler caught the wound, 615
And lightnings darted from the moony round,
Then, by his hand with rushing thunder thrown,
On Oran's helmet burst a mighty stone,
That, bounding onward 'gainst a warrior's side,
Crush'd his strong ribs, and shed a plenteous tide.   620
Stunn'd by the staggering blow, the leader fell,
Writh'd with the pain, and gave a hideous yell ;
Furious he lay, with heaving, panting breath,
Roll'd up his whitening eyes, and frown'd in death ;
Cursing the shield, which seiz'd his nimble dart,   625
And stopp'd its passage to the warrior's heart :
Swift on his throat descends th' indignant blade,
Bursts the black gore, and leaps the grisly head.

Loud o'er the tumult rose the Hero's cry ;
The host all quakes, the distant groves reply---   635
Rush on, bold heroes, conquest crowns the day ;
Now spring to fight, and seize the trembling prey.
This arm on Oran drove the final wound ;
Let shouts of triumph shake the hostile ground :

Wealth, and fair peace, the generous contest **yields,** 635
And wreaths of glory bloom in bloody fields.----
As in th' enkindled wood fierce winds arise,
And storms of fire are blown across the skies ;
In blazing trains, the towering pines descend,
And rushing thunders all the forest rend : 640
So, loud and furious, Israel throng'd the fight,
And their blue armour flash'd a dreadful light ;
O 'er the pale rear tremendous Joshua hung ;
Their gloomy knell his voice terrific rung ;
From glowing eyeballs flash'd his wrath severe, 645
Grim Death before him hurl'd his murdering spear ;
Heads, sever'd from their necks, bestrew'd his **way,**
And gushing bodies round his footsteps lay.

Meantime Ai's sounding portals wide unfold,
And fierce to combat bursting bands are roll'd ; 650
In dreadful pomp ascends the widening train ;
Battalions on battalions cloud the plain :
There glowing Zimri wings his rapid force,
And eager thousands darken round his course,

Ai's ghastly sons the smoking walls survey'd, 655
And wild amaze each pallid front array'd ;
Here lay in gore their brethren, and their sires ;
There sunk their mansions in terrific fires ;
Before, behind, their foes increas'd alarms ; 659
They rais'd one shriek, and dropp'd their useless **arms :**
Where'er an opening rank receiv'd the day,
Or dust obscure disclos'd a glimmering ray,
Borne by light fear, they left the lingering wind,
They fled, they flew, nor cast a look behind ;
Oft on the spear's protended point they ran ; 665
While throng'd resistless, meeting man with **man,**
Steel stretch'd to steel, and shield to shield oppos'd ;
On every side the power of Israel clos'd.
So thick they throng'd, no spear could miss its **course ;**
In vain no falchion spent its ardent force : 670

Less heard and less, resounded piercing cries,
And dust besprinkled ceas'd to fill the skies.
So, when tall navies lift imperial sails,
And hope th' indulgence of propitious gales,
When the cold north's fierce wind the main deform, 675
And, fill'd with thunders, rolls the raging storm,
Heav'd from the bottom, foaming billows rise,
And climb, and climb, and roar against the skies;
O'er shiver'd masts unroll the surging waves,
And the pale sailors plunge in watery graves.   680
Swift as a whirlwind, o'er the southern plain,
Impetuous Zimri drove the Hivite train:
With prosperous course, they sped their hasty flight,
Sunk in the wood, and vanish'd from the sight.

    And now, obedient to the Chief's command,   685
Round the tall standard throng'd each wearied band;
A smile of transport every face adorn'd,
Their wounds unheeded, and the dead scarce mourn'd.

    Nor knew fair Irad how his parent lay,
But, fir'd with glory, steer'd his careless way;   690
Near the great Chief he mov'd with conscious grace,
And conscious blushes crimson'd o'er his face;
When, pale and ghastly, on the bloody ground,
Stain'd with black dust, and pierc'd with many a wound,
Stiff gore besprinkling all his locks of snow,   695
And a cold cloud around his reverend brow,
Hezron appear'd: at once his nerves congeal'd;
His frozen lips a dumb, dead silence seal'd;
A moveless statue, o'er the sire he hung,
Nor streaming tears releas'd his marbled tongue.   700
Then round the corse impassion'd arms he threw,
And wash'd the clotted gore in filial dew;
Glu'd to the form with strong embraces lay,
And kiss'd, with quivering lips, the senseless clay.
At length the Chief, soft pity in his eyes,   705
Reach'd his kind hand, and forc'd the Youth to rise:

BOOK VI.

Four mournful warriors Hezron's body bore,
And their eyes glisten'd with a tender shower.
  The sun declin'd ; besmear'd with dust, and blood,
Slow o'er the plain the wearied squadrons trode ;   710
When, fair as Phosphor leads the morning train,
Dress'd in new beams, and beauteous from the main ;
Crown'd with white flowers, that breath'd a rich perfume
And cloth'd in loveliness, of gayest bloom,
Rose in soft splendor Caleb's youngest pride,   715
A thousand maidens following at her side.
In snow-white robes of flowing silk array'd,
First of the virgins walk'd the blushing maid ;
Her long, dark hair loose-floated in the wind ;
Her glowing eyes confess'd th' etherial mind ;   720
A wreath of olive flourish'd in her hand ;
A silver lyre obey'd her soft command ;
With sounds harmonious rang the warbled strings,
And thus the maids, and thus Selima sings.
Who comes from Ai, adorn'd with gay attire,   725
Bright as the splendor of the morning fire ?
Fair as the spring, ascends the lovely form,
And dreadful as the blaze, that lights the storm !
Ye maids, with flowerets strew the conqueror's way,
Strike the loud harp, and sing the dreadful day !   730
To Irad's steps the matchless fair-one came,
Her breast quick panting, and her cheeks on flame ;
Her beauteous hand the verdant crown display'd ;
Graceful he bow'd, and plac'd it on his head.
Slow to her train the trembling fair withdrew,   735
The charm'd youths following with a moveless view,
So, wing'd with light, and dress'd in strange array,
The mantling glory of the rising day,
With sweet complacence, such as angels show
To souls unprison'd from this world of woe,   740
Parted soft-smiling from our general sire
Some bright-ey'd Virtue, of the heavenly choir,

X

BOOK VI.

Far in the folar walk, with wanderous flight,
The form celeftial leffen'd on his fight.

   Again the youth his wonted life regain'd;   145
A tranfient fparkle in his eye obtain'd;
A rifing glow his tender thoughts confefs'd,
And the foft motions of his melting breaft.
But foon dark glooms the feeble fmiles o'erfpread;
Like morn's gay hues, the fading fplendor fled;   750
Returning anguifh froze his feeling foul,
Deep fighs burft forth, and tears began to roll.

T H E

CONQUEST of CANÄAN:

B O O K VII.

Argument.

Evening described. Irad's dream. He goes out to the walls of Ai. His lamentation for his father. Reflections on the fate of Ai. Appearance of an army. Irad returns in haste, and alarms the Camp. Joshua, at his request, allots him a body of forces, with whom he goes out to attack the Heathens. Battle by the burning of Ai, between Hazor, &c. and Israel. Irad's exploits. He kills Adnor, and pursues Samlah to the eastern part of the host. Uzal. Shelumiel. Jabin's character, and exploits. He kills Shammah, and Seraiah. Jobab. Confusion of the Israelites. Irad returns and rallies them. He attacks Jobab, with success. Kindling of the neighbouring forest separates the combatants.

The scene of this battle is partly on the plain east of Ai, partly in the forest still eastward, and partly northward of the forest.

The CONQUEST of CANÄAN.

BOOK VII.

O'ER the wide world immeafurably fpread,
   Night, ftill and gloomy, caft a folemn fhade.
  Jn heavens half-clouded ftars unfrequent hung;
Scarce heard, the blaft with mournful murmurs rung;
Above tall, eaftern hills, the moon's pale eye   5
Look'd fad, and dreadful, from the cheerlefs fky.
Her cold, wan face, half-hid behind a cloud,
That wrapp'd the mountains in a fable fhroud,
With feeble luftre ftreak'd the fhadowy plains,
And edg'd her vapoury robes with difmal ftains.   10
All, but the favage race, to fleep retir'd,
And the laft gleams of weftern fkies expir'd.
  Stretch'd in his tent, unhappy Irad lay,
And fad oblivion bore his toils away.
In that ftill hour, when rapt on eagle-wings,   15
To diftant climes bewilder'd fancy fprings,
A death-like flumber feal'd his tearful eyes,
And thus unreal fcenes in vifion rife.
  Through lonely fields, in ruffet gloom array'd,
Loft in mute grief, with weary fteps he ftray'd.   20
A fhadowy light, like evening's dufky ray,
Spread o'er the world, and form'd a twilight day.
Before his wandering path, a northern grove
Shed midnight round, and pierc'd the clouds above:

Slow wav'd the tall, dark pines : a hollow sound   25
Roll'd through the wood, and shook th' autumnal ground.
Dull-murmuring fell the sullen, swelling streams,
Lulling to sleep, and blue in glimmering beams.
With broad, black horrors o'er its bosom spread,
An eastern mountain rear'd its shaggy head ;   30
High hung the hoary cliff ; the cedars height,
Less seen, and less, withdrew beyond the sight.
Strange unknown scenes the regions wild display,
And solitary music slowly dies away.

    From the thick grove, in dark-brown robes reveal'd,
A form stalk'd solemn o'er the shuddering field ;   36
Of other worlds he seem'd ; nor cast an eye
On the brown plain, or on the gloomy sky.
Regardless of the scenes that round him mourn'd,
On Irad's path his sad, slow steps he turn'd ;   40
Pale stood the Youth ; the stately shape drew nigh ;
Gash'd was his cheek, and fix'd his lofty eye ;
Like a light flame, low hung his beard of snow,
And death's cold terrors hover'd on his brow.
'Twas Hezron's self.   With weak, but solemn sound,   45
As sullen graves beneath the foot resound,
His voice began---On fate's dark verge I stand,
Whence thickening dangers roll across thy land.
Night wraps the world ; approaching storms arise,
Hang o'er thy race, and cloud the southern skies.   50
My mouldering bones a colder night detains,
Clos'd in the tomb, and bound in icy chains :
But the wing'd spirit fairer climes surround,
And heaven unfolding bids her songs resound.
Faintly he spoke. By strange, immortal spell,   55
His wounds grew smooth, his sightless garments fell :
His pallid face a sudden beauty fir'd,
And with strong life his changing eye inspir'd ;
O'er his white robes a purple splendor ray'd ;
Long glittering pinions loosely round him play'd ;   60

In dreadful pomp, sublime the Vision stood,
And living fragrance breath'd along the wood.

  At once the hero, startled, rais'd his head ;
Still was his tent, and all the tumult fled :
Again to sleep he clos'd his wearied eyes,   65
And broken slumbers o'er his toils arise.

  Sudden, his name re-echoing from the walls,
A wild, and visionary murmur calls---
Irad awake ; my voice thine ear invades,
From the dark mansions of imprison'd shades ;   70
In southern plains the clarion's thunders rise,
And shouts of triumph fill the rending skies.

  Swift from his couch the Youth astonish'd rose,
(While every vein the dreadful murmur froze)
With active hand his arms around him brac'd ;   75
With nimble feet the glimmering champain pass'd,
And tow'rd Ai's flames, that rag'd with awful force,
Suspense, but fearless, steer'd his lonely course.
Still o'er his head the airy phantom hung ;
Irad awake---the voice unreal rung :   80
Sad grief, and anxious doubt his thoughts oppress'd,
But love's soft whispers still disturb'd his breast.

  Now solemn silence sail'd along the air ;
No bird complain'd ; no echoing voice was near ;
Save the slow murmur of the passing gale,   85
That swept the plain, and sounded through the vale.
The flames dark-glimmer'd on the hero's shield,
And cast long shadows o'er the pallid field :
Round the dread scenes he turn'd regardless eyes,
And thus began, with intermingled sighs---   90

  And art thou fled forever ? this thine end,
Thou best of parents, and thou surest friend ?
And could'st thou fall, a prey to murdering war ?
What cruel demon drove my feet so far ?
Was no kind angel hovering o'er the throng ?   95
Where look'd the Power, thy virtue serv'd so long ?

Thy foul fo pure---thy life fo firmly juft---
Scarce Heaven's own law could more demand from duft.
Why, O thou righteous Mind ? but ceafe my tongue,
Nor blame the dread decree, that cannot wrong.　　100
Mine the fole fault---and mine the fingle blame---
Wild with the magic of that phantom, fame.
Didft thou for this the guilty fhield beftow,
To leave thee naked to the fatal blow ?
Didft thou for this the fword accurs'd impart,　　105
That fhould have plung'd beneath the murderer's heart ?
Far other love, far other faithful cares
Nurs'd my young limbs, and watch'd my rifing years ;
My early fteps, from pleafure's flippery road,
Lur'd with foft fmiles, and led them up to GOD ;　　110
Thy own bright actions prompting to purfue,
To virtue charm'd me, and to glory drew ;
With Jofhua's felf my wifhes forc'd to vie,
Boaft of mankind, and chofen of the Sky.

　　Pale, in the vifions of the guilty bed,　　115
Thy form affrights me, and thine eyes upbraid.
There fcenes of dire diftrefs thy words unroll,
Doom'd for my life, and opening on my foul.
Or does thy mind its lov'd employ purfue,
To guard from ill, and hidden dangers fhew ?　　120
Perhaps thy thoughts, beyond the filent tomb,
Watch, as in life, thy nation's fecret doom ;
Some rufhing fate unknown difcern afar,
Some threatening ambufh, or fome wafting war.

　　Perhaps the firft of maids thy care demands,　　125
And claims her fafety from aerial hands.
Ah ! knew the fair what crimes to me belong,
Her lovely voice had fpar'd th' applauding fong ;
A breaft more pure her melting arms embrac'd,
And the bright garland worthier temples grac'd.　　130
　　Thus fpoke the chief, when now his fteps were nigh
Ai's awful flames, that wav'd acrofs the fky ;

BOOK VII.

All pale, and gloomy, climb'd the dreadful blaze,
And fmoky volumes curl'd above the rays ;
A dreary gleam enroll'd the fhady ground,   135
And the brown land-fcape faintly rofe around.
Touch'd by the folemn fcene, the hero cried---
Where haplefs Ai ! is now thy towery pride ?
Where now thy manly fons, whofe finewy arms
Rofe, a ftrong bulwark 'gainft impending harms 140
Where now the heaven-topp'd fpire ? the gilded wall ?
Thy kings, thy heroes ? whelm'd in ruin all---
Deftruction's clouds fail'd blackening o'er thy light,
And wide oblivion's never-ending night.

Where yon tall dome fhoots forth the greedy flame,145
Perhaps fome hero hop'd a deathlefs name.
Oft when return'd from war, his tender race
Climb'd his fond knee and afk'd the fweet embrace :
Oft, with a parent's gliftening eye, he view'd
His face, his virtues in their forms renew'd.   150
Perhaps fome daughter, darling of his care,
Beam'd, like Selima faireft of the fair :
And could thofe flames fome lovely maid deftroy,
A nation's glory and a parent's joy ?
Could babes, fweet-fmiling, claim no hand to fave, 155
But find, unwept, a furnace for a grave ?

Thus mourn'd his generous heart the doom fevere,
And paid loft Ai the tribute of a tear.
Like ocean's long, deep roar, a rufhing found
Burft from the wood, and pour'd along the ground ; 160
At once wide trembled o'er the awful fields
The fudden gleam of fpears, and helms, and fhields,
Impetuous roll'd unfeen the rattling car,
And banner'd terrors wav'd th' approach of war.
Loud rung bold Irad's voice ; the dreadful found   165
Stopp'd the long hoft, and fhook th' affrighted ground ;
Thrice, like the burft of thunder, hoarfe he cried ;
Thrice, ftood the hoft ; and thrice the fky replied :

Y

The cry wav'd solemn through the winding vales ;
Night shook, and murmurs fill'd the rushing gales.　170
The southern guards soon caught the boding sound,
And spread th' alarm the startled camp around ;
Loud as tall billows rend the rocky shore,
Rose the sonorous clarion's bursting roar :
Swift to the camp the hero wing'd his way,　175
Rous'd all the host, and scatter'd wild dismay---
Arm, warriors, arm ! to instant battle fly !
The foe's at hand ! ye combat, or ye die.
Swift to these tents unnumber'd bands repair ;
Hark ! how the trumpet fills the troubled air !　180
In southern fields ascends the wasting war,
And fierce as whirlwinds rolls the rapid car.
Arm, ere our camp be wrapp'd in one broad flame,
And Israel's manly thousands want a name,

　Thus, round the host, his animating cry　185
Urg'd sleep's oblivious hand from every eye ;
Each waking mind the strange alarm appalls ;
Arm, warriors, arm ! each startled hero calls :
From tent to tent the wild confusion flies ;
Shouts rend the plains ; groans murmur ; shrieks arise ;
A rushing noise invades the listening ear ;　191
In swift succession half-seen forms appear ;
Shrill rings the rattling mail ; the trump's big sound
Cleaves the dun heaven, and shakes the gloomy ground.
Round a broad flame, that, by the Chief's command,
Shoots lofty spires, and gleams along the sand,　196
Deep throng the squadrons ; high the standards stream,
And wave, and glimmer, in the livid beam.
There, while the terrors of the lovely fair
Froze every breast, and breath'd a wide despair,　200
A quickening glow the Leader's voice inspir'd ;
Hush'd were their cries ; their lessening fears retir'd ;
Through every bosom thrill'd a new delight,
And brac'd each sinew for the manly fight.

Now, rang'd in ranks, the hoft expectant flood,   205
Prepar'd for combat, fteel'd to death and blood ;
Sudden, before the Chief, with panting breaft,
The generous Youth preferr'd his bold requeft---
Near Ai's red flames I fteer'd my carelefs way,
Robb'd of wifh'd flumbers, and to grief a prey,   210
When fheath'd in gleaming arms, a mighty train,
Pour'd from the wood, and cover'd all the plain :
On foaming courfers, chiefs impel the war,
Or whirl the terrors of the wafting car.
And wilt thou, Chief divine, from Irad hear   215
The dictates of a mind, that knows no fear ?
Shall this young arm again the lance command,
And lead to fight a ftrong, undaunted band,
To Ai's wide ruins wing our active courfe,
And tempt the fury of barbarian force ?   220
Shall thine unconquer'd fword the camp defend,
And ward the fate, if fhame our fteps attend ?
Safe in thy prudence fhall the race endure,
And Jofhua's name our wives, and fons fecure.
Lo, drefs'd in fteel, we wait thy ruling breath !   225
Counfel is ruin, and delay is death.
Go, in JEHOVAH's name---the Chief replied---
Forth ftalk'd the Youth, and warm'd with martial pride ;
O'er fouthern fields the bands appointed fteer'd,
Squar'd in juft ranks, and not a warrior fear'd.   230
    Now where Ai's fons beftrew'd the plain, they came,
Faintly illumin'd by the diftant flame ;
No foe appear'd : the world more gloomy grew,
And, loft in clouds, etherial realms withdrew ;
Save where lone ftars diffus'd a feeble beam,   235
Like the far taper's folitary gleam :
Slow winds breath'd hollow through the dark profound,
And deepening horror brooded o'er the ground.
    Eaft of proud Ai, an ancient foreft ftood,
And fouthward far was ftretch'd the lofty wood ;   240

North lay fair plains ; and next the walls, array'd
With fcatter'd trees, a fpacious level fpread.

   Now near the burning domes, the fquadrons ftood,
Their breafts impatient for the fcenes of blood :
On every face a death-like glimmer fate,   245
The unblefs'd harbinger of inftant fate.
High thro' the gloom, in pale and dreadful fpires,
Rofe the long terrors of the dark-red fires ;
Torches, and torrent fparks, by whirlwinds driven,
Stream'd thro' the fmoke, and fir'd the clouded heaven.
As oft tall turrets funk with rufhing found,   251
Broad flames burft forth, and fweep the etherial round,
The bright expanfion lighten'd all the fcene,
And deeper fhadows lengthen'd o'er the green.
Loud thro' the walls that caft a golden gleam,   255
Crown'd with tall pyramids of bending flame,
As thunders rumble down the dardening vales,
Roll'd the deep folemn voice of rufhing gales :
The bands admiring gaz'd the wonderous fight,
And Expectation trembled for the fight.   260

   At once the founding clarion breath'd alarms ;
Wide from the foreft burft the flafh of arms ;
Thick gleam'd the helms ; and o'er aftonifh'd fields,
Like thoufand meteors, rofe the flame-bright fhields.
In gloomy pomp, to furious combat roll'd   265
Ranks fheath'd in mail, and chiefs in glimmering gold ;
In floating luftre bounds the dim-feen fteed,
And cars unfinifh'd, fwift to cars fucceed :
From all the hoft afcends a dark-red glare,
Here in full blaze, in diftant twinklings there ;   270
Slow waves the dreadful light, as round the fhore
Night's folemn blafts with deep concuffion roar,
So rufh'd the footfteps of th' embattled train,
And fend an awful murmur o'er the plain.

   Tall in th' oppofing van, bold Irad ftood,   275
And bid the clarion found the voice of blood.

Loud blew the trumpet on the sweeping gales,
Rock'd the deep groves, and echoed round the vales ;
A ceaseless murmur all the concave fills,   (hills.
Waves thro' the quivering camp, and trembles o'er the
  High in the gloomy blaze the standards flew ;   181
Th' impatient Youth his burnish'd falchion drew ;
Ten-thousand swords his eager bands display'd,
And crimson terrors danc'd on every blade.
With equal rage, the bold, Hazorian train   285
Pour'd a wide deluge o'er the shadowy plain ;
Loud rose the songs of war, loud clang'd the shields,
Dread shouts of vengeance shook the shuddering fields ;
With mingled din, shrill, martial music rings,
And swift to combat each fierce hero springs.   290
So broad, and dark, a midnight storm ascends,
Bursts on the main, and trembling nature rends ;
The red foam burns, the watery mountains rise,
One deep unmeasur'd thunder heaves the skies ;
The bark drives lonely ; shivering and forlorn,   295
The poor, sad sailors wish the lingering morn :
Not with less fury rush'd the vengeful train ;
Not with less tumult roar'd th' embattled plain.
Now in the oak's black shade they fought conceal'd ;
And now they shouted thro' the open field ;   300
The long, pale splendors of the curling flame
Cast o'er their polish'd arms a livid gleam ;
An umber'd lustre floated round their way,
And lighted falchions to the fierce affray.
Now the swift chariots 'gainst the stubborn oak   305
Dash'd ; the dark earth re-echoes to the shock.
From shade to shade the forms tremendous stream,
And their arms flash a momentary flame.
Mid hollow tombs, as fleets an airy train,
Lost in the skies, or fading o'er the plain ;   310
So visionary shapes, around the fight,
Shoot thro' the gloom, and vanish'd from the sight ;

Thro' twilight paths the maddening coursers bound,
The shrill swords crack, the clashing shields resound.
There, lost in grandeur might the eye behold   315
The dark-red glimmerings of the steel, and gold ;
The chief ; the steed ; the nimbly-rushing car ;
And all the horrors of the gloomy war.
Here the thick clouds, with purple lustre bright,   319
Spread o'er the long long host and gradual sunk in night ;
Here half the world was wrapp'd in rolling fires,
And dreadful vallies sunk between the spires.
Swift ran black forms across the livid flame,
And oaks wav'd slowly in the trembling beam :
Loud rose the mingled noise ; with hollow sound,   325
Deep-rolling whirlwinds roar, and thundering flames re-
    As drives a blast along the midnight heath,   (found.
Rush'd raging Irad on the scenes of death ;
High o'er his shoulder gleam'd his brandish'd blade,
And scatter'd ruin round the twilight shade.   330
Full on a giant hero's sweeping car
He pour'd the tempest of resistless war ;
His twinkling lance the heathen rais'd on high,
And hurl'd it, fruitless, through the gloomy sky ;
From the bold Youth the maddening coursers wheel, 335
Gash'd by the vengeance of his slaughtering steel,
'Twixt two tall oaks the helpless chief they drew ;
The shrill car dash'd ; the crack'd wheels rattling flew ;
Crush'd in his arms, to rise he strove in vain,
And lay unpitied on the dreary plain.   340
    Now Samlah's hands to war the chariot guide,
Fair, beauteous, tall, fam'd Hamor's youngest pride ;
O'er Achsaph's towers he stretch'd a potent sway,
And saw surrounding realms his rod obey.
Adnor, an elder birth, proud grandeur spurn'd ;   345
Lord of his soul, inferior realms he scorn'd ;
Nor felt one pang, nor shew'd one envious frown,
When doating Age to Samlah gave the crown.

Round his young fteps he caft a kind furvey,
And taught the bleffings of an equal fway ; 350
The pride of arts allur'd him to purfue ;
To wifdom form'd him, and to virtue drew ;
To reafon's rules his ftormy paffions wrought,
And fhone, a pattern of the truths he taught.
From Jabin's loins a matchlefs virgin fprung, 355
And every voice with Salma's praifes rung.
Her, Adnor led to fhare his brother's throne,
And made, delighted, Samlah's blifs his own.
Five weeks the prince beheld in tranfport glide,
Blefs'd in the beauties of his lovely bride : 360
Heedlefs of war he dwelt, 'till Jabin's voice
Rous'd him to arms, and call'd to ruder joys.
Now, where bold Irad fcatter'd blood and fate,
In the fame car the friendly brothers fate ;
When Adnor thus---Oh fly yon mifcreant's arm ; 365
Nor tempt the terrors of the fweeping ftorm !
Its wonted aid my broken fpear denies---
With a fierce look, th' impatient youth replies---
Me doft thou urge to bafe, unmanly flight ?
Leap from the chariot ; hide in covering night ? 370
Shall Salma hear ? fhall Samlah's growing name
Wafte with the pangs of never-ending fhame ?
He faid, and furious, urg'd his rapid car,
Crufh'd the firm ranks, and fhouted to the war ;
On Irad's courfe he drove ; the hero turn'd, 375
And a brown glimmering from his buckler burn'd :
'Twixt the bold leaders pour'd an ardent band ;
Sword clafh'd on fword, and hand rofe up to hand ;
They fell ; new fquadrons o'er their corfes rife,
And louder tumults echo from the fkies. 380
Imperious Samlah lifts a haughty cry---
Hence, on your lives, prefuming daftards fly !
Who dares tranfgrefs fhall find a fudden doom :
Give Samlah place---give kings, and heroes room---

He fpoke.   His friends, all anxious for their king,   385
Still crowd the war, and fwift to danger fpring ;
Loud fung the vengeance of his pointed fteel,
And a bold veteran, deeply wounded, fell ;
Enrag'd, the bands on either fide retreat,
And leave the furious monarch to his fate.   390
   Swift from the chariot faithful Adnor fprang ;
On Irad's fhield his rufhing falchion rang :
The Youth's quick wheeling, thro his fhoulder glides ;
Drops the cleft arm, and gufh the living tides.
He funk ; and Irad, touch'd with pity, cried---   395
Ah youth ! whofe bofom glows with generous pride,
To fcenes of endlefs gloom thy fpirit flies ;
Wing, wing thy voice, for pardon, to the fkies !
Oh, Sire of all, may this brave warrior's mind,
In life's fair climes, fome lowly manfion find !   400
   He fpoke.   The chief his anfwering mind addrefs'd---
If foft compaffion warm thy friendly breaft,
Oh hear ! nor fpurn a dying brother's prayer !
Let Samlah's tender years thy pity fhare !
Oh may a fire, a bride, thy bofom move !   405
The charms of beauty, and the calls of love !
Thus the kind youth, and fainting, as he cried,
He liv'd for Samlah, and for Samlah died.
So frown'd dread night on Abraham's fatal plain,
When thou, Montgomery, pride of chiefs, waft flain.
Spare, fons of freedom ! fpare that generous tear ;   411
To heaven refign, nor name the doom fevere---
Great, brave, and juft, to ward Columbia's fhame,
He hunted toil, in fields of growing fame ;
Alive, fair Victory ne'er forfook his fide ;   415
He liv'd in triumph, and in glory died.
Still bards fhall fing, to earth's remoteft clime,
He bled for all, and every heart for him.
   Glued to his fide, t' untimely fate a prey,
There bright Macpherfon breath'd his life away.   420

Round the fair youth in vain soft graces glow'd,
And science charm'd him to her sweet abode;
In vain fond parents hop'd his steps again,
And worth approv'd, and realms admir'd, in vain.
Yet patriot virtue writes the glory high,   425
With such a chief, in such a cause, to die.

Soft spoke the chief---O youth! thy virtuous bloom
Ask'd a lot milder, and a later tomb.
Is there no blissful seat, by Heaven assign'd
To the fair efforts of a clouded mind?   430
To life well-acted, can no grace supply
A sweet remission, and a happy sky?
But thou, base coward, claim'st th' avenging sword;
Could'st thou look on, and see thy brother gor'd?
That best of brothers, whose concluding breath   435
Restrains the falchion, and delays thy death?
Pale Samlah heard, and o'er th' embodied wall
He rush'd, regardless of his brother's fall,
From rank to rank with panting breast he flew,
Where the war open'd, and the coursers drew;   440
Behind, fierce Irad drove his dreadful way,
And left at distance far the pallid ray;
Ten thousand spears around him pierce the gloom;
Ten thousand warriors rush to hastening doom;
Through the black ether smoky volumes flow,   445
And with brown light their skirts all-umber'd glow;
Far o'er conflicting trains the sheets descend;
The deep night thickens, and the shades extend.
There Uzal brave a stubborn fight maintain'd,
And crown'd with matchless strength, retreat disdain'd:
Dan's mighty chief---On Ai's inglorious plain,   451
When vanquish'd Israel left their kindred slain,
His stiff, strong buckler brav'd the fierce affray,
Shelter'd the flight, and cover'd all the way.
Now, in the centre, shrill his armour rung,   455
Where the darts shower'd, and where the javelins sung,

Z

But ftill his dauntlefs footfteps onward drove ;
Nor throng'd battalions could thofe footfteps move.
On all fides round, a thoufand twilight forms
Invade the war, and ftrike their ringing arms ;   460
Here, 'gainft the chief, prepar'd to pierce his foe,
The lance unheeded aim'd the fatal blow ;
There, whilft the warrior liften'd to th' alarm,
High o'er his helmet hung th' uplifted arm.
Unnumber'd bucklers twinkle round the field,   465
In light now dreadful, now in fhades conceal'd.
Still more remote, involv'd in deeper gloom,
Where hands unnotic'd dealt the frequent doom,
Shelumiel fought ; the prince of Simeon's trains,
Fam'd in the contefts of a thoufand plains.   470
  Meantime, dark Hazor's fons to battle roll'd,
And vaft Madonians, wrapp'd in barbarous gold :
Thefe, with their leaders, near the dreadful ray,
Whirl'd the fwift car, and drove their rapid way.
There, drefs'd in gold, tremendous Jabin fhone,   475
And wing'd the terrors of his moving throne.
He Hazor's realms with mighty fceptre fway'd,
And his proud nod unnumber'd hofts obey'd.
A genius vaft, with cool attention join'd,
To wifdom fafhion'd his fuperior mind :   480
No fcene unnotic'd 'fcap'd his fearching view ;
The arts of peace, and arts of war, he knew ;
To no kind wifh, or tender tear, a prey ;
But taught by keen difcerament equal fway :
Intereft, of all his life th' unfhaken guide,   485
Unmov'd by paffion, and unmov'd by pride.
He firft, inventive, to the wafte of war
Led the tall fteed, and drove the dreadful car.
To arms, beneath the ftandard, veterans train'd,
And every movement, every feint, explain'd :   490
Clofe, left his conduct watchful chiefs fhould arm ;
Slow to decide, and vigorous to perform ;

BOOK VII.

With firm, fierce bravery forc'd his foes to fly,
And gave one law---to conquer, or to die.
   Now his great mind, by long succeffes fir'd,   495
To matchlefs fame, and fingle rule, afpir'd ;
In the fame caufe, beneath his banner join'd,
His voice, his art, this countlefs hoft combin'd,
In night's concealing hour, prepar'd th' affray,
And promis'd triumph, ere the dawning ray.   500
High in his flame-bright car his fpear he rais'd ;
A crimfon glory from his armour blaz'd ;
Conquer, he cried, or fall, ye dauntlefs bands,
The nobleft heroes of a thoufand lands.
Shall this brave hoft to Ifrael yield the night ?   505
Few in their numbers ; timorous in the fight---
Shall we, inglorious, blot our ancient fame ?
Forbid it virtue, and forbid it fhame.
Lo here the man, ye chofe to guide your path,
Prepar'd for glory, or prepar'd for death ;   510
This arm fhall guide you through the daftard band ;
Firft in the fight, as firft in fway, I ftand.
   He fpoke, and fiercely wing'd his rapid car ;
As fierce the fquadrons rufh to glorious war ;
All dropp'd the javelin : all the falchion wheel'd ;   515
A copious flaughter drench'd the glimmering field ;
From their dire arms a fearful fplendor came,
And o'er their faces wav'd the gloomy flame.
Hand join'd to hand, the vengeful thoufands rag'd ;
Man challeng'd man, and fword with fword engag'd ; 520
The victors rufh'd ; the pierc'd in anguifh cried ;
No flight ; no fear ; they conquer'd, or they died ;
For Ifrael's dauntlefs fons maintain'd the field,
And chief with chief the dread affault repell'd ;
Round the wild region mingled horrors reign'd ;   525
Nor thofe would yield, nor thefe the victory gain'd.
   Firft, in the van, imperious Jabin's car
Bore down whole troops, and broke the thickening war.

BOOK VII.

High o'er the reſt his dreadful voice was heard ;
High o'er the reſt his lofty form appear'd ; 530
His ſhield, a crimſon moon, before him ſpread,
And o'er his viſage hovering horrors play'd ;
His ſteeds, like rapid winds, impatient flew ;
His ſword the firſt, his ſpear the diſtant, ſlew ;
Round the dark chariot countleſs weapons hung, 535
And groans, with ſullen murmur, ceaſeleſs rung ;
Rank after rank he turn'd to hated flight,
And joyful Hazor throng'd the ſtubborn fight.

Before this dreadful path, two heroes ſought,
And warm'd with vengeance, countleſs wonders wrought.
Sons of one ſire, that in the deſert fell, 541
When impious Korah bade the hoſt rebel.
The helpleſs orphans genbrous Caleb bred,
In arms inſtructed, and to combat led.
With mutual flame their friendly boſoms lov'd ; 545
In peace together liv'd, in war together mov'd.

Now, ſide to ſide, the manly heroes ſtood,
And ſable torrents from their falchions flow'd ;
When Shammah thus---thou beſt of friends, behold
Yon heathen's car, in gloomy terror roll'd. 550
How his fierce courſers wing their rapid way !
How his keen falchion cleaves the yielding prey !
Say, ſhall our force the mighty Chief defy,
His arm experience, and his falchion try ?
Or death, or triumph, ſhall the deed await ; 555
And what is death, in Iſrael's dubious fate ?

To prove fierce danger for his maker's laws,
And proffer life to ſave his country's cauſe,
Thou know'ſt, brave chief, Seraiah quick replied---
The good man's duty, and the brave man's pride. 560
He ſpoke, and fiercely plunging thro' the war,
Hew'd a wide path, and burſt upon the car,
Nor Shammah ſtay'd. On Jabin's ſpacious ſhield
His rapid lance Seraiah's hand impell'd ;

Thro' the thick orb the point no paffage found, 565
Its fhade dark-quivering in the flamy round.
With a fhort flafh, acrofs the thickening air
The furious Heathen drove the greedy fpear;
Swift on Seraiah's helmet funk the fteel;
His red arms rang; the hero groan'd and fell. 570
With pangs, bold Shammah faw his brother's doom,
And wheel'd his fiery falchion thro' the gloom;
From Jabin's hand a fecond javelin fped,
Sung thro' his ear, and pierc'd his gufhing head;
Shrill rofe the conqueror's fhout; and all around 575
The plains remurmur, and the woods refound.

Now, more remote from Ai's decreafing light,
Slow mov'd a giant to the dreadful fight.
As when dun fmoke, o'er all th' horizon fpread,
Pours round the fetting moon a crimfon fhade, 580
Diftain'd with blood, her broad, and dreadful eye
Looks death, and ruin, from the fhuddering fky:
So gleams the circuit of his flame-bright fhield,
And cafts wide terror thro' the quaking field,
A beam-like fpear commands his horrid way, 585
And all, before him, fhun the dire affray.

And now fierce Ifrael's fons, with fad furprize,
To find brave Irad turn'd their boding eyes.
Far round they gaz'd; his form no more appear'd;
They liften'd; but his voice no more was heard. 590
Then every bofom fudden fears appal;
Their nerves all ftiffen, and their falchions fall;
A timorous fight their frozen hands fuftain,
And fighs, and backward looks, confefs their pain.
With fhouts of triumph, fwift the Heathens roll'd, 595
And a bright terror flafh'd from flamy gold;
A thoufand moony fhields before them burn'd;
Ranks fell at once, and troops to flight were turn'd;
Each fatal ftep increas'd the piles of flain,
And boundlefs ruin ravag'd all the plain. 600

As when a storm in midnight pomp extends,
And a broad deluge on the world defcends,
From fteep to fteep, difdaining every goal,
Swell'd with hoarfe thunders, mountain-torrents roll ;
The vales all echo to the dreadful found ; 605
The torne rocks roar ; the cracking trees refound.

 Meantime bold Irad far had crofs'd the fight,
And Samlah vanifh'd with aufpicious flight :
Round the dread region gaz'd the Youth ferene,
And eyed the grandeur of the folemn fcene. 610
Unnumber'd phantoms crowd the dufky war ;
The half-feen hero, and unfinifh'd car :
Black were the fhades, as midnight in the tomb,
And floating glimmerings fpread a fearful gloom.
Now roll'd the diftant cries an awful found ; 615
Now nearer clamors fhook th' embattled ground.
At once, from weftern fields, a fhout afcends ;
The plains all tremble, and the concave rends :
Quick turn'd the chief, while fad alarms infpire,
And faw dark forms, that pafs'd along the fire ; 620
Slow tow'rd the camp the fhouting fquadrons move,
And long pale fpires tremendous wave above.

 Ah wretch ! he cried---to childifh heat a prey !
How foon wild paffion drove my fteps aftray !
What chief, lefs vain, fhall lay th' increafing fear ? 625
Who cheer the bands, my prefence ought to cheer ?
Ah ! fhould difgrace, and dire defeat, enfue,
No more this guilty face fhall Jofhua view ;
Thefe eyes ne'er open on a hoft undone,
But death, or glory, by this arm be won. 630

 Thus as he fpoke, he crofs'd the deep array ;
To his known form they yield an eafy way :
Red flafh his arms ; and high above the field,
Gleams the drear luftre of his orbed fhield.
So, pale, and dreadful, thro' the midnight fhade, 635
Sails a broad meteor o'er the mountain's head :

Dim rife the cliffs; and on the kindling air,
Stream the long terrors of its fanguine hair.
His voice refounding thro' the gloomy fight,
Reviv'd their strength, and turn'd th' increafing flight.
Fly, daftards, fly; defert your Maker's laws;   641
Your name difhonor; yield your country's caufe;
But come, ye friends of Ifrael's injur'd name,
Sons of the fkies, and heirs of deathlefs fame!
Know, round the diftant plains, by chiefs infpir'd,   645
By virtue prompted, and by vengeance fir'd,
Bold, manly warriors, never taught to yield,
Cleave their fell foes, and fweep the dufty field;
Let this bright pattern every breaft inflame;
Here lift your fwords, where Irad leads to fame.   650
   Thus every rank his voice invites to arms;
His prefence actuates; his example charms;
From band to band, with nimble courfe, he flies,
Wheels the long hoft, and wakes intenfer cries;
Thick flath the falchions; thick the javelins rain;   655
And fhooting banners tremble o'er the plain;
In every fcene, alert, the youth appears;
Each chief, each rank, his cry with tranfport hears;
Shouts fiercely burfting liftening earth appall,
And hovering Conqueft yet fufpends her fall.   660
   And now bold Irad, thro' the thickeft war,
Drove the tall chief, and darkly rolling car,
When, lo! the giant full before him ftood,
Involv'd in death, and cover'd o'er with blood:
Like fome vaft wave, approach'd the horrid form,   665
Heedlefs of fpears, and raptur'd with the ftorm.
His wonderous fize th' admiring Youth beheld,
And fnatch'd a lance that glitter'd on the field;
Loud rang the weapon on the monfter's brow;
Backward he quick recoil'd, and bending low,   670
Stood ftaggering. Irad wav'd his dreadful fword,
Springing impetuous; fwift between them pour'd

Two gloomy chariots, of their lords defpoil'd,
And fierce around them thoufand heroes toil'd:
No more the chief could find his deftin'd prey,   675
But turn'd, and mingled in the fierce affray.

    Now loud, and folemn, thro' the roaring vales
Swell'd the hoarfe murmurs of the founding gales,
With deep confufion fhook the cliff's tall brow,
And rufh'd tempeftuous on the world below ;   680
From grove to grove the blaft impatient flies,
Rends the ftiff oak, and howls along the fkies,
On Ai's broad flames, with wild dominion, falls,
And pours ten thoufand thunders round her walls.
More wide, more bright, the folding fires afcend,   685
Heave the dun fmoke, and far in ether bend ;
The glittering brands, by rapid whirlwinds driven,
Stream, like dim meteors, o'er the blacken'd heaven ;
Swift through the woods red paths expanding roll ;
Long heavy volumes thicken round the pole ;   690
From all the concave fparks in torrents rain,
And fiery tempefts rufh along the plain.

    Far through the groves the furious flames had fpread,
And thoufand fires rofe fcatter'd in the fhade,
Ere Hazor's bands (fo eager rag'd the fight)   695
Beheld, with fad amaze, the fearful fight.
Then Jabin's voice, terrific, bade retire,
And the glad warriors fled the widening fire.
Ifrael purfued ; but Jabin's deathful arm
Whole troops repell'd, and brav'd the wafting ftorm : 700
With the fierce giant, o'er the rear he rofe,
And cool'd the vengeance of his ardent foes,
Then to the fight, that ftill, with dreadful fway,
Rent eaftern plains, brave Irad wing'd his way.
Part of the foes, that in the wood remain'd,   705
Had fled the heat, and fafe recefles gain'd ;
Part, lodg'd in open fields, maintain'd the war,
And fhouts rebellow'd tore the murmuring air.

BOOK VII,

Sudden, o'er all the bands, refounds a cry---
Fled are our friends ; we conquer, or we die :   710
Lo round the wood the kindling torrents burn ;
Fix here our ranks ; no warrior can return---
   Then fierce defpair the dauntlefs bofom fir'd,
Wing'd the keen falchion, and the arm infpir'd ;
The chiefs exhorted, threaten'd, fhouted, cried :   715
The ranks rufh'd onward, met the fteel, and died ;
For Ifrael's fons a movelefs fight maintain,
Glued to the field, and cleaving man to man ;
Brave Irad's dreadful voice the heroes arm'd,
Strung every nerve, and every weapon warm'd ;   720
On friend, and foe, alike the blind fword fell ;
And the fon funk beneath the parent's fteel.
Wild, and more wild, the ruin rag'd around ;   (ground ;
Shouts rung ; groans murmur'd ; thunders rock'd the
Through the rent concave rufh'd the loud acclaim,   725
Swell'd with the roaring wind, and fierce refounding flame.
At length a heathen's voice---Retire, retire,
Where yon black opening parts the raging fire---
Quick, at the found, along the glimmering fhade,
Thro' the wide foreft panting heroes fled,   730
In different courfes, where the moory ground
Cleft the deep blaze, and form'd a verdant mound.
Swift as the rapid blaft, the youthful train
Nimbly precipitated o'er the plain ;
On every fide, the flames. with wild career,   735
Roar'd near their path, and added wings to fear ;
None turn'd a gazing eye ; but, with blefs'd flight,
Stream'd thro' the grove, and fcap'd the vengeful light.
   Behind, his path pale age more flow dragg'd on.
And wifh'd, in vain, impending fate to fhun ;   740
Now here, now there, with feeble fteps, they turn'd ;
And here, and there, the fire terrific burn'd.
From tree to tree it flew ; and all around
The moulder'd pines, with hoarfely rufhing found,

Fell thundering. Kindled ruins hedg'd their path; 745
Behind them swift pursued the blazing death ;
Before, beside, and bending o'er their head,
The bright, and scorching splendors fiercely play'd ;
Weak, and more weak, the cries of anguish came,
Drown'd in the roaring fury of the flame. 750

To the dire forest Israel's sons pursued,
And heathen blood their reeking swords imbrued ;
Then by the chief's command return'd from fight,
Th' attentive squadrons eyed the wondrous sight,
Far sound the dreadful region, trees on high, 755
Wave their tall blazing summits in the sky ;
Thro' the dark air, in crimson terror, sail
Broad sheets of flame, and bend along the gale ;
Loud, and more loud, the raging whirlwind pours ;
From wood to wood the rushing deluge roars ; 760
Then, up vast eastern hills with fury driven,
Rolls o'er aerial cliffs, and kindles heaven :
The mountain groves, a long, long ridge of fire,
Shoot their tall flames, and thro' the clouds aspire.
O'er dim-seen rocks, brown plains, and glimmering streams
Floats the pale lustre of the trembling beams ; 766
The camp astonish'd casts a quivering gaze,
And distant towns are lost in dumb amaze :
Retir'd the squadrons, range in dread array,
And watch the splendors of approaching day.— 770

THE

CONQUEST of CANÄAN:

BOOK VIII.

ARGUMENT.

Morning. Joshua joins Irad. Jobab's character, and challenge. Irad accepts it, and kills Jobab. Battle. Irad kills Samlah, and engages Jabin. His death. Judah routed with great slaughter. Death of Uzal, and Shelumiel. Caleb, with a large division, marches out, rallies Judah, and renews the battle. Irad's death throws the whole army into confusion. Joshua inspirits them, and makes great havoc of the enemy. Zimri's exploits. He kills the king of the Hittites, and routs them. Joshua kills the king of Shimron, and routs the centre. Jabin, perceiving the other divisions of the army defeated, orders a retreat, which is performed with regularity. Joshua's lamentation over Irad. Scene of Selima's distress at the sight of his corpse. Evening.

The CONQUEST of CANÄAN.

BOOK VIII.

O'ER misty hills the day-star led the morn,
    And streaming light in heaven began to burn;
Wide scenes of woe the boundless blaze display'd,
Where the steel triumph'd, and the deluge spread.
On wasted plains unnumber'd corses lay,   5
And smokes far scatter'd climb'd upon the day,
Still clouded flames o'er eastern mountains rise,
And Ai's broad ruins sadden all the skies.
    When lo! in glimmering arms, and black array,
Like storms low-hovering in th' etheriatl way,   10
Far round the north a gloomy cloud ascends,
Its horror deepens, and its breadth extends.
Compact and firm, as mov'd by one great soul,
A front immense, the widening squadrons roll;
Thick shoot the spears; the trembling helmets beam,
And waving bucklers cast a moony gleam.   16
As the dire comet, swift through ether driven,
In solemn silence climbs the western heaven;
His sanguine hair, portending fearful wars,
Streams down the midnight sky, and blots the stars;   20
Pale death and terror light the dusky gloom,
And quivering nations read their sudden doom.

So in the flaming van great Joshua rose,
And shot red glories on the wondering foes.
At his command the trumpet sounded high,   25
Aerial ensigns dancing in the sky ;
Near and more near, they trac'd a dreadful way,
Join'd Irad's host, and stretch'd in long array.

    From Hazor's ranks that now before the wood,
In three embattled squares, refulgent stood,   30
Great Jobab strode.   In Madon's realms he reign'd :
Red was his eye, his brow with blood distain'd ;
A beam his spear ; his vast, expanded shield
Shot a bright morning o'er the crimson field ;
His head sublime a mighty helmet crown'd ;   35
His quivering plumes with sable horror frown'd ;
Six cubits from the earth, he rais'd his frame ;
His wish was battle, and his life was fame.

    Proud was his father ; prouder was the son :   39
Nought mov'd his pride ; the tear, nor piercing groan ;
Unmatch'd his force, he claim'd a matchless fame,
And every combat deck'd his brightening name.
Princes, his captiv'd slaves, before him bow'd,
Stalk'd in his train, and round his chariot rode ;
While their fair partners, first in triumph led,   45
Held the rich cup, or grac'd the brutal bed.
Oft had surrounding realms his aid requir'd,
Ere Zimri's hand Ai's hapless turrets fir'd ;
But still their prayers, and still their gifts were vain,
Till Joshua's glory rous'd his fierce disdain.   50
Else had no proffer mov'd his haughty mind,
That deem'd himself the champion of mankind,
When the joint wishes of the various band
To nobler Jabin gave the first command.
But Joshua's triumphs fill'd his anguish'd ear ;   55
Fir'd at the sound, he snatch'd the deathful spear,
Resolv'd at once to prove the hero's might,
And claim, alone, the wreaths of single fight,

'Twas he, when Irad rais'd his dreadful voice,
And inmoſt Hazor trembled at the noiſe, 60
When prudent Jabin urg'd a nightly ſtorm,
Ere the Youth's voice the ſlumbering camp ſhould arm:
Bade his vaſt ſquadrons in the wood delay,
Nor lift a ſpear, till morn ſhould lead the day.
Shall this brave hoſt th' unmanly path purſue, 65
Fight ambuſh'd foes, and baſely creep from view?
Shall Jobab, like the thief, to conqueſt ſteal,
And bravery call, what coward minds can feel?
And now, from Jabin the proud chief demands,
To lead, as firſt in place, the central bands. 70
He, coolly wiſe, reſigns the ſhadowy name,
And, pleas'd with ſubſtance, boaſts a nobler fame.
Forth from the hoſt, in freely pomp, he ſtrode,
And 'twixt th' embattled lines ſublimely ſtood.
His towering ſtride, vaſt height, and awful arms 75
Chill'd all his foes, and ſcatter'd wide alarms:
When thus the chief---Ye ſons of Iſrael know
The dauntleſs challenge of no common foe.
If in your hoſt three heroes can be found,
(Be Joſhua one) to tempt this dangerous ground, 80
Here ſhall they learn what ſtrength informs the brave,
And find no God can ſhield them from the grave.
Stung with the inſult caſt upon his God,
To the great Leader Irad nimbly ſtrode,
And thus---Shall yonder heathen's haughty cry 85
Dare Iſrael's hoſt, and Iſrael's God defy?
Let me this boaſter whelm in inſtant ſhame,
Avenge my nation's cauſe, my Maker's name.
Exalted Youth! the ſmiling Chief replied,
This elder arm ſhall crop his towering pride. 90
Scarce in thy breaſt has manhood fix'd her ſeat;
Blot not thy bloom, nor urge untimely fate.

Line 60) See Book 7, Line 165.

Brave as thou art, his ſtrength muſt win the fight,
And Iſrael's glory ſink in endleſs night.

 Think not, he cried, of Irad's tender age,   95
Nor heed the mockery of yon heathen's rage.
This hand, though young, ſhall boaſt a conquering day ;
Blind is wild rage, and pride an eaſy prey.
Here too ſhall Joſhua's potent prayers be given,
And the bleſs'd aid, that Virtue hopes from Heaven. 100
Should Irad periſh, none the wound ſhall know ;
Should Joſhua fall, our race is whelm'd in woe :
Heaven gave his choſen to thy guardian care,
To rule in peace, to ſave in dangerous war ;
On thee alone our fates ſuſpended lie,   105
With thee we flouriſh, and with thee we die

 Oh beſt of youths ! provoke not haſty doom,
Nor ruſh impetuous to an early tomb.
I lov'd thy ſire, the good, the juſt, the brave---
And ſhall this voice conſign thee to the grave? 110
Swift thy name ripens into matchleſs praiſe ;
My ſon, my choſen, ſtill prolong thy days.
In future fields thy arm ſhall brighter ſhine ;
Thine be the glory, but the danger mine.

 Ah grant my wiſh ! th' impatient Youth replies, 115
While two full tears ſtand gliſtening in his eyes---
This arm, unhurt, ſhall bid the monſter bleed ;
Angels will guard my courſe, and Heaven ſucceed.
My ſpear, when night her lateſt darkneſs ſpread,
Had ſunk him breathleſs in the field of dead ; 120
But ſome kind ſpirit ſav'd his life, till morn
Should grace the fight, and Irad's name adorn.
Aid me, oh aid me, Hezron's every friend !
Your voice, your wiſhes, muſt the Leader bend.

 Won by his earneſt cries, the generous Chief 125
Forc'd his conſent ; but could not hide his grief.
A ſigh ſteals ſilent from his bleeding breaſt,
As his ſlow tongue permits the ſad requeſt.

Wrapp'd in bright arms, while smiles his joy reveal'd,
The Youth stalk'd fearless o'er the horrid field ;   130
The host, with rapture, view'd his lofty stride,
The leap alert, the port of conscious pride ;
But each grave chief, by long experience wise,
With faltering accent, to his comrade cries---
I fear, I fear, lest, on the bloody sand,   135
The bold Youth perish, by yon monster's hand.
What bravery can, fair Irad will perform,
But can the opening floweret meet the storm ?
Ah, that such sweetness, such etherial fire
Should fall, the victim of a heathen's ire !   140
Thy votary's course, all-gracious Heaven, survey !
Let some kind angel hover round his way !
    Now near the scene bold Irad urg'd his course,
Where Jobab triumph'd in resistless force ;
When the huge warrior, swell'd with angry pride,   145
With bended brow, and voice contemptuous, cried---
Art thou the champion of thy vaunting race ?
Shall this poor victory Jobab's falchion grace ?
Go, call great Joshua, long to war inur'd,
Whose arm hath toils, whose skill hath hosts endur'd, 150
With him, ten chiefs ; this hand shall crush them all ;
Shame stains the steel, that bids a stripling fall ;
Retire, ere vengeance on thy helmet light ;
Fly to yon troop, and save thy life by flight.
    His haughty foe the Youth undaunted heard ;   155
Vain, empty threats his bosom never fear'd ;
O'er the vast form he turn'd his smiling eyes,
And saw unmov'd the livid vengeance rise.
Then, with a rosy blush of conscious worth,
Calm from his tongue his manly voice broke forth--- 160
Do threats like these become a hero's voice ?
Can courage find a vent in empty noise ?
To every brave man give the well-earn'd praise,
Nor think on scoffs a bright renown to raise ;

B b

True bravery claims a noble generous fame ;　　165
But the base wretch from vaunts expects his name.
Let shame, let truth, those coward words recall ;
Thou seek'st my life ; I glory in thy fall.
To me thy pride to me thy threats are vain ;
Heaven sees alone whose arm the prize shall gain.　　170
And know, wheree'er may light his angry rod,
I fear no boaster that defies my GOD.
　　Now shield to shield, and lance to lance, they stand ;
With taunts imperious shout the heathen band ;
While hopeless Israel heaven with prayer assails,　　175
And grateful incense fills the rising gales.
Stung by the just reproof, with whizzing sound
The giant plung'd his javelin in the ground :
For passion, ever blind, impell'd his arm,
Steer'd a wild course, and sav'd the youth from harm;　180
He, calm and fearless, with a pleas'd surprise,
Survey'd its curious form and mighty size ;
Then 'gainst his foe, with sure, unerring eye
Drove the swift lance, and lodg'd it in his thigh.
Enrag'd, the warrior saw his bubbling gore,　　185
Writh'd with keen anguish, and the javelin tore.
The flesh pursued ; a copious, sable stream
Pour'd from the wound, and stain'd the steely gleam ;
Then high in air he shook his sunlike shield,
And wav'd his falchion o'er th' astonish'd field.　　190
With matchless force the vengeful weapon fell ;
The wary hero nimbly shunn'd the steel ;
And while his foe with foaming fury cried,
Oft pierc'd his arm, and wounded oft his side.
Wild, and more wild, the giant's strokes resound,　　195
Glance from the shield, and plough the cleaving ground ;
Till, gathering all his strength for one vast blow,
Dark as a storm, he rushes on his foe ;
Lightly the hero springs ; the monster falls,
Like sudden ruins of a turret's walls ;　　200

BOOK VIII.

Full on his neck defcends the gladfome blade,
And from the trunk difparts the grifly head.

Loud fhouts of joy, from Ifrael's thoufands driven,
Burft o'er the plain, and fhook the walls of heaven:
Amaz'd the heathens faw their champion loft,   205
And a wide, fullen groan was heard from all the hoft.

Alert, bold Irad feiz'd the giant's fhield,
His fword, his fpear, and bore them thro' the field;
At Joshua's feet, with felf-approving fmiles,
He caft the grandeur of the glittering fpoils;   210
The hoary warriors gather'd round his way,
And gaz'd and wonder'd at the curious prey;
Then blefs'd the chief, with tranfport in their eyes,
And own'd th' affiftance of aufpicious Skies;
While youths unhappy rais'd lefs ardent prayers,   215
And wifh'd the deed, and wifh'd the glory, theirs.

Led by foft impulfe tow'rd th' imbattled train,
Rov'd fad Selima down the fpacious plain.
Afar fhe ftood, and caft an anxious eye,
And ftrove in vain her favourite to defcry.   220
At once, with diftant din, the fhouts afcend,
And painful fears her tender bofom rend;
Slow tow'rd the camp her lingering fteps inclin'd;
But oft the fair-one caft a look behind.

Now the long thunders of the clarion found,   225
Reclam'd from hills, and plains, and groves around,
O'er the dire field the rufhing fquadrons driven,
Extend their fhady files, and blacken heaven:
High in the central front great Joshua ftands,
And fhoots wide terror thro' th' aftonifh'd bands;   230
Mid eaftern thoufands Zimri towers along,
And Irad fhines before the western throng.

Unfurl'd, the fudden banners ftream afar,
And, wrapp'd in thunder, joins the dreadful war;
Wide roll the volumes of the duft around,   235
And clouds on clouds envelope all the ground.

As floods, increas'd by long defcending rains,
Pour a brown deluge o'er the wintery plains,
Loud from a thoufand hills, the torrents join,
Where azure bonds the river's courfe confine ;   240
The maddening ice, in boundlefs ruin driven,
Burfts, like the thunders of a falling heaven ;
The white rocks foam ; the gloomy blafts arife,
Tofs the wild ftream, and roar along the fkies.
So clos'd the fquadrons of th' unnumber'd foes ;   245
So ftormy fhouts and hollow groans arofe.

    Long in an even ballance hung th' affray,
Nor thofe would loofe, nor thefe could gain, the day.
'Till Irad's rapid path, like heaven's red fire,
Shot through the ranks, and bade the foe retire ;   250
With joy, their chief furrounding warriors view,
And troops on troops the generous courfe purfue.

    At diftance fmall, proud Samlah's glittering car,
Whirl'd by white courfers, tempts the grifly war ;
O'er all the plain, with piercing found, arife   255
His ftern injunctions, and his conquering cries.
With fhouts bold Irad darts along the field,
Now bright in arms, and now in duft conceal'd,
From rank to rank the well-known chief purfues,
And oft his flafhing fteel in blood imbrues.   260
Vain, impious wretch, he cried, thy nimble flight,
And vain the covert of furrounding might.
Once haft thou fled the fwift-purfuing fpear,
But fled'ft in vain, for vengeance finds thee here.
Learn from this hand what fate betides the knave,   265
Who yields, unmov'd, a brother to the grave.
If now thy feet efcape the righteous doom,
Let Heaven protect thee to a peaceful tomb !

    In dread amaze aftonifh'd Samlah ftood ;
From his pale face retir'd the freezing blood ;   270
His wild eye ftar'd , all briftling rofe his hair ;
Quick from his quivering hand the ufelefs fpear

BOOK VIII.

Dropp'd ; his teeth rattled, and the falling reins
At random trembled on the coursers' manes ;
Behind he gaz'd, and found no path to fly ;   275
For aid he panted, but no aid was nigh.
Deep in his back was lodg'd the fatal steel ;
His breathless form, before the rolling wheel,
Plung'd headlong ; mournful rung a pitying groan,
So fair, so mild his beauteous aspect shone :   280
Even Irad, touch'd by Adnor's kind request,
Felt soft emotions stealing through his breast.

    Then swift he wheel'd the lightening of his sword ;
Behind him, Judah's host like torrents pour'd ;
Shrill rose the tumult of the fields around,   285
Trembled through heaven and wav'd along the ground :
With souls undaunted, both the hosts contend ;
Spears fill the air, and shouts the concave rend.

    Far distant, Joshua moves his awful form,
Swells the confusion, and directs the storm.   290
Beyond him, Zimri, swift as rapid fire,
Darts through the fight, and bids the foe expire.
A mingled horror clouds the dreadful plain ;
Here rush the fighting, and there fall the slain.

    Now the mid sun had finish'd half his course,   295
When Irad raging with resistless force,
And far before him breathing wide dismay,
On Jabin's chariot drove his rapid way.
Brave youths around him throng'd the crimson fight,
Eyed the bless'd chief, and smil'd a fierce delight ;   300
From every sword increasing vengeance fell,
And Death sate hovering o'er the sanguine steel.
Thron'd in proud state, the savage Monarch rode ;
Like two red stars his wrathful eye-balls glow'd ;
Hoarse from his voice a dreadful thunder came,   305
And his bright armour flash'd a sudden flame.
Two steeds, bedropp'd with gore, and pale to view,
Emblems of death, his smoaking chariot drew.

Cheer'd by his hand, the coursers swiftly sprang;
Beat by their hoofs, the brazen bucklers rang;   310
Tow'rd Irad's path the heathen wing'd his way,
And, boding conquest, snuff'd the fancied prey.

  Unmov'd, th' angelic Youth, with wearied hands
Pav'd his red path, and drove the circling bands---
Stay, lovely hero! stay; thy course forbear;   315
Enough that sword has rul'd the glorious war---
Ah stay, till Israel's sons thy steps surround;
Return, return, and be with glory crown'd!

  Great Jabin stood, and o'er the bloody field
Rais'd the broad terrors of his flaming shield;   320
His grimly brow, all blacken'd o'er with dust,
Frown'd like a storm, and froze the trembling host;
Near beauteous Irad stream'd the sounding car,
And opening squadrons yield the dreadful war.

  The foaming Chief, serene the Youth beheld,   325
And rear'd his javelin o'er the purple field;
Shrill sung the lance along the dusty sky,
Bor'd the strong shield, and pierc'd the Monarch's thigh.
Enrag'd, to earth the haughty Warrior sprang;
His red eyes flam'd; his arms descending rang;   330
With lofty action, each his hand uprais'd;
The falchions flash'd; aghast the squadrons gaz'd;
Two generous youths between them nimbly broke,
And bow'd their lives beneath the fatal stroke.
Their lovely heads (their helmets cleft in twain)   335
Died the keen swords, and spouted on the plain.
More fierce the Monarch's disappointed ire
Glow'd in his face, and blaz'd with gloomy fire.
In Irad, innocence serenely mild,
And beauty's sweetness with soft splendor smil'd;   340
Round his fair forehead beams of bravery play,
Nor stain'd with rage, nor mingled with dismay.

  Again in ether rose the dreadful steel;
Again it lighten'd, and again it fell;

The Heathen's, ringing, leap'd from Irad's shield;
The Youth's in fragments, treacherous, strew'd the field.
Held by a chief, swift-leaping from the band,
A second falchion touch'd his reaching hand,
When---lovelieſt Youth! why did thy buckler's bound
Shield but thy breaſt? why not thy form ſurround?   350
Where ſtood thy friends? was no kind hero near,
To guard thy life, and ſtay Selima's tear?---
From ſome baſe arm unſeen, in covert flung,
Through his white ſide a coward javelin ſung,
He fell---a groan ſad-murmur'd round the hoſt,   355
Their joy, their glory, and their leader loſt.
    Forth from the train a youth impatient ſprung,
Spread his fond arms, and round the hero clung,
With ſoft endearments ſtay'd the fleeting breath,
And wiſh'd to ſave him from the hand of death.   360
But Jabin's ſword, driven through his friendly ſide,
Stain'd his white armour with a ſpotleſs tide:
In kind imbrace their heaving boſoms lay,
And all life's blooming beauty died away.
Through fields of air, their ſocial ſpirits join'd   365
Wing'd their light way, nor loſt a look behind;
While two bright forms, on roſy pinions borne,
Sail'd round their path, and op'd the gates of morn.
    Mid countleſs warriors Irad's limbs were ſpread,
Even there diſtinguiſh'd from the vulgar dead.   370
Fair as the ſpring, and bright as riſing day,
His ſnowy boſom open'd as he lay;
From the deep wound a little ſtream of blood
In ſilence fell, and on the javelin glow'd.
Grim Jabin, frowning o'er his hapleſs head,   375
Deep in his boſom plung'd the cruel blade;
Foes, even in death, his vengeance ne'er forgave,
But hail'd their doom, inſatiate as the grave;
No worth, no bravery could his rage diſarm,
Nor ſmiling love could melt, nor angel-beauty charm.

With dreadful found, he rais'd his voice on high, 381
Froze the pale bands, and thunder'd thro' the sky--
Hafte, warriors, hafte ; your conquering arms difplay;
Here gafps their leader, to the dogs a prey.
See the flaves fly ; ere evening's dufky hour, 385
The beafts fhall rend them, and the hawks devour.
Receive, illuftrious Oran ! here receive
The poor, the fole reward, thy prince can give.
This victim firft ; a nation foon fhall come
To pay due honours at thy facred tomb, 390
Wide ftreams of gore in rich libations flow,
And fhades unnumber'd wait thy call below.
Here, daftards, here the worthlefs carcafe yield,
Nor wait the vengeance of a future field.
To day this raptur'd hand your camp fhall burn, 395
And fires, and wives, and fons to mingled afhes turn.

　　Thus fpoke the haughty Chief: with flafhing eyes,
To fiercer fight infpir'd the warriors rife ;
Clouds after clouds in gloomy pomp afcend,
And ftormy clamours troubled ether rend. 400
The thickening tempeft Judah's hoft furvey'd,
And wedg'd their volumes in the dufty fhade ;
Man lock'd with man, and helm with helm combin'd,
And fword with fword in glimmering order join'd,
A long dread front, impervious, hides the fields, 405
Cloth'd with the grandeur of a thoufand fhields.

　　Firft, in the flaming van to vengeance rofe
Bold Irad's train, and dar'd their ardent foes.
Their young, brave minds immortal fame infpires ;
Each glowing thought the patriot's virtue fires ; 410
Serene they fmil'd to fee the ruin nigh ;
In death they triumph'd, but they fear'd to fly.

　　O'er the dark deep, as fome tall wave impends,
Its white foam hiffes, and its point afcends ;
'Gainft hoary rocks the burfting ruins roar, 415
Shake all the main, and echo round the fhore,

BOOK VIII.

So Jabin's car with gloomy terror flew,
And crufh'd the ranks that near him rafhly drew;
Roll'd in one mighty mafs, the heathen force,
The fwift-wing'd chariot, and the foaming horfe,   420
O'er all the lovely band refiftlefs fly,
And countlefs warriors round their Irad die.
Thus, on the ftream's fair bank in beauty rife
Young, towering trees, and feel indulgent fkies;
In fpring's mild beam their lovely boughs afpire,   425
Wave o'er the flowers, and call the plumy choir:
At once the floods defcend, the torrents roar;
The trees lie withering on the wafted fhore.

    All firmly brave, imbrown'd with duft and blood
'Gainft the rude tempeft Judah's veterans ftood;   430
Fix'd, even to death, their nation to defend,
With ftout, ftiff ftrength, the ftubborn ranks contend;
To fate undaunted many a hero fprings.
The fhouts redouble, and the concave rings.
Full in the front brave Uzal movelefs ftood,   435
His falchion reeking with inceffant blood;
Fight, warriors, fight, or fall---he faid, nor more;
But wheel'd his arm, and ftepp'd in floods of gore;
Above his feet the purple torrents ran,
And high before him man was pil'd on man.   440
So thick the fwords around his helmet hung,
That fword clave fword; aloud his armour rung;
Panting he ftood; in floods the fweat diftill'd:
Nor moves the Hero, nor the fquadrons yield.

    From his bright car, that rattling pour'd along,   445
With fhouts, and threatnings, Jabin fir'd the throng;
Man leap'd o'er man: from every fide they rufh'd;
Bold warriors fell, by other warriors crufh'd;
'Till, hurl'd by Jabin's hand, a javelin flew,
Pierc'd Uzal's heart, and life's fair current drew,   450
Pleas'd, the great hero gave his parting breath;
My nation own'd my life, and now demands my death.

Thus hung with wounds, a prey to favage steel,
In Princeton's fields the gallant Mercer fell.
When first his native realm her sons decreed,   455
In flavery's chains, with want and woe to bleed,
Check'd, through his bosom fond remembrance ran.
The cause of freedom was the cause of man.
In that fair cause he bar'd his manly breast,
The friend, the hope, the champion, of th' oppress'd,
From height to height on glory's pinions rose,   461
Bless'd by his friends, and prais'd by generous foes;
Swift flew the shaft; the eagle ceas'd to rise,
And mourning millions trac'd him down the skies.

He fell; the throng, that press'd against his shield, 465
Plung'd in one heap, and spread along the field;
Bucklers on bucklers rang; steel clash'd on steel;
Their own swords gash'd them, wounding as they fell.
In one broad ruin lay the mingled crowd,
And cries, and hollow groans were heard aloud.   470
So some tall prop, that bears extended walls,
Mouldering, gives way; the mossy structure falls,
The long beams thundering echo round the skies,
Earth shakes beneath, and clouds of dust arise.
Thus sunk the warriors, some to rise no more,   475
Some, nimbly bounding, bath'd their spears in gore.

Now haughty Jabin lifts a louder cry,
The tall hills echo, and the fields reply.
Fly, dastards, fly; death haunts your impious way;
Your proud name sinks; your squadrons swift decay: 480
Where now 's the chief, that led your hosts abroad?
Your far-fam'd bravery, and fictitious GOD?
Call the dread Power, that cleft th' Egyptian wave,
To mourn your fate, and ope your heads a grave.
Pour on, my heroes, while yon friendly light   485
Shines in the heaven, and joys to view the fight
He spoke, and onward wing'd his dreadful form;
Hazor behind him, like an evening storm,

That rides on gloomy blaſts above the hills,
And wakes the thunder of the mountain rills, 490
Roll'd blackening. Iſrael's ſons in ſad diſmay,
Bent tow'rd the camp their ſlow, unwilling way.

Enrag'd Shelumiel rais'd his angry voice,
But rais'd in vain; no hero heeds the noiſe:
Hoarſe with ſhrill cries, and wild with deep deſpair, 495
He ruſh'd reſiſtleſs on the thickeſt war,
From Jabin's lance a grateful exit found,
Sunk in his arms, and ſtiffen'd on the ground.

Far from the fight, deſpoil'd of helm and ſhield,
Slept beauteous Irad on the mournful field; 500
Deaf to the groans, and careleſs of the cries:
His hair ſoft-whiſtling o'er his half-ſhut eyes.
On either ſide his lifeleſs arms were ſpread,
And blood ran round him from the countleſs dead.

Even there, two warriors, ruſhing o'er the plain, 505
O'er crimſon torrents, and o'er piles of ſlain,
Stopp'd, when the lovely form aroſe to ſight,
Survey'd his charms, and wiſh'd no more the fight.

Ah! hapleſs Youth! cried one, with tender voice,
The Gods' fair offspring, form'd for milder joys! 510
A face like thine the gentleſt thoughts muſt move,
The gaze of Beauty, and the ſong of Love.
Sleep on, fair hero! for thy corſe muſt lie
Bare to the fury of a ſtormy ſky.

Thus he. His friend, by ſofter paſſions warm'd, 515
By grief afflicted, and by beauty charm'd,
Cries ſadly---No; for when my ſteps return,
This bleeding breaſt thy early fate ſhall mourn;
The melting ſong declare-thy hapleſs doom,
And my own hand erect thy head a tomb. 520

But now, outſpread o'er all the northern plain,
In ſable grandeur roll'd a countleſs train,
With trembling ſpears, with waving bucklers, bright,
And the quick gleams of interrupted light.

B O O K VIII.

When Joshua strode the heathen host to dare,   525
To guard the camp was prudent Caleb's care.
He, coolly wise, had summon'd all the train,
Dispos'd in ranks, and guided o'er the plain,
All arm'd for war, at distance meet to stay,
And wait the changes of the dreadful day,   530
In even scale while dubious combat hung,
And far in southern fields the tumult rung,
Silent, they listen'd to the blended cry,
And heard faint shouts in distant murmurs die.

But now th' approaching clarion's dreadful sound   535
Denounces flight, and shakes the banner'd ground ;
From clouded plains increasing thunders rise,
And drifted volumes roll along the skies.
At once the chief commands ; th' unnumber'd throng,
Like gathering tempests, darkly pour'd along :   540
High on the winds, unfurl'd in purple pride,
Th' imperial standard cast the view aside ;
A hero there sublimely seem'd to stand,
To point the conquest, and the flight command ;
In arms of burnish'd gold the warrior shone,   545
And wav'd and brighten'd in the falling sun.

Swift tow'rd the fight approach'd th' impatient throng,
And wider pour'd the thickening dust along ;
Loud, and more loud, victorious clamours grow,
And, more distinguish'd, breathe the sounds of woe ;   550
Pale Judah's sons a yielding fight maintain,
And many a face looks backward o'er the plain,
When Caleb's mighty voice, in thunder driven,
Starts all the host, and rends the clouded heaven.
What dismal scenes, enrag'd the hero cries---   555
Convulse this heart, and pierce these bleeding eyes !
Shall Judah's race, my brethren and my boast,
Flee, vanquish'd, driven, before a heathen host?
Can men, can warriors own so black a part,
The best of chiefs, your Joshua to desert ?   560

Say with what pangs will Heaven the wretches try,
That know no honour, and that feel no tie ?
On yon bright plain, the conquering Chief behold,
Troops wing'd before him, cars tumultuous roll'd,
With Heaven's imperial sword the fight commands, 565
And drives fierce ruin o'er decreasing bands !
Say, shall the Man, who fights, who bleeds for all,
See your base flight, and perish in your fall ?
The Chief, as angels kind, as angels true,
Sink in the doom, he warded long from you ? 570
Fly then ; but know, a few short furlongs past,
Yon camp wild flames, and savage swords shall waste ;
Besmear'd with streaming blood, your parents lie,
And, dash'd on stones, your gasping infants die ;
Your wives, betray'd by such base culprits, feel 575
Abuse, more dreadful than the griding steel ?
No arm, no sword the falling nation save,
But this dire evening ope our common grave.
Can these dread scenes even dastards fail to arm ? 579
Spring from the trance, and burst the sleepy charm ;
Rise, rise like men ; with shame, with vengeance burn ;
Wipe foul disgrace, and swift to fight return.
And ye brave chiefs, that never knew to yield,
Or turn a backward foot from glory's field,
But, led by me, the van's bright honours claim, 585
Smile at fair death, and shrink from torturing shame ;
Lift high th' avenging sword, from pity free,
And cleave the wretch that basely dares to flee.
  He spoke : the sound their manly bosoms fir'd,
Wheel'd their long ranks, and every arm inspir'd ; 590
Even cowards now to generous combat arm'd,
And fainting heroes with new vengeance warm'd :
Fierce Hazor's sons with equal fury driven,
Like one wide cloud, that shades the skirts of even,
Rush'd dark and dreadful : ranks, by ranks impell'd, 595
Felt the keen lance, and heap'd the streaming field.

Pois'd in a dire fufpenfe, the combat hung ;
Swords clafh'd, mail rattled, ftriking bucklers rung ;
Here his bold ranks great Caleb's arm infpir'd:
There Jabin's mighty hand his warriors fir'd :　　　600
No more the foaming fteeds could trace their way,
So thick the fquadrons wedg'd their black array :
Loud tumults roar, the clouded heavens refound,
And deep convulfions heave the labouring ground.

Meantime, great Jofhua, lightening o'er the plain,
Hedg'd his dire path with heaps of ghaftly flain ;　　606.
Back roll'd the fquadrons ; death's encircling fhade
Involv'd his courfe, and hover'd o'er his head.
At once a quivering voice fair Irad nam'd,
Announc'd his ruin, and the flight proclaim'd ;　　610
From ranks to trembling ranks, the mournful found
Wak'd a fad groan, and breath'd a gloom around,
With livid palenefs clouded every face,
Congeal'd each vein, and ftopp'd the growing chace.
On the far camp they turn'd a frequent view ;　　615
Their fainting falchions fcarce the fight renew :
Throng'd in a blackening ftorm, the foe defcends ;
Swift drive the chariots ; far the duft extends :
With fmiles, bold heathens hail commencing flight :
Their lances fhower ; their eye-balls flafh delight.　620
Loud as old ocean beats the rocky fhore,
Loud as the ftorm's deep-burfting thunders roar,
Vaft fhouts unrolling rend th' etherial round,
Trembles all heaven, and fhakes the gory ground.

Amaz'd, the Hero faw the wild defpair :　　625
Nor knew the caufe, 'till Irad fill'd the air ;
Irad, re-echoing with a fearful noife,
Pal'd the blank face, and froze the faltering voice.
Loud o'er the bellowing fhouts refounds his cry---
My fons, my heroes, whither will ye fly ?　　630
Will ye purfue the camp ? defert the flain ?
And leave your Irad on the bloody plain ?

BOOK VIII.

Alas! you fly to more tremendous fates;
There ruin feeks you, and bafe death awaits:
There, in fad horror, will your eyes behold   635
Flames round your camp, your wives, your children roll'd:
Let vengeance roufe, let Ifrael's name infpire,
Let danger fteel you, and let Irad fire,
Turn, turn, this inftant feals your final doom;
You gain the day, or fall without a tomb.   640

 He faid, and wav'd his broad, enfanguin'd fhield;
Turn, warriors, turn, refounds along the field;
A new-born bravery fires the meaneft foul:
Thick fpears protend; ranks lengthening onward roll:
Lefs loud fierce whirlwinds through the valley pour: 645
Lefs loud broad flames the fpiry town devour,
When, wing'd by blafts, red conflagrations rife,
Blaze in the cloud-capp'd towers, and fcorch the fkies,
Black drifts of duft fmoke through the vaft profound;
Shouts hoarfely rage, and hollow groans refound.   650
As, when through ether's fields dark ftorms are driven,
The fwift-wing'd flame, defcending, kindles heaven,
Scath'd by the dreadful ftream, the huge pines fall,
And burfting glory wraps the fmoking ball;
O'er the tall mountains rolls the voice of GOD,   655
The plains all tremble, and the forefts nod:
So fwift, fo bright, the rufhing hero pour'd;
With every ftroke his fword a life devour'd;
Full on his foes he bore refiftlefs ftorm,
Pale fquadrons opening to his angry form;   660
His fhield blaz'd horror, and his lofty hand
Fell, with fwift ruin, on the leffening band;
Gafh'd by his hand, the courfers burft their reins,
And hurl'd their riders on the bloody plains;
Gafh'd by his hand, the proftrate riders die;   665
Crack the round wheels, the fplendid trappings fly.

 Meantime, far eaftward Afher crouds the war,
Nor heeds the terrors of the rattling car.

Swift as on wings of fire a meteor driven,
Mounts o'er the hills, and sweeps the nightly heaven, 670
When the pale wanderer, lost in devious ways,
With bristling hair, starts at the sudden blaze,
Rush'd rapid Zimri through the parting host ;
Mark'd by his eye the hapless foe was lost ;
O'er quivering ranks his sword incessant hung ;   675
Loud in their ears his voice funereal rung
Death's hideous peal ; hard-following on the sound
Sunk the last stroke, and corses cloath'd the ground.
    Now while the Hittites fled the dire alarm,
Their haughty king withstood th' invading arm.   680
Shrill rose the thunders of his piercing cry,
Lost in deaf ears, and echoing through the sky ;
With swifter steps, his warriors urg'd their flight,
And dark behind them rush'd pursuing night.
Fierce on the king's bright car, with rapid force,   685
Resistless Zimri drove his dreadful course ;
The dauntless monarch cast his mighty spear,
That sung, and trembled through th' enlighten'd air ;
Full on brave Zimri's helm the polish'd steel
Clash'd harmless, and to earth, rebounding, fell.   690
Regardless of the shock, the nimble chief
Sprang to the car ; no sword could lend relief ;
Caught by his arm, the heathen beat the ground ;
Wide on his bosom sunk the fatal wound ;
The greedy blade, deep-plunging, gash'd his side,   695
And down his buckler pour'd a bubbling tide.
    Wing'd with fierce ardour, Zimri mounts the car,
And calls his heroes to the crimson war.----
Rush on to conquest, every generous band,
Lo the bless'd triumphs of this happy hand !   700
Here, through his side the sword indignant thrust,
Their furious leader, gasping, bites the dust.----
Fly, miscreants, fly, and let your lives remain
To grace the falchions of a future plain.

From dovelike foes what warrior hopes a name? 705
So cheap the purchafe, victory fcarce is fame.---
Thus, loud and taunting, rofe the hero's cry;
Swift rufh his bands; the heathen fwifter fly:
High in the chariot, in dread pomp reveal'd,
His gloomy hand the firey fteeds impell'd; 710
In dufty clouds the hofts are fnatch'd from fight,
And Death, and Zimri, darken o'er the flight.
  While thus brave Afher trod the conquering plain,
And drove wild ruin on the heathen train,
In the dire centre, to refiftlefs war 715
Proud Shimron's monarch urg'd the thundering car.
In early youth, he faw fierce Jabin's hand
Seize his fair crown, and rule his fertile land;
Then to the victor's court a captive brought,
In arms was train'd, in arts politic taught, 720
Won by foft wiles, his throne of Jabin held,
And bade his realm imperial tributes yield.
There, fir'd to glory by the monarch's voice,
He mock'd his pattern, and obey'd his choice,
And hop'd from conduct, form'd by rules fo juft, 725
Alone to reign, when Jabin flept in duft.
  Full on his lofty breaft the flafhing fhield
Gleam'd a bright terror through the clouded field:
As when the Sun, o'er fcorch'd Peruvia's plain,
Difeafe, and Death, and Horror in his train, 730
Unveils his crimfon face, diftain'd with blood,
Burns the brown hills, and fickens every flood.
Loud rang the hero's voice; his lances flew,
And every lance the foremoft warrior flew.
On him great Jofhua glanc'd a darkening eye, 735
And rufh'd impetuous, with a deathful cry:
His fword, fwift-circling, hew'd his difmal way,
Fell'd ranks at once, and broke the deep array.
Amaz'd, the heathen caft a look behind,
And thus in doubt, explor'd his mighty mind --- 740

D d

Shall I refifting dare that arm of death,
And reach his heart, or nobly yield my breath;
Or with fome diftant band the foe engage
Where bravery fails, and turn the battle's rage?
This arm, this fpear may fpill his hated life;   745
And O what wreaths fhall crown the happy ftrife!
What bright rewards fhall Jabin's hand beftow!
What matchlefs honours round my temples flow!
I claim the conteft--hence bafe flight and fhame--
To fight is glory, and to die is fame.   750

   He fpoke; while Ruin, riding thro' the plain,
Burft o'er his ranks, and mark'd her path with flain:
On Jofhua's helm fhe fate; tremendous hung
His arm on high, his voice like thunder rung:
Near the bright car he wheel'd his ftreaming blade,   755
And duft around him caft a night-like fhade.
Full on his buckler clafh'd the heathen's fpear,
Pierc'd the thick plates, and flafh'd behind in air;
Grazing his fide, it cut the folded garb,
And drops of crimfon ftain'd the polifh'd barb.   760
With joy, the king his faithful javelin view'd,
Leap'd from his car, and with his fword purfued.
Then Jofhua's hand uprear'd his falchion high,
Its flames bright-circling in the dufky fky;
Firft his foe's arm dropp'd on the bloody field;   765
The fecond ftroke divides his glittering fhield;
Full on his throat the fierce avenging blade
Sinks; the freed fpirit flits to midnight fhade.

   "Pour on to glory"--rung the Leader's voice,
The trembling hoft fhrunk backward at the noife;   770
Sad Shimron's fons beheld their monarch dead,
Rais'd one deep howl, and, wing'd with horror, fled.
Throng'd in a gloomy ftorm, their head-long foes
Round the dire flight with lifted falchions rofe;
Broad ftreams of blood o'er-ran the fcenes of death,   775
And fullen groans proclaim'd the parting breath.

BOOK VIII.

As boiling Etna rolls a flood of fire
Down her rough rocks ; and plains, and towns expire,
Lick'd by the flames, exhaling rivers rise,
And crumbling groves smoke upward to the skies,   780
Swift pours the blazing deluge on the shore,
The scorch'd main foams, the hissing billows roar :
So fierce and dreadful, flew the victor host,
In night involv'd, in dusty volumes lost.
Squadrons thick-strown were scatter'd o'er the fields, 785
And helms, and swords, and spears, and sanguine shields.
   Huge piles of slaughter gathering round his course,
On Shimron Joshua wing'd his mighty force.
Like two red flames his vivid eye-balls glow,
And shoot fierce lightenings on th' astonish'd foe ;   790
Before, expanded, his meteorous shield
Blaz'd a broad ruin thro' the stormy field ;
Round the wild war his flashing terrors fly ;
Cars burst before him ;---steeds, and heroes die.
So rush'd an angel down the midnight gloom,   795
When Egypt's first-born sunk in one broad tomb ;
High in dark clouds th' avenging Vision hung,
His path, like distant thunder, hoarsely rung ;
Flames shot before him, whirlwinds roll'd around,
Bow'd the tall hills, and heav'd the trembling ground.
Not with less terror blaz'd the Leader on ;   800
'Twas ruin all and one unbounded groan ;
None look'd behind, none turn'd a hearkening ear ;
Nor hills, nor streams impede the full career :
High o'er the ragged rocks they nimbly bound,   805
Dash thro' the floods, and scower the level ground :
First in the tumult, Youth impels his flight :
Springs o'er the field, and scapes pursuing night :
Pale Age with quivering limbs, and slow-drawn pace,
Feels the keen sword, and sinks beneath the chace.   810
   Far distant, Zimri, like a sweeping storm,
Grim in the chariot rais'd his gloomy form ;

Still on the hindmost fell his fateful sword;
Earth shook, air trembled, heaven with thunder roar'd
Oft, from the car descending to the plain,   815
He stream'd, like lightening, o'er the ghastly slain,
Then swiftly rose, and on the heathens sped,
His wheels dark-rolling o'er th' unnumber'd dead.

    Meantime, with all the rage of combat fir'd,
While throngs of warriors round his steps expir'd ; 820
While now, first disobedient to his call,
The balanc'd victory doubted where to fall :
While Caleb's arm with youthful vigor warm'd,
Sham'd Judah's thousands and their vengeance arm'd :
From rank to rank impatient Jabin flew,   825
Drove these with threats, and those with praises drew.

    But now the eastern plain loud thunders rend ;
The shrill cars rattle ; hoarser cries ascend ;
Progressive clouds, in thickening volumes driven,
Roll tow'rd the south, and shade the dusty heaven.   830
From the tall car the Chief survey'd the field,
And every circling scene at once beheld,
Even the far wood, with sudden flashes bright,
And the dire omens of tumultuous flight.
Around the war he cast a searching view,   833
Saw the day lost, and all its evils knew ;
Deep from his inmost soul burst forth a sigh,
And momentary sadness gloom'd his eye.
But soon his brow resum'd a cheerful grace,
And living ardour fir'd his artful face.   840
Full well the monarch knew that fears begun,
From breast to breast, like glancing lightenings, run ;
That one rank fled instructs a host to fly,
And cowards' eyes teach heroes' hearts to die---
Then, ere his friends the dire event divine,   845
Or Judah's sons their kindred victors join,
A wise retreat his mighty mind ordain'd,
And thus the rage of war his voice restrain'd.

Hear, all ye chiefs; brave Hazor's bands that guide,
Your nation's pillars, and your monarch's pride.   850
Your matchless deeds this raptur'd eye has told,
And fame's bright hand to diſtant years enroll'd.
But ſee, o'er weſtern hills the ſun's low fire
Cuts ſhort the day, and bids the hoſt retire.
Firm be your ranks, man faſt inlock'd with man,   855
The rear led onward, fix'd the generous van ;
At once let chief with chief inſpir'd combine,
And 'gainſt the foe extend th' embattled line ;
Brace firm the ſhield ; the moveleſs ſpear protend;
Join hand and heart, and every rank defend.   860
Your prince behold ; when Hazor claims the ſtrife,
My wounds are tranſport, and a toy my life.

   The hero ſpoke : as by one ſoul inſpir'd,
Swift to their well-known poſts the chiefs retir'd ;
At once, by banners rang'd, to brave the ſtorm,   865
Firm, dreadful lines th' experienc'd ſquadrons form.
Dire o'er the van-guard, ſhield with ſhield combin'd,
Spear lock'd with ſpear, th' undaunted leaders join'd ;
'Gainſt Judah's hoſt, with ridgy terrors bright,
Roſe a long wall, and flaſh'd a fearful light.   870
O'er the tremendous ſcene the Monarch's car
Pour'd death around, and rul'd the griſly war :
Fierce on the foe, where'er their ſteps purſue,
From rank to rank the mighty warrior flew ;
Hearts form'd of ſtubborn ſteel his deeds appall ;   875
The diſtant tremble, and the nearer fall ;
Till Caleb's voice commands the chace to ſtay,
And yields his foes an unmoleſted way.

   Then, ſtill and ſlow, while Judah's hoſt admir'd,
In gloomy ſtrength the ſullen ſtorm retir'd.   880
So, when in heaven propitious breezes riſe,
And on the deep the nimble veſſel flies,
Shagg'd with brown ſnades, that o'er the billows lower,
In grim, dark pomp recedes the clifted ſhore ;

Less seen, and less, the awful scenes decay,   885
And lost in blue confusion fade away.
  With gore all hideous, and with dust imbrown'd,
In the dire front terrific Jabin frown'd ;
His lifted arm prepar'd the fatal blow,
And menac'd vengeance to th' approaching foe.---   890
So, forward driven by earth's convulsive pangs,
The tall, hoar cliff in dubious terror hangs ;
High pois'd in dread suspense, its hovering brow
Lowers swift destruction on the world below :
Amaz'd, the swain, while sudden fears appall   895
Starts, as the tottering ruin seems to fall.
Enjoy, he cried, imperious foes, enjoy
The fancied triumph, combat shall destroy :
But know, ye boasters, soon this arm shall tear
The short-liv'd crown, your haughty temples wear ; 900
Soon your vain chiefs, your nation want a name,
And all your glories sink in endless shame.
  But now, sublime in crimson triumph borne,
The sacred standard mock'd th' etherial morn ;
Wide on the winds its waving splendors flow'd,   905
And call'd the warriors from the distant wood.
Behind great Joshua, Hazor's sons to dare,
Pour the bold thousands to the western war,
Beyond Ai's walls, the lessening heathen train
In well-form'd squadrons cross the distant plain ; 910
Part still in sight their shady files extend ;
Part fill the wood, and part the hills ascend ;
To cease from toil the prudent Chief commands,
And balmy quiet sooths the wearied bands.
  Half lost in mountain groves, the sun's broad ray 915
Shower'd a full splendor round his evening way ;
Slow Joshua strode the lovely Youth to find ;
Th' unwilling bands more slowly mov'd behind.
Soon as the matchless form arose to view,
O'er their sad faces shone the sorrowing dew ;   920

Silent they ftood. To fpeak the Leader tried,
But the choak'd accents on his palate died.
His bleeding bofom beat with inward pains,
And leaden languors ran along his veins.

Ah, beft and braveft of thy race! he faid,   925
And gently rais'd the pale, reclining head---
Loft are thy matchlefs charms, thy glory gone--
Gone is the glory which thy hand hath won.
In vain on thee thy nation caft her eyes;
In vain with joy beheld thy light arife;   930
In vain fhe wifh'd thy fceptre to obey;
Vain were her wifhes; vain the deftin'd fway.
Oh! Irad, lovelieft Irad, nature's pride!
Would Heaven, myfelf for thee, for thee had died!
Nor more; the thoughts lay ftruggling in his breaft; 935
But tears, expreffive tears forbade the reft.
Borne by fix chiefs, in filence, o'er the plain,
Fair Irad mov'd before the mournful train;
Great Jofhua's arm fuftain'd his fword, and fhield;
Th' afflicted thoufands lengthening thro' the field.   940
When, crown'd with flowers, the maidens at her fide,
With gentle fteps advanc'd great Caleb's pride.
Her fnowy hand, infpir'd by reftlefs love,
Of the lone wild-rofe two rich wreaths inwove;
Frefh in her hand the flowers rejoice to bloom,   945
And round the fair-one fhed the mild perfume.
O'er all the train her active glances rov'd;
She gaz'd, and gazing, mifs'd the Youth fhe lov'd;
Some dire mifchance her boding heart divin'd,
And thronging terrors fill'd her anxious mind.   950
As near the hoft her quickening footfteps drew,
The breathlefs hero met her trembling view;
From her chill'd hand the headlong rofes fell,
And life's gay beauty bade her cheeks farewell;
O'er her fair face unmeaning palenefs fate,   955
And, funk to earth, fhe felt no haplefs fate.

With anguiſh Caleb ſaw her fading charms,
And caught the favourite in his haſtening arms.
Reviv'd with piercing voice, that froze his ſoul,
She forc'd the big, round tear unwiſh'd to roll;   960
By all his love, beſought him ſoon to lead
Where cruel friendſhip ſnatch'd his lovely dead.
In vain the chief his anguiſh ſtrove to hide,
Sighs rent his breaſt, and chill'd the vital tide.

To Joſhua then, whoſe heart beſide her mourn'd,   965
With gaze of keen diſtreſs, the charmer turn'd.--
Oh, generous Chief, to miſery ever kind,---
Thou lov'ſt my ſire--ſupport his ſinking mind!
Thy friendly wiſh delights to leſſen woe---
See how his tears for fallen Irad flow!   970
He claims thy friendſhip---generous hero, ſee,
Loſt to himſelf, his fondneſs bleeds for me.----
To view the hapleſs Youth, diſtreſs'd he fears.
Would wound my ſoul, and force too copious tears.
But lead, oh lead me, where the Youth is borne!   975
Calm is my heart, nor will my boſom mourn---
So cold that heart, it yields no pitying ſigh---
And ſee no tear bedews this marbled eye.

She ſaid, and look'd reſiſtleſs; ſoft reclin'd
On Joſhua's arm, ſhe forc'd his melting mind.   980
Preſſing her hand, he trac'd a gentle way,
Where breathleſs Irad, loſt in ſlumbers lay.
From the pale face his chilling hand withdrew
The decent veil, and gave the Youth to view.
Fix'd o'er the form, with ſolemn gaze ſhe hung,   985
And ſtrong, deep ſighs burſt o'er her frozen tongue.
On Joſhua then ſhe caſt a wiſhful look;
Wild was her tearleſs eye, and rolling ſpoke
Anguiſh unutterable. Thrice ſhe tried
To vent her woes, and thrice her efforts died.   990
At length, in accents of ecſtatic grief,
Her voice bewilder'd, gave her heart relief.

BOOK VIII.

Is this the doom we dread ?---is this to die ?
To fleep ?---to feel no more ?---to clofe the eye ?---
Slight is the change---how vain the childifh fear,   995
That trembles, and recoils, when death is near ?
I too, methinks, would fhare the peaceful doom,
And feek a calm repofe in Irad's tomb.
This breath I know, this ufelefs breath muft fail,
Thefe eyes be darken'd, and this face grow pale--   1000
But thou art pale, oh Youth ! thy lot I crave,
And every grief fhall vanifh in the grave.

    She ceas'd, the tender chief without delay,
Soft preffing, kindly forc'd her fteps away.
Slow tow'rd the camp, with folemn pace, they drew ;
The corfe moves on ; the mournful bands purfue.   1006
Pale Uzal follows, virtuous now no more ;
And brave Shelumiel, black with clotted gore.
Unnumber'd tears their haplefs fate bewail,
And voice to voice refounds the dreadful tale.   1010
But Irad, matchlefs Irad, call'd in vain,
Breathes wide a folemn fadnefs round the plain :
Unhappy, to their tents the hoft retir'd,
And gradual ; o'er the mountains day expir'd.

THE

CONQUEST of CANÄAN.

BOOK IX.

ARGUMENT.

Evening. Interview between Selima and her parents. Morning. Diſtreſs of the Camp. Joſhua directs Zimri to bury the dead. Funeral of Irad. Burial of the dead. Hareſhab informs Joſhua of a combination of the ſurrounding nations againſt Gibeon, and ſolicits his aſſiſtance. Story of Elam and Mina. Hareſhab is directed to wait until the divine pleaſure ſhall be known. Evening. Joſhua walks out on the plain, northward of the camp, and hears Selima lamenting the death of Irad. Affected by the ſcene, he breaks out into a ſoliloquy on his diſtreſs, and is reproved by an angel, who delivers him a meſſage from the Moſt High, and directs him to prepare for a viſion of futurity.

THE CONQUEST OF CANÄAN.

BOOK IX.

NOW fober evening hung her curtains round,
    And gloomy fadnefs brooded o'er the ground.
All pale, and folemn, rofe the languid moon,
And fhed a feeble twilight from her throne.
Sad in her tent, the feeling maiden fate,   5
Fed on her woes, and figh'd her haplefs fate.
Diffolv'd in tears, her tender parents came,
To fhare her grief, and ftay life's parting flame.
Like dull, cold lights, that hover o'er the tomb,
A lone lamp languifh'd round the filent room :   10
Befide her couch, two lorn attendants ftay'd,
And drooping, lingering, eyed th' unconfcious maid.
O'er the fad fcene the pair attentive hung ;
Then round the favourite form all-anxious clung :
Her tearlefs eye-balls fcarce the virgin turn'd,   15
But, fix'd in blank defpair, her flumbering Irad mourn'd.
    Awake ! oh wake ! the tender mother cry'd---
My child ! my darling ! nature's lovelieft pride !
Awake, and hear ! oh hear thy mother's call !
Behold thefe tears for thee in anguifh fall !   20
Ah fee thy fire, with mighty woes opprefs'd !
His fighs hard-burfting from his heaving breaft !

BOOK IX.

Turn, turn thine eye! thy hapless parents save!
Nor speed our footsteps to the dreary grave!

   She spoke. O'erwhelm'd in bitterness of fate,   **25**
Still the sweet maiden unregardful sate:
Fix'd on the parent, droop'd her failing eyes,
And deep, and heavy, heav'd her long-drawn sighs.
Again the mother, lost in sad amaze,
Cast on her woes a strong, expressive gaze,   **30**
And thus---O child of parents once too bless'd!
Let not such anguish tear thy bleeding breast.
Swell not, with other pangs, thy miseries dire,
A dying mother, and a widow'd sire:
The balm of patience summon to thy soul: **35**
Let Heaven's high voice excessive grief controul.
He call'd, from earth's dark wild, the Youth away;
And call'd complacent, to the world of day.
To nobler scenes his mind seraphic flies,
To bliss, to Hezron, angels, and the skies.   **40**
   Thus spoke the parent. Struggling rose the fair,
And look'd unmeasur'd woe, and blank despair:
Again she languish'd; to the couch she fell,
And life sad-lingering seem'd to bid farewell.
Pierc'd to the soul, the tender father stood,   **45**
And, lost in woes like her's, the darling view'd,
He saw the mild reproof her sense recall,
Her strength reviv'd her tears in silence fall;
A beam of glimmering hope his grief allay'd,
And thus, with grave, but gentle voice, he said---   **50**
O child of love! sweet daughter of delight!
Let not that death-like gaze our souls affright.
Arise to thought! to sense, and reason, rise!
Nor dumb and marbled grieve against the Skies.
Such mighty woes no earthly loss requires;   **55**
Not Irad claims them, nor true love inspires.
All is not lost; thy parents still survive:
And for thy bliss, and in thy life, they live.

He spoke.   Again the virgin, whelm'd in woes,
With slow, and forceful effort feebly rose.   60
His voice rever'd arous'd her quickening soul,
Loos'd her sad tongue, and taught her tears to roll;
Pressing her mother's hand, with head reclin'd,
She thus disclos'd the anguish of her mind.
O best of parents, e'er to daughter given!   65
Lov'd, next to Irad! reverenc'd, next to Heaven!
Let not these frowns your hapless child destroy,
Bereft of every hope, and every joy!
What hand, what power, can Irad's breath restore?
Those eyes shall beam, that face shall smile, no more;
That voice ne'er warble music's sweetest sound;   71
And that pale form must moulder in the ground.
'Tis this, awakes the anguish of your mind;
But ye can weep, and weep to Heaven resign'd.
Not so your daughter: form'd of feebler frame,   75
Grief rends her soul, and damps the vital flame.
Yet even her heart but shares the common pain,
Partakes the tears of all, and breathes their sighs again.
Far round all Israel cast attentive eyes,
And see for him the general anguish rise.   80
See his own son the childless sire forget;
The childless mother only weeps his fate:
His fate alone the virgin's shrieks proclaim;
And the poor, wailing infant lisps his name.
Even lifeless nature mourns him, wrapp'd in gloom,   85
O'ercast with woe and conscious of his tomb.
I saw the sun forlorn, and slow, retire;
I saw the silent evening sad expire;
In shades of double gloom ascend the night,
And the stars languish, with a mournful light.   90
How cold yon moon extends her widow'd beam!
Announcing death, and pale with sickening gleam!
How faint her feeble glimmering spread the plain!
How still, and lonely, light the azure main!

While thus impaſſion'd, lifeleſs nature all,   95
In ſpeechleſs ſorrow, mourns the hero's fall;
Shall I, belov'd, beyond all merit dear,
His beſt Selima, and his choſen fair,
Shall I, O ſire! with common anguiſh weep?
And o'er his grave, with dull indifference, ſleep?   100
Dumb fields, and ſenſeleſs foreſts would reprove
Such baſe oblivion of ſo bright a love.

  Pleas'd, the great ſire beheld her thoughts return,
And heard her melting accents Irad mourn;
And thus---O brighteſt, lovelieſt of thy kind,   104
Grac'd with each charm, that robes the angel's mind,
More dear than ever child to ſire was dear,
As virtue lovely, and as truth ſincere!
Think not thy parents on their darling frown,
Or feel a thought leſs tender than thy own.   110
Like thine, our wiſhes the bleſs'd Youth approv'd;
Like thee, we choſe him, and like thee, we lov'd.
But O all beauteous daughter! ſhall thy ſire
Behold thee, whelm'd in boundleſs grief expire?
Or ſee thy life to hopeleſs anguiſh given?   115
Or hear thee murmur 'gainſt a righteous Heaven?
Again to earth could thy fond Youth remove,
His heart would chide thee, and his voice reprove;
Bid thee, ſubmiſſive, to thy Maker fall,
Embrace his hand, and wake at duty's call;   120
Bid thee to him thy patient thoughts reſign,
And blame thy wanderings, with a love like mine.
From grief's exceſs, thy parent would reſtrain,
Aſſert Heaven's right, and fix the bounds of pain.

  Ah ſire rever'd! the pleading maid returns---   125
No common loſs thy hapleſs daughter mourns.
Search the wide world. Can all her regions boaſt
One youth ſo fair, ſo bright, ſo early loſt?
How Age admir'd him! how all Iſrael lov'd!
The world applauded! and the Heavens approv'd! 130

B O O K IX.

His form was all, the brightest thoughts can frame;
His mind was all, the fondest wish can claim;
Whate'er is great, or good, or soft, or fair,
Refin'd, or lovely, fix'd its mansion there.
Even he, whose hand the sacred sceptre bears, 135
Is but an Irad, of maturer years.
It is, O 'tis, as if, in yon fair clime,
Some prince of angels, bright in glory's prime,
Transcending every peer, in worth supreme,
Mitred with truth, and sunn'd with virtue's beam, 140
In youth's gay morn, in beauty's endless bloom,
And life, superior to the potent tomb,
Had clos'd his smiles, while Heaven refus'd to save,
And sunk his glories in the dreary grave.
What tears, for such a loss, would seraphs shed? 145
Tears, rich as theirs, should mourn their rival dead.

 And where, O where shall poor Selima find
One beam of light to cheer her drooping mind?
All sad, I wander round the earth, and skies;
But no soft solace meets my failing eyes. 150
To friends I fly: those weeping friends I see
Sunk in the deep despair, that buries me.
For him, O kindest, tenderest mother! rise
Thy heart-felt anguish, and thy hopeless sighs.
Thy tears, all-gentle sire! resistless shed, 155
Approve my grief, and weep the hero dead.
No cheering hope your fondest love can give,
Sooth your sad child, or make her Irad live.
Then bid me mourn; this last relief bestow,
And yield my bosom to the peace of woe. 160

 Oppress'd with grief, the feeling sire rejoin'd---
Sweet, lovely charmer of thy father's mind!
From earth, from friends, thy hope can never flow;
Too poor, to yield the balm of real woe.
When real ills invade; when Want annoys; 165
When hissing Shame, with lingering death destroys;

F f

When pain torments, or sickness wastes our bloom;
Or friends too dear desert us, for the tomb :
This barren world no solace can supply :
But all earth's portion is to weep, and die.   170
Yet there are springs whence hope and comfort rise,
Springs of pure life, and flowing from the skies :
Thence gentle Mercy sends her treasures down;
And bright Religion makes the bliss her own.
To famish'd Want she spreads a boundless store,   175
With that unbless'd, the heir of worlds is poor :
Repentant Shame she bids to crowns aspire,
Grace ever new, and glory ever higher :
On earth, in heaven, her wealth and honours rise,
Ennoble angels, and enrich the skies.   180
Decay and Pain to cheerful peace she leads,
With patience arms them, and with comfort feeds ;
And points the realms, where Health and Beauty bloom,
And Life, with smiles of triumph, braves the tomb.
When Friends, if Virtue's friends from earth retire,   185
And waste the bosom, with corroding fire ;
She sees those friends again immortal live,
Rise from the grave, and dying worlds survive,
To each the form, the mind, of angels given,
Fair sons of light, and habitants of heaven.   190
She too, and she alone, a Friend secures,
That through all times, and in all scenes, endures
At hand, to hear, to love, to bless, to save,
In life, and death, and worlds beyond the grave ;
As heaven o'er earth sublime, all friends above,   195
In power in wisdom, truth, and boundless love.
    In grief, even vast as thine, his hand can heal,
And teach the heart its anguish not to feel.
Bright from the tomb, she sees thine Irad rise
To peace, and life, and glory in the skies ;   200
One little moment separate from thy arms ;
Again to meet thee, with superior charms ;

To hail thy rising soul, from realms above ;
To smile as angels, and as Heaven to love.

Then, O thou child of truth ! to her controul　　205
Resign the tumults of thy troubled soul.
She on thy wounds shall shed her healing power,
Thy faith revive, thy wonted peace restore ;
With softest music charm the passing day ;
Bid Heavenly visions o'er thee nightly play ;　　210
The tents of angels round thy curtains spread :
Invite the guardian cherub to thy bed ;
Calm, with sweet slumbers, every stormy care,
And dry, with downy hand, the plaintive tear.
She too shall life's rough path with flowers adorn ;　215
With spring's mild splendor, cheer the wintry morn ;
Thy yielding feet, in strong temptations save ;
Welcome grim death, and triumph o'er the grave ?
To brighter scenes, in happier regions, fly,
And lift to thrones of glory, in the sky.　　220

The parent spoke.　The hapless maiden sate
Forlorn, and sad, bewailing Irad's fate.
Silenc'd, but not reliev'd, her drooping mind
Fail'd not to sigh, nor yet to Heaven resign'd :
At length with vast, and heavy woes oppress'd,　225
She sunk in slumbers of tumultuous rest.

Mild rose the morn ; and, round the tented plain
The cries of thousands mourn'd their kindred slain.
In silent woe the hoary parent stood,
And wail'd his hopes, all sunk in fields of blood ;　230
His sons, sweet charm of nature's evil day,
Fair light of age, and life's most pleasing stay,
Now left him helpless, and alone, to find
Some foreign aid to sooth a drooping mind.
Strong pangs of sorrow fix'd his speaking eye,　235
And his rack'd heart heav'd deep the heavy sigh.
The pale, sad widow cast a tender view
On her sweet race, and shed the plaintive dew.

Touch'd with her woes, the beauteous orphans mourn'd,
And artless tears their infant cheeks adorn'd.　　　240
The bride deplor'd a young, fond husband's doom,
Snatch'd from her arms, and banish'd to the tomb;
Her joys all ended in one dreadful day;
Her brightest hopes forever swept away;
No prospect left her, but long years of woe;　　　245
No wish, but ransom from these realms below.

　　These scenes, with anguish, pierc'd the Leader's breast,
Blank'd his fair prospects, and his soul depress'd.
Yet still, before the host, a cheerful grace,
With blameless art, array'd his tranquil face.　　　250
In all their pains, to him they cast their eyes;
Like a fond sire, he heard their plaintive cries:
From his calm brow they caught the placid smile,
Forgot their miseries, and despis'd their toil.

　　Now in the silence of his tent, alone　　　255
He mourn'd their fears, and made their grief his own,
When Zimri came, with anxious care oppress'd,
And Joshua thus his faithful friend address'd.

　　Hear'st thou what sorrows fill the murmuring air?
The warriors' groans? and terrors of the fair?　　　260
What tears of anguish every face bedew!
What throngs of orphans crowd upon the view!
Oh heavy, heavy pangs Jehovah's hand
On this sad heart, and on his chosen band!
Ah, where is Hezron? chief of spotless name!　　　265
His life so virtuous! and so pure his fame!
How soon, O pride of nature, art thou fled
To the dark, lonely mansions of the dead!
How soon to thy compeers, thine angels, given,
All-beauteous Irad! fairest plant of heaven!　　　270
But still superior grace may point a way,
Through the long darkness to the promis'd day.

　　These mournful thoughts with prudent care conceal;
Nor let thy guarded brow a pain reveal.

Thy face they watch, the motions of thine eye,   275
Know all thy fears, and number every ſigh.
When leaders ſmile, their looks the hoſt inſpire;
Are leaders brave? the vulgar catch the fire;
With us they faint, they tremble, and they grieve;
With us they joy, they dare, they die, they live.   280

But now more ſolemn ſcenes thy care demand;
Chooſe twice ten thouſand of the warrior band;
To yonder hapleſs field thy footſteps ſpeed,
And pay the laſt, ſad honours to the dead.
In one broad pit, our ſlaughter'd friends entomb;   285
Nor grudge our foes the ſame unenvied doom:
Let men, let brave men, ne'er refuſe the brave
The humble bleſſing of a peaceful grave.

I go, the darling hero's fate to cloſe,
And bid the matchleſs Youth a ſweet repoſe: 290
'Tis all we can, the friendly tear to ſhed,
And raiſe the light tomb o'er his lovely head.

With ſoft affections, thus the mighty Chief;
And Zimri ſlow retir'd, with anſwering grief.
Meantime, grave warriors, in black robes array'd,   295
And many a youth, and many a lovely maid,
Along the northern green, the Chief purſued;
Flowers grac'd their hands, and tears their cheeks bedew'd
For now brave Irad clos'd his final doom,
Borne to his darkſome, everlaſting home.   300

Behind the bier, that ſlow, and ſolemn mov'd,
Penſive Selima follow'd him ſhe lov'd;
On the ſad coffin fix'd a ſtedfaſt eye;
Nor dropp'd a tear, nor breath'd a tender ſigh.
Her dark-brown hair a wreath of roſes crown'd;   305
Her robes of ſable flow'd along the ground:
A flower, juſt opening to the morning dew,
Bluſh'd in her hand, and brighten'd to the view.

Now in the grave the breathleſs Youth was laid:
Sadly ſerene advanc'd the lovely maid;   310

With fpeaking eyes, bewail'd her haplefs doom,
And dropp'd the floweret in the lonely tomb.
High on the plain the funeral earth was fpread;
The turf's gay verdure flourifh'd o'er his head:
Each gentle face deplor'd his lot fevere,   315
And fpoke th' expreffive language of a tear.

Near the fair maiden ftood th' exalted Chief,
Fix'd in mute woe, and great in manly grief.
No ill-tim'd comfort would he ftrive to lend,
Nor ape the flatteries of the fpecious friend: 320
Yet the foft texture of his heart could feel---
Why fhould he ope the wound he could not heal?

As thus their bofoms wail'd his haplefs end,
And mourn'd, as each had loft his chofen friend;
Admir'd why Heaven had made fuch worth in vain,   325
And why confin'd it to the dreadful plain;
His generous deeds in deep difpair ran o'er,
And faw him live, and fpeak, and act, no more;
Through the fad filence of the folemn fcene,
The bands of Zimri crofs'd the gloomy green.   330
Unnumber'd widows, on the field, they found,
Whofe fons, whofe hufbands, ftrew'd the crimfon ground:
Slow mov'd the fair-ones round the dreadful plain,
Wafh'd the black gore, and prov'd the countlefs flain;
And when the partners of their joys they knew,   335
They cleans'd their ftiffen'd wounds in briny dew;
Wail'd their hard lot, that fwept, in life's gay bloom,
Each hope, each rapture, to the fullen tomb;
With tears of anguifh, envied earth its truft,
And grudg'd the grave the lov'd the precious duft.   340

Three days, above the undiftinguifh'd dead,
Their friends, and foes, the gather'd earth was fpread.
A hill of ftones, fad wound to human pride!
Juft mark'd the place, where countlefs warriors died.

As there, in future years, the lonely fwain   345
Drove his fmall flock, to feed the grafs-grown plain,

BOOK IX.

Near the rough maſs, in ſolemn thought, reclin'd,
Thus ſad reflections fill'd his pondering mind.
Ah proud inglorious man! whoſe inſect life
Is loſt in pain, in vanity, and ſtrife.   350
What mighty toils, to gain immortal fame!
What waſtes, what ſlaughters, build the darling name!
Yet this rude tomb, this ſhapeleſs pile, contains,
Of chiefs, of kings, the poor, the ſole remains.
This prize to win, muſt nations then expire?   355
And ſeats of peace, and joy, be whelm'd in fire?
Oh Heaven, in pity, looſe the ties, that bind
To man's black race, a juſt and honeſt mind!
   Low ſunk the ſun. As now the chief return'd
From midſt the camp, and hapleſs Iſrael mourn'd,   360
Hareſhah ſad, beſide his tent, he found;
Proſtrate he fell, and reverent kiſs'd the ground.
Upraiſ'd by Joſhua's hand, again he ſtood,
And thus his fear in plaintive accents flow'd.
Hail mighty prince! to thee alone tis given,   365
To taſte the favour of indulgent Heaven;
To guide, with proſperous hand, the race he choſe,
And hurl deſtruction on reſiſting foes.
Thou know'ſt, with thee how Gibeon's ſons are join'd;
What views unite us, and what covenants bind;   370
This, through the circling realms by fame was ſung,
And round each realm, th' alarm of vengeance rung:
To waſte her domes the general voice decreed,
And millions haſte t' atchieve the barbarous deed.
Salem's imperious ſons, in proud array,   375
And haughtier Hebron, thither bend their way;
In martial pomp unnumber'd Lachiſh ſhines,
And Jarmuth brave with ſavage Eglon joins;
With theſe, fierce nations ſpeed from realms unknown,
Near the firſt glimmerings of the dawning ſun.   380
There too, O Prince! tremendous Jabin ſtands,
Brings all his chiefs, and leads his veteran bands,

BOOK IX.

Wings the dread lightenings of the war around,
And rolls his thunders o'er th' embattled ground.   284

   From these dread powers, so numerous, and so brave,
Nought less than Heaven, and thy own hand, can save.
Worne with long years, Aradon's trembling arm
Ill wards the vengeance of so fierce a storm.
And,---O exalted Prince! prepare to hear
A tale more sad than ever pierc'd thine ear---   390
In the dark grave is generous Elam laid,
And near him sleeps the Heaven-instructed maid.

   How fell the lovely pair? the Leader cried;
And, with sad voice, the stranger chief replied.
When cheerful morn walk'd forth in golden air,   395
Rode the young hero, and his blooming fair,
With nimble hounds, that bade the forest roar;
To chace the buck, to wound the bristly boar;
On two white steeds they bounded o'er the plain,
And gayly round them pranc'd a youthful train.   400
No coats of steely mail their limbs invest;
No buckler sparkles o'er the fearless breast;
Thro' sylvan shades they trac'd an easy way:
Each mind was sunshine, and each face was gay.

   At once, with dreadful din before them rose   405
The trump of death, and shout of savage foes.
From the thick covert burst a barbarous throng,
Rang clashing arms, and scream'd a hideous song;
His gallant friends, a young, but chosen few,
The prince, serenely brave, around him drew;   410
With firm, bold breast, they fought, and at his side
In death they triumph'd, for with him they died.

   As thro' his bosom sung the fatal steel,
He rais'd his hand, and wav'd along farewell:
On the sweet maid his eye all-wishful hung,   415
And half-form'd accents ceas'd upon his tongue.
Quick round the youth a tender arm she threw,
Fell as he fell, and wish'd to perish too.

BOOK IX.

The quivering form she press'd, in icy death,
Kiss'd his pale lips, and suck'd his parting breath.   420
No more her careless thoughts attempt to fly ;
No more her ear attends the horrid cry :
Close to the wound her snowy hand applied
Withdrew the lance, and stopp'd the purple tide.
A grim barbarian to the fair-one came,   425
Pierc'd her white side, and forc'd the vital stream ;
With one weak gasp, on Elam's bosom laid,
Her bloom all vanish'd, and her spirit fled.

   In distant fields, we heard the trumpet's sound,
And strode impatient to the fatal ground.   430
On the sad scene, by favouring shrubs conceal'd,
A youth, unarm'd, the dire event beheld:
He, drown'd in tears, disclos'd the fierce affray,
And shew'd where Mina, and her Elam, lay.
On the cold earth, the wither'd leaves he press'd ;   435
The fair yet panting at his lifeless breast.
Her hand was feebly laid against the spear,
Still in her side, and in her eye a tear.
So blooms a flower beside th' autumnal stream,
And waves, and wantons, in the solar beam,   440
Nor knows the frost, that in the midnight sky
Lurks for its charms, and bids its beauty die.

   The hapless pair in snow-white robes array'd,
To the same grave our friendly hands convey'd.
Kind youths, and virgins, there at dawn appear,   445
Strew fragrant flowers, and drop the tender tear ;
There the sad wild rose yields its withering bloom,
And melancholy music mourns their doom.
Pierc'd thro' his thigh, and weltering on the ground,
A savage wretch, beneath an oak, we found.   450
By favours won, he shew'd th' impending doom,
What bands are gather'd, and what heroes come.
To spy these realms, he cried, from Hebron's land,
Thro' many a forest rov'd our warlike band-.

Led by bold Hoham, from far diftant fhores,   455
Thence countlefs hofts invade yon fhining towers ;
There giant Zedeck's lofty car is roll'd ;
There beams young Piram in refulgent gold ;
High rais'd in air, ten thoufand ftandards play,
And chiefs unnumber'd hail the deathful day.   460

   Thus fpoke the wretch.   As o'er yon mountain's brow
I fteer'd my path, and eyed the world below,
From diftant fields, the trump's approaching found
Wav'd o'er the plains, and fill'd the groves around ;
Swift tow'rd the walls long, dufty volumes came,   465
And dreadful gleams of interrupted flame ;
On high the banners danc'd ; a mighty train,
With lines immeafurable, hid the plain.

   Oh, by the covenant, which thy voice hath given,
By the bleft favour of all-bounteous Heaven,   470
That Heaven, which makes thee his peculiar care,
Aid our weak race, and grant our righteous prayer !

   Thus mourn'd the chief, while Caleb flow drew nigh,
His anguifh'd bofom heaving many a figh ;
His foul, in filence, mourn'd the haplefs pair,   475
All-lovely Irad and his beauteous fair ;
When Jofhua fad the hoary fage addrefs'd---
Great prince, this night Harefhah is thy gueft.
His voice a mournful tale from Gibeon brings;
How 'gainft her walls Canäan arms her kings.   480
Our aid he claims ; an aid by covenant doe ;
But ah, what griefs our haplefs race purfue !
Again th' Eternal arm our courfe withftands,
Cuts off our chiefs, and flays our haplefs bands.
Firft Hezron flept : then virtuous Uzal fell,   485
And brave Shelumiel bade the world farewel,
Next lovely Irad found a haplefs doom ;
And now fweet Mina feeks an early tomb.
Should ftill new courfes unadvis'd be tried,
Frefh wrath may kindle, and frefh ills betide.   490

BOOK IX

Let then this chief in peace with thee retire,
'Till Heaven his counsels, and our course, inspire.
   He spoke.   Harefhah with the sage withdrew,
While the sun lingering flowly left the view;
The mourning Hero fought a flight repose,   495
And broken flumbers o'er his eye-lids rose.
   Now Night, in vestments rob'd of cloudy die,
With fable grandeur cloth'd the orient fky,
Impell'd the fun, obfequious to her reign,
Down the far mountains to the western main :   500
With magic hand, becalm'd the folemn even,
And drew day's curtain from the fpangled heaven.
At once the planets fail'd around the throne ;
At once ten thoufand worlds in fplendor fhone :
Behind her car, the moon's expanded eye   505
Rofe from a cloud, and look'd around the fky :
Far up th' immenfe her train fublimely roll,
And dance, and triumph, round the lucid pole.
Faint fhine the fields, beneath the fhadowy ray ;
Slow fades the glimmering of the weft away ;   510
To fleep the tribes retire ; and not a found
Flows through the air, or murmurs on the ground.
   The Chief, arifing, o'er the darkfome green
Turn'd his flow fteps, and view'd the fplendid fcene;
With wondering gaze, furvey'd the vaulted even,   515
The half-feen world, and all the pomp of Heaven.
Wide arch'd the palace of th' Almighty hand,
Its walls far-bending o'er the fea, and land :
Round the vaft roof, from antient darknefs fprung,
In living pride, immortal tapers hung :   520
The lamp on high an endlefs luftre fhed,
And earth's broad pavement all beneath was fpread.
From diftant hills, red flames began to rife,
Topp'd the talls towers, and climb'd the kindling fkies :
Thick ftream'd the tranfient ftars ; and all around   525
A ftill, mild glory rob'd the twilight ground.

B O O K IX.

Now tow'rd the north he bent his wandering way,
Each scene revolving of the busy day,
When lo! soft sounds his startled ear assail,
Soft as the whisper of the flowing gale.   530
Now mournful murmurs slowly-pensive rise;
Now languid harmony in silence dies:
Now nobler strains, with animating fire,
Warm the bold raptures of the living lyre.

Whither, O whither is thy beauty gone!   535
To what far region? to what world unknown?
No lone, drear shades of everlasting gloom,
Verg'd on the confines of the icy tomb,
No frozen climes, extend impervious bounds,
Confine thy walks, and bar thy active rounds,   540
Forbid thy upward flight at large to rove,
And climb the mountains of eternal love.

Far other scenes thy lovely spirit claim;
Far other mansions own thy lasting fame.
Borne on light wings, I see thy guardian come,   545
Unchain thy mind, and point the starry home:
With joy, he clasps thee in immortal arms,
Waves his young plumes, and smiles etherial charms;
Through fields of air, he wins his purple way,
And rosy choirs, delighted, round him play.   550

There, o'er bright realms, and pure, unchanging skies,
Suns gayly walk, and lucid morns arise;
Crown'd with new flowers, the streams perpetual roll,
And living beauty blooms around the pole.
Will there, alas! the soft enchantment end?   555
And can no love to those fair climes ascend?
It can; it will; for there the bless'd improve
Their minds in joy, and where's the joy, but love?

Canst thou forget, when, call'd from southern bowers,
Love tun'd the groves, and spring awak'd the flowers,
How, loos'd from slumbers by the morning ray,   560
O'er balmy plains we bent our frequent way?

BOOK IX.

On thy fond arm, with pleasing gaze, I hung,
And heard sweet music murmur o'er thy tongue ;
Hand lock'd in hand, with gentle ardour press'd,   565
Pour'd soft emotions through the heaving breast,
In magic transport heart with heart entwin'd,
And in sweet languors lost the melting mind.

  'Twas then, thy voice, attun'd to wisdom's lay,
Shew'd fairer worlds, and trac'd th' immortal way ; 570
In virtue's pleasing paths my footsteps tried,
My sweet companion, and my skillful guide ;
Through varied knowledge taught my mind to soar,
Search hidden truths, and new-found walks explore :
While still the tale, by nature learn'd to rove,   575
Slid, unperceiv'd to scenes of happy love.
'Till weak, and lost, the faltering converse fell,
And eyes disclos'd what eyes alone could tell ;
In rapturous tumuls bade the passions roll,
And spoke the living language of the soul.   580

  With what fond hope, through many a blissful hour,
We gave the soul to fancy's pleasing power ;
Lost in the magic of that sweet employ
To build gay scenes, and fashion future joy !
We saw mild Peace o'er fair Canäan rise,   585
And shower her pleasures from benignant skies.
On airy hills our happy mansion rose,
Built but for joy, nor room reserv'd for woes.
Round the calm solitude, with ceaseless song,
Soft roll'd domestic ecstasy along :   590
Sweet as the sleep of Innocence, the day,
By raptures number'd, lightly danc'd away :
To love, to bliss, the union'd soul was given,
And each, too happy ! ask'd no brighter heaven.
Yet then, even then, my trembling thoughts would rove,
And steal on hour from Irad, and from love,   596
Through dread futurity all-anxious roam,
And cast a mournful glance on ills to come.

Hope not, fond maid, some voice prophetic cried---
A life, thus wasted down th'unruffled tide :   600
Trust no gay, golden doom, from anguish free,
Nor wish the laws of Heaven revers'd for thee.
Survey the peopled world ; thy soul shall find
Woes, ceaseless woes, ordain'd for poor mankind.
Life's a long solitude, an unknown gloom,   605
Clos'd by the silence of the dreary tomb.

   For soon, ah soon shall fleet thy pleasing dreams ;
Soon close the eye, that, bright as angels, beams
Grace irresistible.   To mouldering clay
Shall change the face, that smiles thy griefs away ;   610
Soon the sweet music of that voice be o'er,
Hope cease to charm, and beauty bloom no more :
Strange, darksome wilds, and devious ways be trod,
Nor love, nor Irad, steal thy heart from God.
And must the hours in ceaceless anguish roll ?   615
Must no soft sunshine cheer my clouded soul ?
Spring charm around me brightest scenes, in vain ?
And Youth's angelick visions wake to pain ?
Oh come once more, with fond endearments come ;
Burst the cold prison of the sullen tomb ;   920
Thro' favourite walks, thy chosen maid attend ;
Where well-known shades for thee their branches bend :
Shed the sweet poison from thy speaking eye ;
And look those raptures, lifeless words deny !
Still be the tale rehears'd, that ne'er could tire ;   625
But, told each eve, fresh pleasure could inspire :
Still hop'd those scenes, which love and fancy drew ;
But, drawn a thousand times, were ever new !

   Yet cease, fond maid ; 'tis thine alone to mourn :
Yield the bright scenes, that never can return.   630
Thy joys are fled, thy smiling morn is o'er ;
Too bless'd in youth, thou must be bless'd no more.
The hope, that brighten'd, with all-pleasing ray,
Shone, but to charm, and flatter'd, to betray.

B O O K IX.

No more fair Irad heeds my tender strain ;   635
Dull is the voice, that never call'd in vain ;
Vain the cold languish of these once lov'd eyes ;
And vain the fond desire, that bids him rise.
In life's gay scenes, their highest grace before,
Thy mind, O Youth divine ! must share no more ;   640
Alike unnotic'd, joys and tumults roll,
Nor these disturb, nor those delight, thy soul.

Again all bright shall glow the morning beam ;
Again soft suns dissolve the frozen stream :
Spring call young breezes from the southern skies,   645
And, cloath'd in splendor, flowery millions rise.
In vain to thee--No morn's indulgent ray
Warms the cold mansion of the slumbering clay.
No mild etherial gale, with tepid wing,
Shall fan thy locks, or waft approaching spring :   650
Unfelt, unknown, shall breathe the rich perfume,
And unhear'd music wave around thy tomb.

A cold, dumb, dead repose invests thee round ;
Still as the void, ere nature form'd a sound.
In thy dark region, pierc'd by no kind ray,   655
To roll the long, oblivious hours away.
In these wild walks, this solitary round,
Where the pale moon-beam lights the glimmering ground
At each sad turn, I view'd thy spirit come,
And glide, half-seen, behind a neighbouring tomb ;   660
With visionary hand, forbid my stay,
Look o'er the grave, and beckon me away.

But vain the wish ; for still, around thy tomb,
This faithful hand shall bid the wild rose bloom ;
Each lonely eve, Selima hither rove,   665
And pay the tribute of unalter'd love ;
Till, O fond, lovely youth ! these eyes shall close,
Seal'd in the silence of a long repose :
Beneath one turf our kindred bodies lie,
And lose, unpain'd, this melancholy sky.   670

With thee, well-pleas'd, the final pang I'll brave;
With thee Death smile, and lightsome be the grave;
O'er earth's broad fields, till heaven forget to reign,
And suns benighted vanish in the main;
This dark recess the cherub then shall find,   675
And wake a form, angelic as thy mind.

   Distress'd, kind Joshua heard her moving strain,
But still walk'd onward o'er the shady plain;
Why should his face her mournful thoughts molest,
Tho' soft compassion warm'd his feeling breast;   680
No comfort could he lend, nor joy impart,
While slumbering Irad own'd her tender heart.

   And now his footsteps slow and softly rove,
Thro' the black silence of th' extended grove;
Alternate moon-beams feebly pierce the shade,   685
And o'er his path a glimmering horror spread;
Strange, awful objects dimly rise around,
And forms unfinish'd cloath the gloomy ground.
With mournful thoughts the prospect well combin'd,
And sooth'd the wanderings of a drooping mind.   690
Around he cast his melancholy eyes,
And pleas'd, beheld the solemn scenes arise;
Scenes tun'd in conceit with his sadden'd soul,
To grief resign'd, and pity's soft controul;
The gloom, the silence, gave a kind relief;   695
Peace sprung from trouble, and delight from grief?
His heart impassion'd mourn'd his daughter's doom,
Her charms, her virtues, banish'd to the tomb.
Then hapless Irad all his woes renew'd,
And copious tears afresh his cheeks bedew'd: 700
At length, the tumults of his struggling breast
Unwish'd, unbidden accents thus express'd.

   Oh, when shall Israel's countless sorrow's cease?
And war once more resign to lasting peace?
Each rising morn, more dreadful woes appear,   705
And each sad evening prompts a larger tear.

Why did pale terror Judah's race appal ?
Why princes, chiefs, and generous thoufands fall ?
Ah ! why did Heaven to me commit the fway,
And bid his fons this feeble arm obey ?   710
Oh had the Power divine for me ordain'd
Some humble manfion, in a lonely land ;
Where the trump's voice was never never heard ;
Nor falchion drawn, nor favage flaughter fear'd !
In quiet then my life had pafs'd away,   715
Blefs'd without pride, and without fplendor gay ;
In death, my foul ferenely met her doom,
And my own children built my humble tomb.
   At once a wild, and vifionary found,
With fudden murmurs, fill'd the grove around ;   720
The ftrange alarm now loud and louder grew,
And through the foreft burfting fplendor flew ;
A Form, the brighteft of the morning choir,
Drew near, in all the pomp of heavenly fire ;
Twelve ftars of glory crown'd his awful head ;   725
His fun-bright eyes the forky lightening fhed ;
Serene, but dreadfully ferene, he ftood,
And a dire trembling feiz'd the confcious wood.
As when a ftorm the dark horizon fills,
Long, folemn thunders roll o'er diftant hills ; 730
So, from the Vifion's voice, a fearful found
Appall'd his ear, and fhook the ftartled ground.
Chief of thy race ! from heaven's eternal King,
At his command, this facred charge I bring.
I AM THE LORD. I form'd the earth, and fky,   735
Illum'd the fun, and hung his flames on high ;
Bade worlds, in millions, ftar th' etherial plain,
And built the fecret chambers of the main.
My voice, the heaven, and heaven of heavens obey ;
And Ocean, Earth, and Hell, confefs my fway.   740
Through worlds, on worlds, in Being's mighty bounds,
That roll through fpace' illimitable rounds ;

H h

Where skies, o'er skies, unmeasur'd arches bend,
And stars, o'er stars, in endless pride ascend ;
Where the sun's searching beam hath never ray'd,   745
Nor scarce an angel's pinion'd fancy stray'd ;
My power, my wisdom, with divine controul,
Surveys, preserves, directs and moves. the whole.
All these, with all their scenes, th' eternal Mind,
Ere angels sung, or heaven began, design'd.   750
Whate'er my voice ordain'd to being came,
Touch'd by th' immortal, all-inspiring flame.
In all, though man, with vain, benighted eye,
Of insect ken, unnumber'd blots descry,
From hell's deep caves, to heaven's sublimest bound, 755
No stain, no fault, no error, can be found.
    Whose thoughts shall then my boundless wisdom blame?
Whose wishes rise against my holy Name ?
My spirit form'd thee in the silent womb,
And wrote, with Mercy's hand, thy favourite doom; 760
Thy soul awak'd, thy infant limbs inspir'd,
With truth illum'd thee, and with virtue fir'd ;
Bade all my sons thy sceptred rule obey,
And stretch'd thy glory with the solar ray.
And shall thy heart my bounteous hand distrust,   765
And mourn that warriors mingle with the dust ?
What though brave Irad from the world retir'd,
Tho' numerous bands around his steps expir'd ;
Without a fear, without a pang, resign ;
That virtuous Youth, and all those bands, were mine.770
With songs the grace adore, that rais'd thy mind,
From the low confines of the bestial kind,
Where countless throngs plod on their base pursuits,
Above, and just above, their kindred brutes,
To that sublimest honour, man can know,   775
To bless my sons, and shew my praise, below.
    Forgive, O Heaven ! forgive---the Hero cried ;
And milder thus the Vision's voice replied.

BOOK IX.

O Chief of Ifrael ! let no rebel thought 779
Accufe the wonders, God's right hand hath wrought.
While his almighty arm thy courfe fuftains,
Afk not what numbers crowd embattled plains.
From the broad circuit of her various lands,
He call'd to fight Canäan's countlefs bands :
He bids thee fearlefs tempt the martial field, 785
And truft the covert of his guardian fhield.
For there, in virtue's caufe, thy God fhall arm,
And pour the vengeance of the baleful ftorm ;
The fun ftand ftill ; the moon thy voice obey ;
And the bright angel fweep thy foes away. 790
    But now to nobler fcenes thy views extend !
See long futurity in pomp afcend !
The varying doom of Ifrael's wayward race ;
How truth exalts them, and how crimes debafe ;
Their arts, their arms, their towns, and towers, behold,
Fields of fair flocks, and domes inchaf'd with gold ! 796
High Heaven around them fpreads his bleffings far
Or proves, and fcourges, with vindictive war !
There too, fucceffive, fee the wonders rife,
That guard, and blefs, the Children of the fkies ; 800
Thy own bright Ifrael ; Heaven's immortal race,
Sav'd by his Son, and fainted by his grace ;
To Jacob's chofen feed at firft confin'd,
Then wide, and wider, fpread to all mankind !
With more than mortal ken, thy raptur'd foul 805
Shall fee far diftant times in vifion roll ;
When Abraham's fons, from earth's remoteft end,
To Salem's heaven-topp'd mountains fhall afcend ;
When round the poles, where frozen fplendors play,
In noontide realms, that bafk in brighter day, 810
On fpicy fhores, where beauteous morning reigns,
Or Evening lingers o'er her favourite plains,
From guilt, from death, reviving nations rife,
And one vaft hymn of tranfport fills the fkies.

Beyond these scenes, shall nobler wonders shine,   815
Climes of sweet peace, and years of joy divine,
Where truth's fair sons extend the golden wing
Thro' morn e'er-rising, ever changing spring ;
Where unborn Beauty, round whose awful throne,
All splendors fade, and suns are dark at roon,   820
Smiles o'er broad regions ever-brightening day,
Fair nature quickening in th' ecstatic ray :
The soul, pure effluence of th' all-beaming Mind,
With virtue diadem'd, with truth refin'd,
With bliss supreme, with radiance yet unknown,   825
Begins, a star, and brightens to a sun ;
Life, Love, and Rapture, blossom in her sight,
And Glory triumphs o'er the world of light.

T H E

CONQUEST of CANÄAN:

BOOK X.

Argument.

*Vision of futurity. Prospect of the land of Canäan. Pros-
perous events after the war is finished. Apostacy after
the death of Joshua, and consequent judgements. Troubles
by Cushan-rishathaim, Hazor, Midian, Ammon, and the
Philistines. Samson. Civil War. Philistines' Kings.
David's combat with Goliath. War with Ammon, and
Syria. Joab. David's glory. Jerusalem. Temple.
Dedication. Solomon. Division of the kingdom. De-
struction of Israel by Shalmaneser, and of Judah by Ne-
buchadnezzar. Restoration. Messiah. his Birth Bap-
tism, Miracles, Trial, Death, Resurrection, and Ascensi-
on. Destruction of Jerusalem by the Romans. Preach-
ing of the Gospel by the Apostles, and succeeding Minis-
ters. Prospect of America. Slavery of the eastern Con-
tinent. Glory of the Western Millennium. Calling of
the Jews. Signs which forebode the end of the World.
Resurrection, Conflagration, General Judgement, and
consummation of all things. Prospect of heaven, and a
happy immortality. Angel departs, and Joshua returns
to the camp.*

THE CONQUEST OF CANÄAN.

BOOK X.

THE Vision ceas'd. At once the foreft fled,
 At once an unknown region round them fpread,
Like the ftill fabbath's dawning light ferene,
And fair as blifsful Eden's living green.
High on a hill they ftood, whofe cloudy brow   5
Look'd o'er th' illimitable world below.
In fhining verdure eaftern realms withdrew,
And hills and plains, immingling, fill'd the view:
From fouthern forefts rofe melodious founds ;
Tall northern mountains ftretch'd cerulean bounds ;   10
Weft, all was fea; blue fkies, with peaceful reign,
Serene roll'd round th' interminable plain.
Then thus the Power. To thee, blefs'd man, 'tis given,
To know the thoughts of all-confidering Heaven :
Scenes form'd eternal in th' unmeafur'd Mind,   15
In yon bright realms, for Abraham's race defign'd,
While the great promife ftands in heaven fecure,
Or earth, or feas, or fkies or ftars endure.

He ſpoke.   At once a ſpacious land is ſeen,
Bright with young cornfields, and with paſtures green; 20
Fair ſhine the rivers; fair the plains extend;
The tall woods wave, and towering hills aſcend;
Ten thouſand thouſand flooks around them ſpread,
Sport o'er the lawns, and crop the verdant blade;
Bleſs'd ſwains with muſic charm their uſeful toil,   25
The cheerful plowmen turn the ſable ſoil;
The vine, glad offspring of the ſun, aſpires,
And ſmiles, and purples, in th' indulgent fires;
The vales, with humble pride, gay coats adorn,
And pleaſure dances in the beams of morn;   30
Spring, hand in hand with golden Autumn join'd
Lives in the flowers, and wantons in the wind.

    Then ſpacious towns exalt their ſtately ſpires,
Bend their long walls, and light unnumber'd fires;
Here all the pomp of haughty ſtructures ſhines,   35
Youth crowds the dance, and Age in council joins;
There, built by virtue, ſmoking altars riſe,
And clouds of incenſe fill the morning ſkies.
When thus the Hero---Say, O Power divine!
What bright and happy ſcenes before me ſhine,   40
Tell, if thoſe regions Iſrael's bliſs diſplay,
And flocks, and fields, and cities own their ſway.

    Juſt are thy thoughts---the Seraph's voice return'd,
While roſy beauty round his aſpect burn'd,
In theſe fair climes ſhall Iſrael fix her ſeat,   45
End her long toils, and find a calm retreat,
Then all the bleſſings, mortals here can know,
From GOD's good hand, in plenteous ſtreams, ſhall flow.
In pureſt beams ſhall genial ſuns deſcend;
And moons, and ſtars, their ſofteſt radiance lend: 50
The gales waft health; kind flowers the plains renew;
Morn yield her fragrance; eve her balmy dew;
With autumn's prime the wintery froſt conſpire;
With ſprings mild influence ſummer's ſcorching fire;

To nurſe the land of virtue's lov'd receſs,   55
And bleſs the nation, Heaven delights to bleſs.
  Theſe ſcenes of blisful peace ſhalt thou enjoy,
Nor grief diſturbs, nor circling foes annoy.
But when death calls thee to divine abodes,
They fly from Heaven, and ſeek Canäan's gods ;   60
To ſtocks, to ſtones, with ſtupid reverence, bow,
Burſt every tie, and perjure every vow.
Then war ſhall thunder from the realms around ;
Then ſuns malignant parch the ſterile ground ;
The fields ſhall waſte ; the flocks to duſt decay, 65
And fierce diſeaſes ſweep their tribes away.
Yet ſhall his bounty ſainted guardians raiſe,
And ſhed rich bleſſings on their peaceful days ;
Wak'd to new life, the land forget to mourn,
And fruitful ſeaſons to the plains return.   70
  Behold theſe ſcenes expanding to thy ſoul !
From orient realms what blackening armies roll !
See their proud Monarch, in yon glimmering car,
Leads his ſtrong hoſt, and points the waſte of war.
Till, rais'd by Heaven, the youth, whoſe early bloom, 75
Gives a fair promiſe of his worth to come,
That ſecond Irad, Othniel, lifts his hand,
And ſweeps the heathens from his waſted land.
  In awful pomp, ſee Hazor's bands ariſe,
Shade the far plains, and lower along the ſkies !   80
An unborn Jabin ſways thoſe ſpacious ſhores,
And on theſe climes that raging deluge pours.
The little band, thou ſeeſt thy nation ſends ;
Lo, how the hoſt innumerable bends !
Before Jehovah's wrath the millions fly,   85
Drop their weak arms, and lift a leſſening cry.
  Behold, in ſouthern ſkies, what clouds appear !
There Midian's ſons the bloody ſtandard rear :

Line 71) See Judg. 3. Ch. L. 79) Jud. 4, L. 87) Jud. 7.

I i

BOOK X.

Before them, Ruin marks her ravag'd way;
Fire sweeps the plains, and smoke involves the day!　90
Behold yon Angel, rapt on wings of light,
Flames, like a meteor, down the face of night!
His fearful hand accelerates their doom,
And their own weapons plunge them to the tomb.

Beyond fair Jordan, that broad, azure stream,　95
What moony shields, what throngs of lances, gleam!
In long, dark lines, see Jephthah's spreading host
Benight the heavens, and dusk the shady coast!
Lo, wing'd with fear, the ranks of Ammon yield,
Mount their bright cars, and fly the sanguine field!　100

From those dread scenes, now southward turn thine eyes;
Behold, what clouds of Philistines arise!
Ordain'd the terror of Canäan's climes,
The sting of guilt, the scourge of daring crimes;
Illum'd with spears, the gloomy squadrons roll,　105
Dust shades their path, and darkness hides the pole.

See Gaza's thousands, rang'd in black array,
Spread their wide volumes on the setting day!
Behold brave Samson sweep the dreadful plain!
Their falchions flame, their spears are hurl'd, in vain;
Swift from his fateful arm their squadrons fly,　111
And shields behind them glimmer on the sky.

Now, where yon haughty pile in pomp ascends,
His strong-wrought nerves the eyeless hero bends;
The columns shake, the cloudy temple falls,　115
And dusty ruin veils the smoking walls,

See, where proud Gibeah's turrets strike the skies,
On every side embattled armies rise!
There Civil Discord calls her sons to war,
And waves her banner through the troubled air;　120
Against one tribe the swords of all unite,
Destruction hovering o'er the crimson fight.

Line 95) Jud. 11.　L. 101) Jud. 13. &c.　L. 107) Jud. 15, 16.
L. 117) Jud. 20.

B O O K X.

See, like a ſtorm, the Philiſtines again
Roll o'er yon hills, and crowd the darkening plain !
Lo Iſrael flees ! the haughty heathens dare,   125
Pollute the ark ; nor know th' Almighty's there.
The ſacred Prophet lifts his ſuppliant hands,
And calls down vengeance on the impious bands ;
Aghaſt they hear tremendous thunders riſe,
And from the lightenings turn their trembling eyes ;   130
The fields are redden'd with a ſanguine die,
The vanquiſh'd triumph, and the victors fly.

Thus ſcenes of varied life thy nation prove,
Reſtrain their crimes, and fix their wandering love.
At length, impatient of their Maker's hand,   135
Their tribes, with union'd voice ; a king demand.
Firſt choſen to the throne, of truth forlorn,
Blaſting the promiſe of his opening morn,
Saul, impious tyrant, holds the ſacred ſway,
And Iſrael's hapleſs ſons his rod obey.   140
But now the ſcenes a longer view demand ;
Behold what wonders to thine eyes expand !

The hero gaz'd ; at once two mountains roſe,
O'erſpread by ſquadrons of embattled foes.
Proud, from the ſouthern hill a giant ſtrode,   145
Dar'd his pale foes, and brav'd the arm of GOD.
Vaſt were his limbs, for war and ruin made ;
His towering ſtature caſt a long, dark ſhade ;
His eye glar'd fury, and his buckler's gleam,
Flam'd, like a cloud before the ſetting beam.   150
A youth, in nature's prime, oppos'd his arm,
To the dire threatenings of the lowering ſtorm :
Soft round his aſpect roſy beauty ſmil'd,
Bold but not raſh, and without terror mild.
By his ſtrong hand, like rapid lightening, flung,   155
Full on the giant's front a pebble ſung ;

Line 123) 1 Sam. 7. L, 143) 1 Sam. 17.

Like some tall oak, the mighty warrior fell,
And with shrill thunders rang his clashing steel.
At once the heathens fled ; their foes pursued,
And boundless death the crimson fields bestrew'd.   160
 Then thus the Guide---Here David's skilful hand,
Sinks vast Goliath in the bloody sand.
Call'd, from the peace of sylvan shades unknown,
To rule an empire, and to mount a throne,
This beauteous youth shall stretch a prosperous sway,   165
And bid rude realms, and conquer'd kings, obey ;
Where fertile shores the proud Euphrates laves,
Where yon broad ocean rolls its lucid waves,
Beyond the limits of the Syrian reign,
Or where far southward spreads the crimson main.   170
 Behold, in dreadful pomp, from northern skies,
What gloomy clouds, what thronging squadrons rise !
Kings in the flaming van exalt their forms,
Borne in swift cars, and wrapp'd in dazzling arms ;
Here Ammon's sons unnumber'd crowd the fields ;   175
There Syria's millions wave their glimmering shields.
 See Israel moves in glory to the fight !
See Joab, circled with a blaze of light !
His lofty port, his firm, undaunted eye,
Shoot terror round, and bid the millions fly.   180
 Again what crowds the distant plains invade !
How the world darkens in the sable shade !
Aloft in air the dancing banners fly,
And throngs of lances tremble in the sky.
High in the front majestic David stands,   185
Leads on the conquest, and the fight commands,
Bids death before him sweep the dreadful plain,
And rolls his chariot o'er th unnumber'd slain.
 Nor less shall peace adorn his righteous sway ;
The proud shall tremble, and the rich obey ;   190
With equal hand, great Justice hold the scale ;
In every council Wisdom's voice prevail ;

Line 17 1) 2 Sam. 10.

The fields grow fat, beneath the culturing hand,
And smiling plenty wanton round the land.
Then spacious towns, with wealth and pomp supplied, 195
Shall bend long walls and lift their spiry pride ;
O'er all imperial Salem's splendors rise,
The boast of earth, and emblem of the skies.
He spoke : tall mountains rear their summits high,
Crown'd with fair spires, that vanish in the sky ;   200
Upheave huge walls : imperial arches bend,
And golden turrets to the clouds ascend.
So, when dun night begins in heaven to rise,
A long, dark cloud surrounds the northern skies ;
Forth from its spacious womb effulgent stream   205
Tall spires of glory, columns bright of flame ;
There shine gay walls illumin'd towers ascend,
Wave round th' immense, and o'er the concave bend ;
Expanding, reddening, the proud pomp aspires,
And stars faint-tremble through the wonderous fires. 210
Thus wide, thus bright, the splendid scene expands,
Rich with the treasures of surrounding lands;
The long streets wind ; the lofty domes ascend ;
Fair gardens bloom, and cryftal fountains bend ;
From flowery millions rich perfumes arise,   215
Load the sweet gales, and breathe upon the skies.
    There, crown'd with towers, and wrapp'd in golden
A bursting dome the wondering Chief descried,   [pride,
On eastern hills its front aerial stood,
Look'd o'er the walls, and distant regions view'd ;   220
There glow'd the beauty of the artists' minds ;
There gates, there spires, there columns, he design'd ;
There, with strong light, etherial wisdom shone,
There blended glories mock'd the noonday sun,
A bright, celestial grandeur towers display'd;   225
And verdant courts, expansive, round them spread.

Line 217) See 2 Chron. 6. 7.

There call'd from circling realms, a gladfome train,
In gayeft robes, unnumber'd, hid the plain.
Soft rofe their fongs ; the harp's bewildering found,
Breath'd mild inchantment through the domes around,
On fhining altars gifts of virtue lay,   231
Rich incenfe fum'd, and fmoke embrown'd the day.
High o'er the reft, a prince majeftic ftood,
And robes of fplendor loofely round him flow'd ;
Spread were hit hands ; his face, to earth declin'd, 235
Spoke the calm raptures of a pious mind ;
His voice, on balmy winds, like incenfe, driven,
Rofe, fweetly fragrant, to approving heaven :
At once, as earthquakes, rumbling, rock the ground,
Slow roll'd a long, deep roar the dome around ;   240
O'er the tall towers a cloud convolving fpread,
Bedimm'd the fkies, and wrapp'd the world in fhade ;
Fierce from its womb terrific lightenings came,
The gifts exhaling in the rapid flame ;
The train fell proftrate ; fhook the bright abode,   245
And trembling earth confefs'd the prefent God.
    Then thus the Guide---This prince, to David born,
With folemn pomp fhall Salem's towers adorn ;
To God's great name, this glorious pile fhall raife,
Fair type of Heaven, and feat of lafting praife.   250
    In his blefs'd reign, fhall peace extend her fway ;
The poor dwell fafely, and the proud obey ;
Ifrael, fecure, in happy fields recline,
Pluck their own figs, and tafte their plenteous wine ;
The fwain fole monarch of his lands fhall reign,   255
And own the products of the grateful plain.
On fame's light wings, his glory fhall be borne,
Where fmiles fair eve, or blooms etherial morn ;
From diftant regions kings enraptur'd throng,
Drink facred truth, and catch the heavenly fong :   260
To him, her boundlefs wealth fhall Egypt yield ;
To him, Sabea ope the fpicy field ;

BOOK X.

In morn's fair iflands, fweets celeftial blow ;
Wide ocean's realms with pearly fplendors glow :
 The loom its purple, earth its gems, unfold,   265
And teeming fulphur kindle into gold.

 Long fhall bright wifdom gild his profperous day,
Till magic beauty charm his heart aftray ;
Wifdom, beyond the narrow thoughts of man,
In clouds involv'd, and bounded by a fpan ;   270
Wifdom, that nature's myfteries fhall controul,
And rule the nobler kingdom of the foul.

 At length, when death his fpirit fhall demand,
Two guilty kings fhall fway Canäan's land,
Both to the fatal love of idols given,   275
And both rejected by an angry Heaven:
While their mad kingdoms oft in fight contend,
And flames lay wafte their fields, and wars their cities rend.

 Then fhall th' Eternal's awful vengeance rife,
His wheels defcend, his chariot fhake the fkies   280
Before his breath the fon's of Ifrael fly,
Like chaff when whirlwinds fweep th' autumnal fky,
To realms, whofe beauty endlefs frofts deform,
To heavens that thunder with eternal ftorm :
Where o'er yon fiery cliffs, that bound the fkies,   285
Dejected funs with feeble influence rife,
At diftance hovering round the unblefs'd fhore,
Where glimmering ice forbids the waves to roar.

 Yet ftill, while Judah owns his awful fway,
And pious kings their facred homage pay,   290
Safe in the covert of his guardian hand,
Shall happy fubjects fhare a peaceful land ;
Till rous'd to wrath by infolence of crimes,
He rolls deep horror o'er Canäan's climes.

 On that dread morn, fhall Salem hear from far   295
The trump's fhrill clamour, and the founding car ;
Hofts train'd to blood her fhining feats furround,
And all her glories totter to the ground.

Adieu ! adieu ! thou darling of the skies ;
Thy towers begin to shake ; thy flames begin to rise. 300
    Where once the palace raptur'd eyes descried,
And the tall temple rear'd its splendid pride,
Round mouldering walls the nightly wolf shall howl ;
Sad ruins murmur to the wailing owl ;
In domes, once golden, creeping moss be found ;   305
The long, rank weed o'erspread the garden's bound ;
The wild Idumean cast a mournful eye
On the brown towers, and pass in silence by.

    Nor let deep sorrow pain thy pitying eyes ;
Lo fairer scenes in quick succession rise !   310
Soon shall the temple crown the sacred hill,
Bright domes ascend, and fields around them smile ;
Thy nation gather ; great Messiah shine,
And earth be honour'd with a King divine.

    From Edom's realms, what mighty form ascends !   315
How the vale blossoms ! how the mountain bends !
How shine his limbs, in heaven's immortal pride !
How beams his vesture in the rainbow died !
'Tis he ! 'tis he ! who saves a world undone ;
The Prince of glory ! God's eternal Son !   320
O'er conscious hills he wins his beauteous way ;
The plains are transport, and all nature gay.

    O sons of men !---th' indulgent Saviour cries---
My raptur'd voice invites you to the skies.
No more to Jacob's narrow race confin'd,   325
A bliss unmeasur'd flows for all mankind ;
The life, the youth, of climes forever bless'd ;
Increasing glory, and seraphic rest.

    Say, what the gain in pleasure's paths to stray,
Where poison blossoms, and where serpents play.   330
Ambition's lofty steep with pain to climb,
Where guilt, and anguish, swell with every crime ;

Line 323) Isaiah 63.

To wafte, in weary toils, man's little doom,
For treafures, ravifh'd by the neighbouring tomb.
Should earth's broad realms beneath your fceptre roll,
Can worlds exchang'd redeem the deathlefs foul ?   336
Rife then, oh rife, from fin's oblivious fleep !
Lo, wide beneath you gapes th' unfathom'd deep !
Explore, with me, the undeceiving road,
That blooms with virtue, and that leads to GOD.   340
　　What though dire pain, and grief, and fad difmay,
And all earth's fury hedge the arduous way ;
Thofe griefs, thofe pains, my feet before you brave,
The world's fell hatred, and the gloomy grave ;
I feel fuperior wifdom's peace refin'd,   345
And the fair morning of a guiltlefs mind ;
The toils of faith, rewarding as they rife ;
Befriending feraphs, and complacent Skies.
　　And O the end ! the bright, immortal end !
Heaven's gates unbar, and angel hofts attend.   350
Each hour more fweet, for you her rivers roll ;
A fky, ftill brightening, arches round her pole ;
Fair, and more fair, her funny manfions glow ;
Pure, and more pure, her airs etherial blow ;
Her hoft, in growing youth, ferenely fhines ;   355
Her glory quickens, and her world refines.
In that fair world, to e'er-beginning joy,
Each hour increafing, ting'd with no alloy,
Reft from each toil, relief from every care,
Conqueft of death, and triumph o'er defpair,   360
To your own peers, your lafting home, afcend,
To blifs' fair fountain, virtue's faithful friend,
Thofe peers heaven's fons, that home the bright abode,
That fount an ocean, and that friend a GOD.
To thefe fair realms to lift the contrite mind,   365
To give blefs'd faith, and purchafe peace refin'd,
To man's loft foul the ftamp of heaven recall,
And build again the ruins of the fall,

　　　　　　K k

From God's high throne he comes to every woe,
The world his dungeon, and mankind his foe,   370
Heaven's wrath for thankless wretches dares assume,
Ascends the cross, and tries the darksome tomb.

    Lo these dread scenes expanding to thine eye!
Behold yon cloudy pomp invest the sky!
What hosts of angels wave their flamy wings!   375
The world is silent---hark, what music rings!---
All hail, ye happy swains! this sacred morn,
Of David's race, the promis'd Saviour's born;
In Bethlehem's inn, behold the parent maid,
Her heavenly offspring in a manger laid!   380
See, see, in yon blue track, his star ascend!
Adore ye angels! heaven in homage bend!
From earth one cloud of mingling incense rise!
Peace to the world, and glory to the skies!

    Before the harbinger behold him stand,   385
And take the sacred sprinkling from his hand;
On wings of flame the etherial dove descend,
And the glad train with reverent homage bend!
Far round th' immense approving thunders roll,   389
And God's own son belov'd resounds from pole to pole.

    See, at his touch, the fainting form respires;
The pale-eyed leper glows with purple fires;
Light as the hart, th' exulting cripple springs,
And the dumb suppliant new-born praises sings;
Unusual sounds the cleaving ear surprise,   395
And light, and prospect, charm expanding eyes;
The dungeon bursts; the prisoner leaps to day,
And life recall'd reanimates the clay!

    At his commands, what throngs of demons flee,
To yon far gulf, that blackens o'er the sea!   400
Lo, in the skirt of yonder fading storm,
Obscurely sailing, many a dreadful form!

    Line 373) Luke 2.   L. 385) Mat. 3.

From its deep womb, what sullen murmurs rise !
And what pale lightenings feebly sweep the skies !
   But O ! what love the harden'd soul can gain !   405
Fair truth compels, Messiah charms, in vain.
Untaught, unmov'd, by hate and fury driven,
His nation rise against the heir of heaven,
Before a heathen's bar tumultuous hale ;
Nor worth can move, nor innocence avail.   410
Behold the milder glories round him shine !
What peace serene ! what constancy divine !
How silently sublime ! how meekly great !
How virtue's splendor shades the glare of state !
   By friends denied, by poor vile worms contemn'd, 415
Judg'd without law, and without guilt condemn'd,
While men, while demons, in fond triumph rise,
The Prince of life, the Lord of angels, dies.
At once dire earthquakes heave the shuddering ground,
Rend the hard rocks ; the mountains quake around ; 420
Far o'er the world blank midnight casts her shade,
And trembling rise the nations of the dead :
Pain'd, from the scene the conscious sun retires,
And nature's voice proclaims---A God expires.
   But not the earth his sacred form confines ;   425
The bands dissolve ; the grave its trust resigns ;
His fair, transforming limbs new life inspires ;
Heaven's youth informs, and Godlike beauty fires ;
From the dark tomb he wings his lucid way,
Ascends the sky, and glads the climes of day.   430
As thy bold arm, to Israel's chosen band,
Thy foes extinguish'd, gives the promis'd land ;
Call'd by thy name, shall he to realms of gloom
Drive vanquish'd Death, and triumph o'er the tomb,
To that bless'd land, the true Canäan, rise,   435
And guide his chosen children to the skies.
   Then o'er his foes shall fearful vengeance break ;
Heaven shine in arms ; earth's listening regions quake ;

B O O K X.

The fond, vain triumph unknown woes deſtroy,
And clouds of ruin blaſt the tranſient joy.   440
   Behold, in weſtern ſkies, the ſtorm aſcend,
Its terrors blacken, and its flames extend !
There hide the whirlwinds, ſoon ordain'd to roll ;
There ſleep fierce thunders, ſoon to rock the pole.
But firſt dread ſigns the guilty world alarm ;   445
A ſanguine horror ſhades the ſun's bright form ;
In fields of air, unreal hoſts contend ;
Shrill arms reſound, and cars the concave rend :
From hell's black ſhores the Peſtilence aſpires,
Roams the wide earth, and breathes her baleful fires ; 450
Whole regions wither in her ſickening flight,
And hoſts, and nations, periſh in a night :
Far round the ſhuddering ſky pale meteors glare,
And raging Diſcord ſounds the trump of war.
   Then countleſs millions ſeize the bloody ſhield,   455
And Death's black enſign glooms the fading field.
Lo, Zion's domes what grimly hoſts incloſe !
See ſun-bright eagles lead her gathering foes !
High o'er her walls, what threatening engines riſe !
And hark, what clamours murmuring mount the ſkies ;
With clouds, purſuing clouds, the terrors grow ;   461
More fierce the blaze, more dark th' invading woe.
But why ſhould diſmal ſcenes diſtreſs thy ſight,
Or grief unnerve thee for th' impending fight ?
   Meantime, from land to land with ſpeed convey'd, 465
Meſſiah's ſons his truth and bleſſings ſpread.
On countleſs realms, to guilt and darkneſs given,
Aliens from life, and reprobate of Heaven,
The ſacred Spirit ſheds his healing power,
And ſkies indulgent heavenly bounty ſhower.   470
Low at his name the raptur'd nations bend ;
By him perfum'd, unnumber'd prayers aſcend ;

Line 441) Mat. 24. L. 455) Taking of Jeruſalem by the Romans.
L. 465) Preaching of the Goſpel by the Apoſtles. &c.

BOOK X.

To heaven his name from earth's great houshold flies,
And one vast cloud of incense cheers the skies.

From Salem's favour'd hills, the bliss shall stray, 475
Glad every land, and stretch to every sea ;
But chief far onward speed its western flight,
And bless the regions of descending light.

Far o'er yon azure main thy view extend,
Where seas, and skies, in blue confusion blend, 480
Lo, there a mighty realm, by heaven design'd
The last retreat for poor, oppres'd mankind !
Form'd with that pomp, which marks the hand divine,
And clothes yon vault, where worlds unnumber'd shine,
Here spacious plains in solemn grandeur spread ; 485
Here cloudy forests cast eternal shade :
Rich vallies wind ; the sky tall mountains brave,
And inland seas for commerce spread the wave ;
With nobler floods, the sea-like rivers roll,
And fairer lustre purples round the pole. 490
Here, warm'd by happy suns, gay mines unfold
The useful iron, and the lasting gold ;
Pure, changing gems in silence learn to glow,
And mock the splendors of the covenant bow :
On countless hills, by savage footsteps trod, 495
That smile to see the future harvest nod,
In glad succession, plants unnumber'd bloom,
And flowers unnumber'd breathe a rich perfume ;
Hence life once more a length of days shall claim,
And health, reviving, light her purple flame. 500
Far from all realms this world imperial lies ;
Seas roll between, and threatening storms arise ;
Alike unmov'd beyond Ambition's pale,
And the bold pinions of the venturous sail :
Till circling years the destin'd period bring, 505
And a new Moses lifts the daring wing.

Line 479) Vision of America.

BOOK X.

Through trackless seas, an unknown flight explores,
And hails a new Canäan's promis'd shores.

   On yon far strand, behold that little train
Ascending, venturous, o'er th' unmeasur'd main.   510
No dangers fright : no ills the course delay ;
'Tis virtue prompts, and GOD directs the way.
Speed, speed, ye sons of truth ! let Heaven befriend,
Let angels waft you, and let peace attend !
O smile thou sky serene ! ye storms retire !   515
And airs of Eden every sail inspire !
Swift o'er the main, behold the canvas fly,
And fade, and fade, beneath the farthest sky ;
See verdant fields the changing waste unfold ;
See sudden harvests dress the plains in gold :   520
In lofty walls the moving rocks ascend,
And dancing woods to spires and temples bend !

   Meantime, expanding o'er earth's distant ends,
Lo, Slavery's gloom in sable pomp descends ;
Far round each eastern clime her volumes roll,   525
And pour, deep-shading, to the sadden'd pole.
How the world droops beneath the fearful blast ;
The plains all wither'd, and the skies o'ercast !
From realm to realm extends the general groan ;
The fainting body stupifies to stone ;   530
Benumb'd, and fix'd, the palsied soul expires,
Blank'd all its views, and quench'd its living fires ;
In clouds of boundless shade, the scenes decay ;
Land after land departs, and nature fades away.

   In that dread hour, beneath auspicious skies,   535
To nobler bliss yon western world shall rise.
Unlike all former realms, by war that stood,
And saw the guilty throne ascend in blood,
Here union'd Choice shall form a rule divine ;
Here countless lands in one great system join ;   540

   Line. 509] Settlement of North America, by the English, for the
enjoyment of Religion. L. 525) Slavery of the eastern Continent.
L. 535) Freedom and glory of the North American States.

BOOK X.

The sway of Law unbroke, unrivall'd grow,
And bid her blessings every land o'erflow.

In fertile plains, behold the tree ascend,
Fair leaves unfold, and spreading branches bend!
The fierce, invading storm secure they brave, 545
And the strong influence of the creeping wave,
In heavenly gales with endless verdure rise,
Wave o'er broad fields, and fade in friendly skies.
There safe from driving rains, and battering hail,
And the keen fury of the wintry gale, 550
Fresh spring the plants; the flowery millions bloom,
All ether gladdening with a choice perfume;
Their hastening pinions birds unnumber'd spread,
And dance, and wanton, in th' aerial shade. 555

Here Empire's last, and brightest throne shall rise;
And Peace, and Right, and Freedom, greet the skies:
To morn's far realms her ships commercing sail,
Or lift their canvas to the evening gale;
In wisdom's walks, her sons ambitious soar,
Tread starry fields, and untried scenes explore. 560
And hark what strange, what solemn-breathing strain
Swells, wildly murmuring, o'er the far, far main!
Down time's long, lessening vale, the notes decay,
And, lost in distant ages, roll away.

When earth commenc'd, six morns of labour rose, 565
Ere the calm Sabbath shed her soft repose.
Thus shall the world's great week direct its way,
And thousand circling suns complete the day.
Past were two days, ere beam'd the law divine;
Two days must roll, ere great Messiah shine; 570
Two changeful days, the Gospel's light shall rise;
Then sacred quiet hush the stormy skies.
O'er orient regions suns of toil shall roll,
Faint lustre dawn, and clouds obscure the pole:

Line 565) The Jews have an ancient tradition of this nature.

=56   B O O K   X.

But o'er yon favourite world, the Sabbath's morn,   575
Shall pour unbounded day, and with clear splendor burn.

   Hence, o'er all lands shall sacred influence spread,
Warm frozen climes, and cheer the death-like shade;
To nature's bounds, reviving Freedom reign,
And Truth, and Virtue, light the world again.   580

   No more in arms shall battling nations rise;
Nor war's hoarse thunders heave the earth and skies;
No hungry vulture, from the rock's tall brow,
Eye the red field, and slaughtering host, below;
No famine waste; no tender infant fear;   585
The meek-eyed virgin drop no painful tear;
Soft to the lyre the trumpet sink refin'd,
And peace' mild music still the stormy mind:
The savage, nurs'd in blood, with wondering eye,
Sees all the horrors of the desert fly :   590
Dread war, once rapturous, now his soul affrights;
Sweet peace allures, and angel love delights;
His melting thoughts with softer passion glow;
His tears steal gently o'er the plaint of woe;
To virtuous toils his feet instinctive turn ;   595
Or seek the temple in the smiles of morn;
Each stormy purpose truth's mild rays serene,
And spring celestial clothes the waste within.

   See, round the lonely wild, with glad surprise,
Strange verdure blooms, and flowery wonders rise!   600
Hark how the sounds of gushing waters roll!
What new Arabias breathe upon the soul!
On russet plains returning Sharon blows;
Her fragrance charms; her living beauty glows;
Each mount a Lebanon in pomp ascends,   605
And, topp'd with cloudy pride, the cedar bends;
To meads, to sports, with lambs the wolf retires,
Sooth'd his wild rage, and quench'd his gloomy fires,

   Line 577) Beginning of the millennium. See Isaiah and the other
prophets.

BOOK X.

The viper fierce, the hissing asp, grow mild,
Refuse their prey, and wanton with the child:　　610
New hymns the plumy tribes inraptur'd raise,
And howling forests harmonize to praise.

Shine soft, O sun ! ye skies around them smile !
Your showers propitious balmy heavens distil !
In every waste what cheerful domes arise !　　615
What golden temples meet the bending skies ;
To yon bright world what clouds of incense roll ;
How Virtue's songs breathe sweet from pole to pole !

Through earth's wide realms let solemn silence flow !
Be hush'd thou main ! ye winds forget to blow !　　620
JEHOVAH speaks---Beneath the farthest skies,
My trump shall sound, my sacred standard rise ;
From morn to eve the lucid banner shine,
And saints, ecstatic, hail th' illustrious sign.
Wak'd from the slumbers of the world unknown,　　625
See raptur'd Sion mount the starry throne,
Round her fair gates, her thronging sons behold,
Dress'd in white garments, and adorn'd with gold !

Arise, O child of fostering heaven, arise ;
Queen of the world, and favourite of the skies ;　　630
In sunny robes, with living splendor, shine ;
Be all thy vestments as thyself divine !

Seize the loud harp, arouse the breathing string ;
Exalt thine eyes, and hymns of transport sing ;
Behold thy ruin'd walls again ascend ;　　635
Thy towers shoot up ; thy spacious arches bend ;
Thy gardens brighten ; streams reviving roll,
And gales of paradise intrance the soul.

Where long, long howl'd the solitary blast,
O'er the brown mountain, and the dreary waste ;　　640
Where famish'd wolves proclaim'd their nightly roam,
And raging lions found a bloody home ;

Line 619) Calling of the Jews.

L l

Again glad funs command thy towers to burn,
And o'er thy fplendors burfts the raptur'd morn ;
In vales of fragrance hymns of angels ring ;   645
The mountains leap ; the confcious forefts fing ;
To thy fair realms the bloom of Eden given
Tranfcends the morn, and rivals opening heaven.

    Lo, from the weft, and eaft, and fouth, and north,
In countlefs millions, Gentile throngs break forth !   650
Their garlands bloom ; their golden offerings blaze ;
Their harps inftinctive tremble to thy praife.
For thee, what prayers from gathering lands afcend !
What fuppliant nations at thine altars bend !
With what foft mufic founds th' etherial fong !   655
What love, what ecftacy, attunes the tongue !
How gay the heavens ! how fair the earth ferene !
How joy illumes, how incenfe charms the fcene !
Lo, in each face primæval beauty glows !
In every vein primæval vigour flows ;   660
In every bofom brightens peace refin'd,
And endlefs funfhine lights th' unclouded mind ;
Without one terror, fhuts the willing eye
And the foul wafts in flumber to the fky.
See mighty Juftice lifts his awful reign !   665
Behold new Jofhuas fway thy realms again !
Again the Prophet lights the earthly gloom ;
Heaven's gates difclofe, and climes beyond the tomb ;
To earth glad angels fpeed their beauteous flight,
And call their fellows to the domes of light !   670
    In eaftern climes, where funs begin to roll,
Or where clear fplendors gild the fparkling pole,
Or where, illum'd by nature's faireft ray,
Smile the blefs'd regions of defcending day,
Unnumber'd fhips, like mift the morn exhales,   675
Stretch their dim canvas to the rufhing gales.
Behold, afcending, cloud-like, in the fkies,
How their fails whiten ! how their mafts arife !

BOOK X.

The world all moves ! the far-extended main
Is loft beneath th' immeafurable train !   680
Here earth impatient all her treafures yields,
Fruits of gay mines, and fweets of fpicy fields :
Fair robes of filken fplendor mock the morn,
And fun-bright gems with changing luftre burn.

   Exult, O earth ! ye heavens with joy furvey   685
Her charms, her glories, hold the lingering day !
Lo, wrapp'd in fparkling gold, thy wide walls burn ;
Thy ftones to pearls, thy gates to diamonds, turn,
Thy domes to palaces, thy feats to thrones,
To queens thy daughters, and to kings thy fons.   690

   Awake, awake, ye tenants of the tomb !
Burft your cold chains, and hail your deftin'd home !
Lo, the night fades ; the fky begins to burn,
And ruddy fplendor opes the living morn !
See tombs, inftinctive, break the fleepy charm,   695
And gales divine the duft imprifon'd warm ;
From finifh'd flumbers changing patriarchs rife ;
Life crowns their heads, and tranfport fires their eyes ;
Drefs'd in the youth of heaven, again are join'd
The form angelic and the fainted mind.   700

   From blifs to blifs the circling hours fhall flow ;
With my own fmiles the pure expanfion glow,
Bright as the moon, the ftars inveft the pole ;
Bright as the fun, the moon fublimely roll ;
Unmeafur'd glories round the fun arife,   795
And every morn light nations to the fkies.

   Long, long fhall thefe fair fcenes the bofom charm,
And light, and love, refining nature warm ;
Till earth flow-mouldering hear the great decree,
And time's laft waves approach th' unfathom'd fea.   710
There o'er wild regions, round the diftant pole,
Shall war's tremendous voice begin to roll,

Line 707] Signs which forbode the end of the world. See Mat.
24, and Rev. 19.

BOOK X.

From hell's dark caverns Discord fierce ascend,
Resound her trump, and startled nature rend ;
All heaven re-echo to the deep alarms,   715
And maddening nations swiftly rush to arms.
See, high in air, her banner, wide unfurl'd,
Streams in black terror o'er the trembling world ;
From pole to pole the rage of combat flies,
And realms 'gainst realms with ardent vengeance rise ! 720
To scenes of slaughtering Fight the millions pour ;
Loud thunders roll, and flashing swords devour ;
On delug'd plains unnumber'd corses lie,
And shouts, and groans, immingled, cleave the sky.
To Cities then she steers her dusky way ;   725
The turrets shake, the walls in smoke decay :
O'er the tall domes, and spires in gold array'd,
Where Pomp sate thron'd, and Joy and Friendship play'd,
Fierce drives the nimble flame ; the whirlwinds throng,
Howl through the walls, and drive the storm along.   730
Now to the Fields she wings her rapid force,
The world involving in her wasting course ;
Before her car, a fiery tempest flies ;
Behind, long hosts interminably rise ;
From her pale face th' etherial orbs retire ;   735
Deep heaves the ground ; the blackening groves expire ;
Horror, and wild dismay, the earth appall,
And one unbounded ruin buries all.
    Mid these dire scenes, more awful scenes shall rise ;
Sad nations quake, and trembling seize the skies.   740
From the dark tomb shall fearful lights ascend ;
And sullen sounds the sleeping mansion rend ;
Pale ghosts with terror break the dreamer's charm,
And death-like cries the listening world alarm.
Then midnight pangs shall toss the cleaving plains ; 745
Fell Famine wanton o'er unburied trains ;
From crumbling mountains baleful flames aspire ;
Realms sink in floods, and towns dissolve in fire ;

In every blaft, the fpotted plague be driven,
And angry meteors blaze athwart the heaven. 750
Clouds of dark blood fhall blot the fun's broad light,
Spread round th' immenfe, and fhroud the world in night,
With pale, and dreadful ray, the cold moon gleam ;
The dim, lone ftars diffufe an anguifh'd beam ;
Storms rock the fkies ; afflicted ocean roar, 755
And fanguine billows die the fhuddering fhore :
And round earth thunder, from the almighty throne,
The voice irrevocable--- IT IS DONE.

   Rous'd on the fearful morn, fhall nature hear
The trump's deep terrors rend the troubled air ; 760
From realm to realm the found tremendous roll,
Cleave the broad main, and fhake th' aftonifh'd pole ;
The flumbering bones th' Archangel's call infpire ;
Rocks fink in duft, and earth be wrapp'd in fire ;
From realms far-diftant orbs unnumber'd come, 765
Sail thro' immenfity, and learn their doom :
And all yon changelefs ftars, that, thron'd on high,
Reign in immortal luftre round the fky,
In folemn filence fhroud their living light,
And leave the world to undiftinguifh'd night. 770
   Hark, what dread founds, defcending from the pole,
Wave following wave, in fwelling thunders roll !
How the tombs cleave ! What awful forms arife !
What crowding nations pain the failing eyes !
From land to land behold the mountains rend ; 775
From fhore to fhore the final flames afcend,
Round the dark poles with boundlefs terror reign,
With bend immeafurable fweep the main,
From morn's far kingdoms ftretch to realms of even,
And climb, and climb, with folemn roar to heaven. 780
What fmoky ruins wrap the leffening ground !
What firey fheets fail through the vaulted round !

Line 759) Refurrection and Conflagration. 787] Laft Judgement.

Pour'd in one mass, the lands, and seas, decay;
Inroll'd, the heavens, dissolving, fleet away;
The moon departs; the sun's last beams expire,　785
And nature's buried in the boundless fire.

　Lo, from the radiance of the bless'd abode,
Messiah comes, in all the pomp of God!
Borne on swift winds, a storm before him flies;
Stars crown his head, and rainbows round him rise;　790
Beneath his feet, a sun's broad terrors burn,
And cleaving darkness opes a dreadful morn:
Through boundless space careering flames are driven;
Truth's sacred hosts descend, and all the thrones of heaven.
See crowding millions, call'd from earth's far ends, 795
See hell's dark world, with fearful gloom, ascends,
In throngs incomprehensible! Around
Worlds after worlds, from nature's farthest bound,
Call'd by th' Archangel's voice, from either pole,
Self-mov'd, with all created nations, roll.　　　800
From this great train, his eyes the just divide,
Price of his life, and being's fairest pride;
Rob'd by his mighty hand, the starry throngs
From harps of transport call exstatic songs.

　Hail, heirs of endless peace! ordain'd to rove　805
Round the pure climes of everlasting love.
For you the sun first led the lucid morn;
The world was fashion'd, and Messiah born;
For you high heaven with fond impatience waits,
Pours her fair streams, and opes her golden gates;　810
Each hour, with purer glory, gayly shines,
Her courts enlarges, and her air refines.

　But O unhappy race! to woes consign'd,
Lur'd by fond pleasure, and to wisdom blind.
What new Messiah shall the spirit save,　　　815
Stay the pent flames, and shut th' eternal grave?
Where sleeps the music of his voice divine?
Where hides the face, that could so sweetly shine?

Now hear that flighted voice to thunder turn !
See that mild face with flames of vengeance burn ! 820
High o'er your heads the ftorm of ruin roars,
And, round th' immenfe no friend your fate deplores.

Lo, there to endlefs woe in throngs are driven,
What once were angels, and bright ftars of heaven !
The world's gay pride ! the king with fplendor crown'd!
The chief refiftlefs, and the fage renown'd ! 826
Down, down, the millions fink ; where yon broad main
Heaves her dark waves, and fpreads the feats of pain :
Where long, black clouds, emblaz'd with awful fire, 829
Pour fullen round their heads, and in dread gloom retire.

Then, tumult's hideous din forever o'er,
All foes fubdued, and doom'd to rife no more,
Sin forc'd from each fair clime to final flight,
And hell's dark prifon lock'd in endlefs night ;
To heaven's extremes diviner peace fhall roll, 835
And fpread through countlefs worlds, beyond each diftant
Crown'd with glad triumph, from the toils of war, [pole.
On angel's wings, fhall fail Meffiah's car ;
To the great Sire his conquering hand reftore
Th' etherial enfigns of unmeafur'd power ; 840
Prefent his fons, before the palace bright,
And feek the bofom of unborrow'd light.

Then fcenes, in heaven before unknown, fhall rife,
And a new æra blefs th' angelic fkies ;
Through boundlefs tracts, a nobler kingdom fhine, 845
Nor Seraphs' minds conceive the pomp divine.
All realms, all worlds above, combin'd in one ;
The heaven of heavens the bright, eternal throne;
The fubjects faints ; the period endlefs fpring ;
The realm immenfity, and GOD the king. 850

As fix'd, unchang'd, yon central world of fire
Leads on fublime the planetary choir,

Line 831) Confummation of all things.

Lights all the living lamps, and round the sky,
In midnight splendor calls the moon to fly ;
Creates their smiles, instructs their orbs to roll,   855
Fair eye of nature, and the world's great soul ;
So, in the beams of clear perfections shrin'd,
Shall his great Source, the Uncreated Mind,
Through all the Morning Stars that round him glow,
Rove in his smiles, and at his altar bow,   860
Through countless trains, where worlds unnumber'd rise,
And cloth'd in starry pomp superior skies,
Pure rays of endless peace indulgent shine,
And warm immensity with love divine.

Love's mighty chain shall boundless beings bind,   865
Join world to world, and mind unite with mind ;
O'er the great houshold heaven's eternal pride,
From age to age, th' Almighty Sire preside ;
Around his awful throne, with searching eyes,
See fairer sons, and priests, and kings, arise ;   870
Bid his own essence in their hearts revive,
His beauty brighten, and his glory live :
From harps etherial living raptures fall,
Heaven fill th' immense, and GOD BE ALL IN ALL.

In glory wafted down the lucid pole,   875
See Salem's walls their solemn scenes unroll !
Less beauteous charms the lovely spouse array,
When beams of rapture light the bridal day.
Behold, new skies serenely round her glow ;
Pure fragrance breathes, and purple splendors flow :   880
In pomp ascends the ever-rising morn,
And starry rainbows round her chariot burn !

There, from the distant wave, no suns arise ;
No moon's pale radiance gleams in evening skies ;
Round the broad region, with unfading ray,   885
JEHOVAH smiles immeasurable day :

Line 875) Prospect of heaven, and a happy immortality.

BOOK X.

With living luſtre, fruits celeſtial glow,
And ſtreams of life in endleſs beauty flow.

In robes of angels, ſee the choſen ſhine;
Waft on the floods, or walk in light divine;　　890
Or taſte the changing tree, whoſe fruit ſupplies
The youth of heaven, and beauty of the ſkies!

There, dreſs'd in bloom, and young in roſy years,
Th' immortal Father of mankind appears:
In clear effulgence, Iſrael's Prophet ſhines,　　895
And no dark veil his eager wiſh confines:
With ſmiles of joy ſerene, the Friend of God
Counts his glad ſons, and opes the bleſs'd abode.

To theſe fair realms thy footſteps ſhall aſcend;
Here crowns await thee, and bright robes attend;　　900
At nature's call, thy guardian ſeraph come,
And guide his choſen to th' eternal home;
Before the ſacred throne, thy thoughts appear,
Thy virtuous toils, thy truth, and love, ſincere;
His witneſs'd favourite, God with ſmiles approve,　　905
And join to nations of immortal love.

O bliſsful hour! when, freed from bonds of clay,
Thy path commences to the climes of day;
When from the ſun thy wing begins to riſe
Through the broad regions of unmeaſur'd ſkies,　　910
When time's dark years behind thy flight ſhall roll,
And all eternity invade thy ſoul.

In that bleſs'd hour, the ſons of light ſhall come,
And ſhout thee welcome to thy deſtin'd home;
With heightening beauty bloom each angel mind,　　915
Glow with pure joy, and yearn with love refin'd;
In ſtrains divine, impaſſion'd ſeraphs tell
How with dire treaſon heavenly nations fell;
What deeds renown'd have grac'd the fair abode;
Truth that endur'd, and zeal that rais'd to God;　　920
How round th' expanſion worlds unnumber'd ſprung,
And hoſts etherial ſky-born praiſes ſung;
The peace, the charms, to vernal Eden given,
Converſing angels, and approving Heaven.
In that bleſs'd hour, ſhall ſaints of antient days,　　925
Lights of mankind, and heirs of deathleſs praiſe,

M m

Diſcloſe how Adam's ſons the world o'erſpread,
Borne to far iſles, and o'er wide ſeas convey'd ;
How the lone ark the ſeeds of nations bore,
And boundleſs ocean toſs'd without a ſhore ;   930
Embattled hoſts the patriarch's faith o'ercame,
Nor votive Iſaac quench'd the living flame ;
Through the long devious deſert Iſrael rov'd ;
The angel wreſtled, and the brother lov'd.
Rapt in thy bleſs'd arrival, there ſhall glow   935
The faithful partners of thine every woe ;
Their hopes, their fears, their toils, with thee run o'er,
Pains far retir'd, and griefs that haunt no more ;
His long-lov'd friend unſpotted Hezron join,
Add ſong to ſong, and mingle bliſs with thine ;   940
Irad, divineſt flower ! to meet thee riſe,
And caſt rich fragrance round delighted ſkies.
    With this great concourſe loſt in joys ſerene,
No tongue can utter, and no fancy feign,
Diſſolv'd in friendſhip, chain'd to friends, divine,   945
Whoſe thoughts, whoſe converſe, every power refine,
Thy unknown ages ſwift ſhall glide away,
Loſt in th' immenſe of never-ending day.
Thro' heaven's expanded field thy feet ſhall rove,
Th' all-beauteous region of ecſtatic love ;   950
Her gates of pearl, her towers of gems, behold,
Her ſtreets, her manſions, of pellucid gold.
Where each fair gate cherubic watchmen guard,
And God, approving, ſhowers the vaſt reward.
    There ſhalt thou feel, when, freed from ſin's alloy, 955
Souls lift their pinions to the climes of joy,
Around all heaven what ſpeechleſs tranſports roll,
Blend ſmile with ſmile, and mingle ſoul with ſoul ;
There hail, ecſtatic, to the bright abode,
The crowns, the trophies, of Meſſiah's blood.   960
    There God's own hand ſhall lift the curtain high,
And all earth's wonders open to thine eye :
In time's myſterious reign, thy ſoul purſue
Power ever glorious, wiſdom ever new ;
See boundleſs good, Creation's ſingle end,   965
And God his own, and being's, faithful friend ;

BOOK X.

In all, the prefent God refulgent fhine,
And boundlefs glory fill the work divine.

    Fed with perennial fprings of blifs refin'd,
Divine effufions of th' All lovely Mind,   970
With endlefs ardour fhall thy fpirit glow,
And love immenfe from heaven's great fountain flow;
Unbounded grace fill unconfin'd defire,
Warm thy rapt bofom, and thy fongs infpire.

    Each hour, thy fpreading thoughts fhall fwift improve;
Each hour increafe the tranfports of thy love;   975
With morning beauty, Youth around thee fhine,
Implant new fenfes, and the old refine;
From height to height thy rifing wifhes grow,
And, at their birth, the full enjoyment flow;   980
No care, no want, th' expanding blifs deftroy,
But every thought, and fenfe, and wifh, be joy.

    From thefe blefs'd fcenes thy flight fhall oft defcend,
And, with thy kindred angels, man attend.
What fweet complacence fhall thy bofom warm,   985
To fpread fair truth, and every woe to charm;
Guard the lone cot, where faith delights to dwell;
Or wake pure fervors in the fecret cell;
Or watch that houfe, where ftrong devotions rife;
And prayers as incenfe cheer the morning fkies;   990
Where fons to faints, to angels daughters, grow,
And peace, and virtue, build a heaven below.
When fear alarms, fhalt thou that fear allay;
When grief diftreffes, fmile the pangs away;
When pain torments, the pious eyelids clofe,   995
Make foft the bed, and breathe ferene repofe;
Guide the departing foul to yonder fkies,
And teach the young immortal how to rife.
Through fcorching fands fhalt thou the wanderer bring,
Waft balmy gales, and point the cooling fpring;   1000
Or lure declining feet from flowery ways,
Seal the charm'd ear, and turn the fatal gaze;
Or with rude whirlwinds the rough main deform;
Or roll the thunders of the mountain ftorm;
Or on the fanguine plain fublimely ftand,   1005
Direct the triumph, and the flight command;

Or o'er some realm in glorious pomp preside,
To saints a guardian, and to kings a guide.

    Nor shall one world thy bounded view confine ;
But round all being stretch thy flight divine,   1010
To worlds dispers'd o'er worlds, ambitious rise,
The golden planets of sublimer skies.

    Far o'er thy little earth, to man's weak eye,
Encircling roll the glories of the sky.
Yet know, bless'd prince though thus apparent all,   1015
The moon moves singly round this darksome ball,
The earth, with those fair fires of wandering light,
That shed soft lustre o'er the darksome night,
All worlds alike, with countless nations crown'd,
In circling course, the sun's bright orb surround.   1020
Still their glad faces to his splendor turn,
Imbibe his beams, and meet the grateful morn.

    This mighty scene thy mind with awe inspires,
With beauty raptures, and with wonder fires.
But O thou man belov'd ! yon vault survey,   1025
Where stars in millions blind the midnight ray ;
In space' broad fields so far the pomp retires,
Yon sapphire concave scarce their twinkling fires :
Hence vainly deem'd the gems of inborn light,
Ordain'd to tremble through the gloom of night :   1030
In near approach, those stars, with constant rays,
Shoot round th' expansion, noon's excessive blaze,
Confine the empire of surrounding night,
And reign, and glory, in immortal light.   1034
For know, bless'd favourite, suns are those fair flames ;
Worlds round them roll, and day perpetual beams :
Those worlds unnumber'd circling moons adorn,
And with long splendors comets mid them burn.
As in the world of minds, with golden chain,
Attractive Love extends her blissful reign,   1040
In one pure realm all sainted beings joins,
God with his sons, his sons with God combines :
The bond to all of pure perfection given,
The life, the beauty, peace, and joy of heaven :
So this stupendous frame, by him alone   1045
Who calls their names, supported, number'd, known,

BOOK X.

These countless systems in one system join'd,
Their size, their distance, with nice art design'd,
A great, attracting power, on all impress'd,
Connects, moves, governs, and forbids to rest.   1050

By this great power, impelling and impell'd,
All worlds move on through space' unmeasur'd field.
Around their planets moons refulgent stray ;
Around their suns those planets trace their way ;
Around your central heaven all systems roll :   1055
And one great circling motion rules the whole.
O scene divine, on those bright towers to stand,
And mark the wonders of th' Eternal hand ;
To see thro' space unnumber'd systems driven,
Worlds round their suns, and suns around the heaven; 1060
To see one ordinance worlds and suns obey ;
Their order, peace, and fair, harmonious way ;
Their solemn silence : varying pomp divine ;
Their fair proportions, and their endless shine !
Some nearer rolling in celestial light ;   1065
Some distant glimmering tow'rd the bordering night ;
'Till far remov'd from thought the regions lie,
Where angels never wing'd the lonely, verging sky,

On the clear glass as smiles the beauteous form,
And youth's fair light, and eyes of glory, charm ; 1070
As lucid streams, with face serene, unfold
Spring's gayest prime, and flowers that bloom in gold ;
As boundless ocean's smooth, resplendent plain
Rebeams the skies, and all their wonderous train,
No part, no wave, but feels the sun's broad ray,   1075
And glows, reflective, with surrounding day :
So round th' immense, on fair creation's breast,
In endless pomp the GODHEAD shines impress'd ;
His love, his beauty, o'er all nature burns ;
Each sun unfolds it, and each world returns ;   1080
Each day, each hour, the glory bright improves,
And GOD, with ceaseless smile, th' immortal image loves.

Wing'd with pure flame thro' space' unmeasur'd rounds,
Thy soul shall visit being's farthest bounds ;
When orbs begin, instruct their mass to roll ;   1085
For changing seasons fix a steady pole ;

Teach eve to purple, golden morn to rife,
And light new funs in folitary fkies.

 Upborne from world to world, fhalt thou behold
How ever-varying wonders GOD unfold ;   1090
In each new realm, with growing blifs purfue
Scenes unimagin'd, nations ever new ;
See fome through highborn virtues fwiftly foar,
Some humbler duties, humbler thoughts explore ;
To every race, new thoughts new fenfes bring ;   1095
On every plain, new vegetations fpring ;
O'er virtue's fons eternal morning bloom ;
O'er guilt's vile throngs afcend eternal gloom ;
O'er mingled nations mingling feafons roll,
And peace, and tumult, wrap the changing pole.   1100

 To endlefs years, thy mind, infpir'd, fhall rife
Thro' knowledge, love, and beauty, of the fkies ;
To heights angelic, archangelic, foar,
'Till man's faint language paint the heights no more :
When borne to glory, wing'd to flights fupreme,   1105
Thy foul fhall reach creation's firft extreme,
Beyond all thought affume her laft abode,
And feek the bofom of th' involving GOD.

 The Vifion ceas'd. At once the fcenes decay'd,
His bright form vanifh'd and his glories fled :   1110
Swift to the camp th' exulting Chief return'd,
While the glad day-ftar in the orient burn'd.

THE

CONQUEST of CANÄAN:

BOOK XI.

ARGUMENT.

Morning. *Hareshab returns to Gibeon.* *Army assembles,*
Speech of Caleb. *Hanniel.* *Joshua's advice to him;*
his reply. *Joshua's prayer.* *Cloud rolls before the ar-*
my toward Gibeon. *Prospect of the Heathen host beyond*
the city. *Speech of Joshua on that occasion.* *Israelites*
descend from the mountain. *Jabin prepares for battle,*
and arranges the heathen army on the bank of a small ri-
ver. *Gibeonites ascend the walls to view the battle.*
Aradon marches his troops out to meet Joshua, who gives
the command of them to Almiran. *Arrangement of the*
combatants. *Joshua by a stratagem draws the Heathens*
from their advantageous post. *General engagement.* *Jo-*
shua's exploits. *He kills Medan and Talmon.* *Zedeck ral-*
lies the heathens; but is forced down the bank, and killed.
Egon. *Joshua, seeing Hazor strongly posted on the bank,*
moves down the river and rescues Almiran, kills Piram,
and routs Jarmuth. *Japhia.* *Exploits of Zimri.* *He*
kills Hobam, and puts Hebron into confusion. *Jabin*
rallies them, and kills Hanniel. *Asher retires.* *Joshua*
leaves his division to engage Hazor; and rallies Asher.
Combat between him and Jabin. *Heathens routed.*
Storm of Hail. *Israelites return to their camp and are*
met by their wives and children singing praise to the
Creator. *Conclusion.*

The CONQUEST of CANÄAN.

BOOK XI.

NOW rofe in heaven the great, the final day,
  Where fates of chiefs, and kings, and kingdoms lay
Morn drefs'd in golden pride the cliffs on high,
Stream'd o'er the groves, and brighten'd round the fky :
No cloud, no mift, obfcur'd the blue ferene ;   5
And peace, and filence, hufh'd the folemn fcene.
  To Caleb's tent alert the Hero ftrode,
And rous'd Harefhah to the field of blood.---
With active hafte to Gibeon's prince repair ;
To range his thoufands be his inftant care :   10
Ere the glad fun climb half th' etherial main,
Shall Heaven's broad ftandard tremble on the plain.---
Far o'er the weftern field, with keen delight,
He wing'd his courfe, and vanifh'd from the fight.
  And now once more the clarion's dreadful found   15
Infpires to arms, and fhakes the banner'd ground :
To arms the martial thoufands raptur'd fpring ;
Their fongs refound, their clafhing bucklers ring :
Roll'd on the winds, imperial enfigns play,
And wav'd their fplendors to the burfting day.   20
  Now join'd in marfhall'd ranks the generous train,
And gloomy columns darken'd o'er the plain ;
When, rob'd in white, their hoary fathers came,
Great in paft fields, and heirs of deathlefs fame.

N n

One was their voice, and from their reverend eyes,   25
The bold heroic flame began to rise ;
The soul stood struggling in the heaving breast,
And every limb their vigorous thoughts exprest.
When Caleb thus---The great concluding day
Now calls to arms, and Heaven directs the way :   30
What tho' unnumber'd hosts against us rise,
And with proud madness brave insulted Skies ;
Shall cumbrous throngs the meanest arm dismay ?
Or one base thought distain the glorious day ?
Think how bold Abraham swept the midnight plain,   35
While realms oppos'd, and millions fought, in vain ;
How two brave patriarchs, in one friendly gloom,
Sunk Shechem's towers and op'd a nation's tomb ;
Think how these sires for you unbroken toil'd,
Dar'd the rough main, and prov'd the hideous wild ;   40
Made spiry towns, and haughty kings a prey,
And forc'd o'er countless lands resistless way.
See your fond partners in sad grief array'd,
Behold your children claim parental aid !
Your hands their freedom and their fate suspend ;   45
Your swords must conquer, or your race must end.
Nor let these narrow scenes your thoughts confine ;
Claim nobler views and pass the selfish line.
Ages unborn from you shall trace their doom,
Heaven's future Seers, and heroes yet to come ;   50
If slaves, or men, this day your hands decide,
The scorn of nations, or the world's great pride :
Empire and bondage in your bosoms lie ;
'Tis yours to triumph, or tis ours to die.
    He spoke, and silent to th' all-bounteous Skies   55
Stretch'd wide his hands, and rais'd his kindling eyes :
Each glowing visage flash'd disdain around
And hoarse applauses shook the neighbouring ground.
    Bright from the lucid main, the sun's broad eye
Look'd in imperial splendor from the sky ;   60

With war's gay pomp then shone th' embattled plains;
In proud battalions rose the martial trains;
A broken radiance burst from trembling shields,
And haughty heroes stalk'd along the fields.

    Bold Hanniel there in shining armour stood,   65
And hop'd a deathless name in scenes of blood.
He saw the host to final combat rise,
The champions nations, and a realm the prize.
Now wealth allur'd; the rival now alarm'd;
Strong pride impell'd, and splendid conquest charm'd; 70
His wounds, his pains, in quick oblivion gone,
The wish of glory prompts the warrior on;
Pleas'd, his fond fancy flies from silent shame
To plains of triumph, and to wreaths of fame.

    Him Joshua view'd with pity in his breast,   75
And kindly thus the haughty chief address'd---
If, when dread war resounds her hoarse alarm,
Health flush the cheek, and vigor brace the arm,
To fight, the warrior virtue same command,
And knaves alone refuse the needed hand.   80
But thou, brave Hanniel, seek'st the field in vain,
Pale with lost blood, and weak with ceaseless pain,
Unstrung to fight, and impotent to fly,
Useless, alive; nor glorious, should'st thou die.
In fields of frequent strife thy garlands bloom;   85
Let not their verdure wither on thy tomb:
No feeble aid such numerous honours claim,
Nor can base envy crop the growing fame.

    He spoke, impatient Hanniel quick return'd,
And keen resentment in his visage burn'd---   90
While yon bright orb rolls on the mighty doom
Of millions born, and millions yet to come,
What chief, what man, who boasts a reasoning mind,
Will hide in shame, or sleep in tents confin'd?
Let these, if Jacob's race such culprits knows,   95
Shirnk from great scenes, and die in vile repose,

Not such is Hanniel : when my country calls.
I smile at fields of blood, and blazing walls;
Where clarions roar my ready footsteps hie,
Glue to the fight, and ask no strength to fly.　　100
Unbroke by wounds, my voice shall now inspire
The coward's languor, and the warrior's fire ;
This shield, or these frail limbs, well pleas'd, arrest
The lance, that flies to wound a worthier breast.
But Hanniel's glory why should Joshua fear ?　　105
Do rival names alarm thy tender ear ?
On yon broad plain unnumber'd stars arise,
Move in gay ranks, and triumph round the skies ;
Each lends his beam to swell the pomp divine,
Nor grieves that neighbouring spangles brighter shine.
How beauteous thus in Honour's Angel-race,　　111
When some blest æra numerous heroes grace,
Mean self disdain'd, if virtuous all engage
To fill with light the constellated age.
Some shining deed should this right hand atchieve,　　115
Unstain'd, unrivall'd, Joshua's name would live ;
Then wish no more my days consum'd in shame ;
Nor grudge the glory, generous actions claim.
　　The Leader heard, and wish'd that Heaven had join'd
A heart more honest with so bright a mind :　　120
Through his great bosom thrill'd a sudden pain,
Where sweet compassion mix'd with brave disdain.
Sighing he said---How blind is reason's eye,
When Heaven ordains o'er-weening man to die !
　　Now through the host he cast a piercing view,　　125
And every rank, and every station, knew ;
Then, while mute silence hush'd th' adoring bands,
From a tall rock, he rear'd his suppliant hands.---
　　O thou, whose throne, uprais'd beyond all height,
Glews in th' effulgence of unutter'd light,　　130
O'er earth, o'er hell, o'er heaven, extends thy sway ;
Angels, Archangels, Thrones, and Powers obey ;

BOOK XI.

All scenes, all worlds, confess thy hand divine,
And seas, and skies, and stars, and suns, are thine.
  At thy command, to glory nations rise ;   135
At thy command, each guilty kingdom dies ;
At thy command, awakes the trumpet's roar :
Death walks the plain, and earth is drench'd in gore :
Hush'd by thy sovereign nod, the tempests cease ;
Peace is thy choice, and all the world is peace.   140
  This day, O Power supreme ! against the skies,
Sheath'd in dread arms, unnumber'd thousands rise.
As raging flames the shaggy mountains burn,
The groves to dust, and fields to deserts turn ;
So let thy vengeance sweep th' embattled plain, 145
And teach proud monarchs GOD's eternal reign.
  From endless years thy all-encircling mind
To Abraham's race this beauteous land assign'd :
The land, where Truth shall fix her lasting seat ;
Where sky-born Virtue seeks a calm retreat ;   150
Where blest Redemption opes her living morn ;
Where heaven commences, and where GOD is born.
For this thy voice the sacred promise gave ;
For this thy thunders cleft th' Egyptian wave ;
Rich manna shower'd ; with streams the desart smil'd, 155
And the whole heaven descended on the wild.
Still, O unchanging Mind ! thy bounty shower ;
Draw thy red sword, and stretch thine arm of power.
To gain these realms, the crown of long desire,
Let Heaven protect us, and let Heaven inspire ! 160
  He spoke : a rushing voice began to roar,
Like caverns, echoing on the sea-beat shore :
Deep rang the hollow sound : and o'er the train,
The cloud stupendous sail'd along the plain ;
Broad flames, in fierce effusion, round it play'd, 165
Scorch'd the green fields, and brighten'd all the shade :
Tow'rd western hills the fearful gloom retir'd,
And all the splendor in one flash expir'd.

BOOK XI.

Loud rofe the trump ; and rang'd in dread array,
Behind the cloud the fquadrons trac'd their way ;   170
The burnifh'd helm, blue mail, and upright fpear,
Gleam'd o'er the plain, and ftarr'd the kindled air :
High ftrode the Leader in the glorious van,
And round his arms an awful glory ran :
For God enrob'd him with a pomp divine,   175
And bade an angel in his countenance fhine.
Thus, when no cloud obfcures th' autumnal even,
And night's dark hand unveils the vault of heaven,
Crown'd with pure beams, her fons in beauty rife,
And glow, and fparkle, o'er unmeafur'd fkies ;   180
The moon, bright regent, leads th' immortal train,
And walks in pride imperial round the plain.
    Now climb'd the bands the mountain's towering height,
And o'er the fubject region caft their fight ;
There glifter'd Gibeon's domes in trembling fires,   185
And all the grandeur of a thoufand fpires.
Beyond her walls, a far-extended plain
Spread, like the furface of the fleeping main :
A mighty hoft there left the bounded eye,
And loft its diftant terrors in the fky.   190
Full in th' effulgence of the morn's broad beem,
Stretch'd the tremendous front, a ridge of flame,
Of length immeafurable.   Ether wide
Wav'd with a thoufand nations' banner'd pride ;
Tofs'd in gay triumph, lucid enfigns fhone,   195
And caft their various fplendor on the fun :
Swift round the region dim-feen chariots roll'd ;
The far fteeds bounded wrapp'd in twinkling gold ,
With fpears and helms adorn'd of countlefs trains,
Rofe the full pomp of conftellated plains ;   200
And proud with wanton beams, the fun-bright fhields
Join'd like unnumber'd moons, and dazzled all the fields.
    Unmov'd, great Joshua round him caft his eyes,
And faw th' interminable legions rife :

Then thus, while Ifrael hufh'd in filence ftood,   205
Rang'd in juft ranks, and fac'd the field of blood.
Behold, on yon bright plain, embodied ftands
The gather'd force of all Canäan's lands !
Gather'd by Heaven's right hand, and fad defpair,
To crown our arms, and fink in one dread war !   210
Hail my brave fons, with me, th' immortal day,
That opes to blifsful peace the glorious way,
The hour, long number'd in impatient fkies,
The morn, ordain'd with every pomp to rife,
By angels watch'd, by Heaven's dread figns led on,   215
Sinai's fierce flames, and Jordan's walls of ftone.
   Each boundlefs hope let yon fair field infpire :
Each warrior kindle with a leader's fire :
The fpoils of kingdoms each rapt eye behold ;
Enfigns of fame, and fhields of moony gold ;   220
The herds, that wanton round a thoufand rills ;
The flocks, that whiten on a thoufand hills ;
The corn, all verdant o'er unmeafur'd plains ;
The world, where fpring with fmiling plenty reigns ;
Where olives fwell ; where beauteous figs refine ;   225
And warm, and purpling, glows the clufter'd vine.
This day ordains them ours : this mighty day
Through realms unknown fhall ftretch our potent fway ;
Far as the hills, where funs begin to rife ;
Far as the feas, that limit evening fkies ;   230
Till fading years unloofe the fleeping grave,
And time's laft current joins th' eternal wave.
   There too, my fons, fhall boundlefs glory rife,
And yon bright field of conqueft fill the fkies.
Through Ifrael's future tribes the tale fhall ring ;   235
The fage record it, and the prophet fing ;
Our deeds, our honours, wake the flumbering lyre ;
Warm the faint's praife, and wake the hero's fire ;
Rous'd by the theme, new arts of virtue grow ;
New chiefs break forth, and rival wonders flow ;   240

Truth's happy fons rehearfe in raptur'd ftrains,
Far through all climes, and ages, Gibeon's plains ;
To morn's etherial hoft new blifs be given,
And human triumphs tune the harps of heaven.

    For know, when darknefs laft involv'd the fkies,   245
I faw the promis'd land in vifion rife.
I faw fweet peace exalted joys unfold ;
Fair towers afcend, and temples beam in gold ;
Kings, fprung from Jacob's lineage, mount the throne,
And ftretch their fway to years and realms unknown ; 250
Art raife her fceptre ; wifdom's light revive,
And angel Virtue bid our glory live.
I faw Meffiah bright from heaven defcend,
And fpread his fway to earth's remoteft end :
Deep Gentile darknefs yield to light refin'd ;   255
And truth, and virtue, flow to all mankind.
I faw the world, where Powers and Seraphs bright
Shine in pure robes, and rove in endlefs light ;
Where, in new youth, the patriarchs, from their thrones
Hail a long ftarry train of heavenly fons ;   260
Where Abraham's fteps his native fkies fuftain,
And Mofes raptur'd meets his GOD again.

    On you, my fons, thefe mighty fcenes fufpend ;
From you fhall Ifrael's fame and blifs defcend ;
From you fhall princes, heroes, prophets fpring ;   265
From you be born the heaven-appointed king ;
On this great day his earthly kingdom ftand,
Reach thro' all times, and flow to every land ;
To blifs, in diftant ages, nations rife,
The world ennoble, and expand the fkies :   270
Rufh then to glory ; GOD's tremendous arm
Moves in the flaming front, and guides us to the ftorm.

    He fpoke : a fhout convuls'd the mountain's brow,
And burft fonorous o'er the world below :
Each warrior on the plain in fancy ftood,   275
Drove back whole hofts, and rul'd the fcenes of blood ;

Each on his falchion cast a frequent eye,
And thought it bliss, in Israel's cause to die.
As fullen clouds, when blasts in silence rest,
Hang black and heavy on the mountain's breast;   280
Slow sink the volumes down its hoary side,
Shroud all the cliffs, and roll in gloomy pride :
At once the winds arise ; and sounding rain
Pours with impetuous fury o'er the plain :
So the dark hosts descend in deep array,   285
And o'er the champaign drive their dreadful way.

From the far plains, great Jabin's eye beheld
The squadrons, thickening on the distant field,
For when from Joshua's arm his host retir'd,
Stung by disgrace, with fierce resentment fir'd,   290
Some future fight his angry thoughts design'd,
To glut the vengeance of his haughty mind.
To Gibeon's fields he steers his sullen course,
Where circling kings combin'd their gather'd force ;
Chiefs rush'd to conquest from a thousand lands,   295
Whirl'd all their cars, and led their countless bands.
To guide their strength against their dreaded foes
All with one voice the mighty hero chose.
He, pleas'd once more to rule the dreadful plain,
Survey'd the terrors of th' unnumber'd train ;   300
Survey'd a host, beyond his wishes great,
And ask'd the gods to give no happier fate.
In splendid arms confess'd to dreadful view,
To final fight, to final fame, he drew ;
Full on his shield, with various forms inroll'd,   305
OR DEATH, OR CONQUEST---blaz'd in words of gold.

In fields far west, a torrent, with rough waves,
The rocky shore with endless fury laves.
Here, o'er the stream high banks majestic hung,
And with sad murmurs hollow caverns rung ;   310
There, for the squadrons, rushing to th' affray,
Smooth, sloping shores prepar'd an easy way.

O o

B O O K XI.

High on the weſtern margin of the flood,
A wall of fire, Canäan's millions ſtood.
Here Jabin's will ordain'd his hoſt to ſtay,   315
Shields join'd with ſhields, and wedg'd in firm array.
For well he knew, when Iſrael's ruſhing force
Up the rough bank ſhould urge their toilſome courſe,
Their broken ranks would fall an eaſy prey,
And fame, and triumph, cloſe th' important day.   320
    Now Iſrael's hoſt, ſlow-moving o'er the plain,
Succeſſive roll'd, as waves diſturb the main ;
In every face a fix'd, calm bravery ſhin'd ;
And not a hero caſt a look behind.
    High on her ramparts Gibeon's children roſe,   325
Survey'd the fields, and eyed th' impending foes.
Here in fond arms, the tender Mother bare
The babe, ſweet offspring of her anxious care,
Hung o'er its infant charms, and joy'd to trace
The fire's lov'd image in its blooming face :   330
Then on the combat turn'd a boding view,
Wrung her white hands, and ſhed the gliſtening dew.
Here the gay Child, with pleas'd, and wondering eye,
Catch'd the broad ſtandard, ſtreaming in the ſky ;
On the red armour caſt a raptur'd gaze,   335
 And rais'd his artleſs hands, and mark'd the ſplendid blaze.
Here, bath'd in tears, and whelm'd with timorous care,
In woe more lovely, mourn'd the melting Fair ;
O'er Gibeon's hoſt their eyes inceſſant rov'd,
And each, mid thouſands, trac'd the youth ſhe lov'd : 340
Fond hope, ere eve gave champions to his ſteel,
And at her feet his ſhining garlands fell.
Then fear preſents him weltering on the plain,
Soft, healing, female aid implor'd in vain ;
Cloſ'd were thoſe eyes, that beam'd etherial fire,   345
Glow'd with young joy, or languiſh'd ſweet deſire,
Dumb was the voice, that every wiſh could move,
And cold the form, that wak'd unutter'd love.

BOOK XI.

Here hoary Age in new-born pleafure ftood,
And war's dread glories fir'd his languid blood ;   350
Long-buried years rufh'd forward to the view ;
What hofts they battled, and what chiefs they flew :
Each on his brethren gaz'd with glad furprize,
And the great foul ftood kindling in their eyes.

From northern gates her dark battalions pour'd,   355
And many a hero fierce to combat tower'd ;
His warlike thoufands wife Aradon led,
The white locks trembling o'er his ancient head.
Hail, mighty Chief !---the hoary prince began---
Favourite of God, and virtuous friend of man !   360
Bleft be thy fteps, that bring this kind relief
To feeble age, and folitary grief.
In fields of conflict once rejoic'd I ftood,
With death familiar, and with fcenes of blood.
But now fad age my head has whiten'd o'er ;   360
This palfied arm muft wield the fword no more.
To mourn, to weep is all my future doom,
Drawn near to death, and bending o'er the tomb.
Thefe bands thy voice obey ; in danger's field
Their manly bofoms never knew to yield :   370
Nor will their feet, long tried in honour's race,
Now learn to flee, and firft commence difgrace.
But, fix'd to death, their king, their land to fave,
All force will hazard, and all terrors brave.

When round the hoft I turn my weeping eyes,   375
And gaze, and gaze, my foul, with anguifh, cries
Where, where is Elam ? Oh, may no fad doom
Compel thee to a fon's untimely tomb !
A happier life, a brighter lot be thine ;
Tafte all the rapturing joys that once were mine.   380
From childlefs age may Heaven his chofen fave,
Nor bring thy hoary hairs in forrow to the grave !

Great prince ! the Chief, with cheering voice, replied--
Thy nation's father, and thy country's pride !

BOOK XI.

Not singly thou the pangs of grief hast known ; 385
I mourn a daughter, as thou weep'st a son.
From hearts too fond, Heaven call'd the pair away
To fields of bliss, and climes of lasting day.
May every virtue in thy breast refine,
Till those fair climes, and all that bliss be thine. 390

 But now retire, where yon bright chariot stands ;
Let youth and vigour lead thy warlike bands,
For see, to fight Canäan's millions rise !
And hark, what clamors rend the boundless skies !

 The king obey'd. In arms, the ardent throng, 395
Behind Almiran, darkly rush'd along ;
Almiran, Gibeon's noblest, bravest son,
Led the bold heroes, and like lightning shone.

 In three vast squadrons stood the heathens strength,
And rose a mighty front of dreadful length. 400
O'er northern banks, where chariots hoarsely rung,
Like clouds of thunder, haughty Hebron hung :
There too fierce Eglon rush'd with dreadful roar,
Like the long murmurs of the sounding shore.
Nor feebler legions fill the southern plain ; 415
There Lachish, Jarmuth there, the fight sustain ;
To the dire centre numerous nations throng,
And Jabin guides the storm, and swiftly flames along.

 With piercing eyes the Chief his foes descried,
And bade his host in three vast squares divide. 410
'Gainst Lachish Gibeon rolls in proud array ;
'Gainst Hebron Asher bends a dreadful way :
As fires pursue a comet's sanguine form,
Behind great Joshua drives the central storm.

 Now o'er the plain, as ocean pours his tide, 415
Their streaming ensigns rear'd in purple pride,
Far north, and southward stretch'd the chosen train,
And cross'd in gloomy pomp the dreadful plain.
Near, and more near, th' undaunted warriors drew ;
For well the Chief, by sure experience knew 420

BOOK XI.

That nations, taught in fudden fight to rife,
To war by ftealth, and triumph by furprife,
To wiles, vain-glorious, fall an eafy prey,
And, throng'd in tumult wild, are fwept away.
Thence, near the foe he bade the fquadrons move, 425
Tempt with keen taunts, and with proud threatnings prove,
That chiefs, and men, with childifh rage o'ercome,
Might quit the fhore, and hafte to certain doom.

  Now near the ftream the facred thoufands ftood,
Their breafts all panting for the fcenes of blood. 430
At once, as fome black ftorm begins to rife,
A cloud of arrows fill'd the weftern fkies;
The long, afcending gloom all heaven o'erfpread,
And the fields darken'd with a tranfient fhade.
Then ftones on ftones tempeftuous ether pour'd: 435
And darts on darts in quick fucceffion fhower'd:
Now here, now there, expiring warriors fell,
And fhrill beneath them rung the clafhing fteel.

  At once, as mov'd by fear, the Chief withdrew,
And bade his hoft the diftant walls purfue. 440
With joy, the heathens eyed their backward way,
Rais'd a long fhout, and fprang to feize the prey.
Swift rufh'd th' exulting thoufands down the fhore;
For ranks behind, urg'd on the ranks before;
Loud ring the chariots, fwift the courfers bound, 445
And a deep thunder waves along the ground.

  Around, great Jabin caft a mournful view,
And faw his foes retreat, his friends purfue,
His laws contemn'd, that bade the thoufands ftay,
Till o'er the torrent Ifrael urg'd their way; 450
Kenn'd the deep fnare, by Jofhua wifely laid,
And to himfelf with fighs thus fiercely faid.----
I fee, proud chief, I fee thy profperous wiles;
On me fate frowns; on thee propitious fmiles;
But not alone I prove the general doom; 455
Ten thoufand ghofts fhall meet me at the tomb:

Aveng'd, and happy to the shades I'll go,
To bid thy princes quake in realms below.
Thus spoke the king, and deem'd his ruin nigh,
A fearful vengeance reddening in his eye ;   460
Strong, fell despair inflam'd his eager look ;
His bands gaz'd trembling, and his princes shook.
    Meantime with smiles the sacred Chief beheld
His foes rush headlong o'er th' embattled field :
At once his piercing voice restrain'd the flight,   465
Wheel'd his long ranks, and marshall'd to the fight.
At once the trump's tremendous blast ascends
The plains all shudder, and the concave rends ;
Loud as the storm's ten thousand thunders rise,
A shout unmeasur'd rocks the lands and skies ;   470
Again high heaven is gloom'd with stony showers ;
Again all ether darts unnumber'd pours ;
With deep convulsion roars the closing war ;
Fierce bounds the steed ; sonorous rolls the car ;
With one broad ruin heaves the earth amain,   475
And Night, and Death, and Horror, shroud the plain.
So pours a storm on Greenland's frozen shore ;
The hoarse winds rage ; the maddening billows roar ;
When boundless darkness wraps the realms on high,
And flaming meteors stream across the sky :   480
Huge isles of raging ice, together driven,
With bursting thunder rend air, sea, and heaven :
Rocks rise o'er rocks ; o'er mountains mountains roll,
And the world trembles to the distant pole.
Thus o'er the field the dreadful tumult grows ;   485
Alike impetuous, foes encounter foes ;
Where Asher's sons proud Hebron's host engage ;
Or where bold Gibeon pours her torrent rage ;
Or where, around the Chief, immingled rise
Triumphant clamours, and expiring cries.   490
    Long roar'd the tumult of the dubious fight,
And no base coward wish'd inglorious flight :

All fierce to combat rush'd th' undaunted train ;
Nor these the palm would lose, nor those could gain ;
Till cloth'd in terror, Joshua's dreadful arm   495
Began the triumph, and led on the storm.

Two chiefs, whose silver arms confess'd their sway,
Rais'd their broad buklers in his fateful way.
By their fair wives a common sire they claim'd ;
And Medan this, and Talmon that, was nam'd ;   500
Of royal race, from Salem's wall they came,
Their deeds just budding in the field of fame.
Cleft through the side brave Medan gasping fell ;
And Talmon trembling fled the lifted steel.
By his own friends a javelin swiftly hurl'd   505
Plung'd his freed spirit to the nether world ;
Far round the field a shout of joy ascends,
And groans re-murmur from his sadden'd friends.

Then swift the Hero wheel'd his flaming sword ;
Like mountain streams his host behind him pour'd ;   510
Loud roar'd the thunders of the dreadful plain,
Rock'd the tall groves, and fill'd th' etherial main :
Increasing horror rent the world around,
And steeds, and cars, and warriors mingled on the ground.

Now near the stream approach'd the sounding war, 515
When fierce to combat roll'd a splendid car ;
There giant Zedeck rose in dreadful view ;
Two furious steeds the mighty monarch drew ;
With wild impetuous rage, they foam'd along,
And, pale before them, fled the parting throng.   520
From Joshua's course he saw his bands retire ;
His reddening aspect flash'd a gloomy fire ;
With huge, hoarse voice the furious hero cried,
While the plains murmur'd, and the groves replied,
Whatever wretch from this bright combat flies,   525
By the just gods, the impious dastard dies.
Nor hope to 'scape the keen, avenging blade
In the still cot, or in the lonely shade.

Soon ſhall this ſword, with victory crown'd, return ;
And wrath, and vengeance, all your dwellings burn ; 530
Your bodies, limb from limb, this arm ſhall tear,
Nor ſons, nor wives, nor ſires, nor infants, ſpare ;
But bid the hungry hawks your race devour,
And call grim wolves to feaſt in floods of gore.

He ſpoke ; aſtoniſh'd, ſome more nimbly flew ;   535
And ſome to conflict with freſh ardour drew :
Deſpair once more the growing flight repell'd,
And gave new horrors to the gloomy field.

Meantime on Joſhua drove the ſounding car,
And burſt impetuous through the thickeſt war,   540
Rough, heavy, dreadful, by the giant thrown
Flew the vaſt fragment of a craggy ſtone ;
Scarce 'ſcap'd the wary Chief, with ſudden bound,
While the broad ruin plow'd the crumbling ground.
A javelin then the monarch's hand impell'd,   545
That ſung, and trembled, 'gainſt the Hero's ſhield ;
Swift o'er his head a ſecond hiſſing flies,
And a pierc'd warrior groans, and falls, and dies.
At once great Joſhua rais'd his reeking ſword,
And with deep wounds the maddening courſers gor'd ;
Through cleaving ranks the courſers backward flew, 551
And ſwift from fight the helpleſs monarch drew.
To the high ſhore, impendent o'er the flood,
They ruſh'd, as whirlwinds ſweep the rending wood ;
To turn they tried, with ſhort and ſudden wheel ;   555
But tried in vain ; the ſounding chariot fell.
Prone down the lofty bank the ſteeds purſued,
Where ſharp, and ragged rocks beneath were ſtrew'd ;
All ſhrill the giant's ſtriking mail reſounds :
With clattering craſh, the cracking car rebounds ;   560
White o'er his lifeleſs head the waters roar---
Loſt in the ſtream, and doom'd to riſe no more.---
As, when the ſouth's fierce blaſts the main deform,
And roll the pealful onſet of the ſtorm ;

Hung are the heavens with night ; the world around,
Deep-murmuring, trembles to the folemn found ;   566
Full on dread Longa's wild-refounding fhore
Hills, wav'd o'er hills, afcend, and burft, and roar :
Safe in his cot, the hoary failor hears,
Or drops, for fancied wrecks, unbidden tears.   570
A boundlefs fhout, from Ifrael's raptur'd train,
Rent the broad fkies, and fhook the dreadful plain.
For now, their champion, truft, and glory loft,
From Jofhua's vengeance flew fad Salem's hoft ;
Before him nought avail'd the fhields, and fpears, 575
But chiefs, and foaming fteeds, and rattling cars,
Ranks urging ranks, fquadrons o'er fquadrons borne,
Down the bank plung'd ; the bank behind them torne,
Sunk with a rufhing found : great Jofhua's arm
Uplifted, imminent impell'd the ftorm.   580
Alert, he bounded on the yielding fand,
And fcatter'd ruin from his red right hand.
The white waves foam'd around his midway fide,
As fierce he thunder'd thro' the rufhing tide.
Two blooming youths, he dafh'd againft the rock,   585
Where Zedeck's chariot felt the fatal fhock ;
Their gufhing blood ran purple thro' the wave,
And thoufands with them found a watery grave.

   There, mid vile throngs, t' untimely fate a prey,
Young, generous Egon breath'd his foul away.   590
Him Salem's nymphs refounded thro' the vales,
Or fung melodious, to refponfive gales.
He, from the mountain wilds, and cliffs fublime,
Untrod, uncultur'd, from the firft of time,
Drove the fierce beafts, by arms and arts compell'd, 595
To feek their fafety in the lowland field.
By flames unclos'd, by hounds and fwains purfued,
They fled each faftnefs of th' impervious wood ;
Ambufh'd, in vales beneath the favage prey
Rufh'd on the fpear, and yell'd their lives away.   600

Then howling wilds the traveller ceas'd t' appall;
Then night spread harmless round th' unguarded stall
His flocks, the rising swain with joy survey'd,
And slaughter'd lambs defil'd no more the glade.
Egon, each pipe, each voice of music sung;　　605
And Egon's glory courts and caverns rung:
But pass'd was all his fame; by Joshua's hand
Plung'd in the stream, and choak'd with surging sand,
While from the bank the warriors leap'd amain,
Crush'd, drown'd, he mingled with the numerous slain.610
　On the steep, western bank all Hazor stood;
A cloud of fire, high-towering o'er the flood:
Their darts unnumber'd Israel's host invade,
And many an eye is clos'd in death's dark shade.
Swift down the shore a rock with fury fell,　　615
And crush'd two warriors, wrapp'd in shining steel:
Near Joshua's steps the craggy ruin pour'd;
The Hero sprang; the foaming torrent roar'd.
Then stones on stones, with sounding tempest driven,
Fill'd the wide concave of the troubled heaven:　620
Beneath their shields the prudent warriors stood;
All ether rang and foam'd the reddening flood;
'Till mighty Joshua, breathing wide dismay,
Swift down the raging torrent drove his way.
Where southward waves, expanding ceas'd to roar,　625
The stream was bounded by a sloping shore.
Hither the hero bent his awful course;
His host behind him pour'd their mighty force;
Fierce up the shore he rush'd; a dreadful band
Throng'd round their chief, and darken'd all the strand.
　Here brave Almiran, like a sweeping fire,　　631
Urg'd his dread path, and bade his foes expire.
Tall in the gloomy van, the hero sped,
And Lachish pale before him fell or fled:
Such fiery terrors round his visage glow'd;　　635
Such streams of slaughter from his falchion flow'd.

BOOK XI.

'Till, generous youth, an arrow found thy fide,
And down thy armour gufh'd the living tide.
Thy fire had grafp'd his long-neglected fhield,
And follow'd, trembling, to the deathful field :　　640
There on thy deeds he caft an anxious view ;
There touch'd with tranfport, felt his youth renew ;
Then faw thee falling, pale, depriv'd of breath,
Plung'd on the foe, and funk in whelming death.

　　The youth, great Jofhua caught in friendly arms,　645
His fhield averting war's impendent harms ;
Chaf'd by his hand, again he op'd his eyes ;
His lips refpir'd ; his bloom began to rife.
Then Gibeon's fons the mighty Leader fir'd,
And forrow prompted, and revenge infpir'd.　　650
　　Now drefs'd in golden pride, to crimfon war,
Tall, beauteous Piram drove his fhining car.
Born in the ftillnefs of a court ferene,
Where peace, and pleafure led the jocund fcene,
He loath'd dire fight, to gentler thoughts inclin'd ;　655
And love, and mufic, charm'd his feeling mind.
Soft pity touch'd his heart ; and oft a tear
He dropp'd, and mourn'd the human doom fevere ;
Th' unnumber'd ills of wafting pride would rue,
And wifh that kings the fweets of friendfhip knew.　660
Yet, not of fervile kind, his thoughts had foar'd,
In brighter days, and Art's fair realms explor'd.
Such was his foul, as grace from heaven refin'd
Can warm, and ripen, to an angel's mind.
　　To combat now the prince reluctant rode,　　665
When full before him Ifrael's Leader ftood.
Pleas'd, he beheld the graceful form afcend,
And wifh'd the gods had made the Chief his friend.
But vain his wifhes ; by the Hero thrown,
Full on his forehead burfts a founding ftone,　　670
He fell ; his courfers backward rufh'd amain
And fnatch'd the monarch o'er the cloudy plain.

His haplefs fall pale Jarmuth's fons beheld;
Grief froze their hearts, and fear their nerves congeal'd
The Chief purfues ; their trembling bands retire ;   675
Deep groans afcend, and troops on troops expire :
Wide rolls the duft ; the fkies are fnatch'd from fight,
And death hangs dreadful o'er the growing fight.

There, thron'd in ftate, and drefs'd in burnifh'd fteel,
Lachifh' fair prince, Japhia, haplefs fell.   680
He bade foft fongs awake the trembling lyre,
With notes of magic, and with words of fire ;
Such fongs, as Mofes, uninfpir'd, might fing ;
Like him, a bard, a hero, and a king.
But far beyond the pride of pomp, and power,   685
He lov'd the realms of nature to explore ;
With lingering gaze, Edenian fpring furvey'd ;
Morn's fairy fplendors, night's gay curtain'd fhade ;
The high hoar cliff ; the grove's benighting gloom ;
The wild rofe, widow'd, o'er the mouldering tomb ; 690
The heaven-embofom'd fun ; the rainbow's die,
Where lucid forms difport to fancy's eye.
When rous'd to war, and deeds of deathlefs name,
Faint fhone to him the charms of martial fame :
But fir'd to ecftacy, his foul beheld   695
The ftormy grandeur of the troubled field :
The morn, that trembles o'er the fteel-bright plains ;
The whirlwind car, wing'd fteed, and clafhing trains.
Such fcenes the warrior fung.   The fwains around
Hung on th' enchantment of the wildering found :   700
Soft o'er the lyre the voice of mufic pafs'd,
Wild as the woodland warblings of the wafte ;
Each favage foften'd, as the numbers rofe,
Forfook his falchion, and forgot his foes.

As dread before him glow'd the Hero's face,   705
His angel pomp, and heaven-defcended grace ;
He ftopp'd ; he gaz'd ; and with fond fancy warm,
Glued to the folemn glories of his form ;

Swift through his bofom drove the deadly fpear,
And all his beauteous dreams diffolv'd in air.   710

    Meantime far north the fons of Afher pour'd,
And fierce to combat chiefs and heroes tower'd:
There, like a whirlwind, rapid Zimri flew,
And, like a tempeft, countlefs bands purfue :
Clouds after clouds behind him darkly roll,   715
And fhouts of glory heave the murmuring pole.

    As when two feas, by winds together hurl'd,
With burfting fury fhake the folid world ;
Waves pil'd o'er waves, the watery mountains rife,
And foam, and roar, and rage, againft the fkies :   720
So join'd the combat ; ranks, o'er ranks impell'd,
Swell'd the hoarfe tumult of the hideous field ;
Black drifts of duft becloud the gloomy ground ;
Hoarfe groans afcend, and clafhing arms refound.
And now, where Zimri broke th' embodied war,   725
Imperious Hoham drove his founding car ;
Like flames, his rapid courfes rufh'd along,
Forc'd a red path, and crufh'd the thickening throng :
His hiffing lances fhower'd deftruction round,
And ftreaming bodies ftrew'd the crimfon ground.   730
With joy, bold Zimri kenn'd the prince afar
And wing'd his javelin thro' the flafhing air ;
Deep in his throat was lodg'd th' avenging fteel ;
With groans, the monarch panting, ftruggling, fell :
The fword indignant gafh'd his cleaving fide,   735
Freed the pale ghoft, and pour'd the vital tide.

    With fhouts of triumph fwell'd th' etherial main,
And new convulfions fhook the ftormy plain.
The cars rufh'd backward ; foaming courfers bound ;
The fhrill fwords clafh, and hollow groans refound.   740
'Twixt the long banks remurmuring clamors roar,
And eyes unnumber'd wifh the fartheft fhore.
As, fwell'd with rains, th' autumnal ftream afcends,
Foams o'er the rocks, and all the mountain rends,

Heav'd deep, with groans th' uprooted foreſt yields,   745
And huge, unwieldy oaks, plunge cumbrous to the fields ;
So furious Aſher, with reſiſtleſs ſway,
On Hebron burſting broke a dreadful way ;
Swift o'er the floods the warriors eager fly,
And ſteeds, and men, on earth immingled lie.   750

On theſe dire ſcenes great Jabin caſt his view,
And ſaw his friends retire, his foes purſue,
Then, while the ſtorm of war brave Zedeck bore,
He whirl'd his chariot down the weſtern ſhore.
As, ſtain'd with blood, a meteor's midnight beam   755
Cleaves the dun clouds, and trails a length of flame ;
At once, with dreadful burſt, its terrors fly,
And a deep thunder rocks the ſhuddering ſky :
So, thron'd tremendous in his ſun-bright car,
Ruſh'd the impetuous Hero to the war ;   760
Loud to their ears his voice terrific came,
And his fierce eyeballs flaſh'd a withering flame---
Rouſe, rouſe to fight, to triumph bend your way ;
Nor yield theſe ſlaves the wiſh'd immortal day.
Shall Hebron's ſons, that never knew to fly,   765
Now turn inglorious, and like daſtards die ?
Let all your antient deeds each ſoul inſpire,
And each bold warrior emulate his ſire.
This hour propitious brings the glorious doom,
And ſweeps theſe wretches to the coward's tomb.   770

He ſpoke, and furious, with reſiſtleſs force
Burſt on his foes and ſtopp'd their eager courſe :
All Hebron round him ſwift to conflict turn'd,
New life inform'd them, and new bravery burn'd ;
Squadrons on ſquadrons wedg'd their deep array,   775
And darker horrors gloom'd the dreadful day.

Him Hanniel ſaw ; for here in fierceſt fight
With joy he mingled, and diſdain'd baſe flight.
No griding anguiſh now his limb diſtreſs'd ;
No thought, but glory, triumph'd in his breaſt ;   780

Chiefs to his arm had given the parting breath,
And vulgar warriors ftain'd his fword with death.
Alive, impetuous, burn'd the martial flame,
And every hope beat high for endlefs fame.

On Jabin's car th' undaunted warrior flew : 785
The car, like whirlwinds near him fwiftly drew.
This the blefs'd hour the hero deem'd to gain
The garland, wifh'd fo long, but wifh'd in vain.
The Chief of foes his raptur'd eye furvey'd,
The deftin'd victim of his conquering blade. 790
No fear difturb'd, left combat's fickle doom
Should change the lot, and ope another's tomb :
He fmil'd, from Jofhua fure the palm to win,
And felt frefh honours round his temples twine.
At once, by Jabin's hand like lightening driven, 795
A fpear flew nimbly through the dufty heaven ;
Deep in his forehead funk th' unerring fteel ;
Without a groan the haughty warrior fell :
No foul more reftlefs e'er from earth retir'd,
Nor pride more boundlefs e'er in duft expir'd. 800

As, when bold youths, the mount's dim fummit gain'd,
Upheave the huge, hoar crag, with toilfome hand ;
From point to point th' unwieldy ruin tofs'd,
Smokes down the fteep, and grinds the cliffs to duft ;
High bounding, finking headlong, feeks the plain, 805
Cleaves the torne ground, and plows the foaming main ;
Far plunge the crafhing pines ; the wild rocks roar,
Hurl'd with tumultuous fury to the fhore ;
Wide-rolling duft the neighbouring concave fills,
And a long, fwelling roar runs murmuring round the hills.
So down the bank, tremendous Jabin's car 811
Urg'd the pale throng, and drove the founding war :
His foes plung'd headlong in the crimfon wave,
And chiefs, and warriors, found a liquid grave.

While thus in dreadful fight the hofts engag'd, 815
The tumults thicken'd, and the clamours rag'd ;

From Joſhua's terrors Hazor's ſons withdrew,
And diſtant from the ſhore their front renew.
With hideous ſtrength, their ridgy lines aſcend ;
Red flame the ſhields ; ſwords tremble ; ſpears protend :
Pleas'd, the Chief views ; too generous not to know, 821
And own, with praiſe, the merit of a foe.

From a tall rock he caſt his flaſhing eyes,
And ſaw the varied ſcenes of combat riſe.
While every foe bold Gibeon fiercely drove ;   825
The tribes of Zimri backward ſlowly move :
Tow'rd the high walls aſcending volumes roll,
And clouds on clouds ſucceſſive wrap the pole.
Greatly ſerene, he view'd the threatening doom,
Nor veil'd his viſage with a tranſient gloom ;   830
But bade his chiefs, their bands for fight array'd,
Lead on the war, and Hazor's hoſt invade.

Then, where the fields diſplay'd an eaſy courſe,
Along the ſhore he wing'd his rapid force ;
Swift as a tempeſt down the bank he flies,   835
Cuts the red ſtream, and lifts tremendous cries---
Heavens ! what diſhonour pains this bleeding eye ?
See, loſt to ſhame, my friends, my heroes fly !
Turn, turn to triumph ; ſwift to glory turn ;
With generous ſhame let every boſom burn !   840
Shall your brave ſires, that never knew to flee,
With pangs your flight, and tarniſh'd honour, ſee ;
And wiſh high Heaven had lent a milder doom,
And ſwept them childleſs to an earlier tomb ?
Shall Dan, ſhall Aſher, names of long renown,   845
Now loſe the ſplendors of a deathleſs crown !
Forbid it Heaven ! now wipe the hateful ſtain ;
One bold exertion wins th' immortal plain.

He ſpoke : at once, unfurl'd in glorious pride,
The ſacred ſtandard caſt the view aſide ;   850
There Dan's bright eagle, high in pomp diſplay'd,
Stretch'd his long wings, and rear'd his golden head ;

Of gold his form in lucid triumph turn'd,
And ftreamy lightnings round him fiercely burn'd.
At once all Afher furious rufh'd to fight,   855
Each ardent warrior fpurn'd inglorious flight.
With wider ruin heave the trembling fields ;
Cars burft ; cries roar ; groans murmur ; found the fhields.
As in fome foreft two red flames afpire,
And whelm huge pines in floods of furging fire,   860
Then fwift through falling groves together driven
Roll o'er the mountain tops, and kindle heaven :
So, fierce and dreadful, front to front oppos'd,
Mid clouds of duft, the thundering fquadrons clos'd : 864
Earth fhakes ; air rends ; the trembling fkies refound,
And night, and fad difmay, invade th' embattled ground.

For war undaunted Hebron fiercely burn'd,
Nor even in Jofhua's path to flight were turn'd.
Full on his fword they rufh'd, and bravely fell ;
New bands with tranfport fac'd the flaughtering fteel.
Inceffant cries o'er all the combat rung ;   871
Inceffant fpears through darken'd ether fung ;
Swift flew the courfer ; fwift the raging car ;
Hoarfe rofe the tumult of the maddening war ;
Lefs loud through forefts winds impetuous roll,   875
The huge pines fink, and tempeft rends the pole ;
Lefs loud 'gainft Zembla mountain billows roar,
When the ftorm thunders on the frozen fhore.
For Hebron's thoufands Jabin's voice infpir'd,
And Jofhua's deeds the fons of Ifrael fir'd.   880

Now where the Chief terrific fwept the field,
And, cloth'd in terror, ranks on ranks repell'd ;
Whilft a red deluge o'er his footfteps fpread,
And countlefs torrents fpouted from the dead ;
Swift to his path a chief of Afher ran,   885
Wild with difmay, and quivering thus began---
Wing, wing, thou beft of men, thy friendly path---
Oh fave the hero, or avenge his death !---

Now Zimri dies; from yon afcending ground,
I faw fierce Jabin point the fatal wound---　　　890
He fpoke; at once, from all the Heathen train,
A voice of thunder heav'd th' affrighted plain:
Loud as hoarfe whirlwinds torrent flames infpire,
When up the mountains rolls tempeftuous fire;
Loud as th' Almighty's voice, through ether driven, 895
Pales the wide world, and fhakes the walls of heaven;
Long fhouts tremendous from the fields arife,
Burft o'er the hofts, and rend the clouded fkies.
Through Ifrael's thoufands thrills a dire alarm,
When thus great Jofhua nerves each fainting arm--- 900
Urge, my brave warriors, urge the glorious ftrife;
Wheel your red fwords, and fave the leader's life---
Shall Zimri die, whilft each aftonifh'd ftands,
Nor fees thefe falchions ufelefs in our hands?
Alive the fainting hero meets my fight,　　　905
And yet maintains the folitary fight---
　　He fpoke, and furious wheel'd his dreadful fword;
Back roll'd the heathens; ftreams of flaughter pour'd:
Behind him Afher's hoft in deep array
Throng'd darkening; clouds and death involv'd their way;
The bounding fteeds bedew'd their hoofs in blood, 911
And chiefs and monarchs fwell'd the purple flood.
　　Now, where bold Zimri brav'd the deathful ground,
O'erhung with foes, and pierc'd with many a wound,
Whilft labouring, panting, heav'd his frequent breath,
And o'er his helmet flafh'd defcending death;　916
Great Jofhua, flaming, drove th' embattled train;
Their lances flew, their falchions rag'd in vain.
Dire as a peal of thunder fweeps the fkies,
He rufh'd, and Death fate frowning in his eyes:　920
For now brave Zimri fcarce fuftain'd the ftrife;
Sunk on one knee, and wifh'd to fell his life.
'Thro' the thick tumults of the broken war
Impetuous Jabin wing'd his rapid car;

With ruddy beams his lance uplifted ſhone ;   925
His waving buckler mock'd the ſanguine ſun ;
'Twixt the bold chiefs, undaunted at the ſtorm,
Sublime great Joſhua rear'd his mighty form.
   Now front to front the frowning heroes ſtood ;
Their eyes red flames ; their faces dropp'd with blood ;930
Their ſwords the lightning ; two broad moons,their ſhields
Shot a fierce glory through the dreadful fields.
Then Jabin's heart, though form'd of ſtubborn ſteel,
Firſt ſhook with terror, and firſt learn'd to feel.
But rous'd by keen diſdain, and vengeful ire,   935
Quick from his eye-balls blaz'd infernal fire ;
To earth, impatient, from the car he ſprang ;
His breaſt beat high ; his rattling armour rang ;
To die reſolv'd, but as a king to die,
Like ſudden thunder roſe his burſting cry---   940
From this right hand receive, thou baſe-born ſlave,
A death too noble, but a daſtard's grave ;
Torne by the dogs, thy carcaſe here ſhall lie,
Or glut the fowls, that ſweep th' avenging ſky.
The Chief diſdain'd return.   The Heathen's ſteel   945
Full on his helm with rapid fury fell,
Glanc'd by his ſword, it clave the bloody ground ;
Elſe had the Hero known no future wound.
Then with ſwift wheel, through Jabin's yielding ſide
Ruſh'd his keen blade, and pour'd the ſable tide;   950
Aghaſt, their monarch's fall his hoſt beheld,
And ſullen groans rung murmuring round the field.
   Like Heaven's dread thunder Joſhua rais'd his voice ;
Hoſts backward roll'd, earth trembled at the noiſe---
On Gibeon's turrets ſtand thou ſtill, O Sun !   955
Look down, thou Moon, on dreary Ajalon !
Fix'd in high heaven the awful ſplendors ſtood,
And flam'd tremendous on the field of blood ;
From each dread orb enſanguin'd ſtreams aſpire,
The ſkies all mantling in fierce-waving fire ;   960

300

Amaz'd, Canäan's realms the pomp defcried ;
The world grew pale ; the hearts of nations died :
The bounding Hero feiz'd the fhining car,
Snatch'd the long reins, and fhouted to the war :
Behind, fierce Afher fwift to vengeance flew ;   965
All dropp'd their fpears, and all their falchions drew ;
A fudden blaze gleam'd round the dufty gloom,
And plung'd ten thoufand warriors to the tomb.
For now, o'er all the fight, the heathens yield,
And Ifrael triumphs round the dreadful field.   970
High in the van, fublime great Jofhua rode,
Wing'd the dire flight, and fwell'd the tide of blood ;
Aghaft, they fee the lightning of his eyes,
And hear the thunders of his voice arife.
The plains are tumult all, convuls'd affright,   975
Fierce ruin, wild amaze, and raging flight ;
The Chariots ftream ; the fteeds all eager bound,
Stretch o'er the plains, and fweep the rifing ground ;
O'er rocks, o'er floods the thoufands headlong fly,
And fwords, and fpears, and fhields, behind them lie ;
No ftop, nor backward look, nor liftening ear,   981
From plains to forefts pants the full career ;
Behind, the Hero wings his rapid way,
And duft and darknefs fhroud the beams of day.
So, borne in clouds of fire, an Angel's form   985
On impious Sodom drove the dreadful ftorm.
From heaven, in dreadful pomp, the Vifion came ;
Far, far behind him, ftream'd the angry flame ;
The dark-red thunder, from his right hand hurl'd,
Upheav'd the fky, and fir'd the rocking world ;   990
High o'er the ftorm, on wings of light, he rode,
And fail'd, in lucid triumph, to th' approving God.
   Long rufh'd the victors o'er the fanguine field,
And fcarce were Gibeon's loftieft fpires beheld ;
When up the weft dark clouds began to rife,   995
Sail'd o'er the hills, and lengthen'd round the fkies.

A ridge of folding fire their fummits fhone ;
But fearful blacknefs all beneath was thrown.
Swift round the fun the fpreading gloom was hurl'd,
And night, and folitude, amaz'd the world.   1000
    At once the voice of deep-refounding gales
Rung flow, and folemn, in the diftant vales ;
Then through the groves, and o'er th' extended plain,
With ftormy rage the rapid whirlwinds ran :
Red o'er the glimmering hills, with pomp divine,   1005
The lightning's flaming path began to fhine ;
Far round th' immenfe unufual thunders driven,
Proclaim'd the onfet of approaching Heaven ;
Aftonifh'd Nature own'd the ftrange alarm,
And the world trembled at th' impendent ftorm.   1010
O'er the dark fields aghaft Canäan ftream'd ;
Thick in their courfe the fcatter'd bucklers gleam'd :
Behind them, Jofhua urg'd the furious car,
And tenfold horrors hover'd round the war.
    But when the Chief the fpreading ftorm furvey'd, 1015
And trac'd almighty arms in heaven difplay'd ;
With piercing voice, he gave the great command---
Stand ftill, ye chofen fons, admiring ftand !
Behold, what awful fcenes in heaven arife !
Adore the power that brightens in the fkies !   1020
Now God's tremendous arm afferts his laws ;
Now bids his thunder aid the righteous caufe ;
Unfolds how Virtue faves her chofen bands,
And points the vengeance doom'd for guilty lands.   1024
Behold, what flames fhoot forth ! what gloom afcends !
How nature trembles ! how the concave rends !
How the clouds darken ! fee, in yonder fky,
Their opening fkirts proclaim th' Almighty nigh !
    He fpoke, and from the north a rufhing found   1029
Roll'd through the heavens, and fhook th' embattled
At once a rapid path of dreadful flame   [ground :
Burft from the fkies, and pour'd a fanguine ftream :

Thron'd on a dark red cloud, an Angel's form
Sail'd awfully sublime, above the storm.
Half veil'd in mist, his countenance, like a sun,　1035
Inflam'd the clouds, and through all ether shone ;
Long robes of crimson light behind him flow'd ;
His wings were flames ; his locks were died in blood :
Ten thousand fiery shapes were round him driven,
And all the dazzling pomp of opening heaven.　1040
　Now, save Canäan's cries, that feebly rung,
Round the dark plain a horrid silence hung.
Stretch'd in dire terror o'er her quivering band,
Th' etherial Vision wav'd his sun-bright hand ;
At once from opening skies red flames were hurl'd,　1045
And thunders, roll'd on thunders, rock'd the world,
In one broad deluge sunk th' avenging hail,
And, fill'd with tempest, roar'd the hoary vale ;
The headlong whirlwinds boundless nature blend ;
The streams rush backward ; tottering mountains bend ;
Down the tall steep their bursting summits roll,　1051
And cliffs on cliffs, hoarse-crashing, rend the pole :
Far round the earth a wild drear horror reigns ;
The high heavens heave, and sink the gloomy plains :
One sea of lightnings all the region fills :　1055
Long waves of fire ride surging o'er the hills ;
The nodding forests plunge in flame around,
And with huge caverns gapes the shuddering ground.
Swifter than rapid winds Canäan driven,
Refuse the conflict of embattled Heaven.　1060
But the dire hail in vain the victims fly,
And death unbounded shook from all the sky ;
The thunder's dark career ; the Seraph's arm,
Fierce vengeance blazing down th' immense of storm.
From falling groves to burning plains they flew ;　1065
Hail roars around, and angry blasts pursue ;
From shaking heavens almighty arms are hurl'd,
And all the gloomy concave bursts upon the world.

No day like this the guilty earth had known ;
Not Egypt's storm with equal terror shone ;　　1070
No day like this o'er eastern hills shall rise,
Till Gabriel's trump inrolls the sinking skies.
For Heaven's dread stores, reserv'd for death, and war,
Fierce hail, and lightning, fill'd the rending air.
In vain the host attempted still to fly ;　　1075
They fell, they rose again ; but rose to die.
Mid thousand corses, there, beneath his shield,
Stalk'd a lone trembler through the sounding field :
Here, scatter'd wretches roam'd along the plain,
And sheltering bucklers hid their heads in vain.　　1080
On every side resistless foes engag'd ;
The lightning's livid blast around them rag'd ;
While the shrill torrents of th' avenging hail
Rush'd on the pinions of the sweeping gale.
Rare, and more rare, were seen the sinking host,　　1085
'Till, whelm'd beneath the deluge, all were lost.

Thus, when black midnight's terrors earth deform,
From the tall Andes bursts a blazing storm ;
From steep to steep the ridgy flames aspire,
Bend o'er wide realms, and wrap the heavens in fire ;1090
All nature trembles ; tottering mountains rend ;
Down the cliffs thunder ; showers of fire descend ;
Huge hills of ice, dissolv'd, and wastes of snow
Plunge in one deluge on the world below ;
O'er half Peru the floods tempestuous sweep,　　1095
And rocks, and groves, and towns, roll mingled to the deep.
The form began to move ; the clouds gave way,
Their skirts all brightening with the crimson ray ;
Far south, on wings of fire, the Angel flew,
And his clear splendors lessening left the view,　　1100
Down the broad regions of the mid-day skies,
Where glittering domes were seen, and scarcely seen to rise.

Through the long day, Canäan's widows stood,
And look'd, all-anxious, toward the plain of blood ;

Look'd for the hoſt, with victory's garlands crown'd, 1105
Enrich'd with ſpoils, and with fair fame renown'd.
Their hands, to glad their friends with choice repaſt,
Cull'd every ſweet, and wines of daintieſt taſte ;
Oſt as a duſty cloud the whirlwinds rear'd,
In diſtant fields they thought their lords appear'd ; 1110
Then, with new terrors, gaz'd, and gaz'd again,
'Till night, and ſorrow darken'd every plain.

    The ſtorm retir'd ; the enſigns gave command,
And round their Leader throng'd the conquering band.
Here ſparkling eyes with joy and triumph burn'd ; 1115
Here pity ſilent from the ſlaughter turn'd ;
Here for fallen friends the tear was ſeen to flow,
And ſighs oft ſpoke unutterable woe :
While Joſhua's thoughts mount upward to the ſkies,
And fear, and wonder, in his boſom riſe.   1120
The ſtream, the walls they paſs'd ſerenely ſlow,
Climb'd the tall hills, and ſought the plain below ;
There crown'd with flowers, their wives and children came
And ſongs roſe grateful to th' Eternal Name---
Bleſs'd be the Power divine-- rejoic'd they ſung,--- 1125
The green vales echoed, and the foreſt rung---
Bleſs'd be the hand, that clave the conſcious ſea,
And, rob'd in thunder, ſwept our foes away !
Let endleſs bleſſings round our nation riſe,
Cheer all our lives, and waft us to the ſkies !   1130
Thus ſtrains of rapture charm'd the liſtening gales,
While the low ſun-beam glimmer'd on the vales :
To reſt the camp retir'd : ten-thouſand fires
Thro' the calm ſilence rais'd their bending ſpires :
The bright moon roſe ; winds cool'd the chearful even,
And wide magnificence enkindled heaven.   1136

T H E E N D.

E R R A T A.

B. 1, l. 332 read *vesture* glow
337   *lost* to shame
433   *where* pity
451   airy *vision*
644   *wing* explore
725   *bonds* combined
845   *this* flood
B. 2, l. 249   *all* adorn'd
286   *Mock'd* &c
290   *Nor* fair
387   *knowledge* stood
B. 3, l. 114   Smil'd *on*
116   *joys* as
119   *glad* skies
130   *Where*
131   *Where*
147   *Fix'd*
175   *gifts*
203   sink *a prey*
337   were *those*
357   *lonely* wild-rose
540   *Creak*
585   *Thrice*
771   *criers* proclaim
805   Oran's *host*
826   rent the
906   *beauty's* endless
B. 4, l. 45   *and* flow
209   *For* round he *cast*
B. 5, l. 39   *inborn* light
70   prospect *chain'd*
134   *Where*
151   *each* half-form'd
180   *happy* home
484   In *sports*
544   Down *gush'd*
675   virtue's *course*
678   *inglorious* days
738   *cautious*
B. 6, l. 27   *impervious*
186   *clothe* the
675   fierce *winds*
743   *wondrous*
B. 7, l. 135   gleam *enrob'd*
176   *wide* dismay
252   *swept* th'
257   *darkening*
273   *rush*

276 read And *bade*
306   *Dash*
312   *vanish*
539   Before *his*
679   deep *concussion*
B. 8, l. 150   whose *shield*
262   surrounding *night*
648   Blaze o'er
764   *dusty* sky
945   *rejoic'd*
946   *a* mild
962   *the* lovely
B. 9, l. 48   *revive*
67   *those* frowns
79   *For*
197   *her* hand
364   *fears*
411   *breasts*
503   *her* throne
524   *toll* lowers
655   O'er thy
656   *Slow* roll
659   *view* thy
669   *bodies*
673   *heavens*
703   *sorrows*
B. 10, l. 23   *flocks*
29   gay *cots*
41   *these* regions
51   kind *showers*
58   *disturb*
161   *wide* realms
221   *mind*
281   *sons*
399   *command*
503   Alike *remov'd*
711   *Then* o'er
857   clear *perfection*
1026   blend the
1086   fix *the*
B. 11, l. 20   *wave* their
238   and *light*
239   *acts* of
248   *towns* ascend
293   *steer'd*
501   *walls*
697   *trembled*

PAGE 30, Note at the bottom. religious *power,*

TRIUMPH

OF

INFIDELITY:

A

POEM.

PRINTED IN THE WORLD

M,DCC,LXXXVIII.

To Monſ. de Voltaire.

SIR,

YOUR *Creator endued you with ſhining talents, and caſt your lot in a field of action, where they might be moſt happily employed: In the progreſs of a long and induſtrious life, you devoted them to a ſingle purpoſe, the elevation of your character above his.   For the accompliſhment of this purpoſe, with a diligence and uniformity which would have adorned the moſt virtuous purſuits, you oppoſed truth, religion, and their authors, with ſophiſtry, contempt, and obloquy; and taught, as far as your example or ſentiments extended their influence, that the chief end of man was, to ſlander his God, and abuſe him forever.   To whom could ſuch an effort as the following be dedicated, with more propriety, than to you.   The ſubject it celebrates is the moſt pointed attack upon your old enemies; an attack more happily deviſed, at leaſt, than any of yours; as yours were more advantageouſly concerted than the efforts of any of your predeceſſors.   Reaſoning is an unhappy engine to be employed againſt chriſtianity; as, like elephants in ancient war, it uſually, in this caſe, turns upon thoſe who employ it.   Ridicule is a more convenient weapon, as you have ſucceſsfully evinced; but in-*

a 2   *genious*

*genious mifinterpretation is a still more sure and
effectual annoyance ; for the sword and javelin,
however keen, may be dreaded and shunned, while
the secret and deadly dirk is plunged to the heart
of unsuspecting friendship, unhappily trusting the
smooth-faced assassin. Accept then, as due, this
tribute of acknowledgment from the*

WRITER OF THIS POEM.

Audies, & veniet manes hæc fama sub imos.

THE

THE
TRIUMPH
OF
INFIDELITY.

ERE yet the Briton left our happy shore,
Or war's alarming clarion ceas'd to roar,
What time the morn illum'd her purple flame,
Thro' air's dread wilds the prince of darkness
    came.
A cloud his gloomy car; his path around,
Attendant whirlwinds gave a fearful sound,
Before him dragons wound their bloody spires;
Far shot behind him death's Tartarean fires:
To image heaven's high state, he proudly rode,
Nor seem'd he less than hell's terrific God.
While, full before him, dress'd in beauteous day,
The realms of freedom, peace, and virtue lay;
The realms, where heav'n, ere Time's great em-
    pire fall,
Shall bid new Edens dress this dreary ball;
He frown'd; the world grew dark; the moun-
    tains shook,
And nature shudder'd as the spirit spoke.

                   What

What wafted years, with angry voice he cries,
I wage vain wars with yonder hated fkies?
Still, as I walk th' unmeafur'd round of things,
From deepeft ill what good perpetual fprings;
What order fhines, where bleft confufion lay,
And from the night of death, what fplendid day?
How* near me feem'd, ere Bethlehem's wonder
    rofe,
The final victory o'er my ftruggling foes;
All nations won to ignorance, and fin,
Without the Gentile, and the Jew within?
How near, when crofs'd, he met th' accurfed
    doom,
Or lay, extinguifh'd in the mortal tomb?
Yet then, even whilft I felt my pinions rife
Above the arches of a thoufand fkies,
Even then, deep plunged beneath the loweft hell,
As erft when hurl'd from heav'n, my kingdom fell,
And† oh, by what foul means! An angel I,
A god, the rival of yon haughty fky!
They the laft fweepings of the clay-born kind,
The dunghill's offspring, and the reptile's mind.
Yet their creating voice, with ftartling found,
From death and darknefs wak'd the world's wide
    round;
Before it crumbled, mid my groans and tears,
The Pagan fabric of a thoufand years;

                     The

---

* State of infidelity at the birth of ———
† Injuries done to infidelity, by Peter, Paul, and others.

The fpells, the rites, the pomp, the victims fled,
The fanes all defert, and the lares dead.
In vain fierce perfecution hedg'd their way;
In vain dread power's huge weight incumbent lay;
As fand-built domes diffolve before the ftream,
As vifions fleet upon th' awakening beam,
The ftructure fled; while hell was rack'd to fave,
And all my heaven-bright glories fought the
      grave.
Amaz'd,* awhile, I faw the ruin fpread,
My hopes, my efforts, with my kingdom, dead.
But foon I bade the floods of vengeance roll,
Soon rous'd anew my mightinefs of foul,
With arts my own, th' oppofer's power withftood,
And reign'd once more the univerfal God;
Mine, by all poifoning wealth, his fons I made,
And Satan preached, while proud Meffiah fled.
Surpriz'd,† enrag'd, to fee his wiles outdone,
His power all vanquifh'd, and his kingdom gone,
From the ftern North, he hail'd my darling hoft,
A whelming ocean, fpread to every coaft;
My Goths, my Huns, the cultur'd world o'er-ran,
And darknefs buried all the pride of man.
On dozing realms he pour'd his vengeance dread,
On putrid bifhops, and on priefts half dead,
                              Blotted,

* Progrefs of infidelity after the death of Conftantine
the Great.

† Infidels injured unwittingly by their friends, the
northern barbarians.

Blotted, at one great ftroke, the work he drew,
And faw his gofpel bid mankind adieu.
The* happy hour I feiz'd; the world my own:
Full in his church I fix'd my glorious throne;
Thrice crown'd, I fate a God, and more than
    God;
Bade all earth's nations fhiver at my nod;
Difpens'd to men the code of Satan' laws,
And made my priefts the columns of my caufe.
In their blefs'd hands the gofpel I conceal'd,
And new-found doctrines, in it's ftead, reveal'd;
Of gloomy vifions drew a fearful round,
Names of dire look, and words of killing found,
Where, meaning loft, terrifi: doctrines lay,
Maz'd the dim foul, and frighten'd truth away;
Where noife for truth, for virtue pomp was given,
Myfelf the God promulg'd, and hell the heaven.
To this blefs'd fcheme I forc'd the ftruggling
    mind;
Faith funk beneath me; fenfe her light refign'd;
Before rebellious confcience clank'd the chain;
The rack, the wheel, unbofomed all their pain;
The dungeon yawn'd; uprofe the faggot pyre,
And, fierce with vengeance, twin'd the livid fire.
Thefe woes I form'd on earth; beyond the tomb,
Of dreams, I built the purgatorial doom;
Hurl'd round all realms the interdictive peal;
Shut kings from heaven, and nations fcourg'd
    to hell;

All

* New progrefs of infidelity, under the papal hierarchy.

All crimes forgave; thofe crimes indulg'd again;
Difclos'd the right divine to every fin;
To certain ecftafies the faithful led;
Damn'd Doubt, when living; double damn'd,
    when dead;
O'er bold Inquiry bade all horrors roll,
And to its native nothing fhrunk the foul.
Thus, round the Gothic wild, my kingdom lay,
A night, foon clouded o'er a winter's day.
But* oh, by what fell fate, to be entomb'd
Are bright ambition's brighteft glories doom'd?
While now my rival every hope forfook,
His arts, his counfels, and his fceptre broke,
This vaft machine, fo wondrous, fo refin'd,
Firft, faireft offspring even of Satan's mind,
This building, o'er all buildings proudly great,
Than Heaven more noble, and more fix'd than
    fate,
This glorious empire fell; the world grew pale,
And the fkies trembled, at the dreadful tale.
In vain my arm, in vain my fword, I bar'd;
In vain my angels o'er example dar'd,
My priefts, high-fed on all the fpoils of man,
Outran belief and even my hopes outran;
Hell hop'd, and toil'd in vain: Thro' all her coaft,
A general figh declar'd her kingdom loft.

    Blufh, Satan, blufh, thou fovereign of mankind,
When, what thy reptile foes, thou call'ft to mind.

B   New

---

* Injuries done to infidelity by Luther, Calvin, and others.

New fiſhermen, mechanic worms, anew
The unfolded goſpel from my kingdom drew.
From earth's wide realms, beneath the deluge
    bare,
As ſuns reviving bade the ſpring appear,
So, at their ſtartling voice, from ſhore to ſhore,
A moral ſpring my winter cover'd o'er,
The mind new ſprang; rebudding virtue grew,
And trembling nations roſe from death anew.
From them roll'd on, to bleſs this earth's cold
    clime,
A brighter ſeaſon, and more vernal prime,
Where, long by wintry ſuns denied to riſe,
Fair Right and Freedom open'd on the ſkies,
Virtue, and Truth, and joy, in nobler bloom,
Call'd earth and heaven to taſte the ſweet
    perfume,
Pleas'd, to the ſcene increaſing millions ran,
And threaten'd Satan with the loſs of man.
Theſe* ills to ward I train'd my arts anew;
O'er truths fair form the webs of ſophiſm drew;
Virtue new chill'd, in growing beauties gay,
Wither'd her bloom, and puff'd her ſweets away.
Againſt her friends I arm'd new bands of foes;
Firſt, higheſt, all-ſubduing Faſhion roſe.
From courts to cottages, her ſovereign ſway,
With force reſiſtleſs, bade the world obey.
                    The

* Progreſs of infidelity, under the auſpicious influence
of Charles II. and his cotemporaries.

She moulded faith, and fcience, with a nod ;
Now there was not, and now there was, a God.
"Let black be white," fhe faid, and white it feem'd,
"Hume a philofopher ;" and ftraight he dream'd
Moft philofophically. At her call,
Opinions, doctrines, learn'd to rife, and fall ;
Before* her, bent the univerfal knee,
And own'd her fovereign, to the praife of me.
With† her, brave Ridicule, 'twixt ill and good,
Falfhood and truth, fatanic umpire ftood.
He, Hogarth like, with hues and features new,
The form of providence, perfuafive drew:
Round its fair face bade hells black colours rife.
Its limbs diftorted, blear'd its heaven-bright eyes.
At the maim'd image gaz'd, and grinn'd aloud—
" Yon frightful hag's no femblance of a god."
                    B 2   Mean

* Phil. ii, 10, 11.

† The doctrine that ridicule is a teft of truth cannot,
even on the fcheme of infidels juftify their application of it.
Wherever any object, or if you pleafe, propofition, when
feen clearly and certainly in all its nature, parts, and rela-
tions, is evidently abfurd, and ridiculous, it may be an
objection againft its reality, or truth. But a man, in his
natural and proper appearance, may be a beautiful object ;
and a propofition, in its real nature, and neceffary confe-
quences, may contain a truth important and noble, altho'
when a fign-poft painter fhall have drawn one with a pair
of horns and a tail, and an infidel annexed his own dreams
as appendages to the other, all the fraternity of blockheads
will laugh at both.   Anon.

Mean* time my friends, the veterans of my
    caufe,
Rack'd every nerve, and gain'd all hell's
    applaufe,
Thro' realms of cheat and doubt, and dark-
    nefs, ran,
New-made creation, uncreated man,
Taught, and retaught, afferted and denied,
As pamper'd pleafure, or as bolfter'd pride.
Now, groping man in death's dim darknefs trod,
Now, all things kenn'd, with eyelids of a god.
Now, miracles, not God himfelf could fpell;
Now, every monk could grunt them from his
    cell.
Priefts now were dulleft, laft, of mortal things;
Now outflew Satan's felf, on cunning's wings.

No

---

* See the hoft of infidel writers, during the laft age.

Such advantages does Infidelity enjoy over Revelation,
that both fides of moral queftions will equally fupport that,
and weaken this. Thus one Infidel will overthrow Revelation
by proving that there is not one honeft man living; an-
other will as fuccefsfully attack it by afferting, and the
affertions of Infidels are always to be taken for proofs, that
there are honeft men of all religions and opinions. One
fees intuitively that God never did, nor can, reveal his
pleafure to mankind. Another finds the Koran and
Shahftan in the lift of Revelations. Plato's devotion of him-
felf to a courtizan, and Socrate's to Alcibiades were the
effufions of honeft, virtuous hearts; but Paul's dedication
of his life to the [Redeemer was a reverie of enthufiafm.

God

No fyftem here, of truth, to man is given;

There my own doctrines fpeak the voice of
  heaven;

While God, with fmiling eyes, alike furveys

The pagan myfteries, and the chriftian praife.

While here on earth no virtuous man was found,

There faints, like pifmires, fwarm'd the molehill
  round;

Like maggots, crawl'd Caffraria's entrail'd
  forts;

Or mufhroom'd o'er Europa's putrid courts;
            To

God alfo, tho' difhonoured by adoration, prefented to him
in the character of a holy fin-hating God, and incapable of
being pleafed, when invoked in the name of Jefus Chrift,
is yet glorified, when honeft votaries addrefs him, in the
elevated character of an ox, an onion, or a fnake, and is
highly delighted with invocations, when offered in the
pleafing and prevailing name of the devil.

   Happy, happy, happy caufe!
   None but the wife,
   None but the wife,
   Have fuch fharp eyes,
   Or tell fuch lies.   Morgan.

The Devil's Feaft, or the power of falfhood. An ode, by
the very fame Laureat, who wrote another, on the death of
David Hume, Efq. in which, out of compaffion to the Lord
Jefus Chrift, he forbears to tell how effectually faid Hume
has overthrown him

 • (Morgan) An unhappy man, who went to bed one night, and
dreamed he was a great man, and a moral philofopher, which fo turned
his brain with furprife, that he never knew himfelf in the glafs after-
wards; but thought he was a moral philofopher, to the day of his
death.   SCRIBLERUS.

To deiſt clubs familiar dar'd retire,
Or howl'd, and powaw'd, round the Indian ſire,
Such feats my ſons atchiev'd, ſuch honors won;
The ſhores, the blocking, of th' infernal
    throne!
And tho' yon haughty world their worth deny,
Their names ſhall glitter in the nether ſky.

    But ah their wiſdom, wit, and toils were vain,
A balm firſt ſoothing, then increaſing pain.
Thro'* nature's fields while cloud-borne Bacon
    ran,
Doubtful his mind, an angel, or a man;
While high-ſoul'd Newton, wing'd by Heaven
    abroad,
Explain'd alike the works, and word, of God;
While patient Locke illum'd with newborn ray,
The path of reaſon, and the laws of ſway;
While Berkley, burſting like the morning ſun,
Look'd round all parching from his loſty
    throne,
In all events, and in all beings ſhew'd
The preſent, living, acting, ſpeaking God,
Or caſt reſiſtleſs beams, the goſpel o'er,
Union ſupreme of wiſdom, love, and power!
Pain'd, ſhrivill'd, gaſping, from the forceful ray
How crept my mite Philoſophers away?

                          In

* Names of a few ſilly men, whoſe minds were too ſmall
to comprehend the nature and evidences of Infidelity.
                                COLLINS

In vain my Methodiſt, brave Herbert, cried,
And whin'd, and wrote, pretended, pray'd,
   and lied*,
In vain my Shaftſbury, to his maſter true,
Dread †Humble bee! o'er burrs and thiſtles flew;
Incupped, and raviſhed with the fuſsful noiſe,
To praiſe the wondrous flowers, he rais'd his
   voice,
Of nature, beauty, dream'd and humm'd amain,
And ſung himſelf, and buzz'd at truth, in vain.
Ah Bolingbroke, how well thy tatter'd robe,
Poor, Bedlam king of learning's little globe!
Amus'd thy fancy? He, with glory fir'd,
Myſelf in miniature! to heaven aſpir'd
For fame, his heaven, thro' falſhood's realms
   he ran,
And wiſh'd, and watch'd, and toil'd, and hop'd,
   in vain,
Miſread, miſwrote, miſquoted, miſapplied,
Yet fail'd of fame, and miſs'd the ſkies, beſide.
In views, in pride, in fate, conjoin'd with me,
Even Satan's ſelf ſhall drop a tear for thee.

My

* See Lord Cherburg's Cock-Lane-Ghoſt Tale of
Thunder's anſwer to Prayer.   Scriblerus.

† The characteriſtics of which inſect are, buſily to buſtle
about with a great ſhew of ſtatelineſs and mock majeſty,
with a noiſy, ſolemn hum, that ſounds much, and means
nothing, to be forever poring over flowers, but never to
gather, or yield, any honey.
Linnæus—properties of humble bees.

My leaders thefe; yet Satan boafts his fubs,
His Tolands, Tindals, Collinfes, and Chubbs,
Morgans and Woolftons, names of lighter worth,
That ftand, on falfhood's lift, for &c.
That fworn to me, to vice and folly given,
At truth and virtue growl'd, and bark'd at heaven.
Not men, 'tis true, yet manlings oft they won,
Againft their God help'd blockheads oft to fun,
Help'd fops to folly, and help'd rakes to fin,
And* marr'd all fway, by mocking fway divine.
My lift of authors too they help'd to count,
As cyphers eke the decimal amount.
As writers too they profer'd ufeful aid
Believ'd unfeen, and reverenc'd though unread.
Againft their foe no proof my fons defire,
No reafoning canvafs and no fenfe require.
Enough, the Bible is by wits arraign'd,
Genteel men doubt it, fmart men fay it's feign'd,
Onward my powder'd beaux and boobies throng,
As puppies float the kennel's ftream along.
But their defects to varnifh, and, in fpite
Of pride and dignity, refolv'd to write,

I feiz'd

---

* The fame principles, which fuppport or deftroy chrifti-
anity, alike fupport or deftroy political order and govern-
ment. So manifeft is this, that Lord Bolingbroke, when
contending againft thofe whom he efteemc enemies of the
Britifh government, treats them unwittingly, I prefume, as
enemies alfo to chriftianity, and loads them, for their com-
bined folly and perverfenefs, with many epithets of fupreme
contempt.

I feiz'd the work myfelf.   Straight, in a cloud
Of night involv'd, to Scotia's realms I rode.
There, in the cobwebs of a college room,
I found my beft Amanuenfis, Hume,
And bofom'd in his breaft.   On dreams afloat,
The youth foar'd high, and, as I prompted, wrote.
Sublimeft nonfenfe there I taught mankind,
Pure, genuine drofs, from gold feven times refin'd.
From realm to realm the ftrains exalted rung,
And thus the fage, and thus his teacher, fung.
All things roll on, by fix'd eternal laws;
Yet no effect depends upon a caufe:
Hence every law was made by Chance divine,
Parent moft fit of order, and defign!
Earth was not made, but happen'd: Yet, on earth,
All beings happen, by moft ftated birth;
Each thing miraculous; yet ftrange to tell,
Not God himfelf can fhew a miracle.
    Mean time, left thefe great things, the vulgar
          mind,
With learning vaft, and deep refearch, fhould
          blind,
Left dull to read, and duller ftill when known,
My favorite fcheme fhould mould, and fleep,
          alone;
To* France I pofted, on the wings of air,
And fir'd the labors of the gay Voltaire.
              C   He,

* Satan feems guilty of an anachronifm here, Voltaire
being the eldeft writer of the two.   SCRIBLERUS.

He, light and gay, o'er learning's furface flew,
And prov'd all things at option, falfe or true.
The gofpel's truths he faw were airy dreams,
The fhades of nonfenfe, and the whims of whims.
Before his face no Jew could tell what paft;
Or know the right from left, the firft from laft;
Conjecture where his native Salem ftood,
Or find, if Jordan had a bank, or flood.
The Greeks, and Romans, never truth defcried;
But always (when they proved the gofpel) lied.
He, he alone, the bleft retreat had fmelt,
The* Well, where long with frogs, the goddefs
 dwelt;
In China dug, at Chihohamti's† call,
And curb d with bricks, the refufe of his wall.
There, mid a realm of cheat, a world of lies,
Where alter'd nature wears one great difguife,
Where fhrunk, mifhapen bodies mock the eye,
And fhrivell'd fouls the power of thought deny,
Mid idiot Mandarins, and baby Kings,
And dwarf Philofophers, in leading-ftrings,

         Mid

---

* It appears, by the teftimony of all the ancient hifto-
rians, that truth originally lived in a well ; but Voltaire
was the firft geographer, who difcovered where it was
dug——Lord Kaims's fketches of the weaknefs of man ;
article Voltaire.

† The Emperor, who burnt all the ancient records of his
country, and built the great wall to defend it from the
Tartars. Quere—In which inftance did he do his country-
men the moft good ; if the books, he burnt, were like thofe
written by them afterwards ?

Mid senseless votaries of less senseless Fo,
Wretches who nothing even seem'd to know,
Bonzes, with souls more naked than their skin,
All brute without, and more than brute within,
From Europe's rougher sons the goddess shrunk,
Tripp'd in her iron shoes, and sail'd her junk.
Nice, pretty, wondrous stories there she told,
Of empires, forty thousand ages old,
Of Tohi, born with rainbows round his nose,
Lao's long day—Ginseng† alchymic dose—
Stories, at which all Behmen's dreams awake,
Start into truth, and sense and virtue speak;
To which, all, lisping children e'er began
With, "At a time," or "Once there was a man,"
Is reason, truth, and fact; and sanctioned clear
With heaven's own voice, or proof of eye and ear.
He‡ too reveal'd, that candour bade mankind
Believe my haughty rival weak, and blind;

C 2   That

---

* Fo, principal Idol of the Chinese.

† A plant, to which the Chinese ascribe all virtues of
food and medicine, and proved by European scrutiny to be
just as remote from them, as the date of the Chinese empire
from 40,000 years. In the same manner, all Chinese ex-
traordinaries, except a few mechanical ones, when examined,
descend to plain dock and plantain. Yet, when swallowed
by Voltaire, they will help to expel gripes of conscience,
as a decoction of Ginseng will those of the flatulent cholic-
full as well as warm water.

GARTH's alphabetical prophecies, article Ginseng.

‡ See Voltair's Candide, the great purpose of which is
to prove, that whatever is, is *not* right.

That all things wrong a ruling God denied;
Or a fatanic imp that God implied
An imp, per chance of power and fkill poffeft,
But not with juftice, truth, or goodnefs bleft.
Doctrines divine! would men their force receive,
And live to Satan's glory, as believe.

    Nor thefe alone: from every clafs of man,
I gain'd new aids to build the darling plan.
But chief his favorite clafs, his priefts, I won,
To undermine his caufe, and prop my own.
Here Jefuitic art its frauds combin'd
To draw ten thoufand cobwebs o'er the mind.
In poifoned toils the flutterer to inclofe,
And fix, with venom'd fangs, eternal woes.
On fceptic drofs they ftamp'd heavens image
    bright,
And nam'd their will a wifp, immortal light,
Thro' moors, and fens, the fightlefs wanderer
    led,
'Till down he plung'd, ingulph'd among the
    dead.
To life,* Socinus here his millions drew,
In ways, the art of Heaven conceal'd from view,
                    Undeified

---

  * Great men, if clofely examined, will generally be
found ftrongly to refemble each other. Thus Milton,
Homer and Offian were blind. Thus this great man ex-
ceedingly refembled Milton. There was however one or
two trifling circumftances of difference. Milton, for in-
ftance, was ftone-blind in his bodly eyes, but had clear
and intuitive moral optics. In Socinus the cafe was exactly
                        reverfed.

Undeified the world's almighty truſt,
And lower'd eternity's great* ſire to duſt.
He taught, O firſt of men! the Son of God,
Who hung the globe, and ſtretch'd the heavens
    abroad,
Spoke into life the ſun's ſupernal fire,
And mov'd to harmony the flaming choir,
Who in his hand immenſity infolds,
And angels, worlds, and ſuns, and heavens,
    upholds,
Is—what? a worm, on far creation's limb,
A minim, in intelligence extreme.
O wondrous goſpel, where ſuch doctrines riſe!
Diſcoveries wondrous of moſt wondrous eyes!
From him, a darling race deſcended fair,
Even to this day my firſt and chiefeſt care,
When perteſt Prieſtly† calls mankind, to ſee
His own corruptions of chriſtianity.

    Mean time, leſs open friends my cauſe ſuſtain'd,
More ſmoothly tempted and more ſlily gain'd;
Taught eaſier ways to climb the bright abode;
                        Leſs

reverſed. Milton alſo roſe in his moral conceptions, with
no unhappy imitation of the ſcriptural ſublimity: Socinus,
on the contrary, anticlimaxed the ſcriptural ſyſtem down to
nothing.   SCRIBLERUS.

   * Iſai. ix. 6.

   † A celebrated philoſopher of the preſent day, who has
carried chemical compoſition to a higher perfection than
any other man living; for he has advanced ſo far, as to
form a whole ſyſtem of divinity out of fixed air.
                                  SCRIBLERUS.

Lefs pure made virtue, and lefs perfect God;
Lefs guilty vice, the atonement lefs divine,
And pav'd, with peace and joy, the way to fin.
While* thus by art and perfeverance won,
Again the old world feem'd almoft my own.

In this wild wafte, where Albion's lights revive,
New dangers threaten and new evils live.
Here a dread race, my fturdieft foes defign'd,
Patient of toil, of firm and vigorous mind,
Pinion'd with bold refearch to truth's far coaft,
By ftorms undaunted, nor in oceans loft,
With dire invafion, error's realm affail,
And all my hardy friends before them fail.

But my chief bane, my apoftolic foe,
In life, in labours, fource of every woe,
From fcenes obfcure, did heaven his * * * * * * *
    call,
That moral Newton, and that fecond Paul.
He, in clear view, faw facred fyftems roll,
Of reafoning worlds, around their central foul;
Saw love attractive every fyftem bind,
The parent linking to each filial mind;
The end of heaven's high works refiftlefs fhew'd,
Creating glory, and created good;
And, in one little life, the gofpel more
Difclos'd, than all earth's myriads kenn'd before.
Beneath his ftandard; lo what number rife,
To dare for truth, and combat for the fkies!
　　　　　　　　　　　　　　　Arm'd

---

* Oppofition to infidelity by difciples of Peter, Paul, &c.
in this country.

Arm'd at all points, they try the battling field,
With reason's sword and faith's etherial shield.
To ward this fate all irreligion can,
Whate'er sustains, or flatters sinning man;
Whate'er can conscience of her thorns disarm,
Or calm, at death s approach, the dread alarm;
Whate'er like truth, with error cheats mankind;
Whate'er, like virtue, taints with vice the mind;
I preach d, I wrote, I argued, pray'd, and lied,
What could my friends, or even myself, beside?
But, tho' with glad successes often crown'd,
Unceasing fears my troubled path surround.
While with each toil my friends the cause
    sustain,
Their toils, their efforts, and their arts are vain.
  Even plodding * * * * * * did but little good,
Who* taught, the soul of man was made of mud:
Cold mud was virtue; warmer mud was sin;
And thoughts the angle-worms, that crawl'd
    within:
Nor taught alone; but wise, to precept join'd
A fair example, in his creeping mind.
In vain thro † realms of nonsense * * * * * ran
The great Clodhopping‡ oracle of man.

                      Yet

  * See a late American treatise entitled a Philosophical Essay on Matter, in which this great doctrine is fully proved.
  † Otherwise called Oracles of Reason.
  ‡ New name elegantly given to man, in Oracles of Reason.   Anon.
  The annotator above mistakes, in calling this epithet a
                           new

Yet faithful were his toils: What could he more?
In Satans caufe he buftled, bruifed, and fwore;
And* what the due reward, from me fhall know,
For gentlemen of equal worth below.

 To vengeance then, my foul, to vengeance
   rife,
Affert thy glory and affault the fkies.
What tho' dull feers have fung, in dreams
  fublime,
Thy ruin floats along the verge of time,
Tho'† without hands the ftone from mountains
  riven,
Alarms my throne, and haftes the ire of heaven;
Tho'‡ blifs' dread heralds earth's far limits
  round
Pardon, and peace, and joy, ere long fhall found;
How beauteous are their feet! all regions cry,
And one great, natal fong falute the fky:
          Still

---

new name. I could eafily fhew, by a feries of learned de-
ductions, that Clodhopper was the very original name of
mankind, when they wore tails, as Lord Monboddo has
moft ingenioufly proved they did, at their firft creation.
             SCRIBLERUS.

 * In A——n's Journal the writer obferves, he prefumes
he fhall be treated; in the future world as well as other
gentlemen of equal merit are treated: A fentiment, in
which all his countrymen will join him. SCRIBLERUS.

 † Dan. ii. 44—45.

 ‡ Ifai. lii. 7.

Still, fhould I fink, a glorious fate I'll find,
And fink amid the ruins of mankind.

But what bleft onfet fhall I now begin,
To plunge the New World in the gulph of fin?
With fweet declenfion, down perdition's fteep,
How, in one hoft, her cheated millions fweep?
I hail the glorious project, firft, and beft,
That ever Satan's bright invention bleft;
That* on this world my kingdom firft began,
And loft my rival paradife, and man.
Twice fifteen funs are paft, fince C • • • • • • •'s
    mind,
Thro' doctrines deep, from common fenfe refin'd,
I led, a nice, myfterious work to frame,
With love of fyftem, and with luft of fame.
Fair in his hand the pleafing wonder grew,
Wrought with deep art, and ftor'd with treafures
    new:
There the fweet fophifm led the foul aftray;
There round to heaven foft bent the crooked way:
Saints, he confefs'd, the fhorteft rout purfue;
But, fcarce behind, my children follow too.
Even Satan's felf ere long fhall thither hie;
On† cap, huzza! and thro' the door go I!
Now palfied age has dimm'd his mental fight,
I'll roufe the fage his mafter's laws to fight,

D

The

* Genefis iii, 4. *And the ferpent faid unto the woman—*
Ye fhall not furely die. &c.

† Magical incantation ufed formerly by the witches at
Salem, when they went thro' key holes. SCRIBLERUS.

The injuries, long he render'd, to repair
And wipe from heaven's fair book his faith and
  prayer.
To wound the eternal caufe with deepeft harms,
A cheated gofpel proves the fureft arms:
Thofe arms, no hand can, like a preacher's wield;
Falfe friends may ftab, when foes muft fly the
  field.
This M * * * * * proves, in whom my utmoft
  fkill
Peer'd out no means of mifchief, but the will.
He, in hard days, when ribbons gave no bread,
And Spitalfield's brave fons from Tyburn fled,
Scampering from bailiffs, wifely dropp'd the
  fhuttle,
To preach down truth, and common fenfe to
  throttle.
With cunning, oft in fcrapes and buftles tried,
Tongue at-your-fervice, in all ftories plied,
The dirtieft ridicule of things moft holy,
And dirtier flattery of fin and folly,
A mimickry, at which buffoons would blufh,
Religion cent-per-cented, at a rufh,
Boldnefs, that dares to make the Bible lie,
And brafs, that would a foundery fupply,
Mid gather'd rogues, and blockheads, oft he
  ftood,
And rous'd to fun the genuine brotherhood;
Scripture, and argument, oblig'd to yield,
Made learning, fenfe, and virtue, quit the field,
       While

While fainting decency funk down to fee
The defk of God a puppet-fhow for me.

This faid, invefted with the robes of day,
To C* * * * * * *'s dome he wing'd his gladfome
  way,
And fpread delightful to his wilder'd fenfe,
The pride of fyftem, and the increafe of pence.
Forth from its cobwebs ftraight the work he
  drew,
In mould ftill precious, and in duft ftill new.
This darling pet to ufher to mankind,
High blown to ecftafy, the fage defign'd;
And conn'd, with grand-parental love, the day,
When thro' the world the heir fhould make its
  way.

The laughing fpirit feized the lucky hour,
And round Columbia bade the* trumpet roar,
And thus thro' all her regions rang the
  fong—
To† Pandemonia's plains, ye mortals, throng!
Here fhall you, raptur'd, find there is no hell;
A prieft fhall teach it, and the gofpel tell;

D 2   The

---

* Otherwife called Salvation to all men. A treatife,
publifhed as a harbinger to the great one having this
motto on the title page——

  I leave you here a little book,
  For you to look upon,
  That you may learn to lie and fwear,
  When I am dead and gone. SCRIBLERUS.

† Otherwife called the field of mifchief. SCRIBLERUS.

The pleaſing truth, ſo long from earth conceal'd,
To bleſs deſponding guilt, is now reveal'd.
Thus rang the thrilling voice the new world round;
Each villain ſtarted at the pleaſing ſound,
Hugg'd his old crimes, new miſchiefs 'gan deviſe,
And turn'd his noſe up to the threatning ſkies.

The perjur'd wretch, who met no honeſt eye,
But felt his own retreat, his ſpirit die,
Clear'd up his wither'd front, and true he cried
Pve ſometimes been forſworne, and often lied;
But all's a farce; as proves this doctrine new,
For God muſt help the perjur'd, as the true.

Up Florio ſprang; and with indignant woes,
As thus he cried, his ſtartled boſom roſe——
I am the firſt of men in ways of evil,
The trueſt, thriftieſt ſervant of the devil,
Born, educated, glory to engroſs,
And ſhine confeſs'd, the Devil's Man of Roſs.
Here's three to one, I beat even him in pride;
Two whores already in my chariot ride:
Shall then this wretch?—forbid it Florio, heaven!
Shall ſin's bright laurels to this prieſt be given?
No, ſtill on Satan's roll ſhall ſhine my praiſe,
As erſt on C——'s liſts of yeas and nays.

Half pleas'd, the honeſt tar out bolted——
      "whew"!
"Good doctrine, Jack" "Aye, too good to
   "be true."
P···· ſcowling heard, and growl'd—The day's
   our own!
I'll now tell two lies, where I told but one.
                       W······

W****** more hard than flint, in fin grown
    old,
Clinch'd clofe his claws, and grip'd his bags of
    gold.
In vain, he cried, their woes let orphans tell;
In vain let widows weep; there is no hell.
Six, fix per cent, each month, muft now be
    given,
For pious ufury now's the road to heaven.
All who, tho' fair without, yet black within,
Glued to their lips the choice liqueur of fin,
Whofe confcience, oft rebuff'd, with fnaky
    power,
Impoifon'd ftill the gay and gleeful hour,
Check'd the loofe wifh, the paft enjoyment
    ftung,
And oft the alarm of retribution rung,
Thrill'd at each nerve, to find their fears were
    vain,
And fwung triumphant caps at future pain.
    And now the morn arofe; when o'er the plain
Gather'd, from every fide, a numerous train;
To quell thofe fears, that rankled ftill within,
And gain new ftrength, and confidence, to fin.
There the half putrid Epicure was feen,
His cheeks of port, and lips with turtle green,
Who hop'd a long eternity was given,
To fpread good tables, in fome eating heaven.
The leacher there his lurid vifage fhew'd,
The imp of darknefs, and the foe of good;

Who

Who fled his lovely wife's moſt pure embrace,
To ſate on hags, and breed a mongrel race;
A high-fed horſe, for others wives who neigh'd;
A cur, who prowl'd around each quiet bed;
A ſnake, far ſpreading his impoiſon'd breath,
And charming innocence to guilt, and death,
Here ſtood Hypocriſy, in ſober brown,
His ſabbath face all ſorrow'd with a frown.
A diſmal tale he told of diſmal times,
And this ſad world brimful of ſaddeſt crimes,
Furrow'd his cheeks with tears for others ſin,
But cloſ'd his eyelids on the hell within.]
There ſmil'd the ſmooth Divine, unus'd to wound
The ſinners heart, with hell's alarming ſound.
No terrors on his gentle tongue attend;
No grating truths the niceſt ear offend.
That ſtrange new-birth, that methodiſtic grace,
Nor in his heart, nor ſermons, found a place.
Plato's fine tales he clumſily retold,
Trite, fireſide, moral ſeaſaws, dull as old;
His Chriſt, and bible, plac'd at good remove,
Guilt hell-deſerving, and forgiving love.
'Twas beſt, he ſaid, mankind ſhould ceaſe to ſin;
Good fame requir'd it; ſo did peace within:
Their honours, well he knew, would ne'er be
    driven;
But hop'd they ſtill would pleaſe to go to heaven.
Each week, he paid his viſitation dues;
Coax'd, jeſted, laugh'd; rehears'd the private
    news;

Smoak'd

Smoak'd with each goody, thought her cheefe
    excell'd;
Her pipe he lighted, and her baby held.
Or plac'd in fome great town, with lacquer'd
    fhoes,
Trim wig, and trimmer gown, and gliftening
    hofe,
He bow'd, talk'd politics, learn'd manners mild;
Moft meekly queftioned, and moft fmoothly
    fmil'd;
At rich mens jefts laugh'd loud their ftories
    prais'd;
Their wives new patterns gaz'd, and gaz'd, and
    gaz'd;
Moft daintily on pamper'd turkies din'd;
Nor fhrunk with fafting, nor with ftudy pin'd:
Yet from their churches faw his brethren driven,
Who thunder'd truth, and fpoke the voice of
    heaven,
Chill'd trembling guilt, in Satan's headlong
    path,
Charm'd the feet back, and rous'd the ear of
    death.
"Let fools," he cried, "ftarve on, while
    prudent I
Snug in my neft fhall live, and fnug fhall die.
  There ftood the infidel of modern breed,
Bleft vegetation of infernal feed,
Alike no Deift, and no Chriftian, he;
But from all principle, all virtue, free.

                      To

To him all things the fame, as good or evil;
Jehovah, Jove, the Lama, or the Devil;
Mohammed's braying, or Isaiah's lays;
The Indian's powaws, or the Christian's praise.
With him all *natural* desires are good;
His* thirst for stews; the Mohawk's thirst for
 blood:
Made, not to know, or love, the all beauteous
 mind;
Or wing thro' heaven his path to bliss refin'd:
But his dear self, choice Dagon! to adore;
To dress, to game, to swear, to drink, to whore;
To race his steeds; or cheat, when others run;
Pit tortur'd cocks, and swear 'tis glorious fun:
His soul not cloath'd with attributes divine;
But a nice watch-spring to that grand machine,
That work more nice than Rittenhouse can plan,
The body; man's chief part; himself, the man;
Man, that illustrious brute of noblest shape,
A swine unbristled, and an untail'd ape:
To couple, eat, and die—his glorious doom—
The oyster's church-yard, and the capon's tomb.
 There * * * * * * grinn'd, his conscience
  fear'd anew,
And scarcely wish'd the doctrine false or true;
Scarce smil'd, himself secure from God to know,
So poor the triumph o'er so weak a foe.
         In

---

 * Both justified, as all other crimes are, on the great
principle that they are natural.   SCRIBLERUS.

In the deep midnight of his guilty mind,
Where not one folitary virtue fhin'd,
Hardly, at times, his ftruggling confcience
    wrought
A few, ftrange intervals of lucid thought,
Holding her clear and dreadful mirrour nigher,
Where villain glow'd, in characters of fire.
Thofe few the tale difpers'd: His foul no more
Shall, once a year, the Beelzebub run o'er;
No more fhall J——n's ghoft her infant fhow,
Saw his hard nerves, and point the hell below;
Fixd in cold death, no more his eyeballs ftare,
Nor change to upright thorns his briftly hair.
    There Demas fmil'd, who once the Chriftian
    name
Gravely affum'd, and wore with fober fame.
Meek, modeft, decent, in life's lowly vale,
Pleas'd he walk'd on; nor now had grac'd this
    tale;
But, borne beyond the Atlantic ferry, he
Saw wondrous things, his fchoolmates did not fee,
Great houfes, and great men, in coaches carried;
Great Ladies, great Lord's wives, tho' never
    married;
Fine horfes, and fine pictures, and fine plays,
And all the fineft things of modern days.
Camelion like, he loft his former hue,
And, mid fuch great men, grew a great man too;
Enter'd the round of filly, vain parade;
His hair he powder'd, and his bow he made.
            E   Shall

Shall powder'd heads, he cried, be fent to hell?
Shall men in vain in fuch fine houfes dwell?
    There Euclio---Ah my Mufe, let deepeft
        fhame
Blufh on thy cheek, at that unhappy name!
Oh write it not, my hand! the name appears
Already written: Wafh it out, my tears!
Still, Oh all pitying Saviour! let thy love,
Stronger than death, all heights, and heavens
        above,
That on the accurfed tree, in woes fevere,
The thief's dire guilt extinguifh'd with a tear,
Yearn o'er that mind, that, with temptations dire,
Rank appetites, and paffions fraught with fire,
By each new call without, each thought within,
Is forc'd to folly, and is whirl'd to fin;
In confcience fpite, tho' arm'd with hiffing fears,
Strong pangs of foul, and all his country's tears,
Is charm'd to madnefs by the old ferpent's breath,
And hurried fwiftly down the fteep of death.
Burft, burft, thou charm! wake, trembler wake
        again,
Nor let thy parent's dying prayers be vain!
    The hour arriv'd, th' infernal trumpet blew;
Black from its mouth a cloud fulphureous flew;
The caverns groan'd; the ftartled throng gave
        way,
And forth the chariot rufh'd to gloomy day.
On every fide, expreffive emblems rofe,
The man, the fcene, the purpofe to difclofe.
                                        Here

Here wrinkled dotage, like a fondled boy,
Titter'd, and fmirk'd its momentary joy:
His crumbs there avarice grip'd, with lengthen'd
		nails,
And weigh'd clipp'd half pence in unequal
		fcales.
Trim vanity her praifes laugh'd aloud,
And fnuff'd for incenfe from the gaping crowd.
While Age an eye of anguifh caft around,
His crown of glory proftrate on the ground.
There C****** fate ; aloud his voice declar'd,
Hell is no more, or no more to be fear'd.
What tho' the Heavens, in words of flaming fire,
Difclofe the vengeance of eternal ire,
Bid anguifh o'er the unrepenting foul,
In waves fucceeding waves, forever roll ;
The ftrongeft terms, each language knows,
		employ
To teach us endlefs woe, and endlefs joy :
'Tis all a fpecious irony, defign'd
A harmlefs trifling with the human kind :
Or, not to charge the facred books with lies,
A wile moft needful of the ingenious fkies,
On this bad earth their kingdom to maintain,
And curb the rebel, man: but all in vain.
Firft Origen, then Tillotfon, then I
Learn'd their profoundeft cunning to defcry,
And fhew'd this truth, tho' nicely cover'd o'er,
That hell's broad path leads round to heavens
		door.

See

See* *kai's* and *epi's* build the glorious and scheme!
And *gar's* and *pro's* unfol'd their proof supreme!
But such nice proof, as none but those can
    know,
Who oft have read the sacred volume thro',
And read in Greek: but chiefly those, who all
The epistles oft have search'd of cunning Paul.
He, he alone, the mystery seem'd to know,
And none but wizard eyes can peep him thro'.
Then here, at second hand, receive from me
What in the sacred books you'll never see.
For† tho' the page reveal'd our cause sustains,
When search'd with cunning, and when gloss'd
    with pains,
Yet our first aids from human passions rise,
Blest friends to error, and blest props to lies:
And chief, that ruling principle within,
The love of sweet security in sin:

                    Beneath

---

* How much alike are great men, still say I? The
Doctor has found a whole system of divinity, in three or
four Greek adverbs, and prepositions; as Lord Coke had
before discovered, that there is much curious and cunning
kind of learning, in an &c.——   SCRIBLERUS.

† Witness Matthew vii. 13——14 —*Strait is the gate, and
narrow the way, that leadeth to destruction, and no body
there is, who goes in thereat:*

*Because wide is the gate, and broad is the way, that
leadeth unto life, and all they be, who find it.* Murray's new
version of the Bible, very proper to be kept by thieves,
whoremongers, idolaters, and all liars; with others, who
mean to go to heaven, via hell.

Beneath whofe power all pleafing falfhoods, blind
And fteal, with foft conviction, on the mind.
No good more lufcious than their truth fhe
    knows.
And hence their evidence will ne'er oppofe.
Aided by this, fhe mounts th' Eternal Throne,
And makes the univerfe around her own,
Decides the rights of Godhead with her nod,
And wields for him dominion's mighty rod.
Whate'er he ought, or ought not, fhe defcries,
Beholds all infinite relations rife,
Th' immenfe of time and fpace furveys ferene,
And tells whate'er the bible ought to mean;
Whate'r fhe wifhes, fees him bound to do,
Elfe is his hand unjuft, his word untrue.

    Then would you lay your own, or others fears,
Search your own bofoms, or appeal to theirs.
Know, what thofe bofoms wifh Heaven muft
    reveal;
And fure no bofom ever wifh'd a hell.
But, left fuftain'd by underpinning frail,
Our hopes and wits, our proofs and doctrines
    fail,
Admit a hell; but from its terrors take
Whate'er commands the guilty heart to quake.
Again the purgatorial whim revive,
And bid the foul by ftripes and penance live.
And know, with fearch moft deep, and wits moft
    keen,
I've learn'd, that hell is but a fchool for fin;
                    Which

Which yields, to heaven, the foul from guilt
    refin'd,
And, tho' it mars the devils, mends mankind.
And thus the matter ftands. When God makes
    man,
He makes him *here* religious, if he can;
If he cannot, he bids him farther go,
And try to be religious, down below;
But as his failure is his fault, ordains
His foul to fuffer dire repentance' pains,
Repentance, fearful doom of finners vile!
The law's whole curfe, and nature's higheft ill!
If there the wretch repent, the work is done;
If not, he plunges to a lower zone,
A lower ftill, and ftill a lower, tries,
'Till with fuch finking tir'd, he longs to rife;
And finding there the fafhion to repent,
He joins the throng, and ftrait to heaven is fent.
Heaven now his own he claims; nor can the fky
Preferve its honour, and its claim deny.
Thus ftands the fact; and if the proof fhould
    fail,
Let Heaven, next time, fome better proof reveal.
I've done my part; I've given you here the pith;
The reft, the bark and fap, I leave to * * * * *
    Thus fpoke the fage: a fhout, from all the
        throng,
Roll'd up to heaven, and roar'd the plains along;
Confcience, a moment, ceas'd her ftings to rear,
And joy exceffive whelm'd each rifing fear.
                    But

But foon reflection's glafs again fhe rear'd,
Spread out fell fin; and all her horrors bar'd;
There anguifh, guilt, remorfe, her dreadful train,
Tremendous harbingers of endlefs pain,
Froze the fad breaft, amaz'd the withering eye,
And forc'd the foul to doubt the lufcious lie.

Yet foon fophiftic wifhes, fond and vain,
The fcheme review'd, and lov'd, and hop'd
        again;
Soon, one by one, the flames of hell withdrew;
Lefs painful confcience, fin lefs dangerous grew;
Lefs priz'd the day, to man for trial given,
Lefs fear'd Jehovah, and lefs valued heaven.

No longer now by confcience' calls unmann'd,
To fin, the wretch put forth a bolder hand;
More freely cheated, lied, defam'd, and fwore;
Nor wifh'd the night to riot, drink, or whore;
Look'd up, and hifs'd his God; his parent ftung,
And fold his friend, and country, for a fong.
The new-fledg'd infidel of modern brood
Climb'd the next fence, clapp'd both his wings,
        and crow'd;
Confefs'd the doctrines were as juft, as new,
And doubted if the bible were not true.
The decent chriftian threw his mafk afide,
And fmil'd, to fee the path of heaven fo wide,
To church, the half of each fair funday, went,
The reft, in vifits, fleep, or dining, fpent;
To vice and error nobly liberal grew;
Spoke kindly of all doctrines, but the true;

All men, but faints, he hop'd to heaven might
  rife,
And thought all roads, but virtue, reach'd the
  fkies,
 There truth and virtue ftood, and figh'd to
  find
New gates of falfhood open'd on mankind;
New paths to ruin ftrew'd with flowers divine,
And other aids, and motives, gain'd to fin.
 From a dim cloud, the fpirit eyed the fcene,
Now proud with triumph, and now vex'd with
  fpleen,
Mark'd all the throng, beheld them all his own
And to his caufe no friend of virtue won:
Surpriz'd, enrag'd, he wing'd his footy flight;
And hid beneath the pall of endlefs night.

GREENFIELD HILL:

A

POEM

IN

SEVEN PARTS.

BY TIMOTHY DWIGHT, D. D.

NEW-YORK:—PRINTED BY CHILDS AND SWAINE,

1794

To JOHN ADAMS, Efquire,

VICE-PRESIDENT OF THE UNITED STATES
OF AMERICA,

THIS Poem is infcribed with Sentiments of the

higheft Refpeft for his Private Charafter, and

for the important Services he has rendered

his Country,

By his very Obedient,

And Moft humble Servant,

TIMOTHY DWIGHT.

The INTRODUCTION.

I N the Parish of Greenfield, in the Town of Fair-
field, in Connecticut, there is a pleasant and beautiful
eminence, called Greenfield Hill; at the distance of
three miles from Long-Island Sound. On this emi-
nence, there is a small but handsome Village, a Church,
Academy, &c. all of them alluded to in the following
Poem. From the highest part of the eminence, the
eye is presented with an extensive and delightful
prospect of the surrounding Country, and of the
Sound. On this height, the Writer is supposed to
stand. The First object, there offering itself to his
view, is the Landscape; which is accordingly made
the governing subject of the First Part of the Poem.
The flourishing and happy condition of the Inhabit-
ants very naturally suggested itself next; and became
of course, the subject of the Second Part. The
Town of Fairfield, lying in full view, and, not long
before the Poem was begun, and in a great measure
written out, burnt by a party of British Troops,
under the command of Governor Tryon, furnished
the theme of the Third Part. A Field, called the

Pequod Swamp, in which, moſt of the warriors of that nation, who ſurvived the invaſion of their country by Capt. Maſon, were deſtroyed, lying about three miles from the eminence abovementioned, and on the margin of the Sound, ſuggeſted not unnaturally, the ſubject of the Fourth Part.

As the writer is the Miniſter of Greenfield, he cannot be ſuppoſed to be unintereſted in the welfare of his Pariſhioners. To excite their attention to the truths and duties of Religion (an object in ſuch a ſituation, inſtinctively riſing to his view,) is the deſign of the Fifth Part; And to promote in them juſt ſentiments and uſeful conduct, for the preſent life, (an object cloſely connected with the preceding one) of the Sixth.

Many of the ſubjects, mentioned in the Poem, and ſuggeſted by the general ſtate of this Country, eaſily led a contemplative mind to look forward, and call up to view its probable ſituation at a diſtant approaching period. The ſolid foundations, which appear to be laid for the future greatneſs and proſperity of the American Republic, offered very pleaſing views of this ſubject to a Poet; and of theſe the writer has, in the Seventh Part of the Work, endeavoured to avail himſelf.

To contribute to the innocent amuſement of his countrymen, and to their improvement in manners, and in œconomical, political, and moral ſentiments, is the object which the writer wishes to accomplish. As he is firmly persuaded, that his countrymen are furnished by Providence with as extensive and advantageous means of prosperity, as the world has hitherto seen, so he thinks it the duty and the interest of every citizen, to promote it, by all the means in his power. Poetry appears to him to be one, among the probable means of advancing this purpose. "Allow me to make the Songs of a nation," said a wise man, "and who will may make their Laws." Poetry may not, perhaps, produce greater effects in promoting the prosperity of mankind, than philosophy;* but the effects which it produces, are far from being small. Where truth requires little illustration, and only needs to be set in a strong and affecting light, Poetry appears to be as advantageous an instrument of making useful impressions, as can be easily conceived. It will be read by many persons, who would scarcely look at a logical discussion; by most readers it will be more deeply felt, and more lastingly remembered; and, to say the least, it will, in the present case, be an unusual, and for that reason may be a forcible method of treating several subjects, handled in this Poem.

When the writer began the work, he had no design of publishing it; aiming merely to amuse his own mind, and to gain a temporary relief from the

* See Lowth's Lectures on Heb. Po.

preffure of melancholy. Hence it was dropped, at
an early period; when other avocations, or amufe-
ments prefented themfelves. The greater part of it
was written feven years ago. Additions have been
made to it, at different periods, from that time
to the prefent—This will account for the dates of
feveral things mentioned in it, which would otherwife
feem to be improperly connected.

Originally the writer defigned to imitate, in the
feveral parts, the manner of as many Britifh Poets;
but finding himfelf too much occupied, when he
projected the publication, to purfue that defign, he
relinquifhed it. The little appearance of fuch a
defign, ftill remaining, was the refult of diftant and
general recollection. Much, of that nature, he has
rejected, and all he would have rejected, had not
even that rejection demanded more time than he
could afford for fuch a purpofe. Thefe facts will,
he hopes, apologize to the reader, for the mixed
manner which he may, at times, obferve in the
performance.

Greenfield, June 13th, 1794.

GREENFIELD HILL:

A

POEM.

THE ARGUMENT.

SPRING—General Prospect—View of the Inland Country—Of the beauty of Vegetation at the time of Harvest—Of the happy state of the Inhabitants—Men esteemed in New-England according to their personal qualities—State of New-England—Connecticut—State of Society in Europe contrasted to that of New-England—People of New-England exhorted not to copy the Government, Manners, &c. of other nations—Remembrance of the late Councils and Armies of the United States—Prospect of the Country between Greenfield Hill and the Sound—Description of the Sound—Retrospect of the troubles occasioned by the British Marauding Parties—Wish for perpetual Peace—Beauty of the Scenes of Nature—Happiness of a Clergyman in the Country—Address to the Clergy.

GREENFIELD HILL.

PART I.

THE PROSPECT.

FROM southern isles, on winds of gentlest wing,
Sprinkled with morning dew, and rob'd in green,
Life in her eye, and music in her voice,
Lo Spring returns, and wakes the world to joy !
Forth creep the smiling herbs ; expand the flowers ;   5
New-loos'd, and bursting from their icy bonds,
The streams fresh-warble, and through every mead
Convey reviving verdure ; every bough,
Full-blown and lovely, teems with sweets and songs ;
And hills, and plains, and pastures feel the prime.   10

As round me here I gaze, what prospects rise ?
Etherial ! matchless ! such as Albion's sons,
Could Albion's isle an equal prospect boast,
In all the harmony of numerous song,
Had tun'd to rapture, and o'er Cooper's hill,   15
And Windsor's beauteous forest, high uprais'd,
And sent on fame's light wing to every clime.
Far inland, blended groves, and azure hills,
Skirting the broad horizon, lift their pride.
Beyond, a little chasm to view unfolds   20
Cerulean mountains, verging high on Heaven,
In misty grandeur.   Stretch'd in nearer view,
Unnumber'd farms salute the cheerful eye ;
Contracted there to little gardens ; here outspread

Spacious, with paftures, fields, and meadows rich;   25
Where the young wheat it's glowing green difplays,
Or the dark foil befpeaks the recent plough,
Or flocks and herds along the lawn difport.

Fair is the landfchape; but a fairer ftill   30
Shall foon inchant the foul—when harveft full
Waves wide its bending wealth.   Delightful tafk!
To trace along the rich, enamell'd ground,
The fweetly varied hues; from India's corn,
Whofe black'ning verdure bodes a bounteous crop,
Through lighter grafs, and lighter ftill the flax,   35
The paler oats, the yellowifh barley, wheat
In golden glow, and rye in brighter gold.
Thefe foon the fight fhall blefs.   Now other fcenes
The heart dilate, where round, in rural pride
The village fpreads its tidy, fnug retreats,   40
That fpeak the induftry of every hand.

How blefs'd the fight of fuch a numerous train
In fuch fmall limits, tafting every good
Of competence, of independence, peace,
And liberty unmingled; every houfe   45
On its own ground, and every happy fwain
Beholding no fuperior, but the laws,
And fuch as virtue, knowledge, ufeful life,
And zeal, exerted for the public good,
Have rais'd above the throng.   For here, in truth,   50
Not in pretence, man is efteem'd as man.
Not here how rich, of what peculiar blood,
Or office high; but of what genuine worth,
What talents bright and ufeful, what good deeds,
What piety to God, what love to man,   55
The queftion is.   To this an anfwer fair
The general heart fecures.   Full many a rich,
Vile knave, full many a blockhead, proud
Of ancient blood, thefe eyes have feen float down

Life's dirty kennel, trampled in the mud,   60
Stepp'd o'er unheeded, or push'd rudely on;
While Merit, rifing from her humble skiff
To barks of nobler, and still nobler fize,
Sail'd down the expanding stream, in triumph gay,
By every ship faluted.   65

             Hail, O hail
My much-lov'd native land! New Albion hail!
The happieft realm, that, round his circling courfe,
The all-fearching fun beholds. What though the breath
Of Zembla's winter fhuts thy lucid streams,   70
And hardens into brafs thy generous foil;
Though, with one white, and cheerlefs robe, thy hills,
Invefted, rife a long and joylefs wafte;
Leaflefs the grove, and dumb the lonely spray,
And every pafture mute: What though with clear   75
And fervid blaze, thy fummer rolls his car,
And drives the languid herd, and fainting flock
To feek the fhrouding umbrage of the dale;
While Man, relax'd and feeble, anxious waits
The dewy eve, to flake his thirfty frame: 80
What though thy furface, rocky, rough, and rude,
Scoop'd into vales, or heav'd in lofty hills,
Or cloud-embofom'd mountains, dares the plough,
And threatens toil intenfe to every fwain:
What though foul Calumny, with voice malign,   85
Thy generous fons, with every virtue grac'd,
Accus'd of every crime, and ftill rolls down
The kennell'd ftream of impudent abufe:
Yet to high HEAVEN my ardent praifes rife,
That in thy lightfome vales he gave me birth,   90
All-gracious, and allows me ftill to live.

    Cold is thy clime, but every weftern blaft
Brings health, and life, and vigour on his wings;
Innerves the fteely frame, and firms the foul

With ſtrength and hardihood; wakes each bold   95
And manly purpoſe; bears above the ills,
That ſtretch, upon the rack, the languid heart
Of ſummer's maiden ſons, in pleaſure's lap,
Dandled to dull repoſe. Exertion ſtrong
Marks their whole life. Mountains before them ſink   100
To mole-hills; oceans bar their courſe in vain.
Thro' the keen wintry wind they breaſt their way,
Or ſummer's fierceſt flame. Dread dangers rouſe
Their hearts to pleaſing conflict; toils and woes,
Quicken their ardour: while, in milder climes,   105
Their peers effeminate they ſee, with ſcorn
On lazy plains, diſſolv'd in putrid ſloth,
And ſtruggling hard for being. Thy rough ſoil
Tempts hardy labour, with his ſturdy team,
To turn, with ſinewy hand, the ſtony glebe,   110
And call forth every comfort from the mould,
Unpromiſing, but kind. Thy houſes, barns,
Thy granaries, and thy cellars, hence are ſtor'd
With all the ſweets of life: while, thro' thy realm,
A native beggar rarely pains the ſight.   115

    Thy ſummer glows with heat; but choiceſt fruits
Hence purple in the ſun; hence ſparkling flowers
Gem the rich landſchape; double harveſts hence
Load the full fields: pale Famine ſcowls aloof,
And Plenty wantons round thy varied year.   120

    Rough is thy ſurface; but each landſchape bright,
With all of beauty, all of grandeur dreſs'd,
Of mountains, hills, and ſweetly winding vales,
Of foreſts, groves, and lawns, and meadows green,
And waters, varied by the plaſtic hand,   125
Through all their fairy ſplendour, ceaſeleſs charms,
Poetic eyes. Springs bubbling round the year,
Gay-wand'ring brooks, wells at the ſurface full,
Yield life, and health, and joy, to every houſe,

And every vivid field.   Rivers, with foamy courfe,   130
Pour o'er the ragged cliff the white cafcade,
And roll unnumber'd mills; or, like the Nile,
Fatten the beauteous interval; or bear
The fails of commerce through the laughing groves.

With wifdom, virtue, and the generous love   135
Of learning, fraught, and freedom's living flame,
Electric, unextinguifhable, fir'd,
Our Sires eftablifhed, in thy cheerful bounds,
The nobleft inftitutions, man has feen,
Since time his reign began.   In little farms   140
They meafur'd all thy realms, to every child
In equal fhares defcending; no entail
The firft-born lifting into bloated pomp,
Tainting with luft, and floth, and pride, and rage,
The world around him : all the race befide,   145
Like brood of oftrich, left for chance to rear,
And every foot to trample.   Reafon's fway
Elective, founded on the rock of truth,
Wifdom their guide, and equal good their end,
They built with ftrength, that mocks the battering ftorm, 150
And fpurns the mining flood; and every right
Difpens'd alike to all.   Beneath their eye,
And forming hand, in every hamlet, rofe
The nurturing fchool; in every village, fmil'd
The heav'n-inviting church, and every town   155
A world within itfelf, with order, peace,
And harmony, adjufted all its weal.

Hence every fwain, free, happy, his own lord,
With ufeful knowledge fraught, of bufinefs, laws,
Morals, religion, life, unaw'd by man,   160
And doing all, but ill, his heart can wifh,
Looks round, and finds ftrange happinefs his own;
And fees that happinefs on laws depend.
On this heav'n-laid foundation refts thy fway;

On knowledge to difcern, and fenfe to feel, 165
That free-born rule is life's perennial fpring
Of real good. On this alone it refts.
For, could thy fons a full conviction feel,
That government was noxious, without arms,
Without intrigues, without a civil broil, 170
As torrents fweep the fand-built ftructure down,
A vote would wipe it's very trace away.
Hence too each breaft is fteel'd for bold defence ;
For each has much to lofe. Chofen by all,
The meffenger of peace, by all belov'd, 175
Spreads, hence, the truth and virtue, he commands.
Hence manners mild, and fweet, their peaceful fway
Widely extend. Refinement of the heart
Illumes the general mafs. Even thofe rude hills,
Thofe deep embow'ring woods, in other lands 180
Prowl'd round by favages, the fame foft fcenes,
Mild manners, order, virtue, peace, difclofe ;
The howling foreft polifh'd as the plain,

From earlieft years, the fame enlightened foul
Founded bright fchools of fcience. Here the mind 185
Learn'd to expand it's wing, and ftretch it's flight
Through truth's broad fields. Divines, and lawyers, hence,
Phyficians, ftatefmen, all with wifdom fraught,
And learning, fuited to the ufe of life,
And minds, by bufinefs, fharpen'd into fenfe, 190
Sagacious of the duty, and the weal,
Of man, fpring numberlefs ; and knowledge hence
Pours it's falubrious ftreams, through all the fpheres
Of human life. Its bounds, and generous fcope,
Hence Education opens, fpreading far 195
Through the bold yeomanry, that fill thy climes,
Views more expanded, generous, juft, refin'd,
Than other nations know. In other lands,
The mafs of man, fcarce rais'd above the brutes,

Drags dull the horſemill round of ſluggiſh life :   200
Nought known, beyond their daily toil ; all elſe
By ignorance' dark curtain hid from ſight.
Here, glorious contraſt ! every mind, inſpir'd
With active inquiſition, reſtleſs wings
Its flight to every flower, and, ſettling, drinks   205
Largely the ſweets of knowledge.

                         Candour, ſay,
Is this a ſtate of life, thy honeſt tongue
Could blacken ? Theſe a race of men, thy page
Could hand to infamy ? The ſhameful taſk   210
Thy foes at firſt began, and ſtill thy foes,
Laborious, weave the web of lies. 'Tis hence
The generous traveller round him looks, amaz'd,
And wonders at our unexpected bliſs.

  But chief, Connecticut ! on thy fair breaſt   215
Theſe ſplendours glow.   A rich improvement ſmiles
Around thy lovely borders ; in thy fields
And all that in thy fields delighted dwell.
Here that pure, golden mean, ſo oft of yore
By ſages wiſh'd, and prais'd, by Agur's voice   220
Implor'd, while God th' approving ſanction gave
Of wiſdom infinite ; that golden mean,
Shines unalloy'd ; and here the extended good,
That mean alone ſecures, is ceaſeleſs found.

  Oh, would ſome faithful, wiſe, laborious mind,   225
Develope all thy ſprings of bliſs to man ;
Soon would politic viſions fleet away,
Before awakening truth ! Utopias then,
Ancient and new, high fraught with fairy good,
Would catch no more the heart.   Philoſophy   230
Would bow to common-ſenſe ; and man, from facts,
And real life, politic wiſdom learn.

C

Ah then, thou favour'd land, thyself revere!
Look not to Europe, for examples juft
Of order, manners, cuftoms, doctrines, laws,   235
Of happinefs, or virtue.   Caft around
The eye of fearching reafon, and declare
What Europe proffers, but a patchwork fway;
The garment Gothic, worn to fritter'd fhreds,
And eked from every loom of following times.   240
Such as his fway, the fyftem fhows entire,
Of filly pomp, and meannefs train'd t' adore;
Of wealth enormous, and enormous want;
Of lazy finecures, and fuffering toil;
Of grey-beard fyftems, and meteorous dreams;   245
Of lordly churches, and diffention fierce,
Rites farfical, and phrenzied unbelief.
See thick and fell her lowering gibbets ftand,
And gibbets ftill employ'd! while, through thy realms,
The rare-feen felon ftartles every mind   250
And fills each mouth with news.   Behold her jails
Countlefs, and ftow'd with wretches of all kinds!
Her brothels, circling, with their tainted walls,
Unnumber'd female outcafts, fhorne from life,
Peace, penitence, and hope; and down, down plung'd 255
In vice' unbottom'd gulph! Ye demons, rife,
Rife, and look upward, from your dread abode;
And, if you've tears to fhed, diftil them here!
See too, in countlefs herds, the miftrefs vile,
Even to the teeth of matron fanctity,   260
Lift up her fhamelefs bronze, and elbow out
The pure, the chafte, the lovely angel-form
Of female excellence! while leachers rank, and
Bloated, call aloud on vengeance' worms,
To feize their prey, on this fide of the grave.   265
See the foul theatre, with Upaz fteams,
Impoifoning half mankind! See every heart
And head from dunghills up to thrones, moon'd high

With faſhion, frippery, falling humbly down
To a new head-dreſs; barbers, milliners,   270
Taylors, and mantua-makers, forming gods,
Their fellow-millions worſhip ! See the world
All ſet to ſale ; truth, friendſhip, public truſt,
A nation's weal, religion, ſcripture, oaths,
Struck off by inch of candle ! Mark the mien,   275
Out-changing the Cameleon ; pleaſing all,
And all deceiving ! Mark the ſnaky tongue,
Now lightly vibrating, now hiſſing death !
See war, from year to year, from age to age,
Unceaſing, open on mankind the gates   280
Of devaſtation ; earth wet-deep with blood,
And pav'd with corpſes ; cities whelm'd in flames ;
And fathers, brothers, huſbands, ſons, and friends,
In millions hurried to th' untimely tomb ;
To gain a wigwam, built on Nootka Sound,   285
Or Falkland's fruitful iſles ; or to ſecure
That rare ſoap-bubble, blown by children wiſe,
Bloated in air, and ting'd with colours fine,
Purſu'd by thouſands, and with rapture nam'd
National honour. But what powers ſuffice   290
To tell the ſands, that form the endleſs beach,
Or drops, that fill the immeaſurable deep.

  Say then, ah ſay, would'ſt thou for theſe exchange
Thy ſacred inſtitutions ? thy mild laws ?
Thy pure religion ? morals uncorrupt ?   295
Thy plain and honeſt manners ? order, peace,
And general weal ? Think whence this weal aroſe.
From the ſame ſprings it ſtill ſhall ceaſeleſs riſe.
Preſerve the fountains ſweet, and ſweeteſt ſtreams
Shall ſtill flow from them. Change, but change alone,   300
By wiſe improvement of thy bleſſings rare ;
And copy not from others. Shun the lures
Of Europe. Cheriſh ſtill, watch, hold,

And hold through every trial, every fnare,
All that is thine. Amend, refine, complete; 305
But ftill the glorious ftamina retain.
Still, as of yore, in church, and ftate, elect
The virtuous, and the wife; men tried, and prov'd,
Of fteady virtue, all thy weal to guide;
And HEAVEN fhall blefs thee, with a parent's hand. 310

When round I turn my raptur'd eyes, with joy
O'erflowing, and thy wonderous blifs furvey,
I love to think of thofe, by whom that blifs
Was purchas'd; thofe firm councils, that brave band,
Who nobly jeoparded their lives, their all, 315
And crofs'd temptation's whirlpool, to fecure,
For us, and ours, this rich eftate of good.
Ye fouls illuftrious, who, in danger's field,
Inftinct with patriot fire, each terror brav'd;
And fix'd as thefe firm hills, the fhock withftood 320
Of war's convulfing earthquake, unappall'd,
Whilft on your labours gaz'd, with reverent eyes,
The pleas'd and wondering world; let every good,
Life knows, let peace, efteem, domeftic blifs,
Approving confcience, and a grateful land, 325
Glory through every age, and Heaven at laft,
To crown the fplendid fcene, your toils reward.

Heavens, what a matchlefs group of beauties rare
Southward expands! where, crown'd with yon tall oak,
Round-hill the circling land and fea o'erlooks; 339
Or, fmoothly floping, Grover's beauteous rife,
Spreads it's green fides, and lifts its fingle tree,
Glad mark for feamen; or, with ruder face,
Orchards, and fields, and groves, and houfes rare,
And fcatter'd cedars, Mill-hill meets the eye; 335
Or where, beyond, with every beauty clad,
More diftant heights in vernal pride afcend.
On either fide, a long, continued range,

In all the charms of rural nature drefs'd,
Slopes gently to the main. Ere Tryon funk   340
To infamy unfathom'd, thro' yon groves
Once glifter'd Norwalk's white-afcending fpires,
And foon, if HEAVEN permit, fhall fhine again.
Here, fky-encircled, Stratford's churches beam;
And Stratfield's turrets greet the roving eye.   345
In clear, full view, with every varied charm,
That forms the finifh'd landfchape, blending foft
In matchlefs union, Fairfield and Green's Farms
Give luftre to the day. Here, crown'd with pines
And fkirting groves, with creeks and havens fair   350
Embellifh'd, fed with many a beauteous ftream,
Prince of the waves, and ocean's favorite child,
Far weftward fading in confufion blue,
And eaftward ftretch'd beyond the human ken,
And mingled with the fky, there Longa's Sound   355
Glorious expands. All hail! of waters firft
In beauties of all kinds; in profpects rich
Of bays, and arms, and groves, and little ftreams,
Inchanting capes and ifles, and rivers broad,
That yield eternal tribute to thy wave!   360
In ufe fupreme: fifh of all kinds, all taftes,
Scaly or fhell'd, with floating nations fill
Thy fpacious realms; while, o'er thy lucid waves,
Unceafing Commerce wings her countlefs fails.
Safe in thy arms, the treafure moves along,   365
While, beat by Longa's coaft, old ocean roars
Diftant, but roars in vain. O'er all thy bounds,
What varied beauties, changing with the fun,
Or night's more lovely queen, here fplendid glow.
Oft, on thy eaftern wave, the orb of light   370
Refulgent rifing, kindles wide a field
Of mimic day, flow failing to the weft,
And fading with the eve; and oft, through clouds,
Painting their dark fkirts on the glaffy plain,

The ftrong, pervading luftre marks th' expanfe,   375
With ftreaks of glowing filver, or with fpots
Of burnifh'd gold ; while clouds, of every hue,
Their purple fhed, their amber, yellow, grey,
Along the faithful mirror.   Oft, at eve,
Thron'd in the eaftern fky, th' afcending moon,   380
Diftain'd with blood, fits awful o'er the wave,
And, from the dim dark waters, troubled calls
Her dreary image, trembling on the deep,
And boding every horror.   Round yon ifles,
Where every Triton, every Nereid, borne   385
From eaftern climes, would find perpetual home,
Were Grecian fables true, what charms intrance
The fafcinated eye ! where, half withdrawn
Behind yon vivid flope, like blufhing maids,
They leave the raptur'd gaze.   And O how fair   390
Bright Longa fpreads her terminating fhore,
Commix'd with whit'ning cliffs, with groves obfcure,
Farms fhrunk to garden-beds, and forefts fallen
To little orchards, flow-afcending hills,
And dufky vales, and plains ! Thefe the pleas'd eye   395
Relieve, engage, delight ; with one unchang'd,
Unbounded ocean, wearied, and difpleas'd.

  Yet fcarce fix funs are pafs'd, fince thefe wide bounds,
So ftill fo lovely now, were wanton'd o'er
By fails of Britifh foes, with thunders dread   400
Announcing defolation to each field,
Each town, and hamlet ; in the fheltering night
Wafting bafe throngs of plunderers to our coaft,
The bed of peace invading ; herds and flocks
Purloining from the fwain ; and oft the houfe   405
Of innocence and peace, in cruel flames
With fell revenge, encircling.   Now, afar
With fhame retir'd, his bands no more, no more
(And oh may HEAVEN the fond prediction feal)

Shall hoſtile bands, from earth's extended bounds,　410
Th' infernal talk reſume.　Henceforth, through time,
To peace devoted, 'till millenian ſuns
Call forth returning Eden, arts of peace
Shall triumph here.　Speed, oh ſpeed, ye days
Of bliſs divine!　when all-involving HEAVEN,　415
The myſtery finiſh'd, come the ſecond birth
Of this ſin-ruin'd, this apoſtate world,
And clos'd the final ſcene of wild miſrule,
All climes ſhall clothe again with life, and joy,
With peace, and purity; and deathleſs ſpring　420
Again commence her bright, etherial reign.

O who can paint, like Nature? who can boaſt
Such ſcenes, as here inchant the lingering eye?
Still to thy hand, great parent of the year!
I turn obſequious; ſtill to all thy works　425
Of beauty, grandeur, novelty, and power,
Of motion, light, and life, my beating heart
Plays uniſon; and, with harmonious thrill,
Inhales ſuch joys, as Avarice never knew.

Ah! knew he but his happineſs, of men　430
Not the leaſt happy he, who, free from broils,
And baſe ambition, vain and buſt'ling pomp,
Amid a friendly cure, and competence,
Taſtes the pure pleaſures of parochial life.
What though no crowd of clients, at his gate,　435
To falſhood, and injuſtice, bribe his tongue,
And flatter into guilt; what though no bright,
And gilded proſpeᴄts lure ambition on
To legiſlative pride, or chair of ſtate;
What though no golden dreams entice his mind　440
To burrow, with the mole, in dirt, and mire;
What though no ſplendid villa, Eden'd round
With gardens of enchantment, walks of ſtate,
And all the grandeur of ſuperfluous wealth,

Invite the paſſenger to ſtay his ſteed,   445
And aſk the liveried foot-boy, " who dwells here ?"
What though no ſwarms, around his ſumptuous board,
Of ſoothing flatterers, humming in the ſhine
Of opulence, and honey, from its flowers,
Devouring, 'till their time arrives to ſting,   450
Inflate his mind; his virtues, round the year,
Repeating, and his faults, with microſcope
Inverted, leſſen, till they ſteal from ſight:
Yet, from the dire temptations, theſe preſent,
His ſtate is free; temptations, few can ſtem;   455
Temptations, by whoſe ſweeping torrent hurl'd
Down the dire ſteep of guilt, unceaſing fall,
Sad victims, thouſands of the brighteſt minds,
That time's dark reign adorn; minds, to whoſe graſp
Heaven ſeems moſt freely offer'd; to man's eye,   460
Moſt hopeful candidates for angels' joys.

His lot, that wealth, and power, and pride forbids,
Forbids him to become the tool of fraud,
Injuſtice, miſery, ruin; ſaves his ſoul
From all the needleſs labours, griefs, and cares,   465
That avarice, and ambition, agonize;
From thoſe cold nerves of wealth, that, palſied, feel
No anguiſh, but its own; and ceaſeleſs lead
To thouſand meanneſſes, as gain allures.

Though oft compell'd to meet the groſs attack   470
Of ſhameleſs ridicule, and towering pride,
Sufficient good is his; good, real, pure,
With guilt unmingled. Rarely forc'd from home,
Around his board, his wife and children ſmile;
Communion ſweeteſt, nature here can give,   475
Each fond endearment, office of delight,
With love and duty blending. Such the joy,
My boſom oft has known. His, too, the taſk,
To rear the infant plants, that bud around;

To ope their little minds to truth's pure light;   480
To take them by the hand, and lead them on,
In that ftraight, narrow road, where virtue walks;
To guard them from a vain, deceiving world;
And point their courfe to realms of promis'd life.

His too th' efteem of thofe, who weekly hear   485
His words of truth divine; unnumber'd acts
Of real love attefting, to his eye,
Their filial tendernefs.   Where'er he walks,
The friendly welcome and inviting fmile
Wait on his fteps, and breathe a kindred joy.   490

Oft too in friendlieft Affociation join'd,
He greets his brethren, with a flowing heart,
Flowing with virtue; all rejoic'd to meet,
And all reluctant parting; every aim,
Benevolent, aiding with purpofe kind;   495
While, feafon'd with unblemifh'd cheerfulnefs,
Far diftant from the tainted mirth of vice,
Their hearts difclofe each contemplation fweet
Of things divine; and blend in friendfhip pure,
Friendfhip fublim'd by piety and love.   500

All virtue's friends are his: the good, the juft,
The pious, to his houfe their vifits pay,
And converfe high hold of the true, the fair,
The wonderful, the moral, the divine:
Of faints, and prophets, patterns bright of truth,   505
Lent to a world of fin, to teach mankind,
How virtue, in that world, can live, and fhine;
Of learning's varied realms; of Nature's works;
And that blefs'd book, which gilds man's darkfome way,
With light from heaven; of blefs'd Meffiah's throne   510
And kingdom; prophefies divine fulfill'd,
And prophefies more glorious, yet to come,
In renovated days; of that bright world,

D

And all the happy trains, which that bright **world**
Inhabit, whither virtue's fons are gone :　　　　515
While GOD the whole infpires, adorns, exalts,
The fource, the end, the fubftance, and the foul.

This too the tafk, the blefs'd, the ufeful tafk,
To' invigour order, juftice, law, and rule ;
Peace to extend, and bid contention ceafe ;　　　　520
To teach the words of life ; to lead mankind
Back from the wild of guilt, and brink of woe,
To virtue's houfe and family ; faith, hope,
And joy, t' infpire ; to warm the foul,
With love to GOD, and man ; to cheer the fad,　　　　525
To fix the doubting, roufe the languid heart ;
The wandering to reftore ; to fpread with **down,**
The thorny bed of death ; confole the poor,
Departing mind, and aid its lingering **wing.**

To him, her choiceft pages Truth expands,　　　　530
Unceafing, where the foul-intrancing fcenes,
Poetic fiction boafts, are real all :
Where beauty, novelty, and grandeur, **wear**
Superior charms, and moral worlds unfold
Sublimities, tranfporting and divine.　　　　535

Not all the fcenes, Philofophy can boaft,
Tho' them with nobler truths he ceafelefs blends,
Compare with thefe.　The·y, as they found the mind,
Still leave it ; more inform'd, but not more wife.
Thefe wifer, nobler, better, make the man.　　　　540

Thus every happy mean of folid good
His life, his ftudies, and profeffion yield.
With motives hourly new, each rolling day,
Allures, through wifdom's path, and truth's fair field,
His feet to yonder fkies.　Before him heaven　　　　545
Shines bright, the fcope fublime of all his **prayers,**
The meed of every forrow, pain, and toil.

Then, O ye happy few! whom God allows
To ſtand his meſſengers, in this bad world,
And call mankind to virtue, weep no more,   550
Though pains and toils betide you : for what life,
On earth, from pains and toils was ever free ?
When Wealth and Pride around you gaily ſpread
Their vain and tranſient ſplendour, envy not.
How oft (let virtue weep !) is this their all ?   555
For you, in ſunny proſpect, daily ſpring
Joys, which nor Pride can Taſte, nor Wealth can boaſt ;
That, planted here, beyond the wintery grave
Revive and grow with ever vernal bloom.

Hail theſe, oh hail! and be 't enough for you,   560
To 'ſcape a world unclean ; a life to lead
Of uſefulneſs, and truth ; a Prince to ſerve,
Who ſuffers no ſincere and humble toil
To miſs a rich reward ; in Death's dark vale,
To meet unboſom'd light ; beyond the grave   565
To riſe triumphant, freed from every ſtain,
And cloth'd with every beauty ; in the ſky
Stars to outſhine ; and, round th' eternal year,
With ſaints, with angels, and with Christ, to reign.

END OF THE FIRST PART.

GREENFIELD HILL:

A

POEM.

THE ARGUMENT.

*V*IEW *of the Village invested with the pleasing appear-
ances of Spring—Recollection of the Winter—Pleasures of
Winter—Of Nature and humble life—March—Original sub-
ject resumed—Freedom of the Villagers from manorial evils—
Address to Competence, reciting its pleasures, charitable effects,
virtues attendant upon it, and its utility to the public—Con-
trasted by European artificial society—Further effects of Compe-
tence on Society, particularly in improving the People at large—
African appears—State of Negro Slavery in Connecticut—
Effects of Slavery on the African, from his childhood through
life—Slavery generally characterized—West-Indian Slavery—
True cause of the calamities of the West-Indies—Church—
Effects of the Sabbath—Academic School—School-master—
House of Sloth—Female Worthy—Inferior Schools—Female
Visit—What is not, and what is, a social female visit—Plea-
sure of living in an improving state of society, contrasted by
the dullness of stagnated society—Emigrations to the Western
Country—Conclusion.*

GREENFIELD HILL.

PART II.

THE FLOURISHING VILLAGE.

FAIR Verna! lovelieſt village of the weſt;
Of every joy, and every charm, poſſeſs'd;
How pleas'd amid thy varied walks I rove,
Sweet, cheerful walks of innocence, and love,
And o'er thy ſmiling proſpects caſt my eyes,   5
And ſee the ſeats of peace, and pleaſure, riſe,
And hear the voice of Induſtry reſound,
And mark the ſmile of Competence, around!
Hail, happy village! O'er thy cheerful lawns,
With earlieſt beauty, ſpring delighted dawns;   10
The northward ſun begins his vernal ſmile;
The ſpring-bird carols o'er the creſſy rill:
The ſhower, that patters in the ruffled ſtream,
The ploughboy's voice, that chides the lingering team, 15
The bee, induſtrious, with his buſy ſong,
The woodman's axe, the diſtant groves among,
The waggon, rattling down the rugged ſteep,
The light wind, lulling every care to ſleep,
All theſe, with mingled muſic, from below,   20
Deceive intruding ſorrow, as I go.

How pleas'd, fond Recollection, with a smile,
Surveys the varied round of wintery toil !
How pleas'd, amid the flowers, that scent the plain,
Recalls the vanish'd frost, and sleeted rain ;
The chilling damp, the ice-endangering street,　　　　25
And treacherous earth that slump'd beneath the feet.

Yet even stern winter's glooms could joy inspire :
Then social circles grac'd the nutwood fire ;
The axe resounded, at the sunny door ;
The swain, industrious, trimm'd his flaxen store ;　　30
Or thresh'd, with vigorous flail, the bounding wheat,
His poultry round him pilfering for their meat ;
Or slid his firewood on the creaking snow ;
Or bore his produce to the main below ;
Or o'er his rich returns exulting laugh'd ;　　　　　35
Or pledg'd the healthful orchard's sparkling draught :
While, on his board, for friends and neighbours spread,
The turkey smoak'd, his busy housewife fed ;
And Hospitality look'd smiling round,
And Leisure told his tale, with gleeful sound.　　　40

Then too, the rough road hid beneath the sleigh,
The distant friend despis'd a length of way,
And join'd the warm embrace, and mingling smile,
And told of all his bliss, and all his toil ;
And, many a month elaps'd, was pleas'd to view　　45
How well the household far'd, the children grew ;
While tales of sympathy deceiv'd the hour,
And Sleep, amus'd, resign'd his wonted power.

Yes ! let the proud despise, the rich deride,
These humble joys, to Competence allied :　　　　50
To me, they bloom, all fragrant to my heart,
Nor ask the pomp of wealth, nor gloss of art.
And as a bird, in prison long confin'd,
Springs from his open'd cage, and mounts the wind,

Thro' fields of flowers, and fragrance, gaily flies,   55
Or re-affumes his birth-right, in the fkies :
Unprifon'd thus from artificial joys,
Where pomp fatigues, and fufsful fafhion cloys,
The foul, reviving, loves to wander free
Thro' native fcencs of fweet fimplicity ;   60
Thro' Peace' low vale, where Pleafure lingers long,
And every fongfter tunes his fweeteft fong,
And Zephyr haftes, to breathe his firft perfume,
And Autumn ftays, to drop his lateft bloom :
'Till grown mature, and gathering ftrength to roam,   65
She lifts her lengthen'd wings, and feeks her home.

But now the wintery glooms are vanifh'd all ;
The lingering drift behind the fhady wall ;
The dark-brown fpots, that patch'd the fnowy field ;
The furly froft, that every bud conceal'd ;   70
The ruffet veil, the way with flime o'erfpread,
And all the faddening fcenes of March are fled.

Sweet-fmiling village ! lovelieft of the hills !
How green thy groves ! How pure thy glaffy rills !
With what new joy, I walk thy verdant ftreets !   75
How often paufe, to breathe thy gale of fweets ;
To mark thy well-built walls ! thy budding fields !
And every charm, that rural nature yields ;
And every joy, to Competence allied,
And every good, that Virtue gains from Pride !   80

No griping landlord here alarms the door,
To halve, for rent, the poor man's little ftore.
No haughty owner drives the humble fwain
To fome far refuge from his dread domain ;
Nor waftes, upon his robe of ufelefs pride,   85
The wealth, which fhivering thoufands want befide ;
Nor in one palace finks a hundred cots ;
Nor in one manor drowns a thoufard lots ;

E

Nor, on one table, fpread for death and pain,
Devours what would a village well fuftain.   90

O Competence, thou blefs'd by Heaven's decree,
How well exchang'd is empty pride for thee!
Oft to thy cot my feet delighted turn,
To meet thy chearful fmile, at peep of morn;
To join thy toils, that bid the earth look gay;   95
To mark thy fports, that hail the eve of May;
To fee thy ruddy children, at thy board,
And fhare thy temperate meal, and frugal hoard;
And every joy, by winning prattlers giv'n,
And every earneft of a future Heaven.   100

There the poor wanderer finds a table fpread,
The firefide welcome, and the peaceful bed.
The needy neighbour, oft by wealth denied,
There finds the little aids of life fupplied;
The horfe, that bears to mill the hard-earn'd grain;   105
The day's work given, to reap the ripen'd plain;
The ufeful team, to houfe the precious food,
And all the offices of real good.

There too, divine Religion is a gueft,
And all the Virtues join the daily feaft.   110
Kind Hofpitality attends the door,
To welcome in the ftranger and the poor;
Sweet Chaftity, ftill blufhing as fhe goes;
And Patience fmiling at her train of woes;
And meek-eyed Innocence, and Truth refin'd,   115
And Fortitude, of bold, but gentle mind.

Thou pay'ft the tax, the rich man will not pay;
Thou feed'ft the poor, the rich man drives away.
Thy fons, for freedom, hazard limbs, and life,
While pride applauds, but fhuns the manly ftrife: 120
Thou prop'ft religion's caufe, the world around,
And fhew'ft thy faith in works, and not in found.

Say, child of paffion! while, with idiot ftare,
Thou feeft proud grandeur wheel her funny car;
While kings, and nobles, roll befpangled by,   125
And the tall palace leffens in the fky;
Say, while with pomp thy giddy brain runs round,
What joys, like thefe, in fplendour can be found?
Ah, yonder turn thy wealth-inchanted eyes,
Where that poor, friendlefs wretch expiring lies!   130
Hear his fad partner fhriek, befide his bed,
And call down curfes on her landlord's head,
Who drove, from yon fmall cot, her houfhold fweet,
To pine with want, and perifh in the ftreet.
See the pale tradefman toil, the livelong day,   135
To deck imperious lords, who never pay!
Who wafte, at dice, their boundlefs breadth of foil,
But grudge the fcanty meed of honeft toil.
See hounds and horfes riot on the ftore,
By HEAVEN created for the haplefs poor!   140
See half a realm one tyrant fcarce fuftain,
While meagre thoufands round him glean the plain!
See, for his miftrefs' robe, a village fold,
Whofe matrons fhrink from nakednefs and cold!
See too the Farmer prowl around the fhed,   145
To rob the ftarving houfhold of their bread;
And feize, with cruel fangs, the helplefs fwain,
While wives, and daughters, plead, and weep, in vain;
Or yield to infamy themfelves, to fave
Their fire from prifon, famine, and the grave.   150

    There too foul luxury taints the putrid mind,
And flavery there imbrutes the reafoning kind:
There humble worth, in damps of deep defpair,
Is bound by poverty's eternal bar:
No motives bright the etherial aim impart,   155
Nor one fair ray of hope allures the heart.

    But, O fweet Competence! how chang'd the fcene,
Where thy foft footfteps lightly print the green!

Where Freedom walks erect, with manly port,
And all the bleffings to his fide refort, 160
In every hamlet, Learning builds her fchools,
And beggars, children gain her arts, and rules;
And mild Simplicity o'er manners reigns,
And blamelefs morals Purity fuftains.

From thee the rich enjoyments round me fpring, 165
Where every farmer reigns a little king;
Where all to comfort, none to danger, rife;
Where pride finds few, but nature all fupplies;
Where peace and fweet civility are feen,
And meek good-neighbourhood endears the green. 170
Here every clafs (if claffes thofe we call,
Where one extended clafs embraces all,
All mingling, as the rainbow's beauty blends,
Unknown where every hue begins or ends)
Each following, each, with uninvidious ftrife, 175
Wears every feature of improving life.
Each gains from other comelinefs of drefs,
And learns, with gentle mein to win and blefs,
With welcome mild the ftranger to receive,
And with plain, pleafing decency to live. 180
Refinement hence even humbleft life improves;
Not the loofe fair, that form and frippery loves;
But fhe, whofe manfion is the gentle mind,
In thought, and action, virtuoufly refin'd.
Hence, wives and hufbands act a lovelier part, 185
More juft the conduct, and more kind the heart;
Hence brother, fifter, parent, child, and friend,
The harmony of life more fweetly blend;
Hence labour brightens every rural fcene;
Hence cheerful plenty lives along the green; 190
Still Prudence eyes her hoard, with watchful care,
And robes of thrift and neatnefs, all things wear.

But hark! what voice fo gaily fills the wind?
Of care oblivious, whofe that laughing mind?

'Tis yon poor black, who ceafes now his fong,   195
And whiftling, drives the cumbrous wain along.
He never, dragg'd, with groans, the galling chain;
Nor hung, fufpended, on th' infernal crane;
No dim, white fpots deform his face, or hand,
Memorials hellifh of the marking brand!   200
No feams of pincers, fcars of fcalding oil;
No wafte of famine, and no wear of toil.
But kindly fed, and clad, and treated, he
Slides on, thro' life, with more than common glee.
For here mild manners good to all impart,   205
And ftamp with infamy th' unfeeling heart;
Here law, from vengeful rage, the flave defends,
And here the gofpel peace on earth extends.

   He toils, 'tis true; but fhares his mafter's toil;
With him, he feeds the herd, and trims the foil;   210
Helps to fuftain the houfe, with clothes, and food,
And takes his portion of the common good:
Loft liberty his fole, peculiar ill,
And fix'd fubmiffion to another's will.
Ill, ah, how great! without that cheering fun,   215
The world is chang'd to one wide, frigid zone;
The mind, a chill'd exotic, cannot grow,
Nor leaf with vigour, nor with promife blow;
Pale, fickly, fhrunk, it ftrives in vain to rife,
Scarce lives, while living, and untimely dies.   220

   See frefh to life the Afric infant fpring,
And plume its powers, and fpread its little wing!
Firm is it's frame, and vigorous is its mind,
Too young to think, and yet to mifery blind.
But foon he fees himfelf to flavery born;   225
Soon meets the voice of power, the eye of fcorn;
Sighs for the bleffings of his peers, in vain;
Condition'd as a brute, tho' form'd a man.

Around he cafts his fond, inftinctive eyes,
And fees no good, to fill his wifhes, rife :   230
(No motive warms, with animating beam,
Nor praife, nor property, nor kind efteem,
Blefs'd independence, on his native ground,
Nor fweet equality with thofe around ;)
Himfelf, and his, another's fhrinks to find,   235
Levell'd below the lot of human kind.
Thus, fhut from honour's paths, he turns to fhame,
And filches the fmall good, he cannot claim.
To four, and ftupid, finks his active mind ;
Finds joys in drink, he cannot elfewhere find ;   240
Rule difobeys ; of half his labour cheats ;
In fome fafe cot, the pilfer'd turkey eats ;
Rides hard, by night, the fteed, his art purloins ;
Serene from confcience' bar himfelf effoins ;
Sees from himfelf his fole redrefs muft flow,   245
And makes revenge the balfam of his woe.

   Thus flavery's blaft bids fenfe and virtue die ;
Thus lower'd to duft the fons of Afric lie.
Hence fages grave, to lunar fyftems given,
Shall afk, why two-legg'd brutes were made by HEAVEN; 250
HOME feek, what pair firft peopled Afric's vales,
And nice MONBODDO calculate their tails.

   O thou chief curfe, fince curfes here began ;
Firft guilt, firft woe, firft infamy of man ;
Thou fpot of hell, deep fmirch'd on human kind,   255
The uncur'd gangrene of the reafoning mind ;
Alike in church, in ftate, and houfhold all,
Supreme memorial of the world's dread fall ;
O flavery ! laurel of the Infernal mind,
Proud Satan's triumph over loft mankind !   260

   See the fell Spirit mount his footy car !
While Hell's black trump proclaims the finifh'd war ;
Her choiceft fiends his wheels exulting draw,
And fcream the fall of GOD's moft holy law.

In dread proceſſion ſee the pomp begin,   265
Sad pomp of woe, of madneſs, and of ſin !
Grav'd on the chariot, all earth's ages roll,
And all her climes, and realms, to either pole.
Fierce in the flaſh of arms, ſee Europe ſpread !
Her jails, and gibbets, fleets, and hoſts, diſplay'd !   270
Awe-ſtruck, ſee ſilken Aſia ſilent bow !
And feeble Afric writhe in blood below !
Before, peace, freedom, virtue, bliſs, move on,
The ſpoils, the treaſures, of a world undone ;
Behind, earth's bedlam millions clank the chain,   275
Hymn their diſgrace, and celebrate their pain ;
Kings, nobles, prieſts, dread ſenate ! lead the van,
And ſhout " Te-Deum !" o'er defeated man.

Oft, wing'd by thought, I ſeek thoſe Indian iſles,
Where endleſs ſpring, with endleſs ſummer ſmiles,   280
Where fruits of gold untir'd Vertumnus pours,
And Flora dances o'er undying flowers.
There, as I walk thro' fields as Eden gay,
And breathe the incenſe of immortal May,
Ceaſeleſs I hear the ſmacking whip reſound ;   285
Hark ! that ſhrill ſcream ! that groan of death-bed ſound !
See thoſe throng'd wretches pant along the plain,
Tug the hard hoe, and ſigh in hopeleſs pain !
Yon mother, loaded with her ſucking child,
Her rags with frequent ſpots of blood defil'd,   290
Drags ſlowly fainting on ; the fiend is nigh ;
Rings the ſhrill cowſkin ; roars the tyger-cry ;
In pangs, th' unfriended ſuppliant crawls along,
And ſhrieks the prayer of agonizing wrong.

Why glows yon oven with a ſevenfold fire ?   295
Criſp'd in the flames, behold a man expire !
Lo ! by that vampyre's hand, yon infant dies,
It's brains daſh'd out, beneath it's father's eyes.

Why fhrinks yon flave, with horror, from his meat?
Heavens! 'tis his flefh, the wretch is whipp'd to eat.   300
Why ftreams the life-blood from that female's throat?
She fprinkled gravy on a gueft's new coat!

.   .   .   .   .   .

.   .   .   .   .   .

Why croud thofe quivering blacks yon dock around?   305
Thofe fcreams announce; that cowfkin's fhrilling found.
See, that poor victim hanging from the crane,
While loaded weights his limbs to torture ftrain;
At each keen ftroke, far fpouts the burfting gore,
And fhrieks, and dying groans, fill all the fhore.   310
Around, in throngs, his brother-victims wait,
And feel, in every ftroke, their coming fate;
While each, with palfied hands, and fhuddering fears,
The caufe, the rule, and price, of torment bears.

Hark, hark, from morn to night, the realm around,   315
The cracking whip, keen taunt, and fhriek, refound!
O'ercaft are all the fplendors of the fpring;
Sweets court in vain; in vain the warblers fing;
Illufions all! 'tis Tartarus round me fpreads
His difmal fcreams, and melancholy fhades.   320
The damned, fure, here clank th' eternal chain,
And wafte with grief, or agonize with pain.
A Tartarus new! inverfion ftrange of hell!
Guilt wreaks the vengeance, and the guiltlefs feel.
The heart, not form'd of flint, here all things rend;   325
Each fair a fury, and each man a fiend;
From childhood, train'd to every baleful ill,
And their firft fport, to torture, and to kill.

Afk not, why earthquakes rock that fateful land;
Fires wafte the city; ocean whelms the ftrand;   330
Why the fierce whirlwind, with electric fway,
Springs from the ftorm, and faftens on his prey,

Shakes heaven, rends earth, upheaves the cumbrous wave,
And with deſtruction's beſom fills the grave:
Why dark diſeaſe roams ſwift her nightly round,   335
Knocks at each door, and wakes the gaſping ſound.

Aſk, ſhuddering aſk, why, earth-emboſom'd ſleep
The unbroken fountains of the angry deep:
Why, bound, and furnac'd, by the globe's ſtrong frame,
In ſullen quiet, waits the final flame: 340
Why ſurge not, o'er yon iſles it's ſpouting fires,
'Till all their living world in duſt expires.
Crimes ſound their ruin's moral cauſe aloud,
And all heaven, ſighing, rings with cries of brother's blood.

Beſide yon church, that beams a modeſt ray,   345
With tidy neatneſs reputably gay,
When, mild and fair, as Eden's ſeventh-day light,
In ſilver ſilence, ſhines the Sabbath bright,
In neat attire, the village houſholds come,
And learn the path-way to the eternal home.   350
Hail ſolemn ordinance! worthy of the SKIES ;
Whence thouſand richeſt bleſſings daily riſe ;
Peace, order, cleanlineſs, and manners ſweet,
A ſober mind, to rule ſubmiſſion meet,
Enlarging knowledge, life from guilt refin'd,   355
And love to God, and friendſhip to mankind.
In the clear ſplendour of thy vernal morn,
New-quicken'd man to light, and life, is born ;
The deſert of the mind with virtue blooms ;
It's flowers unfold, it's fruits exhale perfumes ;   360
Proud guilt diſſolves, beneath the ſearching ray,
And low debaſement, trembling, creeps away ;
Vice bites the duſt ; foul Error ſeeks her den ;
And God, deſcending, dwells anew with men.
Where yonder humbler ſpire ſalutes the eye,   365
It's vane ſlow turning in the liquid ſky,

F

Where, in light gambols, healthy ftriplings fport,
Ambitious learning builds her outer court;
A grave preceptor, there, her ufher ftands,
And rules, without a rod, her little bands.   370
Some half-grown fprigs of learning grac'd his brow:
Little he knew, though much he wifh'd to know,
Inchanted hung o'er Virgil's honey'd lay,
And fmil'd, to fee defipient Horace play;
Glean'd fcraps of Greek; and, curious, trac'd afar, 375
Through Pope's clear glafs, the bright Mæonian ftar.
Yet oft his ftudents at his wifdom ftar'd,
For many a ftudent to his fide repair'd,
Surpriz'd, they heard him Dilworth's knots untie,
And tell, what lands beyond the Atlantic lie.   380

    Many his faults; his virtues fmall, and few;
Some little good he did, or ftrove to do;
Laborious ftill, he taught the early mind,
And urg'd to manners meek, and thoughts refin'd;
Truth he imprefs'd, and every virtue prais'd;   385
While infant eyes, in wondering filence, gaz'd;
The worth of time would, day by day, unfold,
And tell them, every hour was made of gold.
Brown Induftry he lov'd; and oft declar'd
How hardy Sloth, in life's fad evening, far'd; 390
Through grave examples, with fage meaning, ran,
Whift was each form, and thus the tale began.

    " Befide yon lonely tree, whofe branches bare
Rife white, and murmur to the paffing air,
There, where the twining briars the yard enclofe, 395
The houfe of Sloth ftands hufh'd in long repofe."

    " In a late round of folitary care,
My feet inftinct to rove, they knew not where,
I thither came. With yellow bloffoms gay,
The tall rank weed begirt the tangled way: 400

Curious to view, I forc'd a path between,
And climb'd the broken ſtile, and gaz'd the ſcene."

" O'er an old well, the curb half-fallen ſpread,
Whoſe boards, end-looſe, a mournful creaking made;
Poiz'd on a leaning poſt, and ill-ſuſtain'd,   405
In ruin ſad, a mouldering ſwepe remain'd;
Uſeleſs, the crooked pole ſtill dangling hung,
And, tied with thrumbs, a broken bucket ſwung."

" A half-made wall around the garden lay,
Mended, in gaps, with bruſhwood in decay.   410
No culture through the woven briars was ſeen,
Save a few ſickly plants of faded green ;
The ſtarv'd potatoe hung it's blaſted ſeeds,
And fennel ſtruggled to o'ertop the weeds,
There gaz'd a ragged ſheep, with wild ſurpriſe,   415
And too lean geeſe upturn'd their ſlanting eyes."

" The cottage gap'd, with many a diſmal yawn,
Where, rent to burn, the covering boards were gone;
Or, by one nail, where others endwiſe hung,
The ſky look'd thro', and winds portentous rung.   420
In waves, the yielding roof appear'd to run,
And half the chimney-top was fallen down."

" The ancient cellar-door, of ſtructure rude,
With tatter'd garments calk'd, half open ſtood.
There, as I peep'd, I ſaw the ruin'd bin ;   425
The ſills were broke; the wall had crumbled in ;
A few, long-emptied caſks lay mouldering round,
And waſted aſhes ſprinkled o'er the ground ;
While, a ſad ſharer in the houſhold ill,
A half-ſtarv'd rat crawl'd out, and bade farewell."   430

" One window dim, a loop-hole to the ſight,
Shed round the room a pale, penurious light ;

Here rags gay-colour'd eked the broken glafs;
There panes of wood fupplied the vacant fpace."

" As, pondering deep, I gaz'd, with gritty roar,   435
The hinges creak'd, and open ftood the door.
Two little boys, half-naked from the waift,
With ftaring wonder, ey'd me, as I pafs'd.
The fmile of Pity blended with her tear—
Ah me ! how rarely Comfort vifits here !"   440

" On a lean hammoc, once with feathers fill'd,
His limbs by dirty tatters ill conceal'd,
Tho' now the fun had rounded half the day,
Stretch'd at full length, the lounger fnoring lay:
While his fad wife, befide her dreffer ftood,   445
And wafh'd her hungry houfhold's meagre food,
His aged fire, whofe beard, and flowing hair,
Wav'd filvery, o'er his antiquated chair,
Rofe from his feat ; and, as he watch'd my eye,
Deep from his bofom heav'd a mournful figh—   450
" Stranger, he cried, once better days I knew ;"
And, trembling, fhed the venerable dew.
I wifh'd a kind reply ; but wifh'd in vain ;
No words came timely to relieve my pain :
To the poor parent, and her infants dear,   455
Two mites I gave, befprinkled with a tear ;
And, fix'd again to fee the wretched fhed,
Withdrew in filence, clos'd the door, and fled."

" Yet this fo lazy man I've often feen
Hurrying, and buftling, round the bufy green ;   460
The loudeft prater, in a blackfmith's fhop ;
The wifeft ftatefman, o'er a drunken cup ;
(His fharp-bon'd horfe, the ftreet that nightly fed,
Tied, many an hour, in yonder tavern-fhed)
In every gambling, racing match, abroad :   465
But a rare hearer, in the houfe of God."

" Such, fuch, my children, is the difmal cot,
Where drowfy Sloth receives her wretched lot:
But O how different is the charming cell,
Where Induftry and Virtue love to dwell !"   470

" Beyond that hillock, topp'd with fcatter'd trees,
That meet, with frefheft green, the haftening breeze,
There, where the glaffy brook reflects the day,
Nor weeds, nor fedges, choke its cryftal way,
Where budding willows feel the earlieft fpring,   475
And wonted red-breafts fafely neft, and fing,
A female Worthy lives; and all the poor
Can point the way to her fequefter'd door."

" She, unfeduc'd by drefs and idle fhew,
The forms, and rules, of fafhion never knew;   480
Nor glittering in the ball, her form difplay'd;
Nor yet can tell a diamond, from a fpade.
Far other objects claim'd her fteady care;
The morning chapter, and the nightly prayer;
The frequent vifit to the poor man's fhed;   485
The wakeful nurfing, at the fick man's bed;
Each day, to rife, before the early fun;
Each day, to fee her daily duty done;
To cheer the partner of her houfhold cares,
And mould her children, from their earlieft years.   490

" Small is her houfe; but fill'd with ftores of good;
Good, earn'd with toil, and with delight beftow'd.
In the clean cellar, rang'd in order neat,
Gay-fmiling Plenty boafts her cafks of meat,
Points, to fmall eyes, the bins where apples glow,   495
And marks her cyder-butts, in ftately row.
Her granary, fill'd with harveft's various pride,
Still fees the poor man's bufhel laid afide;
Here fwells the flaxen, there the fleecy ftore,
And the long wood-pile mocks the winter's power: 500

White are the fwine ; the poultry plump and large ;
For every creature thrives, beneath her charge."

" Plenteous, and plain, the furniture is feen ;
All form'd for ufe, and all as filver clean.
On the clean dreffer, pewter fhines arow ;   505
The clean-fcower'd bowls are trimly fet below ;
While the wafh'd coverlet, and linen white,
Affure the traveller a refrefhing night."

" Oft have I feen, and oft ftill hope to fee,
This friend, this parent to the poor and me,   510
Tho' bent with years, and toil, and care, and woe,
Age lightly filver'd on her furrow'd brow,
Her frame ftill ufeful, and her mind ftill young,
Her judgment vigorous, and her memory ftrong,
Screne her fpirits, and her temper fweet,   515
And pleas'd the youthful circle ftill to meet,
Cheerful, the long-accuftom'd tafk purfue,
Prevent the ruft of age, and life renew ;
To church, ftill pleas'd, and able ftill, to come,
And fhame the lounging youth, who fleep at home." 520

", Such as her toils, has been the bright reward ;
For Heaven will always toils like thefe regard.
Safe, on her love, her truth and wifdom tried,
Her hufband's heart, thro' lengthened life, relied ;
From little, daily faw his wealth increafe,   525
His neighbours love him, and his houfhold blefs ;
In peace and plenty liv'd, and died refign'd,
And, dying, left fix thoufand pounds behind.
Her children, train'd to ufefulnefs alone,
Still love the hand, which led them kindly on,   530
With pious duty, own her wife beheft,
And, every day, rife up, and call her blefs'd."

" More would ye know, of each poor hind enquire,
Who fees no fun go down upon his hire ;

A cheerful witneſs, bid each neighbour come;			535
Aſk each ſad wanderer, where he finds a home;
His tribute even the vileſt wretch will give,
And praiſe the uſeful life, he will not live."

"	Oft have the prattlers, GOD to me has giv'n,
The flock, I hope, and ſtrive, to train for Heaven,		540
With little footſteps, ſought her manſion dear,
To meet the welcome, given with heart ſincere;
And cheer'd with all, that early minds can move,
The ſmiles of gentleneſs, and acts of love,
At home, in liſping tales, her worth diſplay'd,		545
And pour'd their infant bleſſings on her head."

"	Ye kings, of pomp, ye nobles proud of blood,
Heroes of arms, of ſcience ſages proud!
Read, bluſh, and weep, to ſee, with all your ſtore,
Fame, genius, knowledge, bravery, wealth, and power, 550
Crown'd, laurell'd, worſhipp'd, gods beneath the ſun,
Far leſs of real good enjoy'd, or done."

Such leſſons, pleas'd, he taught. The precepts new
Oft the young train to early wiſdom drew;
And, when his influence willing minds confeſs'd,		555
The children lov'd him, and the parents bleſs'd;
But, when by ſoft indulgence led aſtray,
His pupil's hearts had learn'd the idle way,
Tho' conſtant, kind, and hard, his toils had been,
For all thoſe toils, ſmall thanks had he, I ween.		560

Behold yon humbler manſion lift its head!
Where infant minds to ſcience door are led.
As now, by kind indulgence looſ'd to play,
From place to place, from ſport to ſport, they ſtray,
How light their gambols frolic o'er the green!		565
How their ſhrill voices cheer the rural ſcene!
Sweet harmleſs elves! in Freedom's houſhold born,
Enjoy the raptures of your tranſient morn;

And let no hour of anxious manhood fee
Your minds lefs innocent, or blefs'd, or free!   570

See too, in every hamlet, round me rife
A central fchool-houfe, drefs'd in modeft guife!
Where every child for ufeful life prepares,
'To bufinefs moulded, ere he knows its cares;
In worth matures, to independence grows,   575
And twines the civic garland o'er his brows.

Mark, how invited by the vernal fky,
You cheerful group of females paffes by!
Whofe hearts, attun'd to focial joy, prepare
A friendly vifit to fome neighbouring fair.   58c
How neatnefs gliftens from the lovely train!
Bright charm! which pomp to rival tries in vain.

Ye Mufes! dames of dignified renown,
Rever'd alike in country, and in town,
Your bard the myfteries of a vifit fhow;   585
For fure your Ladyfhips thofe myfteries know:
What is it then, obliging Sifters! fay,
The debt of focial vifiting to pay?

'Tis not to toil before the idol pier;
To fhine the firft in fafhion's lunar fphere;   590
By fad engagements forc'd, abroad to roam,
And dread to find the expecting fair, at home!
To ftop at thirty doors, in half a day,
Drop the gilt card, and proudly roll away;
To alight, and yield the hand, with nice parade;   595
Up ftairs to ruftle in the ftiff brocade;
Swim thro' the drawing room, with ftudied air;
Catch the pink'd beau, and fhade the rival fair;
To fit, to curb, to tofs, with bridled mien,
Mince the fcant fpeech, and lofe a glance between;   600
Unfurl the fan, difplay the fnowy arm,
And ope, with each new motion, fome new charm;

Or fit, in filent folitude, to fpy
Each little failing, with malignant eye;
Or chatter, with inceffancy of tongue,   605
Carelefs, if kind, or cruel, right, or wrong;
To trill of us, and ours, of mine, and me,
Our houfe, our coach, our friends, our family,
While all th' excluded circle fit in pain,
And glance their cool contempt, or keen difdain: 610
T' inhale, from proud Nanking, a fip of tea,
And wave a curtfey trim, and flirt away:
Or wafte, at cards, peace, temper, health and life,
Begin with fullennefs, and end in ftrife,
Lofe the rich feaft, by friendly converfe given,   615
And backward turn from happinefs, and heaven.

    It is, in decent habit, plain and neat,
To fpend a few choice hours, in converfe fweet;
Carelefs of forms, to act th' unftudied part,
To mix in friendfhip, and to blend the heart;   620
To choofe thofe happy themes, which all muft feel,
The moral duties, and the houfhold weal,
The tale of fympathy, the kind defign,
Where rich affections foften, and refine;
T' amufe, to be amus'd, to blefs, be blefs'd,   625
And tune to harmony the common breaft;
To cheer, with mild good-humour's fprightly ray,
And fmooth life's paffage, o'er its thorny way;
To circle round the hofpitable board,
And tafte each good, our generous climes afford;   630
To court a quick return, with accents kind,
And leave, at parting, fome regret behind.

    Such, here, the focial intercourfe is found;
So flides the year, in fmooth enjoyment, round.

    Thrice blefs'd the life, in this glad region fpent,   635
In peace, in competence, and ftill content;

G

Where bright, and brighter, all things daily fmile,
And rare and fcanty, flow the ftreams of ill;
Where undecaying youth fits blooming round,
And Spring looks lovely on the happy ground;   640
Improvement glows, along life's cheerful way,
And with foft luftre makes the paffage gay.
Thus oft, on yonder Sound, when evening gales
Breath'd e'or th' expanfe, and gently fill'd the fails,
The world was ftill, the heavens were drefs'd in fmiles, 645
And the clear moon-beam tipp'd the diftant ifles,
On the blue plain a lucid image gave,
And capp'd, with filver light, each little wave;
The filent fplendour, floating at our fide,
Mov'd as we mov'd, and wanton'd on the tide;   650
While fhadowy points, and havens, met the eye,
And the faint-glimmering landmark told us home was nigh.

　　Ah, dire reverfe! in yonder eaftern clime,
Where heavy drags the fluggifh car of time;
The world unalter'd by the change of years,   655
Age after age, the fame dull afpect wears;
On the bold mind the weight of fyftem fpread,
Refiftlefs lies, a cumbrous load of lead;
One beaten courfe, the wheels politic keep,
And flaves of cuftom, lofe their woes in fleep;   660
Stagnant is focial life; no bright defign,
Quickens the floth, or checks the fad decline.
The friend of man cafts round a wifhful eye,
And hopes, in vain, improving fcenes to fpy;
Slow o'er his head, the dragging moments roll,   665
And damp each cheerful purpofe of the foul.

　　Thus the bewilder'd traveller, forc'd to roam
Through a lone foreft, leaves his friends, and home;
Dun evening hangs the fky; the woods around
Join their dun umbrage o'er the ruffet ground;   670
At every ftep, new gloom infhrouds the fkies;
His path grows doubtful, and his fears arife:

No woodland fongftrefs foothes his mournful way;
No taper gilds the gloom with cheering ray;
On the cold earth he laps his head forlorn,   675
And watching, looks, and looks, to fpy the lingering morn.

And when new regions prompt their feet to roam,
And fix, in untrod fields, another home,
No dreary realms our happy race explore,
Nor mourn their exile from their native fhore.   680
For there no endlefs frofts the glebe deform,
Nor blows, with icy breath, perpetual ftorm :
No wrathful funs, with fickly fplendour glare,
Nor moors, impoifon'd, taint the balmy air,
But medial climates change the healthful year;   685
Pure ftreamlets wind, and gales of Eden cheer;
In mifty pomp the fky-topp'd mountains ftand,
And with green bofom humbler hills expand :
With flowery brilliance fmiles the woodland glade;
Full teems the foil, and fragrant twines the fhade.   690
There cheaper fields the numerous houfhold charm,
And the glad fire gives every fon a farm;
In falling forefts, Labour's axe refounds;
Opes the new field; and wind the fence's bounds;
The green wheat fparkles; nods the towering corn;   695
And meads, and paftures, leffening waftes adorn.
Where howl'd the foreft, herds unnumber'd low;
The fleecy wanderers fear no prowling foe;
The village fprings; the humble fchool afpires;
And the church brightens in the morning fires !   700
Young Freedom wantons; Art exalts her head;
And infant Science prattles through the fhade.
There changing neighbours learn their manners mild;
And toil and prudence drefs th' improving wild :
The favage fhrinks, nor dares the blifs annoy;   705
And the glad traveller wonders at the joy.

All hail, thou weſtern world! by heaven deſign'd
Th' example bright, to renovate mankind.
Soon ſhall thy ſons acroſs the mainland roam;
And claim, on far Pacific ſhores, their home;   710
Their rule, religion, manners, arts, convey,
And ſpread their freedom to the Aſian ſea.
Where erſt ſix thouſand ſuns have roll'd the year
O'er plains of ſlaughter, and o'er wilds of fear,
Towns, cities, fanes, ſhall lift their towery pride;   715
The village bloom, on every ſtreamlets ſide;
Proud Commerce, mole the weſtern ſurges lave;
The long, white ſpire lie imag'd on the wave;
O'er morn's pellucid main expand their ſails,
And the ſtarr'd enſign court Korean gales.   720
Then nobler thoughts ſhall ſavage trains inform;
Then barbarous paſſions ceaſe the heart to ſtorm:
No more the captive circling flames devour;
Through the war path the Indian creep no more;
No midnight ſcout the ſlumbering village fire;   725
Nor the ſcalp'd infant ſtain his gaſping ſire:
But peace, and truth, illume the twilight mind,
The goſpel's ſunſhine, and the purpoſe kind.
Where marſhes teem'd with death, ſhall meads unfold;
Untrodden cliffs reſign their ſtores of gold;   730
The dance reſin'd on Albion's margin move,
And her lone bowers rehearſe the tale of love.
Where ſlept perennial night, ſhall ſcience riſe,
And new-born Oxfords cheer the evening ſkies;
Miltonic ſtrains the Mexic hills prolong,   735
And Louis murmurs to Sicilian ſong.

Then to new climes the bliſs ſhall trace its way,
And Tartar deſarts hail the riſing day;
From the long torpor ſtartled China wake;
Her chains of miſery rous'd Peruvia break;   740

Man link to man; with bofom bofom twine;
And one great bond the houfe of Adam join:
The facred promife full completion know,
And peace, and piety, the world o'erflow.

END OF THE SECOND PART.

GREENFIELD HILL:

A

P O E M.

THE ARGUMENT.

*I*N the beginning of July 1779, the British, under the command of Sir George Collyer, and Governor Tryon, plundered New-Haven. Thence they sailed to Fairfield, plundered, and burned it. Eighty-five dwelling houses, two churches, a handsome court house, several school houses, together with a great number of barns, out-houses, &c. were consumed by the fire. Many other houses were set on fire; but were extinguished by the returning inhabitants. The distress, occasioned by this act of wanton barbarity, is inconceivable; and the name of Governor Tryon will, on account of it, be remembered with the most finished detestation.

From l. 1, to l. 283, the story is related. The reader is then addressed with a representation of the happiness destroyed at Fairfield, and with an account of the prevalence of war, in ancient, and in modern times; its nature and its effects on the morals and happiness of mankind. This address extends to l. 547, and is succeeded by an Address to the Hero, returning victorious from war. He is first presented with a picture of the miseries of war, on the land; and is then conducted to the shore, to take a survey of maritime war.—Death—Speech of Death—Motives to abstain from war—and Conclusion.

GREENFIELD HILL.

PART III.

THE BURNING OF FAIRFIELD.

ON yon bright plain, with beauty gay,
Where waters wind, and cattle play,
Where gardens, groves, and orchards bloom,
Unconscious of her coming doom,
Once Fairfield smil'd. The tidy dome,   5
Of pleasure, and of peace, the home,
There rose; and there the glittering spire,
Secure from sacrilegious fire.

And now no scenes had brighter smil'd,
No skies, with purer splendor mild,   10
No greener wreathe had crown'd the spring,
Nor sweeter breezes spread the wing,
Nor streams thro' gayer margins roll'd,
Nor harvests wav'd with richer gold,
Nor flocks on brighter hillocks play'd,   15
Nor groves entwin'd a safer shade:
But o'er her plains, infernal War
Has whirl'd the terrors of his car,

H

The vengeance pour'd of wasting flame,
And blacken'd man with endless shame, 20

    Long h~d the Briton, round our coast,
His bolts in every haven tofs'd,
Unceasing spread the trump's alarms,
And call'd the swains to daily arms.
Success his wilder'd eye had charm'd, 25
And hope with strong pulsations warm'd,
And pride, with eagle pinion, borne
Far in the blaze of splendid morn.
With brightest beams, as rainbows rise
To suns, departing from the skies, 30
As morn, in April's fairest form,
Is quench'd, and buried, in the storm;
So brighter all his prospects spread,
Just as the gay enchantment fled.
His efforts clos'd in shame forlorn; 35
His pride provok'd the taunt of scorn;
Sunbright, the transient meteor shone,
And darker left the world, when gone.

    Soft rose the summer's mildest morn;
To yonder beach his fleet was borne; 40
His canvas swell'd, his flag, unfurl'd,
Hung ruin o'er the western world.
Then forth his thickening thousands came;
Their armour pour'd an eager flame,
Confusion fill'd the realm around; 45
The reaper left his sheaf unbound;
The farmer, flying, dropp'd his goad,
His oxen yok'd before the load;
His plough the unfinish'd furrow held,
And flocks unguided roam'd the field, 50
Forth from his shop the tradesman flew,
His musket seizing, to pursue;
From every house, the hurried swains,
Tumultuous, throng'd the bust'ling plains;

At race, the croſſing ſteeds were ſeen,   55
And crouds ſtood cluſtering on the green.

Aghaſt the wretched townſmen fled;
The youth with nimble vigour ſped;
The virgin, wild with throbbing woe,
Flew ſwift, and ſwifter, from the foe;   60
Pale Age ſlow totter'd on behind,
His white hair ſtreaming in the wind;
The boy, with little footſteps, hied,
And hung upon his grandſire's ſide.
Claſp'd cloſe, and cheriſh'd at her breaſt,   65
Her new-born babe the mother preſs'd;
Oft toward the town was glanc'd her eye,
And oft ſhe liſten'd to the cry—
" Haſte, haſte, my babes! the foe draws near;
Fly, leſt he ſlay my children here"—   70
Around, the affrighted charmers ſcower'd,
And ſcream'd, as fierce the cannons roar'd.

The pair, beyond expreſſion lov'd,
Apart, with lingering anguiſh, mov'd:
He toward the war reluĉtant drew;   75
She wav'd the long and laſt adieu.

Through every field, and copſe, aſtray,
The unfriended mourners trac'd their way,
That refuge in the waſte to find,
Denied them by the human kind: 80
While waggons bore, behind the throng,
The tythe of furniture along.

Meantime, in combat's ridgy van,
Dark-lowering, man confronted man;
Tempeſtuous, hoſt with hoſt engag'd;   85
The ſhout of thundering onſet rag'd;
The cannon burſt; the muſquet roar'd;
Long, ſmoky folds through ether pour'd;

Loud rofe the uproar wild ; around,
The world all trembled, at the found :   90
Now hollow groan'd the victim's cries,
And now fhrill victory fill'd the fkies.

But ah ! the rude Columbian hoft
Nor leaders, arms, nor fkill, could boaft ;
To war untrain'd, they feebly bore   95
The phalanx firm of veteran power,
Scatter'd to neighbouring hills away,
And gave the fcarce-difputed day.

Yet, though in battle's rage untaught,
Superior fouls undaunted fought,   100
Atchiev'd, with breaft of generous mould,
Such deeds, as Grecian bards have told,
The patriot prov'd, the laurel gain'd,
The brave avengers of their land.

The work of crimfon flaughter done,   105
A fullen interval came on.
The fwains, efcap'd from threat'ning ill,
Hung, gloomy, round each neighbouring hill :
From houfe to houfe th' invaders flew,
To wafte, to plunder, and purfue.   110
Whatee'r their ruffian ftrength could bear
Ufeful, or pleafant, rich, or rare,
From the poor earner's feeble hand
They fnatch'd, and hurried to the ftrand.

To bruife the head of filver hair,   115
To agonize the imploring fair,
The hufband's breaft convulfe with woe,
The wife to wound with every throe,
The feeble crufh, the humble beat,
And fpurn pale Anguifh from their feet,   120
With grofs affault to tear the heart,
And fmile, and revel, o'er the fmart,

To hifs the groan, to mock the prayer,
Alike their tranfport, and their care.

There Delicacy look'd, to meet   125
Compaffion, at Neronian feet;
Compaffion, puff'd in many a fong,
And prov'd by impudence of tongue;
But found, deceiv'd by Britifh breath,
To hope was woe, to truft was death.   130

Yet let not Indignation rude
Commix the worthlefs with the good:
Sweet Candour fings, with voice benign,
And fmiles to pen the generous line,
Bright fouls there were, who felt for woe,   135
And own'd the merit of a foe;
Bright Britifh fouls, with virtue warm'd,
To reafon; and to kindnefs, charm'd,
Who footh'd the wretch with tendereft care,
Their leaders fpurn'd, and curs'd the war,   140
The forrows wept of life's fhort fpan,
And felt the kindred ties of man.

Yet thefe, even thefe (let Pity's tale
Their errors, while it tells, bewail)
Thought facred Duty's ftern commands   145
Compell'd to ill their ftruggling hands.
Fond man! can Duty bid thee do
What thou muft mourn, and others rue?
Are crimes a debt by Virtue paid?
Is GOD, where confcience fhrinks, obey'd?   150
GOD, who from every ill reftrains,
Tho' greateft good the guilt obtains;
Who, on the world's funereal day,
Will truth's divine award difplay,
Bid heaven, and earth, his vengeance fee,   155
And judge thy guilty lord, and thee?

Meantime, on yonder hills, forlorn,
The townfmen ftood, with anguifh torne,
Anguifh for thofe, they left behind,
To fears, and ills, and foes, confign'd;   160
The hufband, for his darling mate;
The father, for his children's fate;
While prefcience wrung with keeneft throe,
And faft enhanc'd fufpended woe.
When lo! dark-rolling thro' the fkies,   165
Unnumber'd fmokes began to rife:
His manfion, long to each endear'd,
Where peace, and joy, alone appear'd,
Where all the charities of life,
Of parents, children, hufband, wife,   170
With fofter, tendereft bofoms ftrove,
For garlands, in the ftrife of love;
The morn with brighter beauty drefs'd;
The evening gladden'd in the weft;
Bade each gay fun more gaily roll,   175
And twin'd the fympathy of foul;
That manfion, malice' feven-fold ire
Now wrapp'd in fwathes of circling fire,
Scatter'd his darling blifs in air,
And plung'd his heart in deep defpair.   180
O vileft of the crimes of War,
Fell partner of his bloody car,
Dread ill, to guilty mortals given,
To mark the wrath of injur'd HEAVEN;
O Conflagration! curfe intire;   185
The impoifon'd fting of baffled ire;
Of kings, of chiefs, th' immortal fhame;
The rafure of the reafoning name!
From thee, no aid the victor gains;
Nor wealth, nor ftrength, rewards his pains: 190
The fear, he fondly hopes imprefs'd,
Is chang'd to rage, in every breaft:

The victim, maddening with his woe,
With vengeance burns, a deadlier foe.
'Tis thine, to glean the wastes of war,   195
The landscape of HEAVEN's good to mar,
Life's latest refuge to confume,
And make the world a general tomb.

   Say, Mufe indignant! whofe the hand
That hurl'd the conflagrative brand?   200
A foe to human feelings born,
And of each future age the fcorn,
TRYON atchiev'd the deed malign,
TRYON, the name of every fin.
Hell's bafeft fiends the flame furvey'd,   205
And fmil'd, to fee deftruction fpread;
While Satan, blufhing deep, look'd on,
And Infamy difown'd her fon.

   Now Night, of all her ftars forlorn,
Majeftic, up the fky was borne.   210
A cloud immenfe her mifty car,
Slow-fliding thro' the burden'd air;
Her wreathe of yew; a cyprefs wand
Uplifted by her magic hand;
Pale, fhrouded fears her awful train,   215
And fpectres gliding on the plain:
While Horror, o'er the fable world,
His enfigns, thro' the expanfe, unfurl'd.
When lo! the fouthern fkies around,
Expanded wide, with turrets crown'd,   220
With umber'd fkirts, with wary gleam,
Uprofe an awful ridge of flame,
Shed far it's dreary luftre round,
And dimly ftreak'd the twilight ground.
Dark clouds, with many a difmal ftain,   225
Hung hov'ring o'er the gleamy main;
While deep, the diftant, hollow roar
Wav'd, echoing from the illumin'd fhore;

And, from each heaven-directed fpire,
Climb'd bending pyramids of fire.   230

 Meantime, a ftorm, in weftern fkies,
Thick, heavy, vaft, began to rife,
Roll'd fwift, on burden'd winds, along,
And brooded o'er the plundering throng,
In deeper night the heavens array'd   235
And ftretch'd it's pall of boundlefs fhade.
Forth fhot the fierce and lurid flame,
(The world dim-rifing in the beam)
Leffen'd the conflagrative fpires,
And blended, with their light, it's fires.   240
Again new darknefs fpread the main,
The fplendors bright'ning rofe again.
The thunder, with earth-rending found,
Shook every vale, and hill around ;
While, at each paufe, with folemn voice,   245
The murmuring flames prolong'd the noife.
It feem'd, the final day was come,
The day of earth's protracted doom ;
The Archangel's voice began to call
The nations of this guilty ball ;   250
The hills to cleave ; the fkies to rend ;
Tumultuous elements to blend ;
And HEAVEN, in pomp tremendous, came
To light the laft, funereal flame.

 The tumult pafs'd, the morn's meek eye   255
Look'd foft, and filent, from the fky.
Still on their hills the townfmen ftood,
And mark'd the fcene of ftrife, and blood,
Watching the progrefs of the day,
That bore their plundering foes away   260
Tumultuous, to the darkening ftrand
From vengeance fhrunk the guilty band,
With loads of fpoil, retir'd in hafte,
The fpoil of domes, and churches, ras'd ;

Thence, to their ships, by boats convey'd,   265
Their sails unfurl'd, their anchors weigh'd,
Awak'd the Injurer's sullen ire,
And brooded o'er another fire.

Each to his home, the townsmen flew,
Where scenes of anguish met the view.   270
Here spread the sunk, still-blazing wall,
And there stood, nodding to its fall:
Here rose the slow-declining fire,
And smoke, reluctant to expire;
There sable brands lay scatter'd round,   275
And ashes vile defac'd the ground.
The sullen chimney frown'd alone;
The sad winds breath'd a hollow groan:
His joys were fled; his hopes were gone;
His houshold driven to haunts unknown: 280
There peaceful slumber'd Ruin wild,
And Horror rear'd his head, and smil'd.

O thou! whose heart, with kind design,
Explores, and feels this honest line;
Before thee, lo! a village stands,   285
In misery plung'd by hostile hands.
Such, such is war's pernicious rage,
In every form, and clime, and age,
It sweeps, where'er its horrors come,
All human blessings to the tomb.   290
Once, on this little spot, appear'd
Whate'er the life of man endear'd,
Peace, freedom, competence, and health,
Enduring good, and real wealth;
With Innocence, of tranquil breast,   295
Their faithful friend, and constant guest;
While all the village Virtues smil'd,
And play'd, and sung their field-notes wild.
The feast of temperate, houshold joy,
That still delights, that cannot cloy,   300

I

Went round the year. The hufband's toil
Still bade the field and garden fmile;
With green adorn'd the vernal day;
Awak'd the tended flock to play;
Bade Summer lay his golden load,　　　　305
And Autumn drop his blooming good;
Of froft, compell'd the rage to ceafe,
And charm'd the wintry ftorm to peace.
Her toils to his the wife conjoin'd,
With fweeteft unity of mind;　　　　310
Converted, all he earn'd, to good,
The fleece to clothes, the corn to food;
Preferv'd, with watchful eye, the hoard;
With dainties crown'd the cheerful board;
In every labour claim'd her fhare;　　　　315
And burnifh'd joy, and gilded care;
And, with a fweet, fupporting fmile,
Seren'd, and leffen'd, every ill.

Around, fuftain'd, inftructed, fway'd,
Their little flock, as lambkins, play'd,　　　　320
With ftripling fports, and fmiling ftrife,
Deceiv'd the thorny road of life;
Clafp'd the fond heart; the bofom charm'd;
And Labour's icy finews warm'd;
With bloffom'd hopes enchanted pain,　　　　325
And life's brown autumn green'd again.
The lovely fcene the parents view'd,
And daily faw their blifs renew'd,
Beheld themfelves, in theirs, revive,
And thro' fucceeding ages live.　　　　330

Meantime, from houfe to houfe, went round
The cup, with focial pleafure crown'd;
The blifs, good neighbourhood beftows,
Immingling joys, and foothing woes;

The feaft, with fpicy fragrance, cheer'd ;   335
With glee the evening hour endear'd ;
Laid ficknefs on a downy bed ;
And pillow'd foft the weary head ;
Smooth'd the ftern brow of angry Strife,
And added balm to drooping life.   340

Here too, with fond, maternal hands,
The fchool embrac'd her infant bands ;
To wifdom led the early mind,
Affections foft, and actions kind ;
Prepar'd to fill the ufeful part,   345
And form'd to worth the cultur'd heart.

And here, when beam'd the fabbath's ray,
Bright earneft of immortal day,
The bell the folemn warning rung ;
The temple's doors unfolded hung :   350
To pay, each grateful houfhold came,
Its tribute to th' Unutter'd Name ;
And fent with heaven-directed eyes,
United incenfe to the fkies.

Where now, thou Child of Nature ! where   355
Is gone this humble blifs fincere ?
Lo ! guilty War has wafted all,
And Ruin, fummon'd at his call,
Has marr'd the good, th' ETERNAL yields,
And fown with falt the defert fields.   360

Such, Child of Nature ! fuch the fcene,
In every age, and clime, has been.
Since Nimrod firft the fpoil began,
Man ftill has toil'd to ruin man.
Search, fearch, and tell me, what has moft   365
The toils, and powers, of men engrofs'd ?
The nerves of fuffering Labour ftrain'd ?
Invention's richeft channels drain'd ?

Awak'd, and fir'd, the immenfe defign?
Devour'd th' incalculable mine? 370
And wing'd bold enterprife afar
Through danger, death, and ruin? War.
Peace' lowly vale neglected lies,
Unfeen, or pafs'd with glancing eyes.
The cultur'd field, the manfion fweet, 375
Where all the Loves, and Virtues meet,
The calm, the meek, the ufeful life,
The friend of man, the foe of ftrife,
The heart to kindnefs tun'd, are things
Too mean for ftatefmen, chiefs, and kings. 380
For there no twining laurels bloom,
Still verdant o'er the wintry tomb;
No cliffs ambitious tempt to rife,
And climb, and climb, to reach the fkies;
Nor fancy opes that bright abode, 385
Where man's transfigur'd to a god.

Yet *here* whate'er the earth's wide field,
Of comfort, hope, or joy, can yield,
Whate'er benignant SKIES defign'd,
To nurfe the form, or cheer the mind, 390
Our being's fcope, and ufe, and end,
The arts, and acts, that life befriend,
Whate'er adorns the reafoning name,
Or emulates an angel's fame,
The juft, the good, the humble, thrive, 395
And in *this fweet republic* live.

But thefe, too mean for kings, are feen
For all the trains of kings too mean.
For thefe no fenate gold beftows;
O'er thefe no ftatefman bends his brows; 400
No garlands bloom, proceffions glare;
Nor mobs, with idiot wonder, ftare;

No heralds blazon them to fame;
They rife, they fall, without a name.

    Thro' earth's immeasurable bounds,   405
Thro' time's interminable rounds,
Each day has heard the clarion roar;
Each land been bath'd in human gore.
The Egyptian rule, the Affyrian throne,
Was rear'd of fpoils, and realms undone.   410
Greece redden'd earth around with blood,
And pour'd of woe an ocean flood;
Then pointed at herfelf the dart,
And brothers pierc'd a brother's heart.
The Perfian ruin'd half mankind: 415
The Macedonian wept, to find,
While brooding o'er the wrecks of joy,
No new world left him, to deftroy.
The ftructure mark of Rome's dread power!
Its marble bones! its cement gore!   420
Her fway the wafte of human joy;
The art to plunder, and deftroy;
A curfe to earth's extended climes;
A web of madnefs, woes, and crimes!
Her towers were built by galled hands;   425
In blood her proud Pantheon ftands;
Her triumphs fhow'd the tyger's prey;
And corpfes pav'd her Appian way.
In each tall temple's dread abode,
Pale fpectres hover'd round the god,   430
(The injur'd ghofts of countlefs lands,
Cut off from life by Roman hands)
Hung round, and claim'd the fpoils their own,
Shriek'd o'er their native realms undone,
Haunted each fhrine, with livid ftare,   425
And mingled groans with every prayer.

    Nor lefs, in modern days, when art
Has led to nobler fcenes the heart,

When fcience beams with vernal rays,
And lights to blifs ten thoufand ways,   440
The Gofpel, found in every tongue,
Has peace, and fweet falvation, fung,
The tyger charm'd to quit his prey,
And taught the wolf with lambs to play—
Still roars the trump's funereal found ;   445
"To arms," the ftartled hills rebound ;
War's iron car in thunder rolls,
From medial climes, to diftant poles.

Amaz'd, fee Europe, firft of all,
Proud Emprefs of this fuffering ball,   450
The fun of power, and arts refin'd,
The boaft, and beauty, of mankind,
The work of death, and plunder, fpread,
And riot on th' untimely dead !

When, borne by winds of fofteft wing,   455
Returns the life-renewing fpring,
The tempeft flies to earth's far ends,
And HEAVEN in peace and love defcends,
Shines in the fun's ferener ray,
Breathes in the balmy breath of May,   460
Diftills in earth-diffolving fhowers,
And glows in rainbow-painted flowers,
While wifdom works, while goodnefs warms,
In fky-born tints, and angel forms,
The new, the fweet, creation fprings,   465
And beauty blooms, and rapture fings :
Faft fwell the teeming feeds of food ;
The world is heap'd with boundlefs good :
In every fcene, the GODHEAD fmiles,
And man of rage, and luft, beguiles.   470
Then beats the drum its fierce alarm ;
Then millions, fir'd to madnefs, arm,

Fight, plunder, defolate, devour,
And drench the wafted world in gore.

Whofe name rolls down, from age to age ?   475
Whofe fplendours light th' Hiftoric page ?
Who wakes th' inrapt Mæonian fong ?
Who prompts the univerfal tongue ?
The world's great guardian, genius, god ?
The Man of fpoil, the Man of blood.   480
Cæfar, the butcher of mankind,
Loads with his praife each paffing wind ;
The general thief, adulterer, brute ;
His boaft to murder, wafte, pollute ;
Dread rival of Apollyon's fame ;   485
His labours, arts, and praife, the fame.
What moft the heart with vice defiles ;
Of worth difrobes ; of heaven beguiles ?
What bids in ftorms the paffions roll ;
Configns to appetite the foul ;   490
Bids Pride afcend th' ETERNAL's throne,
And claim the univerfe, her own ;
Ambition's vulture-wing expands,
Borne, hungry, keen, o'er fuffering lands ;
The wide world talon'd to his fway,   495
A field of death, and food, and prey ?
What lights, for fell Revenge, the pyre
Of Malice heats the quenchlefs fire ;
And lifts Affaffination's knife
Againft a friend's, or parent's, life ?   500
What ftretches Avarice' gulphy maw,
And opens wide her fhark-tooth'd jaw,
Both India's bowels to devour,
To drink the fea, and gorge the fhore ;
Calls forth, in viper paths, Difguife,   505
And points her thoufand tongues with lies ;
Bold, bronzy Fraud invefts in mail,
And clips his weights, and lops his fcale ;

For Honour's houfe digs Forgery's mine,
And guilds his green, impoifoning coin ;   510
Breaks tyger Rapine's iron cage,
And fends him loofe, to roam, and rage ;
Extortion roufes, from his lair,
The cote t' o'erleap, the flock to tear,
To make the fencelefs poor his food,   515
And eat their flefh, and drink their blood ?
What fires, to phrenzy, Lewdnefs' veins ;
Throws on Adultery's neck the reins ;
Gives high-fed Rape at large to fly,
And makes the world a general ftye ;   520
Peoples a realm with fots, and fwine,
And bids men live, to drink, and dine ;
Tempts burrow'd Atheifm abroad,
To infuriate man, to hifs at God,
To burft each moral bond divine,   525
And nature's magic links disjoin,
The fenfe of common good erafe,
Th' etherial ftamp of HEAVEN deface,
Dog gentle peace, bait generous worth,
Haunt juftice, truth, and law, from earth,   530
And bid in hell's fubjeҫted fire,
Religion's fky built fane expire ?

  What licks the final dregs of joy,
And leaves th' inverted veffel dry ;
Makes earth, of virtue befom'd clean,   535
The cage of every beaft obfcene ;
A ruin'd dome, whofe walls around
The hollow moan of death refound ;
An Afric fand ; a Greenland fhore ;
Where life and comfort fpring no more ;   540
An image dark and drear of hell ;
Where fiends, invok'd familiar dwell ;
Where loft immortals Angels weep ;
Where curfes wake, and bleffings fleep ;

And God, the rebels forc'd t' abhor,   545
Repents his marr'd creation ? War.

    Say, Child of Nature! does thy tear
Start, as thy pain'd eye wanders here?
Thy cheek with manly bluſhes burn?
Thy wonted praiſe to curſes turn?   550
Thy boſom waſte with cankering woe?
And thy heart heave th' indignant throe?

    Go then, ah go! whate'er thy lot;
Be thine the palace, or the cot,
To wield the rod, the yoke to bear,   555
A million, or a crown, to ſhare,
The ſenate's guided hand to ſway,
Or bid the little flock obey,
Go, ere thy heart be chang'd to ſtone,
Or ear find muſic in a groan,   560
Or gold the gates of pity bar,
Hate, curſe, oppoſe, Tartarean war.
Diſdain, deſpiſe, with horror name,
And give to never-dying ſhame,
The King, that thron'd for human good,   565
Conſigns his realm to waſte, and blood;
Senates, that, form'd for general weal,
Sanction the dread decree to kill;
Stateſmen, to tygers chang'd by power,
That ſmile, and feaſt on human gore,   570
And chiefs, that havoc love to ſpread,
And pluck their wreaths from fields of dead.

    But round thee gentle peace diffuſe,
Her morning ſmiles, and evening dews;
Thy ſons with love of peace inform;   575
Their hearts with ſweet affections warm;
Bid them pernicious ſtrife abhor,
And liſp the infant curſe on war.

             K

Far round thee light the genial fire;
Thy neighbours, and thy friends, infpire: 580
United, lift the ardent prayer,
That GOD thy ruin'd race may fpare,
Wake in their hearts affections mild,
Sweet femblance of the meekly child,
MESSIAH's peaceful fway extend,   585
Bid kings, and chiefs, to virtue bend,
Protract of life the little fpan,
And change the reafoning wolf to man.

   And O thou Sage, by Learning taught,
With wifdom and with virtue fraught,   590
Whofe foul the breath of HEAVEN informs;
Whofe heart MESSIAH's fpirit warms;
Sleep, fleep no more. For fuffering men,
Awake thy voice; aroufe thy pen;
The caufe of peace and kindnefs plead;   595
For mifery let thy bofom bleed;
To endlefs hate and fhame confign
The tyger thron'd, the titled fwine;
The charm of threefcore centuries break,
And bid the torpid flumberer wake;   600
Burft with new found the adder's ear,
And make th' infenfate marble hear,
His intereft know, his end difcern,
And o'er his flaughter'd kindred yearn,
Feel the unmeafur'd curfe of war,   605
And all her crimfon fiends abhor:
Tread where th' impaffion'd faviour trode,
And earth fhall hail thee, Child of God.*

   Go too, thou ardent Hero! go,
Frefh from fields of war, and woe,   610

* Allufion to Mat. 5. ix.

From thy proud, triumphal car,
Glittering with the fpoils of war,
While thy wheels majeftic roll
Onward to th' immortal goal;
While thy arms with lightning blaze ; 615
While extatic millions gaze ;
Shouts to heaven thy triumphs wing,
And imagin'd angels fing ;
Leffening in th' immenfe parade,
All preceding glories fade, 620
Cæfar's changing ftar retires,
And eclips'd are Marlborough's fires ;
Caft around thee fearching eyes,
Mark thy fplendours, whence they rife !
See, on fields, with corfes fpread, 625
Thine exulting courfers tread !
See, thy car, with garlands proud,
Rolls thro' ftreams of human blood !
Blood from kindred bofoms pour'd !
Brothers by a brother gor'd ! 630
Forth, from Adam's veins, the ftream,
Living, ran through thee and them.

Mark ! around thy wandering eye,
Wafted fields of culture lie,
Late with plenteous harvefts crown'd, 635
Now in gulphs of ruin drown'd.
There the HEAVENS their bounty fhower'd ;
Seafons there their bleffings pour'd ;
Health and comfort, clothes and food ;
Where is now the boundlefs good ? 640

See yon flames thro' ether bend !
See th' immenfe of fmoke afcend !
Loft, afham'd, the fky retires,
And the fun withdraws his fires.

Cities there in ruin lie ,   645
Towns and villages of joy ;
Temples, where, to virtue given,
Man was form'd for life, and Heaven ;
Domes of pomp, and feats of blifs
Manfions fanctified to peace ;   650
Cots, where harmlefs houfholds dwelt,
And each foft emotion felt ;
Sportive play'd the wanton child,
And white Age look'd on, and fmil'd :
Streets, were cheerful Bufinefs reign'd,   655
Shops, where Toil his houfe fuftain'd ;
Humble wifhes fought, and found
Life, with peace and comfort crown'd.
Where are now the manfions dear ?
Scatter'd in the realms of air.   660
Where are now the happy trains ?
Weltering on the bloody plains.
Ruin'd walls deface the ground ;
Silence broods the domes around ;
Ravens flutter o'er the tomb,   665
Vultures fcream, and tygers roam.

    To the margin of the deep
Bid thy wheels of grandeur fweep.
See th' imperial fail, unfurl'd,
Wave triumphant o'er the world ;   670
Rows of fleeping cannon join'd ;
Streamers glorying on the wind !

    Lo ! the proudly-fwelling gales,
Springing, fill the wanton fails ;
Marfhal'd in fublime array,   675
Winds the fleet its lordly way ;
Ocean greets the awful train,
And expands his glaffy plain.

See the private barks of prey,
Steal behind their creeping way ;   680
Arm'd, with piracy to fpoil
Hard-earn'd fruits of honeft toil ;
By the voice of Law let loofe,
Death and beggary to diffufe ;
With the dye of endlefs fhame   685
Blackening man's unhappy name !

    Thron'd upon th' imperial ftern,
Death's unfinifh'd Form difcern !
Sooty clouds his limbs inclofe ;
Thorns his myftic crown compofe ;   690
In his hand, th' uplifted dart
Haftens to transfix the heart ;
From his fcythe, with lurid gleam,
Pale fulphureous lightnings ftream.

    Hark, his hollow voice refounds,   695
O'er the world's unmeafur'd bounds !
Ocean quakes, thro' all his waves ;
Earth remurmurs, from her caves.

    " Ceafe, fond man ! thy claims refign ;
Earth, with all her realms, is mine.   700
Thron'd with all-fubduing fway,
Here I bid the world obey.
Mine, thefe engines ocean brave ;
Mine, thefe crimfon ftreamers wave ;
Mine, the winds to waft them blow ;   705
Mine, the purple deep below.
O'er the fea, from fky to fky,
Mortals, wing'd by terror, fly :
Here, to fartheft eve, and morn,
Death's refiftlefs arms are borne ;   710
Floating hofts behind you pour ;
Hark ! purfuing thunders roar.

See your cities wrapp'd in fire!
See your sons, and sires, expire!
Infants, recent from the womb,   715
Virgins, matrons, croud the tomb!
Seas divided regions join:
All the watery world is mine."

" I ordain the crimson day;
I the embattled hosts array;   720
Sound the trumpet, beat the alarm,
And the heart with vengeance arm.
I the ruddy standard spread,
Pile the groaning fields with dead,
Light the whelming flame, and sweep   725
Every blessing to the deep.

" Man, delighting to destroy,
Hating peace, and shunning joy,
Man, who feels his life too long,
Child of madness, child of wrong,   730
Man, obsequious to my will,
Loves the glorious work of ill,
Cuts off half his brother's years,
Swells my darling stream of tears,
Bids destruction round him flow,   735
Feasting sweet on human woe."

" Who so great a king as I?
My pavilion is the sky;
Earth my realm, my throne the air;
Winds my coursers; clouds my car: 740
Suns but light me to my prey;
Midnight veils my secret way:
O'er expiring worlds I ride;
Dearth and Plague, before me stride:
Storms, my besom, sweep the wave,   745
And with thousands fill the grave;

Chiefs and kings, my fervants, toil,
Butcher hofts, and countries fpoil :
Mortals every claim refign ;
Earth, air, ocean, all are mine."

750

Why, triumphant Hero ! why
Stares thy wild and tearlefs eye ?
Whence thy pale and fpectred brow ?
Palfied limbs ? and fighs of woe ?
Has the gloomy monarch's dart
Pierc'd with agony thy heart ?
Or has human mifery riven ?
Or the advancing curfe of HEAVEN ?

755

Thou haft fhorten'd life's fhort fpan ;
Thou haft emptied earth, of man ?
Breafts unnumber'd rack'd with fears ;
Eyes unnumber'd drown'd in tears ;
Bidden countlefs trains expire ;
Countlefs cities funk in fire ;
Countlefs hearts with mourning riven ;
Countlefs fouls fhut out of heaven.

760

765

Art thou Atheift ? Spare the fpan,
Kinder Chance allows to man.
Shallow is his cup of blifs ;
Make not, then, the portion lefs :
Grudge not foes a boon fo fmall ;
Spare, oh fpare the little all !

770

But, if rais'd from mole to man,
Thou canft nobler objects fcan,
Lift thy curtain'd eyes abroad,
And difcern the prefent GOD ;
If MESSIAH's folar ray
Through thy night has pierc'd it's way,
And, fubliming fenfe to thought,
Has eternal wonders wrought ;

775

780

Think, oh think, the crimfon tide
Pours from thofe, for whom he died!
He the millions bled to fave,
Thou haft hurried to the grave.
He compels, with dread command,   785
Every heart, and every hand,
Man to clothe, fuftain with food,
And to blefs with every good;
But, obdurate to his call,
Thou haft flain, and robb'd of all.   790

    Think how precious is the hour,
Given, the wanderer to reftore.
Think, the heart fhall ever find
Pity from the ETERNAL MIND,
That has learn'd for man to glow,   795
Smile with joy, and weep with woe,
Give the weary outcaft reft,
Draw the barb from Sorrow's breaft,
And (the fole, alchymic ftone)
Make a brother's weal it's own: 800
While th' unfeeling wretch fhall meet
Vengeance at his MAKER's feet.

    But thy heart, with ill uncloy'd,
Woe has fpread, and peace deftroy'd,
HEAVEN's delightful work undone,   805
And the tafk of Hell begun.
Orphans' cries thy car purfue;
Parents' tears thy path bedew;
Widows' fhrieks thy mufic drown;
Cyprefs wreaths inveft thy crown;   810
Spoils in all thy fplendours glow;
Nurs'd with blood, thy laurels grow;
On the bones of flaughter'd bands
See! thy arch triumphal ftands.

Lo ! in yonder, verging ſkies,   795
Myriad troops of ſpeƈtres riſe ;
Spirits of a diſtant world :
By thy arm to ruin hurl'd.
Briſtling ſtands their bloody hair ;
On thee gleams their angry ſtare ;   800
In pale clouds approaching, ſee
Every finger points at thee !
" Thou," they feebly murmuring cry,
" Thou haſt drunk our cup of joy ;
Ere the mortal race was run,   805
Quench'd in blood our noon-day ſun ;
Halv'd the hour, by Mercy given,
To prepare for life, and heaven ;
And, with all our guilt unpaid,
Plung'd us to the untimely dead."   810

Fainting Hero ! pangs unknown
Break, and break, thy heart of ſtone ;
Short, and ſhorter, pants thy breath,
And thine eye-balls ſwim in death ;
Death thy brow has whiten'd o'er ;   815
Thou art fallen, to riſe no more.

END OF THE THIRD PART.

GREENFIELD HILL:

A

POEM.

THE Pequods *inhabited the branches of the Thames, which empties itself into the Sound, at New London. This nation, from the first settlement of the English Colonists, regarded them with jealousy; and attempted to engage the neighbouring tribes in a combination against them. Several of those tribes were, however, more jealous of the Pequods, than of the English, and rejected their solicitations Not discouraged by these disappointments, they resolved to attempt the destruction of the English, with the strength of their own tribes only; and cruelly assassinated Captains Stone, Norton, and Oldham, as they were trading peaceably in their neighbourhood. The English demanded the murderers; but were answered with disdain, and insult. Upon this, Captain Mason was dispatched into their country with a body of troops; and attacking one of their principal forts, destroyed it, together with a large number of their warriors. The rest of the nation fled. A large body of them came to a swamp, three miles westward of Fairfield. One of their number loitering behind the rest, was discovered by the English troops, then commanded by Captain Stoughton, of the Massachusetts; and was compelled to disclose their retreat. One hundred of them, it is said, surrendered. The rest, bravely resolving to live and die together, were attacked, and chiefly destroyed.* On this piece of History, the following part of the Poem is founded. It is introduced by reflections on the changes, wrought in the world by time. Ancient Empires. Great Britain. America. Story related, with reflections on the savages. Conclusion.*

* See Neale's Hist. N. Eng. and Morse's Geog.

GREENFIELD HILL.

PART IV.

THE DESTRUCTION OF THE PEQUODS.

AH me! while up the long, long vale of time,
Reflection wanders towards th' eternal vaſt,
How ſtarts the eye, at many a change ſublime,
Unboſom'd dimly by the ages paſs'd!
What Mauſoleums crowd the mournful waſte!   5
The tombs of empires fallen! and nations gone!
Each, once inſcrib'd, in gold, with "AYE TO LAST"
Sate as a queen; proclaim'd the world her own,
And proudly cried, "By me no ſorrows ſhall be known."

Soon fleets the ſunbright Form, by man ador'd.   10
Soon fell the Head of gold, to Time a prey;
The Arms, the Trunk, his cankering tooth devour'd;
And whirlwinds blew the Iron duſt away.
Where dwelt imperial Timur?—far aſtray,
Some lonely-muſing pilgrim now enquires: 15
And, rack'd by ſtorms, and haſtening to decay,
Mohammed's Moſque foreſees it's final fires;
And Rome's more lordly Temple day by day expires,

As o'er proud Afian realms the traveller winds,
His manly fpirit, hufh'd by terror, falls;   20
When fome deceafed town's loft fite he finds,
Where ruin wild his pondering eye appals;
Where filence fwims along the moulder'd walls,
And broods upon departed Grandeur's tomb.
Through the lone, hollow aifles fad Echo calls,   25
At each flow ftep; deep fighs the breathing gloom,
And weeping fields, around, bewail their Emprefs' doom.

Where o'er an hundred realms, the throne uprofe,
The fcreech-owl nefts, the panther builds his home;
Sleep the dull newts, the lazy adders doze,   30
Where pomp and luxury danc'd the golden room.
Low lies in duft the fky-refembled dome;
Tall grafs around the broken column waves;
And brambles climb, and lonely thiftles bloom:
The moulder'd arch the weedy ftreamlet laves,
And low refound, beneath, unnumber'd funken graves.

Soon fleets the fun-bright Form, by man ador'd;
And foon man's dæmon chiefs from memory fade.
In mufty volume, now muft be explor'd,
Where dwelt imperial nations, long decay'd.   40
The brighteft meteors angry clouds invade;
And where the wonders glitter'd, none explain.
Where Carthage, with proud hand, the trident fway'd,
Now mud-wall'd cots fit fullen on the plain,
And wandering, fierce, and wild, fequefter'd Arabs reign. 45

In thee, O Albion! queen of nations, live
Whatever fplendours earth's wide realms have known;
In thee proud Perfia fees her pomp revive;
And Greece her arts, and Rome her lordly throne:
By every wind, thy Tyrian fleets are blown;   50
Supreme, on Fame's dread roll, thy heroes ftand;
All ocean's realms thy naval fcepter own;

Of bards, of fages, how auguft thy band!
And one rich Eden blooms around thy garden'd land.

But O how vaft thy crimes! Through heaven's great year, 55
When few centurial funs have trac'd their way;
When fouthern Europe, worn by feuds fevere;
Weak, doating, fallen, has bow'd to Ruffian fway;
And fetting Glory beam'd her farewell ray;
To waftes, perchance, thy brilliant fields fhall turn; 60
In duft, thy temples, towers, and towns decay;
The foreft howl, where London's turrets burn;
And all thy garlands deck thy fad, funereal urn.

Some land, fcarce glimmering in the light of fame,
Scepter'd with arts, and arms (if I divine) 65
Some unknown wild, fome fhore without a name,
In all thy pomp, fhall then majeftic fhine.
As filver-headed Time's flow years decline,
Not ruins only meet th' enquiring eye:
Where round yon mouldering oak vain brambles twine, 70
The filial ftem, already towering high,
Erelong fhall ftretch his arms, and nod in yonder fky.

Where late refounded the wild, woodland roar,
Now heaves the palace, now the temple fmiles;
Where frown'd the rude rock, and the defert fhore, 75
Now pleafure fports, and bufinefs want beguiles,
And Commerce wings her flight to thoufand ifles;
Culture walks forth; gay laugh the loaded fields;
And jocund Labour plays his harmlefs wiles;
Glad Science brightens; Art her manfion builds; 80
And Peace uplifts her wand, and HEAVEN his blefling yields.

O'er thefe fweet fields, fo lovely now, and gay,
Where modeft Nature finds each want fupplied,
Where home-born Happinefs delights to play,
And counts her little flock, with houfhold pride, 85
Long frown'd, from age to age, a foreft wide:

Here hung the flumbering bat ; the ferpent dire
Nefted his brood, and drank th' impoifon'd tide ;
Wolves peal'd, the dark, drear night, in hideous choir ;
Nor fhrnuk th' unmeafur'd howl from Sol's terrific fire. 90

No charming cot imbank'd the pebbly ftream ;
No manfion tower'd, nor garden teem'd with good ;
No lawn expanded to the April beam ;
Nor mellow harveft hung it's bending load ;
Nor fcience dawn'd ; nor life with beauty glow'd ;   95
Nor temple whiten'd, in th' enchanting dell ;
In clufters wild, the fluggifh wigwam ftood ;
And, borne in fnaky paths the Indian fell
Now aim'd the death unfeen, now fcream'd the tyger-yell.

Even now, perhaps, on human duft I tread,   100
Pondering, with folemn paufe, the wrecks of time ;
Here fleeps, perchance, among the vulgar dead,
Some Chief, the lofty theme of Indian rhyme,
Who lov'd Ambition's cloudy fteep to climb,
And fmil'd, deaths, dangers, rivals, to engage ;   105
Who rous'd his followers' fouls to deeds fublime,
Kindling to furnace heat vindictive rage,
And foar'd Cæfarean heights, the Phœnix of his age.

In yon fmall field, that dimly fteals from fight,
(From yon fmall field thefe meditations grow)   110
Turning the fluggifh foil, from morn to night,
The plodding hind, laborious, drives his plough,
Nor dreams, a nation fleeps, his foot below.
There, undifturbed by the roaring wave,
Releas'd from war, and far from deadly foe,   115
Lies down, in endlefs reft, a nation brave,
And trains, in tempefts born, there find a quiet grave.

Oft have I heard the tale, when matron fere
Sung to my infant ear the fong of woe ;

Of maiden meek, confum'd with pining care,   120
Around whofe tomb the wild-rofe lov'd to blow :
Or told, with fwimming eyes, how, long ago,
Remorfelefs Indians, all in midnight dire,
The little, fleeping village, did o'erthrow,
Bidding the cruel flames to heaven afpire,   125
And fcalp'd the hoary head, and burn'd the babe with fire.

Then, fancy-fir'd, her memory wing'd it's flight,
To long-forgotten wars, and dread alarms,
To chiefs obfcure, but terrible in fight,
Who mock'd each foe, and laugh'd at deadlieft harms, 130
Sydneys in zeal, and Wafhingtons in arms.
By inftinct tender to the woes of man,
My heart bewildering with fweet pity's charms,
Thro' folemn fcenes, with Nature's ftep, fhe ran,
And hufh'd her audience fmall, and thus the tale began. 135

" Thro' verdant banks where Thames's branches glide,
Long held the Pequods an extenfive fway ;
Bold, favage, fierce, of arms the glorious pride,
And bidding all the circling realms obey.
Jealous, they faw the tribes, beyond the fea,   140
Plant in their climes ; and towns, and cities, rife ;
Afcending caftles foreign flags difplay ;
Myfterious art new fcenes of life devife ;
And fteeds infult the plains, and cannon rend the fkies."

" They faw, and foon the ftrangers' fate decreed,   145
And foon of war difclos'd the crimfon fign ;
Firft, haplefs Stone ! they bade thy bofom bleed,
A guiltlefs offering at th' infernal fhrine :
Then, gallant Norton ! the hard fate was thine,
By ruffians butcher'd, and denied a grave :   150
Thee, generous Oldham ! next the doom malign
Arrefted ; nor could all thy courage fave ;
Forfaken, plunder'd, cleft, and buried in the wave."

M

" Soon the sad tidings reach'd the general ear;
And prudence, pity, vengeance, all inspire :   155
Invasive war their gallant friends prepare ;
And soon a noble band, with purpose dire,
And threatening arms, the murderous fiends require :
Small was the band, but never taught to yield ;
Breasts fac'd with steel, and souls instinct with fire :   160
Such souls, from Sparta, Persia's world repell'd,
When nations pav'd the ground, and Xerxes flew the field."

" The rising clouds the Savage Chief descried,
And, round the forest, bade his heroes arm ;
To arms the painted warriors proudly hied,   165
And through surrounding nations rung the' alarm.
The nations heard ; but smil'd, to see the storm,
With ruin fraught, o'er Pequod mountains driven ;
And felt infernal joy the bosom warm,
To see their light hang o'er the skirts of even,   170
And other suns arise, to gild a kinder heaven."

" Swift to the Pequod fortress Mason sped,
Far in the wildering wood's impervious gloom ;
A lonely castle, brown with twilight dread ;
Where oft th' embowel'd captive met his doom,   175
And frequent heav'd, around the hollow tomb ;
Scalps hung in rows, and whitening bones were strew'd ;
Where, round the broiling babe, fresh from the womb,
With howls the Powaw fill'd the dark abode,   180
And screams, and midnight prayers, invok'd the Evil god."

" There too, with awful rites, the hoary priest,
Without, beside the moss-grown altar, stood,
His sable form in magic cincture dress'd,
And heap'd the mingled offering to his god,
What time, with golden light, calm evening glow'd.   185
The mystic dust, the flower of silver bloom,
And spicy herb, his hand in order strew'd ;

Bright rofe the curling flame ; and rich perfume
On fmoky wings upflew, or fettled round the tomb."

" Then, o'er the circus, danc'd the maddening throng, 190
As erft the Thyas roam'd dread Nyfa round,
And ftruck, to foreft notes, th' ecftatic fong,
While flow, beneath them, heav'd the wavy ground.
With a low, lingering groan, of dying found,
The woodland rumbled; murmur'd deep each ftream ; 195
Shrill fung the leaves ; all ether figh'd profound ;
Pale tufts of purple topp'd the filver flame,
And many-colour'd Forms on evening breezes came."

" Thin, twilight Forms ; attir'd in changing fheen
Of plumes, high-tinctur'd in the weftern ray ; 200
Bending, they peep'd the fleecy folds between,
Their wings light-ruftling in the breath of May.
Soft-hovering round the fire, in myftic play,
They fnuff'd the incenfe, wav'd in clouds afar,
Then, filent, floated toward the fetting day : 205
Eve redden'd each fine form, each mifty car ;
And through them faintly gleam'd, at times, the Weftern ftar."

" Then (fo tradition fings), the train behind,
In plumy zones of rainbow'd beauty drefs'd,
Rode the Great Spirit, in th' obedient wind, 210
In yellow clouds flow-failing from the weft.
With dawning fmiles, the God his votaries blefs'd,
And taught where deer retir'd to ivy dell ;
What chofen chief with proud command to' inveft ;
Where crept th' approaching foe, with purpofe fell, 215
And where to wind the fcout, and war's dark ftorm difpel."

" There, on her lover's tomb, in filence laid,
While ftill, and forrowing, fhower'd the moon's pale beam,
At times, expectant, flept the widow'd maid,
Her foul far-wandering on the fylph-wing'd dream. 220
Wafted from evening fkies, on funny ftream,

Her darling Youth with filver pinions fhone;
With voice of mufic, tun'd to fweeteft theme,
He told of fhell-bright bowers, beyond the fun,
Where years of endlefs joy o'er Indian lovers run." 225

" But now no awful rites, nor potent fpell,
To filence charm'd the peals of coming war;
Or told the dread receffes of the dell,
Where glowing Mafon led his bands from far:
No fpirit, buoyant on his airy car, 230
Controul'd the whirlwind of invading fight:
Deep died in blood, dun evening's falling ftar
Sent fad, o'er weftern hills, it's parting light,
And no returning morn difpers'd the long, dark night."

" On the drear walls a fudden fplendour glow'd, 235
There Mafon fhone, and there his veterans pour'd.
Anew the Hero claim'd the fiends of blood,
While anfwering ftorms of arrows round him fhower'd,
And the war-fcream the ear with anguifh gor'd.
Alone, he burft the gate: the foreft round 240
Re-echoed death; the peal of onfet roar'd;
In rufh'd the fquadrons; earth in blood was drown'd;
And gloomy fpirits fled, and corfes hid the ground."

Not long in dubious fight the hoft had ftriven,
When, kindled by the mufket's potent flame, 245
In clouds, and fire, the caftle rofe to heaven,
And gloom'd the world, with melancholy beam.
Then hoarfer groans, with deeper anguifh, came;
And fiercer fight the keen affault repell'd:
Nor even thefe ills the favage breaft could tame; 250
Like hell's deep caves, the hideous region yell'd,
'Till death, and fweeping fire, laid wafte the hoftile field."

" Soon the fad tale their friends furviving heard;
And Mafon, Mafon, rung in every wind;

Quick from their rugged wilds they difappear'd, 255
Howl'd down the hills, and left the blaft behind.
Their faftening foes, by generous Stoughton join'd,
Hung o'er the rear, and every brake explor'd;
But fuch dire terror feiz'd the favage mind,
So fwift and black a ftorm behind them lowr'd, 260
On wings of raging fear, thro' fpacious realms they fcowr'd."

(O thou, to earth the fecond bleffing given,
Of heart divine, of afpect angel-fweet,
O meek Religion! fecond-born of Heaven,
Cloth'd with the fun, the world beneath thy feet! 265
Softer than lambs on yonder hillocks bleat,
Thy mufic charms to kindnefs favage man,
Since firft, from Calvary's height, with love replete,
Thy wondrous courfe, in funny fheen, began,
And, o'er the death-ftruck globe, thro' ftartled nations ran. 170

When pride and wrath awake the world to arms,
How heaves thy fnowy breaft with fainting throe!
While luft and rapine trumpet death's alarms,
And men 'gainft men with fiery vengeance glow.
In Europe oft, that land of war, and woe, 275
As her fad fteps the lingering mourner draws,
How flowly did thy feet entangled go,
Chain'd by vile tefts, and prifon'd round by laws;
While bigotry and rage in blood infteep'd thy caufe!

When o'er th' Atlantic wild, by Angels borne, 280
Thy pilgrim barque explor'd it's weftern way,
With fpring and beauty bloom'd the wafte forlorn,
And night and chaos fhrunk from new-born day.
Dumb was the favage howl; th' inftinctive lay
Wav'd, with ftrange warblings, thro' the woodland's bound; 285
The village fmil'd; the temple's golden ray
Shot high to heaven; fair culture clothed the ground;
Art bloffom'd; cities fprang; and fails the ocean crown'd.

As on heaven's facred hill, of hills the queen,
At thy command, contention foul fhall ceafe,   290
Thy folar afpect, every ftorm ferene,
And fmooth the rugged wild of man to peace;
So here thy voice (fair earneft of the blifs!)
Transform'd the favage to the meekly child.
Hell faw, with pangs, her hideous realm decreafe;   295
Wolves play'd with lambs; the tyger's heart grew mild;
And on his own bright work the GODHEAD, look'd and fmil'd.

Hail Elliot! Mayhew hail! by HEAVEN inform'd
With that pure love, which clafps the human kind;
To virtue's path even Indian feet you charm'd,   300
And lit, with wifdom's beam, the dufky mind:
From torture, blood, and treachery, refin'd,
The new-born convert lifp'd MESSIAH's name.
Mid Choirs complacent, in pure rapture join'd,
Your praife refounds, on yonder ftarry frame,   305
While fouls, redeem'd from death, their earthly faviours claim.

Oh had the fame bright fpirit ever reign'd;
Nor trader villains foul'd the Savage mind;
Nor Avarice pin'd for boundlefs breadth of land;
Nor, with flow death, the wretches been confign'd   310
To India's curfe, that poifons half mankind!
Then, O divine Religion! torture's blaze
Lefs frequent round thy tender heart had twin'd;
On the wild wigwam peace had caft it's rays,
And the tremendous whoop had chang'd to hymns of praife. 315

Fierce, dark, and jealous, is the exotic foul,
That, cell'd in fecret, rules the favage breaft.
There treacherous thoughts of gloomy vengeance roll,
And deadly deeds of malice unconfefs'd;
The viper's poifon rankling in it's neft.   320
Behind his tree, each Indian aims unfeen:
No fweet oblivion foothes the hate imprefs'd:

Years fleet in vain: in vain realms intervene :
The victim's blood alone can quench the flames within.

Their knives the tawny tribes in flaughter fteep,　　325
When men, miftruftlefs, think them diftant far ;
And, when blank midnight fhrouds the world in fleep,
The murderous yell announces firft the war.
In vain fweet fmiles compel the fiends to fpare ;
Th' unpitied victim fcreams, in tortures dire ;　　330
The life-blood ftains the virgin's bofom bare ;
Cherubic infants, limb by limb expire ;
And filver'd Age finks down in flowly-curling fire.

Yet favages are men.　With glowing heat,
Fix'd as their hatred, friendfhip fills their mind ;　　335
By acts with juftice, and with truth, replete,
Their iron breafts to foftnefs are inclin'd.
But when could War of converts boaft refin'd ?
Or when Revenge to peace and fweetnefs move ?
His heart, man yields alone to actions kind ;　　340
His faith, to creeds, whofe foundnefs virtues prove,
Thawn in the April fun, and opening ftill to love.

Senate auguft ! that fway'ft Columbian climes,
Form'd of the wife, the noble, and humane,
Caft back the glance through long-afcending times,　　245
And think what nations fill'd the weftern plain.
Where are they now ? What thoughts the bofom pain,
From mild Religion's eye how ftreams the tear,
To fee fo far outfpread the wafte of man,
And afk "How fell the myriads, HEAVEN plac'd here !"　350
Reflect, be juft, and feel for Indian woes fevere.

But ceafe, foul Calumny ! with footy tongue,
No more the glory of our fires belie.
They felt, and they redrefs'd, each nation's wrong ;
Even Pequod foes they view'd with generous eye ,　　355
And, pierc'd with injuries keen, that Virtue try,

The favage faith, and friendfhip, ftrove to gain:
And, had no bafe Canadian fiends been nigh,
Even now foft Peace had fmil'd on every plain,
And tawny nations liv'd, and own'd MESSIAH's reign.) 360

" Amid a circling marfh, expanded wide,
To a lone hill the Pequods wound their way;
And none, but Heaven, the manfion had defcried,
Clofe-tangled, wild, impervious to the day ;
But one poor wanderer, loitering long aftray.   365
Wilder'd in labyrinths of pathlefs wood,
In a tall tree embower'd, obfcurely lay :
Strait fummon'd down, the trembling fuppliant fhow'd
Where lurk'd his vanifh'd friends, within their drear abode."

" To death, the murderers were anew requir'd,   370
A pardon proffer'd, and a peace affur'd ;
And, though with vengeful heat their foes were fir'd,
Their lives, their freedom, and their lands, fecur'd.
Some yielding heard.   In faftnefs ftrong immur'd,
The reft the terms refus'd, with brave difdain,   375
Near, and more near, the peaceful Herald lur'd ;
Then bade a fhower of arrows round him rain,
And wing'd him fwift, from danger, to the diftant plain."

" Through the fole, narrow way, to vengeance led,
To final fight our generous heroes drew ;   380
And Stoughton now had pafs'd the moor's black fhade,
When hell's terrific region fcream'd anew.
Undaunted, on their foes they fiercely flew ;
As fierce, the dufky warriors crowd the fight ;
Defpair infpires ; to combat's face they glue ;   185
With groans, and fhouts, they rage, unknowing flight,
And clofe their fullen eyes, in fhades of endlefs night."

Indulge, my native land ! indulge the tear,
That fteals, impaffion'd, o'er a nation's doom :

To me each twig, from Adam's ſtock, is near, 390
And ſorrows fall upon an Indian's tomb.
And, O ye Chiefs! in yonder ſtarry home,
Accept the humble tribute of this rhyme.
Your gallant deeds, in Greece, or haughty Rome,
By Maro ſung, or Homer's harp ſublime, 395
Had charm'd the world's wide round, and triumph'd over time.

END OF THE FOURTH PART.

GREENFIELD HILL:

A

POEM.

THE ARGUMENT.

SUBJECT introduced. Description of a happy village in New England. Character of the Clergyman. He gives his last advice, and blessing, to his Parishioners—recites his past, affectionate and faithful labours for their salvation, and proposes to close them with his last exhortation—estimates the pleasures of sin, and the value of the present life, and urges them to seek eternal life—informs them, that two endless journeys lie before them—of virtue, which guides to happiness; and of sin, which terminates in misery—and describes the nature of both. As means of salvation, he exhorts them to read the Bible, with diligence and care; to frequent public worship; to establish family religion, in their houses; religiously to educate their children; and to abound in all the duties of charity. He further informs them, that all things are labouring to promote this great purpose; recites to them the affectionate invitations of the Redeemer; and represents his own future happiness, as increased by their salvation. Conclusion.

GREENFIELD HILL.

PART V.

THE CLERGYMAN's ADVICE TO THE VILLAGERS.

—————

WHILE thus, from winter's tranſient death,
The world revives to life, and breath ;
While round me all your bleſſings riſe,
And peace, and plenty, greet my eyes ;
Ah ſay ! ye children of my care,   5
Of every wiſh, of every prayer,
Ordain'd my ſacred charge below,
The ſource of joy, the ſource of woe,
Say, ſhall my heart on landſchapes muſe,
And ſcenes of nobler kind refuſe ;   10
Alone for hapleſs Indians feel ;
Forget, in others woes, your weal,
Unmov'd, behold your footſteps roam,
Nor guide the wayward pilgrim home ?
No, let the moral ſong prevail;   15
Liſt, liſt, to truth's perſuaſive tale.
While Heaven, by hoary Wiſdom ſung,
Inſpires my heart, and tunes my tongue,

Oh hear, and from perdition rife,
And point your pathway to the fkies !　　　　20

　Where weftern Albion's happy clime
Still brightens to the eye of time,
A village lies.　In all his round,
The fun a fairer never found.
The woods were tall, the hillocks green,　　25
The vallies laugh'd the hills between,
Thro' fairy meads the rivers roll'd,
The meadows flower'd in vernal gold,
The days were bright, the mornings fair,
And evening lov'd to linger there.　　　　30
There, twinn'd in brilliant fields above,
Sweet fifters ! fported Peace and Love ;
While Virtue, like a blufhing bride,
Seren'd, and brighten'd, at their fide.

　At diftance from that happy way,　　　　35
The path of fenfual Pleafure lay,
Afar Ambition's fummit rofe,
And Avarice dug his mine of woes.

　The place, with eaft and weftern fides,
A wide and verdant ftreet divides :　　　40
And here the houfes fac'd the day,
And there the lawns in beauty lay.
There, turret-crown'd, and central, ftood
A neat, and folemn houfe of God.
Acrofs the way, beneath the fhade,　　　45
Two elms with fober filence fpread,
The Preacher liv'd.　O'er all the place
His manfion caft a Sunday grace ;
Dumb ftillnefs fate the fields around ;
His garden feem'd a hallow'd ground ;　　50
Swains ceas'd to laugh aloud, when near,
And fchool-boys never fported there.

In the fame mild, and temperate zone,
Twice twenty years, his courfe had run,
His locks of flowing filver fpread,   55
A crown of glory o'er his head.
His face, the image of his mind,
With grave, and furrow'd wifdom fhin'd;
Not cold; but glowing ftill, and bright;
Yet glowing with October light: 60
As evening blends, with beauteous ray,
Approaching night with fhining day.

His Cure his thoughts engrofs'd alone:
For them his painful courfe was run:
To blefs, to fave, his only care;   65
To chill the guilty foul with fear;
To point the pathway to the fkies,
And teach, and urge, and aid, to rife;
Where ftrait, and difficult to keep,
It climbs, and climbs, o'er Virtue's fteep.   70

As now the evening of his day,
Retiring, fmil'd it's warning ray;
He heard, in angel-whifpers, come,
The welcome voice, that call'd him home.
The little flock he nurs'd fo long,   75
And charm'd with mercy's fweeteft fong,
His heart with ftrong affections warm'd,
His love provok'd, his fears alarm'd—
Like him, who freed the chofen band,
Like him, who op'd the promis'd land,   80
His footfteps verging on the grave,
His blefling thus the Prophet gave.

" O priz'd beyond expreffion here,
As fons belov'd, as daughters dear,
Your Father's dying voice receive,   85
My counfels hear, obey, and live !"

" For you my ceaseless toils ye know,
My care, my faithfulness, and woe.
For you I breath'd unnumber'd prayers ;
For you I shed unnumber'd tears ;   90
To living springs the thirsty led,
The hungry cheer'd with living bread ;
Of grief allay'd the piercing smart,
And sooth'd with balm the doubting heart ;
The wayward flock forbade to roam,   95
And brought the wandering lambkin home."

" And now, my toils, my duties done,
My crown of endless glory won,
Ev'n while, invited to the skies,
My wing begins through heaven to rise,   100
One solemn labour still is due,
To close a life, consum'd for you."

" Say, what the gain ? Oh search, and say!—
To tread the fatal, sensual way ?
To bristle down in pleasure's stye ?   105
To heap up silver, mountains high ?
With guilt to climb, with anguish keep,
Ambition's proud, and painful steep ?
Should earth for your enjoyment roll,
Can earth redeem the deathless soul ?"   110

" This little life, my children ! say,
What is it ? A departing day ;
An April morn, with frost behind ;
A bubble, bursting on the wind ;
A dew, exhal'd beneath the sun ;   115
A tale rehears'd ; a vision gone."

" How oft too, in the bright career,
Which Pride, and Pleasure wanton here,
While Hope expands her painted wing,
And all around is health, and spring ;   120

How oft refounds the awful knell,
That feals to life a long farewell,
" " Thou fool ! diffolv'd in guilt and fenfe,
This night, thy foul is fummon'd hence." "

" Yet on this little life depend　　　　125
Bleffings, and woes, which cannot end.
For Faith and Penitence below,
Immortal life and rapture glow ;
For harden'd guilt, eternal ire,
And waves, that furge unfathom'd fire."　　130

" Then rife from death's benumbing fleep !
See, fpread beneath, the yawning deep !
Oh rife ! and let falvation call
Your time, your thoughts, and talents all."

" Two only paths before you fpread ;　　　135
And long the way, your feet muft tread.
This ftrait, and rough, and narrow, lies
The courfe direct to yonder fkies.
And now o'er hills, on hills, you climb,
Deferted paths, and cliffs fublime ;　　　140
And now thro' folitudes you go,
Thro' vales of care, and ftreams of woe.
Tho' oft you wander fad, forlorn,
The mark of fpite, the butt of fcorn ;
Yet your's the fweets, that cannot cloy,　　145
The Saviour's peace, the Seraph's joy ;
While nurture Heaven itfelf fupplies,
And fruits depend, and fprings arife ;
And Health and Temperance, fifters gay,
Defpife the leffening length of way ;　　　150
And fweet, tho' rare, companions fmile,
Deceive the road, and lofe the toil ;
And Hope ftill points th' approaching goal,
As magnets tremble to the pole."

O

" As now at hand the realm appears,   155
Where pains retire, and cares, and tears,
Then fmooths the rough, the rude refines,
The defert blooms, the fteep declines;
Then bright, and brighter, fpreads the plain,
Where Love begins her vernal reign.   160
And fweet as mufic of the fkies,
When hymns of blefs'd Redemption rife,
Your FATHER's welcome hails you home;
The LAMB, the SPIRIT bid you come;
And all the Family around   165
Salute you to the blifsful ground,
The heirs of life, the fons of God,
And trophies of their SAVIOUR's blood."

" Full wide the other path extends,
And round, and round, ferpentine bends.   170
To fenfe, bewitching flow'rets bloom,
And charm, and cheat, with ftrange perfume;
Fruits hang diffolving poifon nigh,
And purpling death inchants the eye.
Companions, frolickfome and gay,   175
Laugh jocund on the downward way,
With wiles entice a thoughtlefs throng,
And, blinded, lead the blind along,
Where fmooth, and treacherous, and fteep,
It flides, impending, to the deep."   180

" At length, where Death dominion holds,
A wide and gloomy gate unfolds—
Thro' folitudes immenfely fpread,
The mourning manfions of the dead,
A dreary tomb, that knows no bound,   185
A midnight hung eternal round,
Their journey winds—No friend appears
To dry the ftream of endlefs tears.

Sweet Hope, that footh'd their pains before,
Returns to foothe their pains no more.   190
Thro' the long night, the eye looks on,
But meets with no returning fun;
While Peace refigns to blank Defpair,
And light is chang'd to darknefs there."

" Then rife, and let falvation call   195
Your time, your thoughts, your talents all !"

" For this, the facred page explore,
Confult, and ponder, o'er and o'er;
The words of endlefs life difcern;
The way, the means, the motives, learn;   200
The hopes, the promifes, enjoy,
That ne'er deceive, that cannot cloy;
Alarms to Guilt's obdurate mind;
Perennial blifs to Faith affign'd;
The precepts, by MESSIAH given;   205
His life, the image bright of Heaven;
His death, felf-ruin'd man to fave;
His rife, primitial, from the grave;
Beyond all other love, his love;
His name, all other names above.   210
All duties to be learn'd, or done,
All comforts to be gain'd, or known,
To do, to gain, unceafing ftrive,
The book of books explore, and live,"

" When fmiles the Sabbath's genial morn,   215
Inftinctive to the Temple turn;
Your houfholds round you thither bring,
Sweet off'ring to the SAVIOUR KING.
There, on the mercy-feat, he fhines,
Receives our fouls, forgets our fins,   220
And welcomes, with refiftlefs charms,
Submitting rebels to his arms.

That chofen, blefs'd, accepted day
Oh never never caft away !"

    " Let order round your houfes reign,   225
Religion rule, and peace fuftain ;
Each morn, each eve, your prayers arife,
As incenfe fragrant, to the fkies ;
In beauteous groupe, your children join,
And fervants fhare the work divine :   230
The voice, as is the intereft, one,
And one the blefling wreftled down."

    " Each toil devote, each care, and pain,
Your children for the fkies to train.
Allure, reprove, inftruct, reclaim,   235
Alarm, and warn, commend, and blame ;
To virtue force with gentle fway,
And guide, and lead, yourfelves, the way.
Teach them, profanenefs, falfhood, fraud,
Abufe to man, affronts to GOD,   240
All things impure, obfcene, debas'd,
Tho' oft with high examples grac'd,
To fhun beyond the adder's breath,
When hiffing inftantaneous death ;
But juftice, truth, and love, to prize,   245
Beyond the tranfports of the fkies."

    " Teach them, that, brighter than the fun,
Th' All-fearching Eye looks flaming on,
Each thought, each word, each act, defcries,
And fees the guilty motives rife ;   250
A Witnefs, and a Judge, that day,
Whofe light fhall every heart difplay.
Live what you teach—the heavenly SEER,
Who fpake, as man ne'er fpake, when here,
Taught all things juft, and wife, and true,   255
Shone, a divine example too."

" To all, around, your bleſſings lend,
The ſick relieve, the poor befriend,
The ſad conſole, the weak ſuſtain,
And ſoothe the wounded ſpirit's pain.   260
To you, think every bleſſing given,
To ſhed abroad the alms of HEAVEN,
To blunt the ſtings of human woe,
And build his kingdom, here below.
Let gentle Peace around you reign,   265
Her influence ſpread, her cauſe ſuſtain:
To railing, anſwers mild return;
Let love, oppos'd to anger, burn:
Contention, ere begun, ſuppreſs,
And bid the voice of party ceaſe.   270
The taleful tongue, the meddling mind,
The jealous eye, the heart unkind,
Far diſtant, far, from you remove;
But ope your doors to Truth, and Love:
The meek eſteem, the humble praiſe,   275
And Merit from her footſtool raiſe."

" By every act of peace, and love,
Thus win your way to climes above.
In this great work, ſee all things ſtrive!
Nature toils that you may live: 280

" Lo, to aid you to the ſkies,
Seaſons roll, and ſuns ariſe;
Promis'd, ſee the ſeed-time come,
And the harveſt ſhouted home!"

" All things, in their ſolemn round,   285
Morn, with peace and beauty crown'd,
Eve, with ſweet, returning reſt,
Toil, with health and plenty bleſs'd,
Help you on the aſcending road,
Pointing, leading, ſtill to God: 290

Joys to endlefs rapture charm;
Woes, of endlefs woe, alarm."

" All things toil, that you may live——
Rulers peace and freedom give:
Seers diviner peace proclaim,   295
Glorious to th' Unutter'd NAME,
Good, to guilty mortals given,
Source of endlefs joy to heaven."

 " See the Sabbath's peaceful morn,
(Sabbaths ftill for you return),   300
Opes the Temple to your feet,
Chaunting founds of Seraphs fweet——
" Heaven unfolds, and GOD is near,
Sinners hafte, and enter here"——
Grace and truth, from worlds above,   305
Fruits of fuffering, dying love,
From the SACRED SPIRIT come,
Wilder'd flocks inviting home."

" Hark, what living mufic plays!
Catch the themes of heavenly praife;
Themes, that tune feraphic ftrings,   310
Notes, the blefs'd REDEEMER fings."

 " " Rife, my fons, and hither hafte!
Wintry time is overpafs'd.
See afar the rains have flown!
See immortal fpring begun!   315
Streams with life and rapture flow;
Fruits with life and rapture glow;
Love the door of life unbars;
Triumphs crown your finifh'd wars: 320
Fondly wait impatient fkies,
O'er you to renew their joys." "

" " Are you naked? here behold
Robes of light, and crowns of gold!

Famiſh'd ? an eternal feaſt !   325
Weary ? everliving reſt !
Friendleſs ? an ALMIGHTY FRIEND !
Hopeleſs ? tranſports ne'er to end !" "

" " Children, penitents, ariſe ;
Haſten to your native ſkies :   330
Your arrival all things ſing ;
Angels meet you on the wing ;
Saints with fairer beauty ſhine ;
Brighter years in heaven begin ;
Round the SUN, that lights the ſkies,   335
More refulgent glories riſe." "

" Thus, O my ſons ! MESSIAH's voice
Allures to never dying joys.
That voice of endleſs love receive ;
Thoſe counſels hear, obey, and live."   340

" Thus, from the climes beyond the tomb
If GOD permit my ſoul to come,
Again my little flock to view,
To watch, and warn, and quicken you,
With tranſport ſhall my boſom glow,   345
To ſee each houſe an heaven below,
My ſons ambitious of the ſkies,
And future ſaints, and angels riſe.
And O, what brighter bliſs ſhall bloom,
To hail you victors o'er the tomb ;   350
To guide you, all th' unmeaſur'd way,
And welcome to the gates of day ;
To hear your bleſſed Euge ſound,
And ſee th' immortals ſmile around ;
To ſtand, to ſhine, by you confeſs'd   355
Your friend your earthly ſaviour bleſs'd ;
To mingle joys, all joys above,
And warm with ever-bright'ning love !"

He spoke.   The filial tear around,
Responsive, trickled to the sound ;
He saw their hearts to wisdom won,
And felt his final duty done—
" Jesus ! my soul receive"—he cried,
And smil'd, and bow'd his head, and died.

360

END OF THE FIFTH PART.

GREENFIELD HILL:

A

P O E M.

THE ARGUMENT.

INTRODUCTION. Farmer introduced. Villagers af-
fembled. He recommends to them an induftrious and œconomical
life, the careful education and government of their children,
and particularly the eftablifhment of good habits in early life;
enjoins upon them the offices of good neighbourhood, the avoidance
of litigation, and the careful cultivation of parochial harmony.
Conclufion.

GREENFIELD HILL.

P A R T VI.

The FARMER's ADVICE to the VILLAGERS.

Y E children of my fondeſt care,
With tendereſt love, and frequent prayer,
This ſolemn charge, my voice has given,
To prompt, and guide, your ſteps to heaven.
Your preſent welfare now demands   5
A different tribute, from my hands.

  Not long ſince liv'd a Farmer plain,
Intent to gather honeſt gain,
Laborious, prudent, thrifty, neat,
Of judgment ſtrong, experience great,   10
In ſolid homeſpun clad, and tidy,
And with no coxcomb learning giddy.
Daily, to hear his maxims ſound,
Th' approaching neighbours flock'd around ;
Daily they ſaw his counſels prove   15
The ſource of union, peace, and love,
The means of prudence, and of wealth,
Of comfort, cheerfulneſs, and health :

And all, who follow'd his advice,
Appear'd more profperous, as more wife.   20

    Wearied, at length, with many a call,
The fage refolv'd to fummon all :
And gathering, on a pleafant monday,
A crowd not always feen on funday,
Curious to hear, while hard they prefs'd him,   25
In friendly terms, he thus addrefs'd 'em.

    " My friends, you have my kindeft wifhes ;
Pray think a neighbour not officious,
While thus, to teach you how to live,
My very beft advice I give."   30

    " And firft, *induftrious* be your lives ;
Alike employ'd yourfelves, and wives :
Your children, join'd in labour gay,
With fomething ufeful fill each day.
Thofe little times of leifure fave,   35
Which moft men lofe, and all men have ;
The half days, when a job is done ;
The whole days, when a ftorm is on.
Few know, without a ftrict account,
To what thefe little times amount :   40
If wafted, while the fame your coft,
The fums, you might have earn'd, are loft."

    " Learn *fmall things never to defpife :*
You little think how faft they rife.
A rich reward the mill obtains,   45
'Tho' but two quarts a bufhel gains :
Still rolling on it's fteady rounds,
The farthings foon are turn'd to pounds."

    " Nor *think a life of toil fevere :*
No life has bleffings fo fincere.
It's meals fo lufcious, fleep fo fweet,   50
Such vigorous limbs, fuch health complete,

A mind fo active, brifk, and gay,
As his, who toils the livelong day.
A life of floth drags hardly on;   55
Suns fet too late, and rife too foon;
Youth, manhood, age, all linger flow,
To him, who nothing has to do.
The drone, a nuifance to the hive,
Stays, but can fcarce be faid to live;   60
And well the bees, thofe judges wife,
Plague, chafe, and fting him, 'till he dies.
Lawrence, like him, tho' fav'd from hanging,
Yet every day deferves a banging."

" Let *order* o'er your time prefide,   65
And *method* all your bufinefs guide.
Early begin, and end, your toil;
Nor let great tafks your hands embroil.
One thing at once, be ftill begun,
Contriv'd, refolv'd, purfued, and done.   70
Hire not, for what yourfelves can do;
And fend not, when yourfelves can go;
Nor, 'till to-morrow's light, delay
What might as well be done to-day.
By fteady efforts all men thrive,   75
And long by moderate labour live;
While eager toil, and anxious care,
Health, ftrength, and peace, and life, impair."

" What thus your hands with labour earn,
To fave, be now your next concern.   80
Whate'er to health, or real ufe,
Or true enjoyment, will conduce,
Ufe freely, and *with pleafure* ufe;
But ne'er the gifts of HEAVEN abufe:
I joy to fee your treafur'd ftores,   85
Which fmiling Plenty copious pours;

Your cattle fleek, your poultry fine,
Your cider in the tumbler fhine,
Your tables, fmoking from the hoard,
And children fmiling round the board.   90
All rights to ufe in you confpire;
The labourer's worthy of his hire.
Ne'er may that hated day arrive,
When worfe yourfelves, or your's, fhall live;
Your drefs, your lodging, or your food,   95
Be lefs abundant, neat, or good;
Your dainties all to market go,
To feaft the epicure, and beau;
But ever on your tables ftand,
Proofs of a free and happy land."   100

" Yet ftill, with prudence, wear, and tafte;
Ufe what you pleafe, but nothing wafte:
On little, better far to live,
Than, poor and pitied, much furvive.
Like ants, lay fomething up in ftore,   105
Againft the winter of threefcore.
Difeafe may long your ftrength annoy;
Weaknefs and pain your limbs deftroy;
On forrow's bed your houfholds lie;
Your debtors fail, your cattle die;   110
Your crops untimely feafons kill,
And life be worn with many an ill."

" Lo too, your little flocks demand
Much from the kind parental hand;
Your fons or learning, trades, or farms;   115
Your daughter's portions, with their charms:
From prudence, this provifion flows,
And all, from little favings, grows."

" And, O *ye fair!* *this toil demands*
The efforts of your faithful-hands.   120

If wealth, your hufband's hearts are wifhing,
Of you, they firft muft afk permiffion.
By HEAVEN conjoin'd, to gain, and have,
'Tis their's to earn; 'tis yours to fave :
Whatever from their labour grows,   125
Careful, you keep, but, heedlefs, lofe."

  " 'Tis folly in th' extreme, *to till*
Extenfive fields, and till them ill.
The farmer, pleas'd, may boaft aloud
His bufhels fown, his acres plough'd ;   130
And, pleas'd, indulge the cheering hope,
That time will bring a plenteous crop.
Shrewd Common-fenfe fits laughing by,
And fees his hopes abortive die :
For, when maturing feafons fmile,   135
Thin fheaves fhall difappoint his toil.
Advis'd, this empty pride expel ;
Till little, and that little well.
Of taxes, fencing, toil, no more,
Your ground requires, when rich, than poor ;   140
And more one fertile acre yields,
Than the huge breadth of barren fields.
That mould, the leaves, for ages, fpread,
Is, long fince, with the forefts, fled ;
That flender ploughing, trifling care,   145
No longer will your fields prepare.
Some new manure muft now be found ;
Some better culture fit the ground.
Oft turn the foil to feel the weather ;
Manure from every quarter gather,   150
Weeds, afhes, Paris-plaifter, lime,
Marle, fea-weed, and the harbour flime.
Like Germans bid your acres thrive ;
But not like ftinting Germans live.

  " Let *every grafs of kindly feed*
Exterminate the noifome weed ;

The clover round your paftures blow ;
The rye-grafs o'er your meadows bow :
Hence the rich mow your barns fhall fill ;
Hence with rich green your paftures fmile ;   160
The ox, untir'd, his toil fuftain,
And fat fteers frifk it, o'er the plain."

  " *Your herds feed well, increafe, amend,*
And from the wintery ftorm defend.
No fource will furer profit give,   165
Or furnifh eafier means to live.
The grazier hugs his cool retreat,
And fmiles, to fee the farmer fweat ;
To fee much labour little yield,
The gleanings of a worne-out field ;   170
While gliftening beeves around him fport,
And drovers to his houfe refort ;
Manur'd, huge fwarths his meadows load,
And heavy harvefts proudly nod."

  " Let *ufeful flocks* your care demand,   175
Beft riches of the happy land.
From them, fhall fwell the fleecy ftore,
And want, and rags, depart your door ;
Your daughters find a fweet employ,
And, finging, turn the wheel with joy :   180
With homefpun rich the loom be gay ;
Your houfholds clad in bright array ;
And female toil more profit yield,
Than half the labours of the field."

  " When firft the market offers well,   185
At once your yearly produce fell.
A higher price you wait in vain,
And ten times lofe, where once you gain.
The dog, that at the fhadow caught,
Mifs'd all he had, and all he fought.   190

Lefs, day by day, your ftore will grow,
Gone, you fcarce know or when, or how;
Intereft will eat, while you delay,
And vermin fteal your hopes away.
In parcels fold, in ways unknown,   195
It melts, and, unobferv'd, is gone.
No folid purpofe driblets aid,
Spent, and forgot, as foon as paid :
The fum, a year's whole earnings yield,
Will pay a debt, or buy a field."   200

" *In time*, whate'er your needs require,
Lay in, of clothing, food, or fire.
Your cellars, barns, and granaries fill ;
Your wood, in winter, round you pile :
Let fpring ne'er fee th' exhaufted mow,   205
Or oxen faint, before the plough ;
Nor fummer, when it's hurries come,
Your wood, in harveft, carted home."

" Along the fide of floping hills,
Conduct your numerous living rills.   210
Thence bid them, fweetly-wandering, flow,
To wake the grafs, in fields below.
Rich meadows in their courfe fhall fpring,
And mowers whet the fcythe, and fing."

" Look round, and fee *your wood's decay'd*,   215
Your fuel fcarce, your timber fled.
What groves remain with care enclofe,
Nor e'er to biting herds expofe.
Your ftore with planted nuts renew,
And acorns o'er each barren ftrew.   220
Tho' fpring now fmiles, yet winter's blaft
Will foon the frozen fkies o'ercaft ;
And, pinch'd, your children crowding nigher,
Hang fhivering o'er the fcanty fire :

Q

Roufe ! your reluctant floth o'ercome,   225
And bid reviving forefts bloom."

" Yearly the houfe, the barn, the fence,
Demand *much care*, and *fome expence.*
Small fums, in time, with prudence paid,
Will profit more than great, delay'd :   230
Each year's decays in time repair,
Nor foolifh wafte, thro' want of care."

" *Neat be your farms :* 'tis long confefs'd,
The neateft farmers are the beft.
Each bog, and marfh, induftrious drain,   235
Nor let vile balks deform the plain ;
No bufhes on your headlands grow,
Nor briars a floven's culture fhow.
Neat be your barns ; your houfes neat ;
Your doors be clean ; your court-yards fweet ;   240
No mofs the fheltering roof infhroud ;
No wooden panes the window cloud ;
No filthy kennel foully flow ;
Nor weeds with rankling poifon grow :
But fhades expand, and fruit-trees bloom,   245
And flowering fhrubs exhale perfume.
With pales, your garden circle round ;
Defend, enrich, and clean, the ground :
Prize high this pleafing, ufeful rood,
And fill with vegetable good."   250

" *With punctual hand your taxes pay,*
Nor put far off the evil day.
How foon to an enormous fize,
Taxes, fucceeding taxes, rife !
How eafy, one by one, difcharg'd !   255
How hardly, in the mafs enlarg'd !
How humbling the intrufive dun !
How faft, how far, th' expences run!

Fees, advertifements, travel, coft,
And that fad end of all, the poft !   260
This gulph of quick perdition flee,
And live, from duns and bailiffs free."

" In *merchants' books, from year to year,*
Be cautious how your names appear.
How faft their little items count !   265
How great, beyond your hopes, th' amount !
When fhelves, o'er fhelves, inviting ftand,
And wares allure, on either hand;
While round, you turn enchanted eyes,
And feel a thoufand wants arife,   270
(Ye young, ye fair, thefe counfels true
Are penn'd for all, but moft for you),
Ere Fancy lead your hearts aftray,
Think of the means you have, to pay;
What wants are nature's; fancy's what;   275
What will yield real good, when bought;
What certain, future means you find,
To cancel contracts, left behind;
What means to make the firft of May
To you, and your's, a welcome day."   280

" To you, let *each returning spring*
That day of certain reckoning bring :
All debts to cancel, books t' adjuft,
And check the wild career of truft.
From frequent reckonings friendfhip grows,   285
And peace, and fweet communion, flows."

" Meanwhile, of all your toil, and care,
Your children claim the largeft fhare.
In health, and ficknefs, much they need,
To nurfe, to watch, to clothe, and feed;   290
Their education much demands
From faithful hearts, and active hands."

" First be *their health* your conftant care ;
Give them to breathe the freeft air :
Their food be neither rich, nor dainty,   295
But plain, and clean, and good, and plenty ;
Their clothes, let changing feafons rule,
In winter warm, in fummer cool,
In your own houfes fpun, and dy'd,
For comfort made, and not for pride.   300
Hardy, not fuffering, be their life,
With heat, and cold, and ftorm, at ftrife ;
Accuftom'd common ills to bear,
To fmile at danger, laugh at fear,
Troubles to brave, with hardy breaft,   305
And feek, thro' toilfome action, reft,
Teach them each *manly art to prize,*
And bafe effem'nacy defpife,
Teach them to wreftle, leap, and run,
To win the palm, and prize it, won ;   310
To feek, in acts like thefe, and find
A nervous frame, and vigorous mind."

" *My country's youth, I fee with pain,*
The cuftoms of their fires difdain,
Quit the bold paftimes of the green,   315
That ftrengthen ftriplings into men,
Grovel in inns, at cards, and dice,
The means of foul difeafe, and vice,
And wafte, in gaming, drink, and ftrife,
Health, honour, fame, and peace, and life."   320

" *With gentler hand, your daughters train,*
The houfewife's various arts to gain ;
O'er fcenes domeftic to prefide ;
The needle, wheel, and fhuttle, guide ;
The peacock's gaudry to defpife,   325
And view vain fports with parents' eyes ;

On things of ufe to fix the heart,
And gild, with every graceful art.
Teach them, with neateft. fimpleft drefs,
A neat, and lovely mind t' exprefs ;   330
Th' alluring female mien to wear ;
Gently to foothe corroding care ;
Bid life with added pleafure glow,
And fweetly charm the bed of woe.
To fhow, the giddy fair-one train'd,   335
With every ugly fpot is ftain'd ;
While fhe, who lives to worth, and duty,
Shines forth, in Wifdom's eye, a beauty."

   " *With fteady hand yonr houfhold fway,*
And ufe them always to obey.   340
Always their worthy acts commend ;
Always againft their faults contend ;
The mind inform ; the confcience move ;
And blame, with tendernefs, and love.
When round they flock, and fmile, and tell   345
Their lambkin fports, and infant weal,
Nor foolifh laugh, nor fret, nor frown ;
But all their little interefts own ;
Like them, thofe trifles ferious deem,
And daily witnefs your efteem :   350
Yourfelves their beft friends always prove,
For filial duty fprings from love.
Teach them, *with confidence t' impart,*
Each fecret purpofe of the heart :   355
Thrice happy parents, children blefs'd,
Of mutual confidence poffefs'd !
Such parents fhall their children fee
From vice, and fhame, and anguifh, free."

   " *Correct not, 'til the coming day*
Has fann'd refentment's heat away.   360

When paſſion rules, 'tis fear obeys ;
But duty ſerves, when reaſon ſways.
In earlieſt years, the rod will mend ;
In later, fails to reach the end.
Still vary : let neglect, diſgrace,   365
Confinement, cenſure, find their place.
Convince, ere you correct, and prove
You puniſh, not from rage, but love ;
And teach them, with perſuaſion mild,
You hate the fault, but love the child." 370

 " *All diſcipline*, as facts atteſt,
In private miniſter'd is beſt.
Vex'd to be ſeen diſgrac'd, and ſham'd,
His paſſion rous'd, his pride inflam'd,
Your child his guilt with care conceals, 375
And pertly talks, and ſtoutly feels ;
From truth, with ſwift declenſion flies,
To arts, equivocations, lies ;
And ſullen broods, with ſad deſign,
O'er ſweet revenge of future ſin.   380
Alone, before the parents bar,
His conſcience with himſelf at war,
Of pride, and petulance, bereft,
Without a hope, or refuge, left,
He ſhrinks, beneath a father's eye, 385
And feels his firm perverſeneſs die ;
Reveres the love, his ſighs implore,
And grateful turns, to ſin no more."

 " *On uniformity depends*
All government, that gains its ends. 390
The ſame things always praiſe, and blame,
Your laws, and conduct, be the ſame."

 " Let no *diſcouragement* deter,
Nor *ſloth* this daily taſk defer.

Sloth and difcouragement deftroy   395
The children's weal, the parents' joy.
For one, who labor lothes, we find
Ten thoufand lothing toil of mind,
That clofe attention, careful tho't,
With every real blefling fraught.   400
Early the ftubborn child transgreffes ;
Denies it ; nor, 'till forc'd, confeffes :
The fault, tho' punifh'd, he renews ;
New punifhment the fault purfues :
His heart by nature prone to fin,   405
Agen he wounds you, and agen ;
Amaz'd, difhearten'd, in defpair,
To fee fo fruitlefs all your care,
And wearied, by fuch fix'd attention
To crimes, that fuffer no prevention,   410
Reluctant, by degrees, you yield,
And leave him mafter of the field."

    " Then with fond hope, that reafon's fway
Will win him from his faults away,
For decent power, alone you ftrive,   415
Refign'd, if decently he'll live."

    " Vain hope! by reafon's power alone,
From guilt, no heart was ever won.
Decent, not good, may reafon make him ;
By reafon, crimes will ne'er forfake him.   420
As weeds, felf-fown, demand no toil,
But flourifh in their native foil,
Root deep, grow high, with vigour bloom,
And fend forth poifon, for perfume ;
So faults, inborn, fpontaneous rife,   425
And daily wax in ftrength, and fize,
Ripen, with neither toil, nor care,
And choke each germ of virtue there.

Virtues, like plants of nobler kind,
Transferred from regions more refin'd,　　　　430
The gardener's careful hand muſt ſow;
His culturing hand muſt bid them grow;
Rains gently ſhower; ſkies ſoftly ſhine,
And bleſſings fall, from realms divine."

" Much time, and pain, and toil, and care,　　　435
Muſt virtue's habits plant, and rear:
Habits alone thro' life endure,
Habits alone your child ſecure:
To theſe be all your labours given;
To theſe, your fervent prayers to HEAVEN.　　　440
Nor faint, a thouſand trials o'er,
To ſee your pains effect no more;
Love, duty, intereſt, bid you ſtrive;
Contend, and yield not, while you live;
And know, for all your labours paſs'd,　　　445
Your eyes ſhall ſee a crop, at laſt.
The ſmith beſide his anvil ſtands,
The lump of ſilver in his hands,
A thouſand ſtrokes with patience gives,
And ſtill unform'd the work perceives;　　　450
A thouſand, and a thouſand more,
Unfiniſh'd leaves it as before;
Yet, though, from each, no print is found,
Still toiling on his ſteady round,
He ſees the ductile maſs refine,　　　455
And in a beauteous veſſel ſhine."

" *Taverns, and ſhops, and lounging places,*
Vile comrades, gaming tables, races,
Where youth to vice, and ruin, run,
Teach them, as pits of death, to ſhun.　　　460
At nine, when ſounds the warning bell,
Uſe them to bid their ſports farewell;

Health, order, temperance, every joy,
As blasts, untimely hours destroy;
At these dread hours, in places vile,
Where all things tempt, betray, defile,
Abroad, to every ill they roam,
But peace, and safety, find at home."

" *From licens'd talk their tongues restrain,*
And bridle, with discretion's rein;
Safety, and peace, reserve affords;
But evil hides in many words.
All wond'rous stories bid them shun,
And the *pernicious love of fun;*
In lies, great stories ever end,
And fun will every vice befriend.
What sports of real use you find,
To brace the form, or nerve the mind,
Freely indulge; such sports, as these,
Will profit youth, as well as please.
But from all arts and tricks dehort,
And check th' excessive love of sport.
All buzzing tales, of private life,
All scandals, form'd on houshold strife,
The idle chatterings of the street,
Early forbid them to repeat;
But teach them, kindness, praise, and truth,
Alone become the voice of youth."

" *Their hearts with soft affections warm;*
Their taste, to gentle manners form;
Let manly aims their bosoms fire,
And sweet civility inspire.
Bid them the stranger kindly greet,
The friend with faithful friendship meet,
And charm of life the little span,
By general courtesy to man."

R

465
470
475
480
485
490
495

495

" *Teach them to reverence righteous fway,*
With life defend, with love obey ;
Nor join that wretched band of fcoffers,
Who rail at every man in office.   500
With freedom's warmth their fouls infpire,
And light their brave forefathers' fire.
Bid them their privileges know ;
Bid them with love of country glow ;
With fkill, their arms defenfive wield,   505
Nor fhun the duties of the field."

" How blefs'd this heaven-diftinguifh'd land !
Where fchools in every hamlet ftand ;
Far fpread the beams of learning bright,
And every child enjoys the light.   510
At fchool, beneath a faithful guide,
In teaching fkill'd, of morals tried,
And pleas'd the early mind to charm
To every good, from every harm,
Learn they to read, to write, to fpell,   515
And caft accompts, and learn them well :
For, on this microfcopic plan,
Is form'd the wife, and ufeful man.
Let him a tafte for books infpire ;
While you, to nurfe the young defire,   520
A focial library procure,
And open knowledge to the poor.
This ufeful tafte imbib'd, your eyes
Shall fee a thoufand bleffings rife.
From haunts, and comrades vile fecure,   525
Where gilded baits to vice allure,
No more your fons abroad fhall roam,
But pleas'd, their evenings fpend at home ;
Allurements more engaging find,
And feaft, with pure delight, the mind.   530
The realms of earth, their tho'ts fhall fcan,
And learn the works, and ways, of man ;

See, from the favage, to the fage,
How nations ripen, age by age;
How states, and men, by virtue rife;   535
How both to ruin fink, by vice;
How thro' the world's great prifon-bounds,
While one wide clank of chains refounds,
Men flaves, while Angels weep to fee,
Some wife, and brave, and blefs'd, are free.   540
Thro' moral fcenes shall stretch their fight;
Difcern the bounds of wrong, and right;
That lothe; this love; and, pleas'd, purfue
Whate'er from man to man is due;
And, from the page of HEAVEN derive   546
The motives, and the means, to live."

   " Nor think the fcope, or task, too great;
Coolly your leifure moments state;
Thefe, nicely reckon'd, will appear
Enough for all, that's promis'd here.   550
Would you still higher proof behold?
Plain facts that higher proof unfold.
I know, and tell it with a fmile,
No narrow lift of men of toil,
Illum'd by no collegiate rays,   555
And forc'd to tread in bufy ways,
Who yet, to read intenfely loving,
And every leifure hour improving,
On wifdom's heights diftinguifh'd stand,
The boast, and blefling, of our land.   560
This myftery learn: in great, or fmall things,
'TIS APPLICATION MASTERS ALL THINGS."

   " *Thus taught, in every flate of life,*
Of child, of parent, hufband, wife,
They'll wifer, better, happier, prove;   565
Their freedom better know, and love;

More pleasures gain, more hearts engage,
And feast their own dull hours of age."

" *Use them, and early use, to have,*
To earn, and what they earn, to save.   570
From industry, and prudence, flow
Relief of want, and balm of woe,
Delightful sleep, enduring wealth,
The purest peace, the firmest health,
True independence of our peers,   575
Support for sickness, and for years,
Security from houshold strife,
The conscience sweet of useful life,
Esteem abroad, content at home,
An easy passage to the tomb,   580
With blessings numberless, that flow
To neighbour, stranger, friend, and foe,
That man to man resistless bind,
And spread, and spread, to all mankind."

Would you for them this good acquire,   585
Prudence, and industry, inspire;
To habit bid the blessings grow;
Habits alone yield good below.
To these untrain'd, whate'er you give,
Whate'er inheritance you leave,   590
To every worthless passion given,
And scatter'd to the winds of heaven,
Will foes, and strangers, clothe, and feed;
While your own children pine with need,
Their friends, pain'd, pitied, slighted, fly,   595
Forgotten live, and wretched die.

" *In this New World, life's changing round,*
In three descents, is often found.
The *first*, firm, busy, plodding, poor,
Earns, saves, and daily swells, his store;   600

By farthings firſt, and pence, it grows;
In ſhillings next, and pounds, it flows;
Then ſpread his widening farms, abroad;
His foreſts wave; his harveſts nod;
Fattening, his numerous cattle play,   605
And debtors dread his reckoning day.
Ambitious then t'adorn with knowledge
His ſon, he places him at college;
And ſends, in ſmart attire, and neat,
To travel, thro' each neighbouring ſtate;   610
Builds him a handſome houſe, or buys,
Sees him a gentleman, and dies."

" The *ſecond*, born to wealth, and eaſe,
And taught to think, converſe, and pleaſe,
Ambitious, with his lady-wife,   615
Aims at a higher walk of life.
Yet, in thoſe wholeſome habits train'd,
By which his wealth, and weight, were gain'd,
Bids care in hand with pleaſure go,
And blends œconomy with ſhow.   620
His houſes, fences, garden, dreſs,
The neat and thrifty man confeſs.
Improv'd, but with improvement plain,
Intent on office, as on gain,
Exploring, uſeful ſweets to ſpy,   625
To public life he turns his eye.
A townſman firſt; a juſtice ſoon;
A member of the houſe anon;
Perhaps to board, or bench, invited,
He ſees the ſtate, and ſubjects, righted;   630
And, raptur'd with politic life,
Conſigns his children to his wife.
Of houſhold cares amid the round,
For her, too hard the taſk is found.
At firſt ſhe ſtruggles, and contends;   635
Then doubts, deſponds, laments, and bends;

Her fons purfue the fad defeat,
And fhout their victory complete ;
Rejoicing, fee their father roam,
And riot, rake, and reign, at home.   640
Too late he fees, and fees to mourn,
His race of every hope forlorn,
Abroad, for comfort, turns his eyes,
Bewails his dire miftakes, and dies."

" His *heir, train'd only to enjoy,*   645
Untaught his mind, or hands, t' employ,
Confcious of wealth enough for life,
With bufinefs, care, and worth, at ftrife,
By prudence, confcience, unreftrain'd,
And none, but pleafure's habits, gain'd,   650
Whirls on the wild career of fenfe,
Nor danger marks, nor heeds expenfe.
Soon ended is the giddy round ;
And foon the fatal goal is found.
His lands, fecur'd for borrow'd gold,   655
His houfes, horfes, herds, are fold.
And now, no more for wealth refpected,
He finks, by all his friends neglected ;
Friends, who, before, his vices flatter'd,
And liv'd upon the loaves he fcatter'd.   660
Unacted every worthy part,
And pining with a broken heart,
To dirtieft company he flies,
Whores, gambles, turns a fot, and dies.
His children, born to fairer doom,   665
In rags, purfue him to the tomb."

" Apprentic'd then to mafters ftern,
Some real good the orphans learn ;
Are bred to toil, and hardy fare,
And grow to ufefulnefs, and care ;   670
And, following their great-grandfire's plan,
Each flow becomes a *ufeful man."*

" Such here is life's fwift-circling round;
So foon are all its changes found.
Would you prevent th' allotment hard,   675
And fortune's rapid whirl retard,
In all your race, induftrious care
Attentive plant, and faithful rear;
With life, th' important tafk begin,
Nor but with life, the tafk refign;   680
To habit, bid the bleffings grow,
Habits alone yield good below."

" But, to complete the blefs'd defign,
Both parents muft their efforts join;
With kind regard, each other treat: 685
In every plan, harmonious meet;
The conduct each of each approve;
Nor ftrive, but in the ftrife of love.
What one commands, let both require;
In counfels, fmiles, and frowns, confpire;   690
Alike oppofe; alike befriend;
And each the other's choice commend.
In fweeteft union thus conjoin'd,
And one the life, as one the mind,
Your children cheerful will obey,   695
And reverence undivided pay;
The daily tafk be lightly done,
And half the houfhold troubles gone:
While jars domeftic weal deftroy,
And wither every hope of joy."   700

" Meantime, let peace around you reft,
Nor feuds good neighbourhood moleft.
Your neighbour's crops with juftice eye,
Nor let his hopes by trefpafs die.
Your fence repair, your herds repel;   705
Much virtue's found in fencing well.

With care his reputation guard;
Sweet friendſhip will that care reward.
No idle tatler e'er receive;
No ſtoried ſcandal e'er believe: 710
What's good, and kind, alone report;
Tell nothing, which can others hurt:
Oblige, lend, borrow—freely all—
Rejoice not in another's fall:
When others need, aſſiſtance lend;   715
Are others ſick? their calls attend;
Their viſits hoſpitably greet,
And pay, with cheerful kindneſs ſweet.
Theſe things, or I miſtake, will form,
And keep the heart of friendſhip warm."   720

" But ſhould contentions riſe, and grudges,
Which call for arbitrating judges,
Still ſhun the law, that gulph of woe,
Whoſe waves without a bottom flow:
That gulph, by ſtorms forever toſs'd,   725
Where all, that's once afloat, is loſt;
Where friends, embark'd, are friends no more,
And neither finds a peaceful ſhore:
While thouſand wrecks, as warnings, lie,
The victims of an angry ſky.   730

" *Each cauſe let mutual friends decide,*
With Common-ſenſe alone to guide:
If right, in ſilent peace be glad;
If wrong, be neither four, nor ſad:
As oft you'll find full juſtice done,   735
As when thro' twenty terms you've run;
And when, in travel, fees, and coſt,
Far more than can be won, is loſt."

" Learn, this concluſion whence I draw.
Mark what eſtates are ſpent in law!   740

See men litigious bufinefs fly,
And loungers live, and beggars die!
What anger, hatred, malice fell,
And fierce revenge their bofoms fwell!
What frauds, fubornings, tamperings rife!   745
What flanders foul! what fhameful lies!
What perjuries, blackening many a tongue!
And what immenfity of wrong!
Where peace, and kindnefs, dwelt before,
See peace, and kindnefs, dwell no more!   750
Ills to good offices fucceed,
And neighbours bid each other bleed!"

  " Efop, the merry Phrygian fage,
Worth half the Wife-men of his age,
Has left to litigants a ftory,   755
Which, with your leave, I'll fet before you."

  "" The bear, and lion, on the lawn,
Once found the carcafe of a fawn.
Both claim'd the dainty; neither gave it;
But each fwore roundly he would have it.   760
They growl'd; they fought; but fought in vain;
For neither could the prize obtain;
And, while, to breathe, they both retreated,
The lawyer fox, came in, and eat it." "

  " And would you ufeful live, and blefs'd,   765
Parochial heats, and jars, deteft.
Like you, their interefts others feel;
Have pride, and paffions, warmth, and will.
Thofe interefts clafh; thofe wills contend;
And fome, where all have votes, muft bend.   770
A yielding fpirit hence maintain;
Let all concede, that all may gain:
Hence, when fierce heat the mafs infpires,
And Party blows her angry fires,

S

For weeks, or months, or years, poſtpone 775
What, prudence tells you, muſt be done :
Time will command the flames to ceaſe,
And party ſoften into peace."

    Thus ſpoke the ſage. The crowd around,
Applauding, heard the grateful ſound : 780
Each, deeply muſing, homeward went,
T' amend his future life intent;
And, pondering paſt delays, with ſorrow,
Reſolv'd, he would begin, to-morrow.

END OF THE SIXTH PART.

GREENFIELD HILL:

A

P O E M.

THE ARGUMENT.

INTRODUCTION. Vision. Scene the margin of the Sound. Genius of the Sound appears, and declares the future Glory of America. Splendour of Europe excelled by the Happiness of America. Happy local Situation of U. S. secure from the political evils of Europe. Magnificence of the works of nature, on this Continent. Healthfulness, and fruitfulness of the Seasons. Country divided into small Farms, equally descending to Children. Unhappy effects of an unequal Division of Property, and of Entailments. Stanislaus. Polish Nobility. State of Property in this Country resumed. Its Effects on Industry, Government, and Policy. U. S. contrasted to ancient Empires. Happiness of U. S. contrasted to Eastern Despotism. Universal Prevalence of Freedom. Unfortified, and therefore safe, state of U. S. Influence of our state of Society on the Mind. Public Property employed for the Public Benefit. Penal Administrations improved by Benevolence. Policy enlarges its scope. Knowledge promoted. Improvements in Astronomical and other Instruments of Science. Improvements of the Americans, in Natural Philosophy—Poetry—Music—and Moral Science. State of the American Clergy. Manners refined. Artificial Manners condemned. American Women. Cultivation advanced. Other Nations visit this Country, and learn the nature, and causes, of our happiness. Conclusion.

GREENFIELD HILL.

PART VII.

The VISION.

From thefe fair fcenes, to wonders more refin'd,
Inftinctive turns the ever bufy Mind:
The prefent profpect but expands her fight;
The prefent joy to others tempts her flight;
Allur'd by each new good, fhe loves to roam,   5
And fpreads her wings, through ages long to come;
Where Time, with hand prophetic, points her way,
And heavenly vifions heavenly fcenes difplay.

As late, when Spring awak'd the flumbering plains,
The foul, extatic, burft her earthy chains,   10
Approaching Morn affum'd her magic power,
And bade her vifions blefs the fairy hour,
In quick review, Columbia's glories fpread;
The paft roll on; the prefent fwift fucceed;
Behind, rank after rank, the future rife,   15
As clouds, fucceffive, paint the changing fkies.

I ftood, methought, befide yon azure plain;
Still hung the concave; peaceful flept the main;
In heaven fufpended, lingering Hefper fhin'd,
And purple evening breath'd her gentleft wind.   20

At once I heard a folemn murmur rife,
As thunders flowly fwell, in diftant fkies;
The waves, difturb'd, in deep convulfion lay;
The world was hufh'd; the airs forgot to play.

At that ftill moment, from his fapphire bed, 25
The Genius of the Sound uprear'd his head:
Slow round his form a cloud of amber roll'd,
Now hid, now fplendent, through it's fkirts of gold.
Gemm'd with new ftars, his feagreen mitre fhin'd;
His fcaly mantle ruftled in the wind; 30
A pictur'd fhield his hand, uplifted, bore,
Grav'd with the femblance of his double fhore:
Unnumber'd fails propitious breezes fwell'd,
And his ftrip'd flag difclos'd th' unfinifh'd field.
Here Longa's bays, and whitening coaft, were feen, 35
Small ifles, around her, wrought in living green;
The loftier Mainland there allur'd the eye,
It's margin winding toward the fouthern fky;
The tall hill heav'd; expanfive fpread the plain;
And groves, and gardens, ftreak'd the fubject main: 40
New Haven's fpires, in fculptur'd filver, rofe,
And York's proud domes, efcap'd the wafte of foes.
Here a new Thames an infant London laves;
Through a new Tempe, roll Connecta's waves;
With foamy ftream, another Avon glides, 45
And Hudfon triumphs in his freighted tides.

He ftood, and thus the folemn filence broke,
And brightening nature liften'd as he fpoke.

" Rife, genial years! and hafte, aufpicious times!
Afcend, and blefs the true, Hefperian climes; 50
O'er happy ifles, and garden'd realms, difplay
Th' advancing fplendours of prophetic day."

" Her themes of pride let favage Europe boaft,
Her bloody enginry, and marfhall'd hoft,

Her haughty flags, with purple ſtain'd, diſplay,   55
The car of triumph, and the pomp of ſway;
Or, wrought with Grecian ſkill, her columns raiſe,
Bend the tall arch, and teach the dome to blaze;
In art's wide regions bid her laurels grow,
And place the crown of ſcience on her brow.   60
Round the mild year, let Albion's verdure run;
Let Gallia's opening vines allure the ſun;
O'er brighter realms, the Turkiſh creſcent riſe,
Waſh'd by fair ſeas, and warm'd by vernal ſkies;
Let richer Ind, and prouder Perſia, tell   65
The diamond cavern, and the pearly ſhell;
Peruvia vaunt her ſtreams, in ſilver roll'd,
And ſunny Darien lift her hills of gold.
Here the beſt bleſſings of thoſe far-fam'd climes,
Pure of their woes, and whiten'd from their crimes,   70
Shall blend with nobler bleſſings, all my own;
Here firſt th' enduring reign of Peace be known:
The voice of ſcepter'd Law wide realms obey,
And choice erect, and freemen hail, the ſway:
The ſun of knowledge light the general mind,   75
And cheer, through every claſs, oppreſs'd mankind;
Here Truth, and Virtue, doom'd no more to roam,
Pilgrims in eaſtern climes, ſhall find their home;
Age after age, exalt their glory higher,
That light the ſoul, and this the life inſpire;   80
And Man once more, ſelf-ruin'd Phœnix, riſe,
On wings of Eden, to his native ſkies."

"To build the finiſh'd bliſs, ſee all things given,
The goods of nature, and the ſmiles of Heaven,
A ſite ſequeſter'd, policy ſublime,   85
The nobleſt manners, and the happieſt time."

"See this glad world remote from every foe,
From Europe's miſchiefs, and from Europe's woe!

Th' Atlantic's guardian tide repelling far
The jealous terror, and the vengeful war,   90
The native malice, envy, pride, and ftrife,
The plagues of rank, the ruft of ufelefs life,
The cumbrous pomp, of general want the fpring,
The clafhing commerce, and the rival king.
See, far remote, the crimes of balanc'd fway!   95
Where courts contract the debt, and fubjects pay;
The black intrigue, the crufh of felf-defence,
Th' enliftment dire, foul prefs, and tax immenfe,
Navies, and hofts, that gorge Potofi whole;
Bribes, places, penfions, and the auction'd foul: 100
Ills, that, each hour, invoke the wrath of God,
And bid the world's wide furface fmoke with blood,
Wafte human good, in flavery nations bind,
And fpeed untimely death to half mankind."

" Profufely fcatter'd o'er thefe regions, lo!   105
What fcenes of grandeur, and of beauty, glow.
It's nobleft wonders here Creation fpreads;
Hills, where fkies reft, and Danubes pour cafcades;
Forefts, that ftretch from Cancer, to the Pole;
Lakes, where feas lie, and rivers, where they roll; 110
Landfchapes, where Edens gild anew the ball,
And plains, and meads, where funs arife, and fall:"

" To thefe bright wonders, Nature's hand fublime
Has join'd the varied joys of circling clime.
Winds pureft breathe; benigneft feafons fmile;   115
And double harvefts gild the bounteous foil;
The choiceft fweets, unnumber'd fruits inhale,
And Flora wantons, on the fragrant gale:
Gains of true gold purfue th' exploring plough,
Wealth, that endures, and good unbought with woe;   120
With richeft ore, the ufeful mountains fhine,
And lufcious treafures fill the teeming brine:

Fell Famine fickens, at th' o'erflowing good,
And, hiffing, flies the native land of food."   125

"See the wide realm in equal fhares poffefs'd !
How few the rich, or poor ! how many blefs'd !
O happy ftate ! the ftate, by HEAVEN defign'd
To rein, protect, employ, and blefs mankind ;
Where Competence, in full enjoyment, flows ;
Where man leaft vice, and higheft virtue, knows ;   130
Where the mind thrives; ftrong nerves th' invention ftring;
And daring Enterprize uplifts his wing ;
Where Splendour fpreads, in vain, his peacock-hues ;
Where vagrant Sloth, the general hifs purfues ;
Where Bufinefs reigns, the univerfal queen ;   135
Where none are flaves, or lords ; but all are men :
No nuifant drones purloin the earner's food ;
But each man's labour fwells the common good."

"O ftate, to my lov'd fons moft kindly given ;
Of all their blifs, the bafis laid by HEAVEN !   140
Curs'd be the heart, that wifhes to deftroy,
Curs'd be the hand, that mines this ground-work joy ;
Hung be his name, in infamy's foul den ;
And let the wide world rife, and fay Amen !"

"Thrice wretched lands ! where, thoufands flaves to one,
Sires know no child, befide the eldeft fon ;   [145
Men know no rights ; no juftice nobles know ;
And kings no pleafure, but from fubjects' woe.
There, wealth from plunder'd throngs by few engrofs'd,
To rich, and poor, alike is virtue loft.   150
The rich, to foul oppreffion born, and bred,
To reafon blinded, and to feeling dead,
From childhood, train'd to wield the iron rod,
Alike regard not man, and fear not GOD.
Science they fcorn, the public bar deride ;   155
And every feud by vengeful force decide ;

T

Honour their deity, and will their law,
In private war, the fword of paffion draw,
O'er wretched vaffals, death and ruin drive,
Whofe only hope, or comfort, was to live ;   160
Unblefs'd, forbid all others blifs to find,
Fools, atheifts, bigots, curfes to mankind."

  " Mean, bafe, deceitful, dead to hope, and fhame,
At war with that hard world, which wars with them,
Like trees, adhefive to their native plain,   165
And given, or fold, as pleafure prompts, or gain,
Dower of a daughter, purchafe of a hound,
Alike remov'd from worth, the poor are found.
Mere tools of fraud, oppreffion, whim, or rage,
No law t' avenge their wrongs, nor friend t' affuage,   170
By paffion tempefted, by inftinct fped,
To' obedience whipp'd, to action hunger-led,
In knowledge brutes, in comfort brutes below,
Forbid to tafte the little good, they know,
They envy the fleek dog, that paffes by,   175
They ftarve, and fteal, blafpheme their GOD, and die."

  "Thrice wretched lands! where wealth and fplendour glow,
And want, and mifery, in dire contraft, fhow ;
On fheds, and pens, where palac'd pride looks down ;
A god the noble, and a beaft the clown ;   180
Where tiffue glares, and rags indecent yawn ;
Feet ftep in blood, and kingly cars are drawn ;
Where Luxury fickens, at Vitellius' feaft,
And wretches ftarve, beneath the hedge, to reft ;
Furs guard the filky form from winter's breath,   185
And the bare crofe defiles the frozen heath ;
Idolatry fans off the vernal breeze,
And fun-ftruck Labour, phrenzied, finks to peace.
Such, Poland! long have mourn'd thy realms of woe ;
Such, Ruffia, fuch, Bohemia! thine are now."   109

  " Hail, Prince of princes! firft of modern thrones,
Hail, Staniflaus! thou king, from nature's fons!

Hail, Child of HEAVEN! whofe large, etherial mind
Look'd into woe, and felt for poor mankind.
Let fame eternal crown thy glorious brows,   195
And ills glance from thee to thy favage foes.
Be thine the peace, the blifs, of doing good,
Delightful earneft of the bleft abode!
Sweet be thy day; thine eve fupremely fweet;
Death, fear, and forrow, laid beneath thy feet: 200
And oh! may HE, for ruin'd man who died,
Approve, accept, and hail thee to his fide,
Who, wielding earthly power, for heavenly ends,
Had'it pity on the leaft, among his friends."

"And ye exalted Poles! whofe generous mind,   205
Offering auguft! your pomp, and power, refign'd,
Pleas'd, with divine benignity to fee
Slaves chang'd to men, and wretches blefs'd, and free;
From the far evening of th' Atlantic fhore,
If fome foft gale fhould waft this whifper o'er,   210
Know, for your weal, all Virtue's children glow,
Joy in your joy, and weep your every woe;
Upward, each day, their prayers with fervour rife,
And wreftle down the promife of the SKIES,"

"In thefe contrafted climes, how chang'd the fcene,   215
Where happinefs expands, in living green!
Through the whole realm, behold convenient farms
Fed by fmall herds, and gay with cultur'd charms;
To fons, in equal portions, handed down,
The fire's bold fpirit kindling in the fon;   220
No tyrant riding o'er th' indignant plain;
A prince, a king, each independent fwain;
No fervile thought, no vile fubmiffion, known;
No rent to lords, nor homage to a throne;
But fenfe to know, and virtue to extend,   225
And nerves to feel the blifs, and bravery to defend!"

"As o'er the lawns the humming nations play,
Feel the foft fun, and blefs reviving May,

From field to field, the fragrant wax explore,
And round each fountain, vifit every flower,   230
Approaching froft, with fteady murmur, fing,
Wake with the morn, and hufband all the fpring :
Thus warm'd with induftry, behold my fwains !
Guide the fmooth plough, and drefs the grateful plains;
From earth's rich bofom, bid all products rife,   235
The blefs'd creation of indulgent fkies ;
The grafs-grown hills with herds unnumber'd crown,
And bid the fleecy nations fill the down ;
O'er countlefs fields, the flaxen treafure fpread,
And call the canvas, from it's hempen bed ;   240
Or bid the loom with all earth's fabric fhine,
The ufeful ftrengthen, and the gay refine,
Or ocean's chambers, with bold hand, explore,
And waft his endlefs treafures to the fhore !"

" Here firft fhall man, with full conviction, know   245
Well-fyftem'd rule the fource of blifs below ;
Invent, refine, arrange, the facred plan,
Check pride, rein power, and fave the rights of man !
Here firft, his favage independence bow,
And, at the public fhrine, fpontaneous vow ;   250
The triumph, here, of Reafon firft difplay,
A nation yielding to elective fway."

" See the charm'd States the glorious Rule complete,
Each haftening to be wife, and good, and great ;
Power, nicely balanc'd, all the parts adjuft,   255
The fource of union, and the feat of truft ;
Whence, men forgotten, Law fupremely reigns,
And juftice flows, a river, o'er the plains !"

" Her fky-crown'd pyramids let Egypt fhow,
The tomb of folly, and the work of woe ;   260
Her walls, her gardens, Babylon difplay,
The pomp of fpoils, and pageant of a day;

Greece, with fierce mobs, and rival fury, tofs'd,
Her bafelefs fway, and tottering freedom, boaft;
Her pride of empire haughty Rome unfold,   265
A world defpoil'd, for luxury, and gold:
Here nobler wonders of the world fhall rife;
Far other empire here mankind furprize:
Of orders pure, that afk no Grecian name,
A new born ftructure here afcend to fame.   270
The bafe, fhall knowledge, choice, and freedom, form,
Sapp'd by no flood, and fhaken by no ftorm;
Unpattern'd columns, union'd States afcend;
Combining arches, virtuous manners bend;
Of balanc'd powers, proportion'd ftories rife,   275
Like Babel's dome, intended for the fkies;
One fpeech, one foul, to every builder given,
And the tall fummit fhrouded high in heaven."

    " In this bright manfion, all my fons fhall find
Whatever rights their GOD has given mankind;   280
To rich, and poor, alike, th' avenues clear;
Its gates, like Salem's, open round the year;
Hence juftice, freedom, peace, and bounty, flow,
Redrefs for injuries, and relief for woe."

    " O blifsful vifions of the happy Weft!   285
O how unlike the miferies of the Eaft!
There, in fad realms of defolating war,
Fell Defpotifm afcends his iron car;
Printed in blood, o'er all the moving throne,
The motto glows, of—MILLIONS MADE FOR ONE.   290
Above, on either fide, the Furies glare,
Their fcorpions brandifh, and their fnakes uprear;
His breath their being, and his fcourge their law,
Unnumber'd haggard flaves the chariot draw;
A villain, black as hell, his mafter guides,   295
A guard of blacker villains round him rides.

As rolls the pomp the wasted kingdom o'er,
With corpses causey'd, and wet deep with gore,
One wide Aceldama the region lies,
And whitening Golgothas immingled rise :　　　　300
While nobles, pamper'd on the spoils of woe,
Resound—" The knee to Heaven's Vicegerent bow." "

" Yet there, even there, Columbia's bliss shall spring,
Rous'd from dull sleep, astonish'd Europe sing,
O'er Asia burst the renovating morn,　　　　305
And startled Afric in a day be born ;
As, from the tomb, when great MESSIAH rose,
Heaven bloom'd with joy, and Earth forgot her woes,
His saints, thro' nature, truth and virtue spread,
And light, and life, the SACRED SPIRIT shed ;　　　　310
Thus, thro' all climes, shall Freedom's bliss extend,
The world renew, and death, and bondage, end ;
All nations quicken with th' ecstatic power,
And one redemption reach to every shore."

" Unlike the East, whose castles rivet sway,　　　　315
Shield the fell guard, and force the realm t' obey,
A nations voice, with pointed cannon, brave,
Meant to defend, but useful to enslave ;
Where foes victorious in dire safety stand,
And fix oppression on a hapless land,　　　　320
Here, without walls, the fields of safety spread,
And, free as winds, ascends the peaceful shade ;
Invasion fierce, interfluent oceans bar ;
Streams hedge the foe, and mountains mock the war.
In each dread pass, with naked side, he stands,　　　　325
To sudden terrors, and to unseen hands ;
On the broad plain, ten thousand ills invade,
The day's hard toils, the night's ill-boding shade ;
Surrounding wilds, incessant, breathe alarms,
And moors, and forests, pour harrassing swarms :　　　　330

Pain'd, at each ftep, he fears himfelf undone,
And each new movement lofes all he won.
Thus fhall my fons their fhelter'd regions fave,
Firm as their hills, and as their fathers brave,
On freedom's force, with generous truft, rely,   335
And afk no fortrefs, but the favouring SKY."

" Warm'd by that living fire, which HEAVEN beftows;
Which Freedom lights, and Independence blows;
By that bright pomp, which moral fcenes difplay,
The unrivall'd grandeur of elective fway;   340
And manners, where effulgent nature fhines,
Nor tinfel glares, nor fafhion falfe refines,
At this beft æra, when, with glory bright,
Full-rifing Science cafts unclouded light,
Up wifdom's heights the foul fhall wing her way,   345
And climb thro' realms of ftill improving day."

" Here wealth, from private mifery wrench'd no more,
To grace proud pomp, and fwell a monarch's ftore,
Aid venal hofts to blaft man's little joy,
And bid fell navies towns and realms deftroy,   350
For public blifs, from public hands, fhall flow,
And patriot works from patriot feelings grow.
See Appian ways acrofs the New World run!
Here hail the rifing, there the fetting, fun:
See long canals on earth's great convex bend!   355
Join unknown realms; and diftant oceans blend;
In the Calm Main, Atlantic tides arife,
And Hudfon wanton under torrid fkies.
O'er all my climes, fee palac'd Science fmile!
And fchools unnumber'd gem the golden foil;   360
For want, for woe, the neat afylum rife,
And countlefs temples call propitious fkies.
By locks immenfe fee broken rivers join'd;
And the vaft bridge my Rhines, and Danubes, bind;

For ufeful fabrics, fpacious domes afcend;　365
Huge engines roll, and ftreams their currents bend."

" Here too, each heart, alive to pity's caufe,
Shall curfe ftill-favage Europe's reeking laws;
That gibbets plant, as erft the foreft ftood;
With horfe-leach thirft, cry, "Give us daily blood;"　370
Void, not of mercy, but of common fenfe,
Commute a human life for thirteen pence;
Poor debtors chain, to glut revenge and pride,
And one man hang, that other men may ride."

" Here firft, fince earth beneath the deluge ftood,　375
Bloodfhed alone fhall be aton'd by blood:
All other crimes, unfit with man to dwell,
The wretch fhall expiate, in the lonely cell:
There awful Confcience, and an anguifh'd heart,
Shall ftretch the rack, and wing the flaming dart;　380
Approaching fiends with lowering vengeance glow,
And gulphs yawn downward to the world of woe.
Half feen, at times, and trembling faint, from far,
Shall dawn fweet Mercy's bright and beamy ftar;
Hope enter, fmite his chains, and fet him free,　385
And fpread her wings, and whifper, " Follow me."
In this dread manfion, fhall the culprit find
His country's laws, not juft alone, but kind;
And fed, and clad, and lodg'd, with comfort, feel
Whatever good deftroys not public weal."　390

" Here too, her fcope fhall Policy extend,
Nor to check crimes be ftill her fingle end.
Her hand fhall aid the poor, the fad confole,
And lift up merit from it's lowly ftool,
Reach to th' induftrious youth the means to thrive,　395
The orphan fhelter, bid the widow live,
Nurfe, with a foftering care, each art refin'd,
That mends the manners, or that lights the mind,

The choking damps of foul defpair expel,
And help afpiring genius to excel."   400

" See, in each village, treafur'd volumes ftand !
And fpread pure knowledge through th' enlighten'd land ;
Knowledge, the wife Republic's ftanding force,
Subjecting all things, with refiftlefs courfe ;
That bids the ruler hold a righteous fway,   405
And bends perfuaded freemen to obey.
Frequent, behold the rich Mufeum yield
The wonders dread of Nature's fruitful field !
See ftrong invention engines ftrange devife,
And ope the myfteries of earth, feas, and fkies ;   410
Aid curious art to finifh works refin'd,
And teach abftrufeft fcience to mankind."

" Up the dread vault, where ftars immenfely roll,
To heaven, Herfchelian tubes conduct the foul ;
Where proud Orion heads th' immortal train,   415
And opes his lucid window through the main ;
Where, far beyond this limitary fky,
Superior worlds of liquid fplendour lie ;
Far other funs diffufe th' unfetting ray,
And other planets roll, in living day.   420
Truth, blifs, and virtue, age by age, refine,
And unknown nations bafk in life divine,"

" Even now fair beams around my concave burn,
The golden Phofphor of th' expanding morn.
See raptur'd Franklin, when fierce tempefts ride,   425
Down the fafe dome innoxious lightnings guide !
The nice machine fee felf-taught Kingfley frame,
That, unexampled, pours th' electric flame !
See Rittenhoufe, and Pope, with art their own,
Roll the fmall fyftem round the mimic fun !   430
See Bufhnell's ftrong, creative genius, fraught
With all th' affembled powers of fkilful thought,

U

His myſtic veſſel plunge beneath the waves,
And glide thro' dark retreats, and coral caves!
While crowds, around them, join the glorious ſtrife, 435
And eaſe the load, that lies on human life."

" Nor leſs their ſtrength ſhall private efforts blend,
My ſons t' illume, refine, exalt, amend.
Thro' Nature's field ſhall bold Inquiry ſtray,
Where Europe's Genius leads the ſplendid way; 440
Tell why the winds with fickle wanderings blow,
Thin vapours ſpring, and clouds condenſing flow;
From what ſtrange cauſe th' etherial phaſes riſe,
And gloom, and glory, change ſo ſoon the ſkies;
How heat through nature ſpreads its chemic power; 445
Wakes the ſoft ſpring, diſſolves the icy ſhower,
In fluid ſplendour bids the metal glow,
Commands the ſtream to roll, the flower to blow,
With golden beauty lights the ſtarry choir,
And warms th' exhauſtleſs ſun with living fire. 450
Or pierce the miſt of elemental ſtrife,
See lazy matter rouſing into life;
It's parts meet, mix, repel, attract, combine,
And mould the plant with infinite deſign;
Or through the grades of nobler life aſcend, 455
And the ſtrange, acting, ſuffering Being blend;
Or ceaſe their hold, to bring new forms to light,
And bid the fairy ſtructure melt from ſight;
Or round the globe it's wondrous ſtrata ſpread,
Faſhion the hills, and vault the ocean's bed; 460
Imblaze the ore, th' enticing gem unfold,
And with pure ſunbeams tinge the laſting gold.
Here too ſhall Genius learn, by what controul,
Th' inſtinctive magnet trembles to the pole;
With curious eye, it's ſyſtem'd errors trace, 465
And teach the myſtic longitude of place:
Or through the bright, Columbian ſcience rove,
Purſue the lightning's path, in realms above,

Or o'er earth's bowels, mark it's filent courfe,
And fee all nature own it's magic force :   470
Or ope more awful wonders to mankind,
Evolve the terrors of the Indian wind,
Tell whence volcanic fires the mount inform,
Whence heave the plains, or burfts the raging ftorm ;
Whence the wide concave angry meteors rend,   475
And fhuddering earth quakes to it's diftant end :
Or, in dark paths, where health's fair ftreamlets ftray,
Thro' plants, and mines, explore their chernic way,
Redrefs the ravage of encroaching clime,
Change the fad curfe, rebuild the wafte of time,   480
Protract man's date, bid age with verdure bloom,
And ftrew with flowers the journey to the tomb."

" See rifing bards afcend the fteep of fame !
Where truth commends, and virtue gives a name,
With Homer's life, with Milton's ftrength, afpire,   485
Or catch divine Ifaiah's hallow'd fire.
No fickly fpot fhall foil the page refin'd ;
Lend vice a charm, or taint the artlefs mind ;
Another Pope inchanting themes rehearfe,
Nor the meek virgin blufh to hear the verfe ;   490
Improv'd, and clouded with no courtly ftain,
A whiter page than Addifon's remain."

" On the bright canvas, fee the pencil trace
Unrivall'd forms of glory, and of grace !
In the fair field, no traits of vilenefs fpring,   495
No wanton lordling, and no bloody king,
No ftrumpet, handed to perpetual fame,
No fcenes of lewdnefs, and no deeds of fhame :
But men, that counfell'd, fought, and bled, for men,
And held, to death, the world-renewing pen ;   500
Scenes, that would Envy of her fnakes beguile,
Deeds, where fond Virtue loves to gaze, and fmile :

Such forms, such deeds, on Raphael's tablets shine,
And such, O Trumbull! glow alike on thine."

" No more shall Music trill, with raptures, o'er   505
The swinish revel, and the lewd amour,
The phrenzied ravage of the blood-stain'd car,
Or the low triumphs of the Sylvan war.
But Sorrow's silent sadness sweetly charm,
With love inspire, with real glory warm,   510
Wake, in Religion's cause, diviner lays,
And fill the bosom with MESSIAH's praise."

" But chief, my sons shall Moral science trace,
Man's nature, duties, dignity, and place;
How, in each class, the nice relation springs,   515
To GOD, to man, to subjects, and to kings;
How taste, mysterious, in the Heavenly plan,
Improves, adorns, and elevates, the man;
How balanc'd powers, in just gradation, prove
The means of order, freedom, peace, and love,   520
Of bliss, at home, of homage fair, abroad,
Justice to man, and piety to GOD."

" For soon, no more to philosophic whims,
To cloud-built theories, and lunar dreams,
But to firm facts, shall human faith be given,   525
The proofs of Reason, and the voice of HEAVEN.
No more by light Voltaire with bubbles fed,
With Hume's vile husks no longer mock'd for bread,
No more by St. John's lantern lur'd astray,
Through moors, and mazes, from the broad highway,   530
Transported men the path of life shall know,
And Angels' food shower round them, as they go."

" The Word of life, a world of stores refin'd,
The dress, the feast, the riches, of the mind,
The bold Divine, commercing, shall explore,   535
Search every realm, and visit every shore,

Thence wines, and fruits, of every taſte, and clime,
Matur'd, and beauteous, in immortal prime,
Thence gems collect, and gold from wiſdom's mine,
Robes of pure white, and ornaments divine,　　　　540
(Whate'er can bid the famiſh'd wretch reſpire,
Or clothe the naked in unſtain'd attire)
To HEAVEN's high altar bring the offering bleſs'd,
And all mankind, his Levites, ſhare the feaſt."

　　For here, alike to want, and wealth, allied,　　545
Plac'd in the mean, 'twixt poverty and pride,
The goal, where faithful virtue moſt is found,
The goal, where ſtrong temptations leaſt abound,
Nor ſloth benumbs, nor luxury betrays,
Nor ſplendour awes, nor lures to dangerous ways,　　550
Where the poor boldly tell their woes ſevere,
Fear no neglect, and find the mingling tear,
From civil toils, cabals, and party-heat,
My ſacred clerks ſpontaneous ſhall retreat;
To others leave to others what is given,　　　　555
And ſhine, the mere ambaſſadors of HEAVEN;
Spread truth, build virtue, ſorrow ſoothe, and pain,
And rear primæval piety again."

　　" The nobleſt Manners too my realms ſhall cheer,
With prudence, frank; obliging, yet ſincere;　　560
Great, without pride; familiar, yet refin'd;
The honeſt face diſcloſing all the mind;
Stanhope abjur'd; the Goſpel own'd alone;
And all, from other's claim'd, to others done
Here nature's ſweet ſimplicity ſhall reign,　　565
And art's foul tincture meet a juſt diſdain;
The waxen mien of Europe's courtly lords;
Love ſpent in looks, and honour loſt in words;
Where ſad ambition, ſickening, toils for ſhow,
And ſmiles, invented, maſk the face of woe;　　570

Where life drags on, a difappointing round,
Where hope's a cheat, and happinefs a found."

" What though, like Europe's titled train to live,
Even in thefe climes, the fplendid trifler ftrive ;
Pine, with a fickly appetite, for fhew,   575
And, every year, the income fpend of two ;
With aukward folly, mimic toilfome fin,
Parade without, and wretchednefs within ;
Yet faint, and few, fhall thefe corruptions fpread,
Seen but to be defpis'd, and hifs'd, and fled.   580
Strong fenfe fhall here the life of reafon yield,
Each whim exploded, and each vice expell'd ;
From fweet affections actions fweet fhall flow,
All that makes joy, and all that quiets woe,
Where nature, friendfhip, love, unrivall'd reign,   585
And form anew the dignity of men."

" And O what beams fhall light the Fair-one's mind !
How the foft eye-ball gliften truth refin'd !
What featur'd harmony mild virtue form !
With what fweet fympathy, the bofom warm !   590
To wifdom pure, by ufeful fcience train'd,
From fafhions, cards, and plays, to reafon gain'd,
To fhow, to flattery, victims now no more,
Vile forms extinct, and idle follies o'er,
Anew to duty fhall the heart be given,   595
Love to mankind, and piety to HEAVEN.
Grac'd with each beauty of th' etherial form,
Led by a heart, with rich affections warm,
Each lovely daughter, fifter, friend, and wife,
Shall call forth rofes, from the thorns of life ;   600
With foothing tendernefs, rough man refine,
Wake gentler thoughts, and prompt to deeds divine ;
Through wifdom's paths, their tender offspring charm,
And bear them upward, with fupporting arm ;

Plant truth's fair feeds ; the budding virtues tend ;   650
And bid the nurfling faint a cherub end.
Like vernal dews, their kindnefs fhall diftil,
Cheer the fad foul, and lighten every ill ;
Breathe balmy comfort round the wretches fhed,
And lay the outcaft in a peaceful bed ;   610
Bid, round their manfions, blifs domeftic rife,
And fix a bright refemblance of the fkies."

" Through this wide world, outfpread from fky to fky,
Thus envied fcenes of rapture meet the eye.
Then, on the borders of this fapphire plain,   615
Shall growing beauties grace my fair domain.
O'er thefe green hills, and in each fmiling dell,
Where elves might haunt, and fays delighted dwell,
From Thames's walks, to Hudfon's verdant ifles,
See, with fair feats, my lovely margin fmiles !   620
No domes of pomp infult the fmiling plain ;
Nor lords, nor princes, trample freeborn man.
Man, the firft title known beneath the fkies ;
A prince, when virtuous, and a lord, when wife.
See, circling each, with fimple luftre, fpread   625
The neat inclofure, and the happy fhade ;
Meads green with fpring ; with Autumn orchards fair ;
And fields, where culture bids all climes appear ,
Gay groves exult ; Chinefian gardens glow,
And bright reflections paint the wave below !"   630

" On this blue plain, my eye fhall then behold
Earth's diftant realms immingled fails unfold ;
Proud Europe's towers, her thunders laid afleep,
Float, in calm filence, o'er th' aftonifh'd deep ;
Peru unfetter'd lift her golden fails,   635
And filken India waft on fpicy gales ;
From death's dull fhade, awaken'd Afric rife,
And roll the products of her funny fkies.

Here shall they learn what manners blifs affure ;
What sway creates it, and what laws secure,   640
See pride abas'd ; the wolfifh heart refin'd ;
Th' unfetter'd confcience, and th' unpinion'd mind ;
To human good all human efforts given ;
Nor war infult, nor bondage anger, HEAVEN ;
No favage courfe of Eaftern glory run ;   645
Atchiev'd no conqueft, and no realm undone."

" Here shall they fee an æra new of Fame,
Where science wreathes, and worth confers a name ;
No more her temple ftand in human gore ;
Of human bones, her columns rife no more :   750
The life, by poets fung, the heavens approve,
Wifdom commend, and future ages love."

" From yon blue wave, to that far diftant fhore,
Where funs decline, and evening oceans roar,
Their eyes shall view one free elective sway ;   655
One blood, one kindred, reach from fea to fea ;
One language fpread ; one tide of manners run ;
One fcheme of fcience, and of morals one ;
And, GOD's own Word the ftructure, and the bafe,
One faith extend, one worfhip, and one praife."   660

" Thefe shall they fee, amaz'd ; and thefe convey,
On rapture's pinions, o'er the diftant fea ;
New light, new glory, fire the general mind,
And peace, and freedom, re-illume mankind."

END OF THE SEVENTH PART.

NOTES TO PART I.

LINE 42. The parish of Greenfield confists of about thirteen fquare miles. On this little tract were found, at the time of the late cenfus, almoft fourteen hundred inhabitants: a population as great, as that of Britain, if the accounts which I have feen, of the extent and population of that country, are juft. The people of Greenfield are almoft all Farmers, and have no advantages for fupport, befides thofe which are common to N. England in general. Thus without any peculiar affiftance from commerce, or manufacturing, an immenfe population can exift on the mere labours of the hufbandman. The people of Greenfield, alfo, very generally abound in the neceffaries and comforts of life. Such are the effects of an equal divifion of property, and of the cultivation of lands by the proprietors.

L. 85. No country has been more unjuftly or contemptibly flandered, than New England.

L. 94. [Firms.] I have ventured to ufe this word, as a verb. It appeared to me better to exprefs the idea intended, than any other word, which I could recollect.

L. 177. A remarkable proof of the mildnefs of manners, in New England, exifted during the late war. The inhabitants were at leaft as much divided, and as directly oppofed, both in opinion and conduct, as thofe of France; and through a much longer period. (a) Yet not one perfon was put to death by the hand of violence, and but one by the hand of civil juftice, during an eight years war, and in a country containing a million of inhabitants.

L. 215. The State of Connecticut exhibits the moft uniform and unmixed manners, to be found in New England; and thofe, which may, with the greateft propriety, be called the national manners of that country.

L. 223. The happinefs of the inhabitants of Connecticut appears, like their manners, morals, and government, to exceed any thing, of which the Eaftern continent could ever boaft. A thorough and impartial developement of the ftate of fociety, in Connecticut, and a complete inveftigation of the fources of its happinefs, would probably throw more light on the true methods of promoting the interefts of mankind, than all the volumes of philofophy, which have been written. The caufes, which have already produced happinefs, will ever produce it. To facts alone, there-

(3) *January* 1, 1793.

X

fore, ought we to resort, if we would obtain this important knowledge. Theories are usually mere dreams; fitted to amuse, not to instruct; and Philosophers, at least political ones, are usually mere Theorists. The common sense of the early Colonists of New England saw farther into political subjects, those at least, which are of great importance to human happiness, than all the Philosophers, who have written since the world began.

L. 225. Nothing can be more visionary, than many modern Philosophic opinions, concerning government. All human systems, respecting practical subjects, unless derived from facts, will ever be visionary, and deserve to be classed with substantial forms, subtil matter, and atomic tendency to exertion. Man is wholly unable, by mere contemplation, to bring into his view a number of principles sufficient to constitute a theory, which can consist with practice. One would imagine, that the universal fate of hypothetical philosophy must long since have taught ingenious men this obvious truth; but the pleasure of making, and defending, systems, is so great, that such men are still employed in building air-castles, and in seriously expecting to inhabit them.

L. 234. If gentlemen, who are natives of Europe, should think this paragraph harsh, or unfounded, the writer requests them so far to turn their attention to the several facts, mentioned in it, as to satisfy themselves, whether the ascription be just, or erroneous. The natives of Great Britain, particularly, will find, in distinguished writers of that country, descriptions of British society, warranting all, that is asserted in this poem: descriptions confirmed, so far, at least, as the author's acquaintance has extended, by those Americans, who have travelled into Britain. The *Task*, one of the most sensible and valuable performances, in the English language, is alone a sufficient justification of no small part of what is here declared.

L. 247. It is, perhaps, not to be wondered at, that the state of society, lately existing in France, should be followed by extensive and ridiculous infidelity; but that such a speech as that said to be uttered, Dec. 1792, by Citizen Dupont, should have been spoken by any man, on any occasion, and before any audience, would hardly have been believed, unless published with high authentication. That it should have been uttered by a man, characterized as a man of weight and influence, is still more astonishing: and that it should have been received, by the Legislative Assembly of a great Nation, with applause, is a fact, which, if it should, unhappily for the honour of human nature, be handed to posterity, will probably be regarded rather as a Provencal legend, than as a reality. Of the like contemptible character are the later declarations of Citizen Lacroix, on the petition of the Quakers and Anabaptists; in which are the following words. "The Constitution is my Gospel, and Liberty is my God. I know no other." These gentlemen appear ambitious of rivalling the character of Aretine, on whose tomb this inscription is said to have been written.

> Here lies Aretine,
> Who spoke evil of every one,
> But his God;
> And in this he must be excused,
> Because he did not know him.

L. 248. I have seen a memorial, said to be presented to his British Majesty, by the Lord Mayor, Aldermen, and Common Council, of London;

in which they declare, that within ten years, 4,800 perfons had, in that city, been convicted of felony. (a)　In New England, which contains more inhabitants than London, it is to be queftioned, whether, in any ten years, fince it was fettled by the Englifh, there have been ten perfons convicted of felony.　A partial account, for this enormous difproportion, may be found in the mildnefs of the laws of New England, which are far lefs fan-guinary, than thofe of Great Britain.　It may alfo be juftly obferved, that London is a city of enormous wealth, and enormous poverty, and a ge-neral receptacle of fharpers and villains from the whole Britifh empire; as well as from feveral other countries.　But it is alfo to be remembered, that a great proportion of the felons, convicted in New England, are natives of Europe.　It is probable, that the fubject cannot be explained in any manner, which will not involve, as its principal caufes, the very great difference, in the refpective places, to be found in the univerfality of happinefs, and in the purity of morais.

L. 267.　[See every heart, &c.]　The fafhions of Europe, efpecially of Britain and France, fuit neither the climate, the convenience, the policy, the property, nor the character, of this country.　The changes of climate in this country require modes of dreffing very different from thofe, which are healthful in France and England.　The Americans are generally people of bufinefs, and, of courfe, muft be greatly and continually incommoded by an adoption of many foreign fafhions.　Our policy naturally teaches us to reject all fervile imitation of the manners of other countries; and all conftant imitation is attended with fervility.　The dignified character of free republicans ought to lead them to defpife a perpetual change in the figure of drefs; to aim only at fuch modes as are convenient, and to per-fevere in them; to fhew their independence, in the choice of their own modes, and their ingenuity in the invention of them; and to manifeft a total fuperiority to the miferable frippery of artificial foeiety.　In the mean time, our pecuniary circumftances would be advantageoufly confulted, by the adoption of drefs, in all refpects fuch as might well confift with our general mediocrity of wealth.　The Friends appear to fhew much good fenfe on this fubject.

L. 279.　War has exifted, in fome, or other, of the countries of Europe, 75 years, out of the 92, which have elapfed, fince the beginning of the prefent century; a century boafted of, as the moft enlightened, refined, and humane, within the knowledge of mankind.　The caufes of thefe wars have, alfo, been generally fuch, as ought to cover the authors of them with deep and perpetual infamy.

L. 296.　Few objects more demand the attention of men of influence, in this country, than the eftablifhment of national manners.　That much may be done, for this purpofe, will not, I prefume, be queftioned.　There are but two, or three countries, in the United States, in which the man-ners have any thing like a general uniformity: the low country of Vir-ginia, the low country of South Carolina, and New England.　The man-ners of Virginia and South Carolina cannot be eafily continued, without the continuance of the Negro flavery; an event, which can fcarcely be expected.　The manners of New England appear to be rapidly fpreading through the American republic; the natives of that country being generally

---

(a)　*In the Lent circuit* (1786) 286 *perfons were capitally convicted in England; and from* 960 *to* 1000 *convicts are now annually tranfported from that country.*

even more tenacious of their manners, when abroad, than when at home. When the enterprize, industry, œconomy, morals, and happiness, of New England, especially of Connecticut, are attentively considered, the patriotic mind will perhaps find much more reason to rejoice in this prospect, than to regret it.

L. 297. [Think whence this weal arose.] The peculiar prosperity of New England in general, and particularly of Massachusetts and Connecticut, undoubtedly arises from the equal division of property, the universal establishment of schools, and their peculiar manner of supporting the gospel.

L. 430. [Ah! knew he but his happiness, &c.] Ah! knew he but his happiness, of men the happiest he, &c.   *Thomson.*

O fortunatos nimium, sua si bona norint,
Agricolas!   *Virgil Georg.* 2.
L. 573. Dan. 12. 13.

———

NOTES to PART II.

LINE 1. This part of the poem, though appropriated to the parish of Greenfield, may be considered as a general description of the towns and villages of New England; those only excepted, which are either commercial, new, or situated on a barren soil. Morose and gloomy persons, and perhaps some others, may think the description too highly coloured. Persons of moderation and candour may possibly think otherwise. In its full extent, the writer supposes it applicable to the best inhabitants only; but he believes the number of these to be great: to others he thinks it partially applicable. Poetical representations are usually esteemed flattering; possibly this is as little so, as most of them. The inhabitants of New England, notwithstanding some modern instances of declension, are, at least in the Writer's opinion, a singular example of virtue and happiness.

It will be easily discovered by the reader, that this part of the poem is designed to illustrate the effects of the state of property, which is the counter part to that, so beautifully exhibited by Dr. Goldsmith, in the Deserted Village. That excellent writer, in a most interesting manner, displays the wretched condition of the many, where enormous wealth, splendour, and luxury, constitute the state of the few. In this imperfect attempt, the writer wished to exhibit the blessings, which flow from an equal division of property, and a general competence.

Wherever an *equal division of property* is mentioned, in this Work, the Reader is requested to remember, that that state of things only is intended, in which every citizen is secured in the avails of his industry and prudence, and in which property descends, by law, in equal shares, to the proprietor's children.

L. 1. Sweet Auburn, loveliest village of the plain!   *Goldsmith.*

L. 12. [The spring bird.] A small bird, called, in some parts of New England, by that name; which appears, very early in the spring, on the banks of brooks and small rivers, and sings a very sweet and sprightly note.

(4) L. 26. [Slump'd.] This word, said, in England, to be of North Country original, is customarily used in New England, to denote the sudden sinking of the foot in the earth, when partially thawn, as in the month of March. It is also used to denote the sudden sinking of the earth under the foot.

L. 28. [Nutwood.] Hickory.

L. 45. And, many a year elapsed, return'd to view.

    Goldsmith.

L. 49. Yes, let the rich deride, the proud disdain.   *Goldsmith.*

L. 52. ——   ——   ——   —— The gloss of art.

    Goldsmith.

L. 68. And parting summer's lingring blooms delayed.

L. 73. Sweet-smiling village! loveliest of the lawn.   *Goldsmith.*
    Goldsmith.

L. 75. In several parts of this country, the roads through villages are called streets.

L. 79, and 80. And every want, to opulence allied,
         And every pang that folly pays to pride.   *Goldsmith.*

L. 91, O luxury! thou curst by heaven's decree.   *Goldsmith.*

L. 91, &c. Men in middling circumstances appear greatly to excel the rich, in piety, charity, and public spirit; nor will a critical observer of human life hesitate to believe, that they enjoy more happiness.

L. 145. [Farmer.] Farmer of revenue: A superior kind of tax-gatherer, in some countries of Europe.

L. 154. By poverty's unconquerable bar.   *Beattie.*

L. 196. [Wain.] Waggon, or cart.

L. 208. Some interesting and respectable efforts have been made, in Connecticut, and others are now making, for the purpose of freeing the Negroes.

L. 221. The black children are generally sprightly and ingenious, until they become conscious of their slavery. This usually happens, when they are 4, 5, or 6 years of age. From that time, they usually sink into stupidity, or give themselves up to vice.

L. 237. If we consider how few inducements the blacks have to ingenious, or worthy efforts, we shall more wonder, that there are, among them, so many, than that there are so few, examples of ingenuity or amiableness.

L. 244. [Essoins.] Excuses.

L. 251, 252. [Home, Monboddo.] Two modern philosophers, who have published several ingenious dreams, concerning the first inhabitants of this world.

L. 285, &c. The facts, alleged in this paragraph, are so generally known, as not to need particular proof.

L. 295. See the speech of Mr. Brissot, in the National Assembly of France, Dec. 1, 1791. If the authority here quoted, for these particular instances of cruelty, exercised on the unhappy Africans, in the West Indies, should be thought doubtful, the reader may find, in the evidence taken, on this subject, by the Committee of the British House of Commons, an immense number of instances, in which inhumanity, equally reprehensible, has been undoubtedly practised on these unhappy people.

L. 301. Of this fact, I was informed by a gentleman of reputation, who assured me that he had sufficient evidence of its reality.

L. 305. In some of the West India Islands, it is a custom, to send, on Monday morning especially, offending slaves to the docks; each carrying a billet, declaring the transgression, and the number of stripes the offender is to receive, and containing a pistareen to pay for the infliction of them.— There the offenders are raised up, successively, by a crane, and stretched by heavy weights, appended to their ancles. In this posture, they are most cruelly tortured by the cowskin, and still more cruelly, it is said, by a briar, called ebony; which is used to let out the blood, where it has been started by the whip.

L. 368. The Academical school, mentioned in the preface.

L. 473, 474. No more thy glassy brook reflects the day :
But, choked with sedges, works it's weedy way :
Goldsmith.

L. 476. The red-breast of America is a remarkably sweet singer.

L. 478. The house, here referred to, stands at some distance from the road.

L. 524. Prov. 31. 11.

L. 532. Prov. 31. 28.

L. 538. Deut. 24. 15.

L. 552. Mrs. Eleanor Sherwood, the excellent person, whose character has been given above, died of the small pox, March 29, 1793; sometime after this character was given.

L. 589. Pier. A looking glass; from it's place. and afterwards from a particular structure, called a pier-glass.

Ibid. All persons declare formal visiting to be unpleasing and burthensome, and familiar visiting to be pleasing; yet multitudes spend no small part of their lives, in formal visiting, and consider themselves as being under a species of obligation to it. In formal visiting, persons go to be seen; in social visiting, to give and to receive, pleasure. If common sense were allowed to dictate, or genuine good breeding to influence, we should immediately exchange form and parade, for sociality and happiness.

L. 617. I do not remember ever to have seen a lady, in full dress, who appeared to be so happy, or to behave so easily, and gracefully, as when she was moderately dressed. An unusual degree of dress seems uniformly to inspire formality, distance, and difficulty of behaviour. Toil, taste, and fancy, are put to exertion, to contrive, and to adjust, the dress, which is expected highly to ornament the person; and the same exertion, appears to be used in contriving, and fashioning, manners, which may become the dress.

L. 712. [Asian sea.] Pacific ocean.

L. 720. [Korean.] Korea is a large peninsula on the eastern shore of Asia.

L. 731. [Albion.] New Albion; a very desirable country, on the western shore of America, discovered by Sir Francis Drake.

L. 735. [Mexic hills.] A range of mountains, running from north to south, at the distance of several hundred miles, westward of the Missisippi,

L. 736. [Louis.] The Missisippi. [Sicilian song.] Pastoral poetry.

NOTES to PART III.

LINE 15. On the plain, on which Fairfield is built, are several eminences of uncommon beauty.

L. 115. There were several acts of gross abuse, and of savage barbarity, practised by the British, when they burned Fairfield.

L. 143. That inferiors, in subordination, are bound to obey all, even the unjust and immoral commands of their superiors, and that the inferior is, in this conduct, justifiable, and the superior alone guilty, is still not unfrequently asserted, and therefore probably believed. When it shall be right to do evil, that good may come, when crimes and virtuous actions, with the guilt, and the merit, of them shall become transferable, when man shall cease to be accountable to his MAKER, and when GOD shall no more rule, with rightful authority, over his own creatures, this doctrine will probably rest on a more solid basis.

L. 181. None of the numerous and horrid evils of war is more wanton, more useless, and more indicative of the worst character, than burning. No nation, by which it is either allowed, or done, ought to make a claim to humanity, or civilization.

L. 231. There was a heavy thunder storm, on the night, in which Fairfield was burned; yet such was the confusion and distress of the remaining inhabitants, that several of them did not perceive it.

L. 168. From Fairfield, the British proceeded to Norwalk; which they burned, the next day. It deserves to be remembered, that, during the conflagration, Governor Tryon had a chair carried to the top of an eminence, in that town, called Grummon's hill; and there, at his ease, enjoyed the prospect, and the pleasure, of the scene. Two churches, 135 dwelling houses, with a proportional number of other buildings, were destroyed, at Norwalk. Eight other towns, in the United States, experienced the same fate; and while immense evil was done to the inhabitants, no benefit accrued, as none plainly could accrue, to their enemies.

L. 365. It is probable, that more of human labour, ingenuity, and property, has been expended in the various business of destruction, than in all the arts, by which peace and happiness have been promoted.

L. 405. Every person, acquainted with the history of the Romans, knows that the temple of Janus was shut, whenever they were in a state of peace, and that this happened but twice, during the first 750 years of their national existence. Mankind in general have been engaged in war, with almost as little intermission.

It would be worth the labour of some friend to mankind, to present the public with a complete view of the time, during which war has existed in Europe, since the destruction of the Roman empire; the number of nations concerned in each war; the sums expended; the debts incurred; the soldiers, sailors, and citizens, destroyed; the cities, towns, and villages, burnt, plundered, and ruined; the miseries, known to be suffered; the most probable causes of the respective wars; and the gain resulting to the respective combatants. Those, who have access to large libraries, would probably find, in them, much of the information, necessary to a design of this nature.

L. 487. The injury, done by war, to the morals of a country, is inferior to none of the evils, which it suffers. A century is insufficient to repair the moral waste of a short war.

L. 553. [Go then, ah go.] It is probable, that whenever mankind shall cease to make war, this most desirable event will arise from the general opposition, made to war, by the common voice. Hence the peculiar importance of diffusing this opposition, as widely as possible, especially by education. If parents, school-masters, and clergymen, would unite their efforts, for this most benevolent and glorious purpose, the effects of such an union, on the rising generation, would probably exceed the most sanguine hopes.

L. 601. Some of the fixed stars are, from evident alterations in their appearance, called changeable stars. The star, Aegol, or Medusa's head, is a remarkable one; and changes, from the first, to the fourth magnitude.

L. 659. The custom of privateering is one of the reliques of Gothic barbarity. No good reason can be given, why commissions, to plunder and destroy houses, should not be given to private persons, as well as to plunder and destroy vessels; to rob on the land, as well as on the sea; and why such persons, as resisted, should not be put to death, in the one case, as well as in the other. Custom, it is presumed, is the only ground of any difference of opinion, with regard to the cases proposed. All privateering is robbery, and murder; and the government, which sanctions privateering, is guilty of authorizing these horrid crimes. Nor can the merchant, who is the proprietor, be excused from his share in the guilt.

NOTES to PART IV.

LINE 8, 9. Rev. 18. 7.

L. 10, &c. Dan. 2, 31, &c. 37, &c.

L. 14. [Timur.] Tamerlane, a Samarcand Tartar; who, in a short time, conquered what is now called Turkey in Asia, Persia, and India; together with several parts of Russia, and Tartary: the whole being an extent of territory larger than the Roman empire.

L. 38. [Demon chiefs.] Demons, according to the opinions of the ancient heathens, were beings of a middle character, between gods and men. The souls of departed heroes were ranked in this class of beings.

L. 43. [Trident.] The fabled sceptre of Neptune, the heathen god of the sea.

L. 118. [Sere.] Furrowed, wrinkled.

L. 131. The heroism, exhibited by our ancestors, in their wars with the Indians, and the patriotism, generally displayed, in their public conduct, have scarcely been excelled.

L. 180. The Indians of this country appear generally to have worshipped an evil dæmon, with a hope of averting his ill offices. This deity was however esteemed inferior to the Great or Good Spirit.

L. 186. Sacrifices of this nature are, at the present time, said to be offered by the Senecas.

L. 190. The Pequods used a religious dance, accompanied with songs, which they performed in a small circular spot, resembling the circus of the ancient Romans.

L. 191. [Thyas.] The priestess of Bacchus. [Nysa.] A city in India, said to be built by Bacchus, in which his worship was especially celebrated.

L. 224. The Indians have generally supposed the future world of happiness to lie in the western regions. The reason seems to be the same with that, which induces the Negroes to believe the happy world situated in Africa; viz. that it was the country, whence they originated. A similar opinion appears to have existed among several, perhaps most, ignorant colonists, for some time, after their emigration.

L. 269. [Sheen.] Brightness.

L. 298. [Elliot, Mayhew.] These excellent men have proved, beyond dispute, that the Indians may be civilized, and christianized, by proper efforts. Their Apostolic piety ought to be remembered, with perpetual honour; and well deserves a public monument, from the State, of which they were ornaments, as well as citizens.

L. 307. The greatest obstacle to christianizing the Indians is now, as it has usually been, their rivetted persuasion, that the British Colonists, in all their correspondence with them, have aimed at their own benefit, not at the benefit of the Indians; at the acquisition of their lands, not at the salvation of their souls: a persuasion founded on too unequivocal and shameful proof. So long as those, who trade with them, are allowed to poison them by all the means of corruption, virtuous men can only regret their miserable condition. It is to be hoped, that the late act of Congress, regulating our correspondence with the Indians, together with several other humane and just measures of the same nature, measures which reflect the highest honour on that Body, will, in a good degree, remove these evils.

L. 311. [India's curse.] Rum.

L. 351. The French settlers of Canada took unceasing and immense pains, to induce the Indians to quarrel with the English Colonists. To this conduct they were influenced not less by religious motives, than by those of policy, and by what has been called national enmity.

L. 362. The hill, to which the Pequods retired, has the appearance of being artificial.

L. 394. The heroism, celebrated by Homer, Virgil, and other Greek and Latin Poets, principally consisted of feats of personal prowess, and the conduct of small parties. Such was the gallantry of the first American Colonists.

Y

NOTES to PART V.

NOTES to PART VI.

PREFATORY NOTE I.

THIS part of the poem, though deſigned, in a degree, for perſons in moſt employments of life, is immediately addreſſed to Farmers. As almoſt all the inhabitants of Greenfield, and of New England, are farmers, it was ſuppoſed by the writer, that this circumſtance naturally directed to ſuch an addreſs.

L. 63. [Lawrence.] A proverbial name, in ſome parts of New England, for a lazy perſon.

L. 148. [Fit the ground.] A cuſtomary phraſe, in ſome parts of New England, to denote the preparatory cultivation of a field, which is to be ſown.

L. 270. It is cuſtomary, in New England, when property is taken by diſtreſs, to advertiſe the ſale of it upon a poſt, erected for that purpoſe.

L. 289. [The firft of May.] The day, on which accounts are ufually adjufted, and pecuniary obligations difcharged, in the ftate of New-York.

L. 297. For more than twenty years, the writer of this poem has been employed in the bufinefs of education, and, in that time, has had, in a greater or lefs degree, the fuperintendence of almoft a thoufand young perfons, of both fexes. Almoft all the fentiments here expreffed, concerning the inftruction, government, and habituation, of children, he has feen often proved to be juft, through the whole courfe of this extenfive experience. He is induced to thefe obfervations by a full, experimental conviction of the entirely theoretical and vifionary nature of feveral modern opinions on the fubject; opinions, publifhed by men, of genius indeed, but wholly inexperienced in education; men who educate children on paper, as a geometrician circumnavigates the globe, in half a dozen fpherical triangles. On fome future occafion, he may, perhaps, take the liberty to offer to the public fome further fentiments, on this copious and very interefting fubject. In the mean time, he believes, that thefe may be fafely adopted by fuch, as have not acquired more extenfive information, and for fuch only are they defigned.

L. 447. No principle of action will ufually be of any fervice to children, unlefs it be made habitual.

L. 451. I believe, that there are very few children, who might not be rendered amiable and worthy, if their parents would begin their efforts in feafon, and continue them fteadily, without, yielding to either floth, or difcouragement.

L. 471. In moft places in New England, the parifh bell is rung, at 9 o'clock, in the evening: a cuftom, which has more influence in promoting good order, than a flight obferver would imagine.

L. 531. There are many focial libraries in Connecticut; and the number is faft increafing. This is vifibly one of the beft means of diffufing knowledge. If the proprietors of each would tax themfelves a fmall fum yearly, they would foon be able to procure a fufficient number of books, to anfwer every valuable purpofe of fuch an inftitution.

L. 567. I once knew a farmer, who fteadily did what was called a good day's-work, and yet employed feveral hours, every day, in reading.

L. 570. Several of the moft ufeful and refpectable men, in America, were privately educated; and fome of them, with very fmall advantages.

L. 637. [A townfman.] In New England, the prudencials of each town are commonly placed under the direction of a fmall number of men, chofen for that purpofe, and called indifferently felectmen or townfmen.

L. 638. A reprefentative; Vulgarly called a member of the houfe.

NOTES to PART VII.

LINE 11. 12. The vifions of the morning were anciently thought to be peculiarly prophetical.

538 (180)

L. 42. [Thames.] The river which empties into the found at New London.

L. 43. [Tempe.] A beautiful valley in Theſſaly. [Connecta.[Connecticut river, which, almoſt through its whole courſe, waters a very fruitful and delightful valley.

L. 45. [Avon.] Houſatonuck, or, as it ought to be written, Hooeſtennuck, or Stratford river.

L. 96. Quicquid delirant reges plectuntur Achivi. *Horace.*

L. 105. The great objects of nature are, in America, viſibly formed on a ſcale, ſuperior to what is found elſewhere. Mountains, lakes, plains, cataracts, &c. exiſt in America, which are wholly unequalled by any, on the Eaſtern continent.

L. 113. 114. The Inconveniencies, ariſing from the extremes of heat and cold, in N. America, are abundantly compenſated by the great variety and richnefs of its productions. The two harveſts, of European grain, and Indian corn (one of which is almoſt always a plentiful one) will probably hereafter, as they have done heretofore, ever forbid even a ſcarcity of the neceſſaries of life.

125. The foundation of all equal liberty is the natural and equal deſcent of property to all the children of the proprietor. Republics cannot long exiſt, but upon this baſis.

L. 145. A very unequal diviſion of property appears ever to have had very baneful effects on the general happineſs of mankind. A great part of the proſperity of Great Britain may be attributed to the inroads made by Henry VII. upon the entailment of eſtates.

L. 150. Prov. 30. 8, 9.

L. 154. Luke 18. 2.

L. 162. Irreligion and ſuperſtition are equally conſequences of great wealth, ignorance, and power, in perſons of different characters.

L. 165, 166. The vaſſals, or loweſt claſs of people, were, anciently, in moſt European countries, and are, at the preſent time, in ſome, ſold with the ſoil.

L. 176. Prov. 30. 9.

L. 183 [Vitellius.] A luxurious emperor of Rome, who had, ſerved up for him at one meal, 2000 fiſh, and 7000 fowl.

L. 192. [Staniſlaus.] The preſent king of Poland. The fate of this prince is exceedingly to be lamented. Having, in a moſt dignified manner, made his country free, and laid a moſt deſirable foundation for it's future happineſs, he was fruſtrated, in the nobleſt of attempts, by the interference of injuſtice and tyranny.

L. 204. Matt. 25. 40.

L. 251. In the United States, the world has, for the firſt time, ſeen a nation eſtabliſhing, diſſolving, and renewing, its ſyſtem of government, with as much peace, order, and coolneſs of deliberation, as commonly appear in the cuſtomary buſineſs of a legiſlature.

L. 282. Rev. 21. 25.

L. 367. [Calm Main] Pacific ocean.

L. 368. [Hudſon.] Hudſon's bay.

L. 378. By the laws of Great Britain, one hundred and ſixty different ſorts of human actions are puniſhable with death. *Blackſtone's Com.*

This fact is a dreadful inſtance of the aſtoniſhing power of eſtabliſhed cuſtom, and hereditary opinion: for the nation in which it is found, is unqueſtionably the moſt enlightened and reſpectable, in Europe.

Since Blackſtone wrote, Capel Loft eſtimates the number of felonies, without benefit of Clergy, at 176; and of felonies with Clergy, at 65.— Of thoſe, who were executed, the Solicitor General declares, that 18 out of 20 do not exceed 20 years of age.

L. 386. It has not yet been proved, than the puniſhment of death can, with either juſtice, or policy, be inflicted for any other crime, beſide murder. From the few experiments, which have been made, folitary confinement appears to be as much more effectual as it is more humane.

The preſent penal ſyſtem of Pennſylvania well deſerves the reſpect and the adoption of every Government. To the original authors of this ſyſtem, among whom feveral of the Friends claim a particular diſtinction, the higheſt honour is due. See, on this ſubject, An Enquiry how far the puniſhment of Death is neceſſary, in Pennſylvania. By William Bradford, eſq. And an Account of the Alteration, and preſent State, of the penal Laws, in Pennſylvania; of the Gaol, &c. By Caleb Lownes.

L. 395, 396. Acts 12. 8. 9.

L. 401. It feems not a little furpriſing, that almoſt the whole buſineſs of diſtributive government ſhould, hitherto, have been to puniſh.

L. 413—416. There is no country, in which law has a more decided, (and if I may be allowed the expreſſion) deſpotic power, than in Connecticut. Yet this power reſts wholly on that general information of the people at large; from which they derive full conviction, that government is neceſſary to the exiſtence, and to the continuance, of all their happineſs.

L. 425. In the fword of the conſtellation, Orion, there is a place, which appears like a window in the ſky; through which the eye apparently penetrating fees, in telefcopes of high powers, a more glorious region, than has been elfewhere difcovered; a region in which perpetual day ſeems to ſhine with ſingular ſplendour.

L. 482. [Indian Wind.] The hurricane.

L. 499, 500. Curs'd be the verfe, how well ſo'er it flow,
That tends to make one worthy man my foe;
Give Virtue fcandal, Innocence a fear,
Or from the ſoft-ey'd Virgin ſteal a tear.   *Pope.*

A perfon of delicacy, and virtue, is naturally led to wonder, that a man of fuch talents, as Mr. Pope poſſeſſed, and entertaining the very juſt fentiments, expreſſed in thefe finiſhed lines, ſhould have written, publiſhed, and left to be handed down to poſterity, a great number of verfes, which he has actually written, and publiſhed. In his Rape of the Lock, there are feveral lines plainly indelicate, and fome grofsly obfcene. In his Eloifa to Abelard, the fentiments are, in fome inſtances, grofs and noxious. Yet thefe are his firſt performances. His Moral Eſſays (particularly the fecond) trefpafs, at times, againſt truth, juſtice and decency. The fame is too often true of his fatires. The Dunciad is, in feveral places, a feverer fatire on the author, than on the objects of his refentment: not to mention feveral of his ſmaller imitations of other poets, and the hideous volume, publiſhed as a ſupplement to his acknowledged works.

No Writer ought ever to publiſh a fentiment, or expreſſion (unleſs when fome fcientifical, or other important purpofe neceſſitates it) which cannot he read, in a mixed company, of Ladies and Gentlemen, without giving pain to the moſt refined and delicate mind.

L. 501, 502. And in our own (excufe fome courtly ſtains)
No whiter page than Addifon's remains.   *Pope.*

The drummer of Mr. Addison offends, not unfrequently, againſt decency. There are alſo, in his other works, a few paſſages, which one could wiſh had been expunged. Theſe facts are a proof of unhappy yielding to the taſte of his times, in a man, who was an ornament to human nature.

L. 503. It is not a little injurious to the honour of human nature, that the elegant arts of Poetry, Painting, and Muſic, have, in Europe, been ſo often proſtituted to the celebration of vile characters, to the diſplay of ſubjects and ſentiments groſs and pernicious, and to the commemoration of facts, which deeply ſtain the name of man.

L. 535. Infidel philoſophers frequently impeach, and affect to deſpiſe, the evidence of teſtimony. Yet their own reaſonings are generally attended with evidence, and moſt uſually founded on evidence, which, in clearneſs and ſtrength, is far inferior to that of teſtimony : a great part of their ſentiments being mere and trifling hypotheſes.

L. 565. Warton, in his Eſſay on the genius and writings of Pope, obſerves, that mediocrity is the ſituation, moſt favourable to the exertions of genius. It is alſo the ſituation, evidently moſt friendly to national, and individual, virtue and happineſs.

L. 583. There is ſomething ſingularly unhappy in the attempts of the Americans to imitate the burthenſome oſtentation of Europe. Americans are not, and probably will not ſoon be, ſufficiently acquainted with the round of European form, and etiquette, to adopt it with either ſkill, or grace. At the ſame time, we have not, and, without entailments, never ſhall in any great number of inſtances have, wealth ſufficient to ſupport the neceſſary expenſe.

Common Senſe, Philoſophy, and Religion, alike condemn ſuch manners, in every inſtance, and view them, as the painful efforts of folly to lift itſelf into reſpectability. The plain manners of Republicans, incomparably leſs burthenſome, and more graceful and pleaſing, are our own native manners : ſuch manners, as made the Gaul eſteem the Roman ſenate an aſſembly of gods ; and the courtier Cineas conſider the citizens of Rome, as a collection of kings.

Senſible travellers, whoſe manners are generally viewed as more finiſhed, and pleaſing, than any other, appear uſually to acquire a contempt, and diſuſe, of ceremony, and to adopt a plainer behaviour, than moſt other men of breeding. A perſevering adoption of plain manners, by men of influence, would give them a general and laſting ſanction ; and prove of more real benefit to the preſent, and future, inhabitants of America, than renowned victories, or immenſe acquiſitions of territory.

It may, perhaps, be ſaid, as it often has been ſaid, though with neither diſcernment, nor truth, that parade is neceſſary to give energy to law, and dignity to government. It may be anſwered, that no laws have greater energy, and no government was ever more reſpected, than thoſe of Connecticut have uſually been, for more than 150 years. Yet in Connecticut, parade is unknown in practice, and deſpiſed by the univerſal opinion.—The truth is, people of mere common ſenſe, and uneducated to ceremony, always deſpiſe it : it's introduction, therefore, is always owing to the vanity, and weakneſs, of men in ſuperior ſtations, or ranks, of life.

L. 597. There is reaſon to believe, that the women, in New England, in all that renders the female character reſpectable, and lovely, are inferior to none, in the world. They blend the uſeful, and the pleaſing, the refined, and the excellent, into a moſt delightful, and dignified union ; and well deferve, from the other fex, that high regard, and polite attention, which form a very refpectable branch of our national manners.

L. 657. One of the greateft improvements, which the prefent age has made, in the progrefs of fociety, is the public diminution of military glory, and the elevation of character, acquired by benevolence. Thus Howard is a name more celebrated, than Cæfar, or Marlborough.

F I N I S.

542

THE READER IS REQUESTED TO CORRECT THE
FOLLOWING ERRORS.

	Line	for	read				
P. I.					558	the	thy
	95	wakes	awakes	**P. IV.** Arg. L. 9. for		tribes	tribe
	172	very	every		2	towards	toward
	176	commands	commends		9	sorrows	sorrow
	241	bis	the		90	shrnuk	shrunk
	288	Bloated	Floated		163	clouds	cloud
	411	talk	task		176	around	around,
	543 after day dele,				177	strew'd	strew'd
P. II.	L.	for	read		187	strew'd	strow'd
	162	beggars,	beggars'		210	in	on
	129	sucking	suckling		291	aspect,	aspect
	390	bardy	bardly		297	GODHEAD,	GODHEAD
	644	e'or	o'er	**P. V.** L. 12.		others	others'
	670	dun	sad		137	strait	straight
	717	Commerce,	Commerce'	**P. VI.** L. 176		the	a
	736	murmurs	murmur		215	wood's	woods
P. III. Argument. last Line dele and					247	garden	gardens
	L.	for	read		372	minister'd	minister'd,
	171	softer	softest		381	parents	parent's
	221	wary	wavy		452	leaves	leave
	412	ocean	ocean's	**P. VII.** L. 186.		crose	corse
	531	haunt	hunt		241	fabric	fabrics
	542	invok'd	invok'd,				

A

DISSERTATION

ON THE

HISTORY, ELOQUENCE, AND POETRY

OF THE

BIBLE.

DELIVERED AT THE

PUBLIC COMMENCEMENT,

AT

NEW-HAVEN.

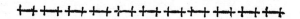

NEW-HAVEN:

Printed by Thomas and Samuel Green,

MDCCLXXII.

A DESSERTATION, &c.

IN a fituation where almoft every theme hath been inge-
niouſly handled, the young fpeaker is left, utterly at a
loſs on which fide to turn himſelf. Learning hath been
panegyrized times innumerable---the particular Scien-
ces have often received their deferved encomiums---nu-
merous inventions have been racked in praife of Œconomy,
Induſtry, Liberty, and *America*---the Eloquence of the Roſ-
trum, and the Bar, hath, both in precept and example, been
handfomely difplayed---a moſt elegant parallel hath been
drawn between the Ancients and the Moderns, the excellen-
cies of each judiciouſly exhibited---the uſe and advantages of
the Fine Arts have been placed in a moſt beautiful, ſtriking
point of view---and this day hath pleafed us with many new
and ingenious thoughts on Education. What fubjeét then
is referved for the prefent hour ? A fubjeét which hath, at
leaſt, novelty to recommend it---a fubjeét, which I flatter
myfelf will be agreeable to *fome* of my audience, and I cannot
but hope, difagreeable to *none*. No perfon hath ever attempt-
ed to entertain this affembly by difplaying the excellencies of
the Fountain of our Religion and Happineſs---(The excellen-
cies I mean, not of its purity and holinefs, which by no means
need a panegyric ; but thofe of fine writing, which, as they
are of lefs importance, fo we fhould naturally expeét they
would have been little attended to.) Could this proceed from
diſlike or inattention ? Surely from inattention. For whilſt
we are enraptured with the fire and fublimity of *Homer*, the
correétnefs, tendernefs, and majefty of *Virgil*, the grandeur of
Demoftbenes, the art and elegance of *Cicero* ; Shall we be blind
to Eloquence more elegant than Cicero, more grand than
Demoftbenes ; or to Poetry more correét and tender than *Virgil*,
and infinitely more fublime than him who has long been ho-
noured,

noured, not unjuftly, with that magnificent appellation " The Father of Poetry ?" Shall we be delighted with the majeftic gravity, the lively, fpirited relations which place *Livy* and *Rob rtfou* on the throne of Hiftory ; with the fine, enthufiaftic morality which obtained *Plato* the furname of " The Divine ;" and fhall we, can we be infenfible to Hiftory far more majeftic, particular Relations far more lively and fpirited than thofe of *Livy* and *Robertfon* ; and to Morality truly divine, whofe glory admits of no comparifon ? Volumes of Criticifm have been written to difplay the beauties of moft of the above Authors, and can a few moments, fpent in an attempt to illuftrate the beauties of the Sacred Scriptures, be thought too many, or tedious ?

The Genius of the Eaftern nations, and particularly of the *Jews*, was in many refpects, different from that of the *Greeks* and *Romans*. Situated in a climate nearer to the vivifying rays of the Sun, his beams acted with a more enlivening influence on the intellectual, as well as vegetable world, and lit up a more bright, glowing Genius in the human breaft. Born in a region which enjoyed this advantage in the happieft degree, and fired with the glorious thoughts and images of Infpiration, can we wonder that the divine writers, though many of them illiterate, fhould fo far tranfcend all others, as well in ftyle, as in fentiment ? Can we wonder that thefe fuperiour advantages fhould be difplayed on every page, in the boldeft metaphors, the moft complete images, and the moft lively defcriptions ? No writers abound fo much in paffionate Exclamation, in that ftriking way of communicating fentiments, Interrogation, or in metaphors taken from fublime objects, and from action, of all others the moft animated. Unincumbered by Critical manacles, they gave their imaginations an unlimited range, called abfent objects before the fight, gave life to the whole inanimate creation, and in every period, fnatched the gracewhich is beyond the reach of art, and which, being the genuine offspring of elevated Genius, finds the fhorteft paffage to the human foul. With all this licenfe no writers have fo few faulty paffages. " But" fays the Critic " they dont defcribe *exactly according to our rules.*" True fir ; and when you can
convince

convince me that *Homer* and *Virgil*, from whom you gather those rules, were sent into the world to give Laws to all other authors ; when you can convince me that every beauty of fine writing *is* to be found, in its higheft perfection, in their works, I will allow the beauties of the divine writers to be faults. 'Till that can be demonftrated, I muft continue to admire the moft fhining inftances of Genius, unparallell'd in force, or fublimity.

In praife of *Homer*, it has been obferved, that he gives *life* to every object which he attempts to defcribe. In the Infpired writings objects are not barely endued with life ; they breathe, they think, they fpeak, love, hate, fear, adore, & exercife all the moft extraordinary emotions of rational beings. *Homer* or *Virgil* can make the mountains tremble, or the fea fhake, at the appearance of a God ; in the *Bible* the mountains melt like wax, or flee away, the Deep utters his voice, and lifts up his hands on high, at the prefence of the LORD of the whole earth. In *other writings* rural fcenes are often addreffed, and receive a momentary animation ; in the *Bible* the heavens and earth are called upon to hear, the winds and ftorms to praife ; the fields rejoice, *Lebanon* fhouts aloud for joy, and the neighbouring forefts warmed to raptures, break forth into fongs of thankfgiving.

Such a Genius muft neceffarily breath an uncommon fpirit, a tranfporting enthufiafm into every production---let us attend to its effects on Hiftory.

The great end of Hiftory is inftruction. To gain the attention of mankind, fomething more is neceffary than a bare, cold relation of diftant events. The earthly part of the human foul is fo difproportionate to the etherial, that every poffible method muft be ufed to extend its regard to any thing, beyond the prefent enjoyment. To awaken our lethargic inclinations, to put in motion the vis inertiæ of our conftitution, is the bufinefs of the Imagination, and the various Paffions. No writers underftood this, as alfo every other part of the human frame, fo well as the facred Penmen. Perhaps, it may not be
unentertaining,

(6)

unentertaining, to trace them in some of the various arts which they have used to catch the attention of the Reader.

Sensible that the Imagination is the principal inlet to the Soul, and that it is far more easily enkindled than the Passions, they passed by no occasion for engaging its assistance. As their subject was better fitted to answer this end, than any other, they have handled it to admiration---they seize every opportunity to introduce transactions, at once new, sublime and wonderful ; for this the frequent awful interpositions of the Deity, in the affairs of *Israel,* gave them the fairest chance--- In every page, we are astonished by glorious and supernatural displays of the divine power---In every page, we are charmed by fanciful, yet just poetical descriptions of a great variety of scenes. By these methods their History has every advantage of Poetry for affecting the Imagination, with this happy circumstance, that it is all reality.

Added to this, though their relations are all directed, more or less, to the illustration of this great Truth " that obedience to God is the path to felicity" they have yet inserted an endless variety of incidents and characters. Convinced thatNovelty hath a most powerful effect on the human mind, they have filled their writings with more new and uncommon events, than are to be found in those of all others united. Convinced that human manners are the most delightful, as well as the most instructive field, for readers of the human race, they have exhibited them in every point of view--Where are characters so naturally drawn ? Where so strongly marked ? Where so infinitely numerous and different ?---To what can the Legislator so advantageously apply for instructions, as to the life and laws of *Moses* ?---Whom can the Prince propose for examples so properly as *Solomon* and *Jehoshaphat* ?---In *Joshua,* and *Joab,* the General, the Hero, are magnificently displayed---In the Prophets and Patriarchs, the Gentleman, the Contemplator may find most excellent patterns, not of gaming, drinking, prophaneness, debauchery, and that unmeaning,unfriendly ceremony which poisons the lip of Hypocrisy ; but of meekness, kindness to inferiors, charity, hospitality, benevolence, and

every

every embelifhment of human nature---In *Jofeph*, the unwary Youth is beautifully taught to fhun the gilded bait of Temptation, and is inftructed that Virtue, fooner or later, will infallibly lift him to the fummit of honour and felicity---Where can the Fair part of the creation find the glorious effects of beauty and virtue fo finely, fo tenderly, fo amiably reprefented, as in *Ruth* and *Efther* ?---*David*'s character, whether as a General, a Ruler, or a Saint, is an exhauftlefs fund of amufement and inftruction---Whom fhould the Clergyman, whom fhould every man imitate, but the Apoftles, but the glorious pattern of excellence, their great MASTER ?

It is an obfervation of *Longinus* " that an Epic poet fhould put as many as poffible, of his fentiments, into the mouths of his heroes." Not, as fome have imagined, to dignify them---do we reverence *Ajax* more than *Homer* ?---but to give them the greater livelinefs. How evident is it, that a man's fentiments ftrike much more from his own mouth, than through the medium of a fecond perfon ? For this reafon, and becaufe we fuppofe *Ajax* to have been better acquainted with circumftances, in which he was an *actor*, than any one who, like the Poet, knew them only by *hearfay* ; we choofe to have his reflections in his own words, rather than in thofe of any relator. What *Homer* has done in Poetry, the Divine writers have done in Hiftory---Great part of their Hiftory is dramatic. By thefe means their characters are drawn not only in a more natural, but more ftriking manner---We don't barely hear of them ; but we fee them ; we hear them fpeak ; they become old acquaintances ; and, at every appearance, we recognize them as fuch. Confining themfelves to fimple narration is what makes a principal difference between the modern and ancient Hiftorians, entirely in favour of the latter.

But this is not all---Senfible that *General Hiftory*, though in many refpects inftructive, is dry and unentertaining---Senfible that *General Defcriptions* leave very faint traces on the Memory ; the writers of Infpiration, contented with giving a plain, concife account of every thing of that kind neceffary to be known (though even this very circumftance hath made
their

their *General Histories* more striking than those of any other nation) hurry on to events more particular, relations more minute. Perhaps not one fourth part of the Sacred History is *General*. To interest the attention, to employ the Memory, it is necessary that we should have a clear, distinct, and perfect idea of any transaction---this can only be given by an exact relation of every minute, important circumstance---and such a relation can only be made of single events.

Reasoning upon principles like these, they have every where inserted narrations of this kind ; and when they have enkindled the Passions, when they have fired the Imagination to a pitch of enthusiasm, they pour into these two great passages to the Soul, truths at once instructive, moral and divine. Are not instances needless ? The story of *Joseph* is too universally admired to allow a comment ; I beg leave to make a few remarks on one less attended to---the subject plain and simple--- the method of handling it inimitable.

Elijah would convince the *Israelites* that the GOD of Heaven is the only Deity. This is the subject. For this purpose, he bids the prophets of *Baal* assemble before all the congregation of *Israel*, and offer a sacrifice to *their* God, whilst he offers a similar one to *his own* : all, at the same time, agreeing that the God, whose fire consumed the oblation, should be accounted the true one. In the morning the prophets of *Baal* erect their altar, prepare their sacrifice, and call on the imaginary Power to kindle it. From morn to noon, this was repeated---no answer was returned. Can their anguish and vexation be more finely imaged than in their leaping on the altar---cutting themselves with knives 'till the blood gushed out ?---Can there be severer sarcasms than those of *Elijah*--- " Cry aloud---spare not---he is a God--either he is talking---or pursuing---or he is on a journey"---and particularly that cutting remark on his Godship---" peradventure he *sleepeth*."

Having allowed them the whole day, near the sunsetting, he builds an altar, digs a trench around it, and, to put the decision beyond a possibility of contradiction, orders twelve

barrels of water to be poured upon the facrifice. The fcene
is now changed. From ridicule, the Prophet afcends to the
higheft folemnity---He calls all the people around him, in-
vokes the DEITY in a concife, but ftriking and awful man-
ner, and is anfwered by a flame from Heaven, which con-
fumes the oblation, with the whole flood of water. What
more folemn, affecting circumftance could have concluded
this relation, than the univerfal voice of the people, refound-
ing in concert, " The LORD, he is the GOD ! The LORD, he
is the GOD !"

I beg leave to mention a few others. The account of Cre-
ation,---ᵃof *Eliezer* and *Rebekah*,--- of the *Ifraelites'* paffage
thro' the Red fea---ᶜof the Law given at *Sinai*---ᵈof *Dathan*
and *Abiram* ;---the Hiftories of *Gideon*, ᶠ*Sampfon*, and ‖*Jeph-
thah* ;---ʰthe ftory of the Levite and his Concubine---ⁱof *Da-
vid* and *Goliath*---ᵏof David and *Jonathan*---of ˡ*Abigail*---ᵐof
Abfalom---ⁿof the dedication of the *Temple*---°of the Queen
of *Sheba*---ᵖof *Elifha* and the *Shunammite*---ᵠof *Naaman* the Sy-
rian---ʳof *Haman* and *Mordecai*---ˢof *Lazarus*---ᵗof the Widow
of *Nain*---ᵘthe Difciples' journey to *Emmaus*---ˣthe birth of
the Saviour---the agony in the garden---and, above all, the
Crucifixion. Each of thefe is handled in a manner mafterly
and inimitable; each of thefe is treated with that peculiar fim-
plicity, which is a grand characteriftic of every fpecies of in-
fpired writing, & which affects the mind more than all the art-
ful, ftudied flourifhes of Rhetoric : though, as it is an object of
univerfal attention, my remarks upon it are the lefs particular.

Nor are the effects of this Genius infpired, lefs apparent in
the Eaftern Eloquence, than in their Hiftory. As I have al-
ready obferved, all thefe hiftorical writings are chiefly dra-
matic and abound in a noble * manly Eloquence. Almoft
an infinite numbers of brave ftriking fenfible fpeeches well
deferve particular notice : But the time will only allow me
to make a few obfervations concerning the Eloquence of St.
Paul.   B   It

ᵃGen. 24. ᵇExod. 14. ᶜExod. 19. &c. ᵈNumb. 16. ᵉJud. 6. &c. ᶠJud·
13. ‖Jud. 11. ʰJudges 19, 20, and 21. There is a remarkable fimilarity
between this ftory and the *Trojan* war.
ⁱ1. Sam. 17. ᵏ1. Sam. 18 &c. ˡ1. Sam. 25. ᵐ2. Sam. 13. ⁿ2. Chron.
6 and 7. °1. Kings 10. ᵖ2. Kings 4. ᵠ2. Kings 5. ʳEfther. ˢSt. John
11. ᵗSt. Luke 7. ᵘSt. Luke 24. ˣSt. Luke 1 &c.
* See Deut. 1. &c. 28. &c. Jofh. C. 14. V. 6. &c. Jofh. C. 22. V. 15.
&c.--2. Chron. C. 13. V. 4. Jofh. 23 and 24. Jud. C. 9. V. 7 &c.
1. Sam. C. 17. V. 44. &c.--Acts C. 2. V. 14. &c. Acts C. 3. V. 12 &c.
C. 4. V. S. &c. C. 5. V. 35. &c. C, 7. C. 13. V. 16. &c. &c. &c.

It is univerfally known, that *Longinus*, a Heathen, by no means well affected to Chriftianity, hath placed this great Apoftle on a lift with *Cicero*, *Demofthenes*, *Efchines*, and others, the moft eminent Orators. What his Elocution was, hath ever been vehemently difputed---to the Critics I leave it---what his Orations were, I think may be determined from thofe recorded in the Acts of the Apoftles.

Of the vehement kind of Eloquence, which raifed *Demof-thenes* to fo high a pitch of Glory, and which alfo abounds in *Cicero* he hath left us no examples ; no occafion, recorded by St. *Luke* being proper for that fpecies of fpeaking : And whether his having excelled them both in every other kind of Oratory, is a fufficient proof that he would alfo have furpaf-fed them in thofe two, the moft common, and the moft eafily attainable, I leave others to determine ; and omitting conjec-tures, will confine my reflections to the inftances of his orato-rical Genius which now remain.

But what pardon can I expect from the Critic, whofe life has been fpent in reading the *Greeks* and *Romans* ; who fcarce-ly knows that there can be any applaufe, befides that which is paid to them, and who doubts whether he may eat, or breathe, unlefs by *Ariftotle's* rules ; when he hears me boldly, unconcernedly prefer St. *Paul's* addrefs to *Agrippa*, for him-felf, before *Cicero's* to *Cæfar*, for *Marcellus* ? As our Chrifti-an Orator knew better than any other man, how to fuit his addreffes to time, place, and audience ; we fhall find that a remarkable circumftance among the excellencies of this, and the other Orations which I fhall notice---a circumftance which defervedly obtains a firft rank among the accomplifhments of a fpeaker. He is now a prifoner, arraigned at the bar of *Feftus*, furrounded by a numerous and fplendid audience---accufers---judges---governors---princes and kings. He be-gins with a compliment infinitely more noble and polite, than all the thick-laid daubing, which *Cicero* has made ufe of, to difplay at once his own meannefs, and *Cæfar's* folly.---Indeed it may be laid down as an unfailing maxim, that the moft ele-gant compliments are ever formed upon truth.---From this he proceeds to ftate the point, opens the cafe, relates his ftory, and adduces the reafons of his conduct, in a manner ftriking---majeftic---convincing. Of the Power of his Eloquence, *Agrippa*, an Heathen, gave him a glorious teftimony, in the ob-fervation---" Thou almoft perfuadeft me to be Chriftian :" Happy, had the word, almoft, been juftly omitted.   But

But I have a mind to trefpafs ftill farther, in a declaration, that his * Farewel to the *Ephefians* is much more beautiful, tender, and pathetic, than the celebrated defence of *Milo.* Never was the power of fimplicity in writing fo clearly, fo finely demonftrated, as in this incomparable Speech. Not a fhadow of art is to be found in it---Scarce a Metaphor, and not one but the moft common, is ufed---Nothing but the natural, unftudied language of affection ; and yet I flatter myfelf, no perfon can read it attentively, without a profufion of tears. Never was the precept of *Cicero* fo perfectly exemplified.--- " To fpeak in fuch a manner, as that all fhould hope they could equal it, and none, upon trial, be able." But this piece will by no means allow a defcant---its beauties are too frequent, in every verfe, in every line, and almoft in every word.

I obferved that of the vehement kind of Eloquence St. *Paul* hath left no examples ; but this remark can by no means be extended to the animated kind in general. What can be more animated than his fpeech to *Elymas* the Sorcerer (which is indeed in a few words feverely invective) unlefs his Oration to the *Athenians* ? I readily confefs, I never was fo much moved by any thing in *Cicero* or *Demofthenes,* as when I have figured to myfelf, the great Apoftle ftanding on *Mars-hill,* in the midft of all the numerous Inhabitants of *Athens,* at that time the Capital of the univerfe for learning and politenefs. Behold on one fide, the young and gay of both fexes, on another, the aged and wife ; on one fide, the rich, adorned with fplendour, on another, in a meaner drefs, the poorer, but not lefs ufeful mechanics and hufbandmen ;--Here, whitened over with age, ftand long rows of venerable Philofophers, here, in their robes of ftate, the more venerable Judges of the *Areopagus* : all in profound filence, liftening to hear fomething of infinite importance. I can almoft hear the glorious man break forth with a force and elocution which made *Felix* tremble, which converted half the world, and induced the inhabitants of *Lyftra* to believe him the very Deity of Eloquence---" God who made the world, and all things that are therein, feeing he is Lord of heaven and earth, dwelleth not in temples made with hands."---And whilft he proceeds in a manner more noble, philofophical, and fublime, than ever delighted any other audience, methinks I can view them, filent as the evening, leaning forward thro' attention, hanging on the words which he utters ; till a clear conviction of the truth of his

affertions

* Acts 20. Verfe 18. &c.

affertions kindles up in their faces, a fmile of fatisfaction and tranfport.

But the effects of this happy Genius, and of Infpiration, are ftill more confpicuous in the Poetry, than even in the Hiftory, or Eloquence of the facred writings. As this cannot be il-luftrated by general remarks, I beg the patience of my audi-ence for a few particulars.

Of Poetry the moft remarkable fpecies are, the Paftoral, Ode, Elegy, Satire, the dramatic and the Epic Poem, and a Mifcellaneous kind, too various to be reduced under any ge-neral name.

Very few ftrokes of a fatirical pen are to be found in the Bible---and even thefe are fhort, but at the fame time cut-tingly fevere. Such, is that ironical farcafm of *Job* to his three friends--- " Doubtlefs ye are the people, and Wif-dom fhall die with you"---his * defcription of his enemies--- || *Ifaiah*'s of an Idol---*Paul*'s obfervation concerning *Ananias*, and fome others : unlefs it fhould be thought that all the reflections on the vice of man are fuch, which I would by no means deny.

Of Paftoral, I fhall only obferve, that *Solomon*'s Song in beauty and tendernefs, is one of the moft complete that can be imagined.

The whole Collection of Prophecies is compofed of poems of the mifcellaneous kind.

As a moft perfect example of the Ode I beg leave to men-tion the 104th Pfalm. The Ode is defined " A fhort Poem, proper to be fung, written in praife of fome beloved object, generally agreeable, tender, or fublime." This Ode has for its fubject, the perfections of the Deity, of all themes the moft fublime and agreeable. The Poet begins with his Pow-er, the moft awful and great of his Attributes, and confe-quently, that which firft engages the attention : from this, he is led to the wonders and bounties of his Wifdom and Pro-vidence. The incidents, chofen to illuftrate thefe Perfections of the Creator, are the moft natural, beautiful, and ftriking. What can be more ftriking than the creation, the heavens, the ocean, the clouds, the winds, the flood, the thunder, the celeftial Hoft, the glory and brightnefs of the DEITY ? What more beautiful than the charms of Nature and profpect, il-luftrating infinite Wifdom and Goodnefs, and particularly, this great truth---That GOD is the univerfal Benefactor of

Being

* Job 50. in the beginning. || Ifaiah 44.

Being ?--Who, after thefe contemplations, can forbear crying out with the poet, in that moft fublime Apoftrophe--- " O Lord ! how manifold are thy Works ! in wifdom haft thou made them all : the earth is full of thy riches !---Who can forbear concluding as he does---" Blefs thou the Lord O my Soul. Praife ye the Lord."

Odes of a more tender kind, are to be found every where amongft the Pfalms ; but I cannot forbear obferving that in the 97th, the above-mentioned 104th, & above all in the 18th, the poet's imagination rifes to fuch a height, as *Pindar, Dryden,* and *Grey* muft look up to, with aftonifhment and defpair.

In the foft, tender ftrain of Elegy, where are fimplicity and Grief fo finely united as in the Lamentations of *Jeremiah* ? What can be more exquifitely pathetic than *David's* Lamentation over *Abfalom* ? What than his Elogium upon the death of *Saul* and *Jonathan* ? His fear left the *Philiftines* fhould hear and rejoice, that the Beauty of *Ifrael* was flain upon the high places---His Apoftrophe to the Mountains of Gilboa--- The excellent character of his Friends, for their Heroifm, in that age a man's greateft glory, and for firmly-united Friendfhip---His elegant addrefs to the Fair-ones of *Ifrael,* to fympathize with him in his diftrefs--His more tender addrefs to his beloved brother *Jonathan,* upon remembrance of their Intimacy---With the repetition of that paffionate exclamation--- " How are the mighty fallen !" are fo many different circumftances, which all contribute to raife this piece to the higheft degree of elegiac perfection.

There is no poem in the Bible, which is ftrictly dramatic, or heroic ; but as the word Epic, commonly ufed for the latter poem, fignifies no more than Narrative, the Book of *Job* may properly come under that denomination. The Action is one---the reftoration of Job to the happinefs, of which he had been deprived by Satan---The Actors, or Speakers are, the Deity, Satan, *Elihu, Job,* his three Friends and Servants. It is almoft wholly dramatic, which gives it a peculiar livelinefs.

Its beauties are infinitely too numerous and various to be mentioned ; but---the bold figures---the ftriking Interrogations---the fine * defcription of Man's frailty---the ‖ Panegyric upon Wifdom---*Job's* § contraft of his former and prefent circumftances---the Introduction, and above all, the Speech of the Deity, are unequalled by any poet, ancient or modern.   Every

* Chap. 14. ‖ Chap. 28. § Chap. 29. 30. &c.

Every one is fenfible of the beauty of Figures. A fingle inftance of the Interrogation will fhew its fine effect in adding livelinefs to every fpecies of writing. The Poet obferves---" Man dieth and wafteth away, yea he giveth up the ghoft, and where is he ?"---What can be more beautiful than *Job's* defcription of his former, and prefent condition ?---The Poets introduction of the CREATOR feems not to have been much attended to, and demands a few remarks.

To give a proper and awful pomp and folemnity to this part of his poem, and to the infinite Being who is now about to appear, the Poet makes *Elihu*, referring to the phenomena of nature around him, deliver himfelf in this manner---" Behold, GOD is great, and we know him not, neither can the number of his years be fearched out. Can any underftand the fpreadings of his clouds or the noife of his tabernacle (i. e. the vifible heavens, poetically fo called.) Behold he fpreadeth his light upon it ; the noife thereof fheweth concerning it, the cattle alfo (then retiring to fhelter) concerning the vapour." And as the thunder was then roaring, he cries out--- " Hear attentively the noife of his voice, and the found that goeth out of his mouth ! He directeth it under the whole heaven, and his lightning to the ends of the earth. Hearken unto this, O *Job* ! ftand ftill, and confider the wondrous works of GOD. And now, *other men* fee not the bright light which is in the clouds ; but the wind paffeth, and cleanfeth them. Brightnefs cometh out of the north ; with GOD is terrible majefty." What can be a more fuitable and glorious attendance upon the CREATOR, than the winds, the rain, the horror and majefty of a ftorm, the fplendour of the lightning, the voice of the thunder, and the brightnefs, or path of flame, which preceeds him as he rides in divine pomp through the the north, and anfwers *Job* out of the whirlwind ? Upon the Speech, which is undoubtedly the moft fublime ever reherfed to mankind, remarks would be impertinence.

As the Epic poem is the moft noble of all others, the whole force of the human Genius is exhaufted in beautifying it with figures, comparifons, and defcriptions.

Many Comparifons are to be found in the Bible, but few of them are extended to any length. As thofe penmen wrote more for Inftruction than Amufement, the Comparifons which they have introduced, being made more for illuftration than beauty, are always fhort, though pertinent and ftriking. If this be thought a deficiency, it is abundantly fupplied by

an

an exuberance of the fineſt Figures which are to be found in writing. Indeed, the Eaſtern Genius was ſo animated, that when thoſe authors ſeized a Compariſon, the warmth of their Imagination inſtantly converted it into the principal ſubjeƈt, and thereby formed a ſhort, and exquiſitely beautiful Allegory ; than whichFigure, nothing is more common in all the ſacred Scriptures---An admirable inſtance may be ſeen in the 5th Chapter of *Iſaiah*.

Of the other principal Figures in compoſition---the Metaphor, the Apoſtrophe, and the Perſonification, as well as the Antitheſis, which was better underſtood, and more happily applied by *Iſaiah*, than by any other Poet, moſt perfeƈt examples are to be found in his awful and ſublime * prophecy concerning the deſtruƈtion of *Babylon*---Particularly in the incomparable Apoſtrophe to that proud city---" How art thou fallen from heaven, O *Lucif.r*, Son of the Morning ! how art thou caſt down to the ground, who didſt weaken the nations !"---This undoubtedly gave *Milton* the firſt thought of ‖ Satan's rebellion, and war.

Can the matchleſs excellence of the ſacred deſcriptions be better illuſtrated, than by comparing the ſublimeſt deſcription of a God, in the ſublimeſt of all the prophane writers of antiquity, with a ſimilar one from the Bible ? That from *Homer*, tranſlated as well as I was able, and, to give it the better appearance,purpoſely cleared of ſeveral puerilities, runs thus---" § *Neptune* emerged from the ſea,and moved with indignation againſt *Jove*, ſate and pitied the *Grecian* hoſt yielding to the force of the *Trojans*. Suddenly, with ſwift ſteps he ruſhed down the broken precipice ; the woods and mountains trembled beneath his immortal feet. Three times he ſtepped, the fourth, he reached the Ægæ. There ſtands his glorious, incorruptible palace of ſhining gold---There he joined his nimble ſteeds, with brazen hoofs and golden manes, cloathed himſelf in gold, aſcended his chariot, and ſkimmed the ſurface of waves. On all ſides, the Whales exulted around their king ; the Sea with joy parted before him ; the ſteeds flew ſwiftly over it, nor moiſtened the brazen axle.

The other from *Habbakkuk* is thus tranſlated.---" God came from *Teman*, and the Holy One from mount *Paran* ; his Glory covered the heavens and the earth was full of his Praiſe. His brightneſs was as the light ; he had horns coming

---

* Iſaiah 13 and 14.

‖ See Par. loſt. B 5 —At length into the limits of the north
They came, and Satan took his royal ſeat

§ Ilias B. 13.　　High on a hill, far blazing, &c.

ing out of his hand, and there was the hiding of his power. Before him went the Peſtilence, and burning coals went forth at his feet. He ſtood, and meaſured the heavens ; he beheld, and drove aſunder the nations ; the everlaſting mountains were ſcattered, the perpetual hills did bow ; his ways are everlaſting. I ſaw the tents of *Guſhan* in affliction, the curtains of the land of *Midian*, did tremble. Thou didſt cleave the earth with thy rivers. The Mountains ſaw thee and trembled, the over flowing of the waters paſſed by, the deep uttered his voice, and lift up his hands on high. The Sun and the Moon ſtood ſtill in their habitation : at the light of thine arrows they went, at the ſhining of thy glittering ſpear."---

Of theſe two paſſages it need only be obſerved, that where the circumſtances are ſimilar, the Prophet is far more lively and ſublime than the Poet, and infinitely ſurpaſſes him in thoſe which are different.

To mention a number of Deſcriptions in the Inſpired writings, would be injuſtice to the reſt ; but how can I paſs by * *Ezekiel*'s, of the Cherubims, ‖ *Daniel*'s, of the Ancient of days, or § St. *John*'s, of the Saviour amid the ſeven golden candleſticks ?

Nothing gives greater weight and dignity to Poetry, than Prophecy. Senſible of this truth *Virgil* has, with great beauty, inſerted ſomething of this kind in the fourth, which is the fineſt of his Paſtorals, and in the ſixth, which is the nobleſt book of his Eneis. But excellent as he is, the Prophets, particularly *Iſaiah* and *John*, in the beauties of this part of writing, ſhine without a competitor.

Inſtead of wild conjectures, inſtead of paſt events, inſtead of Generals and Heroes, inſtead of *Marcellus*, inſtead of the *Roman* City and Empire ; The Prophecies are always certain, the events referred to future ; Their Hero is the *Meſſiah*, the wonderful Counſellour, the mighty God, the everlaſting Father, the Prince of Peace.---The Empire, that of the Univerſe, its extenſion immenſity, its duration eternity.---The City, the new *Jeruſalem*, the Heaven of Heavens, the ſeat of light and bleſſedneſs ; its walls of gold and precious ſtones, its ſplendor that of Almighty God. And this advantage attends all their writings, that every poſſible Reader, every one of us is infinitely more intereſted in the ſubject, than the *Romans* were in that of *Virgil* ; as we are candidates for an immortal exiſtence in that region of felicity, where the Sun doth not give light by day, nor the Moon by night, but the Lord himſelf is an everlaſting Light, and the God of *Zion* her Glory.

* Ezek. 1. ‖ Dan. C. 7. V 9. § Revel. 1.